Techniques of Structured Problem Solving

Second Edition

Arthur B. VanGundy, Ph.D.

VNR VAN NOSTRAND REINHOLD
New York

Copyright © 1988 by Van Nostrand Reinhold
Library of Congress Catalog Card Number 87–6168
ISBN 0–442–28847–6

Printed in the United States of America

Van Nostrand Reinhold
115 Fifth Avenue
New York, New York 10003

Chapman & Hall
2-6 Boundary Row
London SE1 8HN, England

Thomas Nelson Australia
102 Dodds Street
South Melbourne, Victoria 3205, Australia

Nelson Canada
1120 Birchmount Road
Scarborough, Ontario M1K 5G4, Canada

16 15 14 13 12 11 10 9 8 7 6 5 4 3

Library of Congress Cataloging-in-Publication Data

VanGundy, Arthur B.
    Techniques of structured problem solving.

    Bibliography; p.
    Includes index.
    1. Problem solving. I. Title.
HD30.29.V36   1988   658.4′03   87–6168
ISBN 0–442–28847–6

To
my parents,
Arthur B. and Sara J. VanGundy

Preface to Second Edition

I started working on the first edition of this book in 1979. Since then, I have gained additional experience in using the techniques and the creative problem-solving process. I also have uncovered many new techniques. Some of these were new to me, while others were developed more recently. As my knowledge base and experience with the techniques increased over time, I gradually began to notice various errors of commission and omission in the first edition. Thus, I was pleased when I was asked to revise it.

The second edition differs from the first in at least five ways. First, there are the usual changes in grammar, sentence syntax, and word usage that accompany a second critical reading. Most of these changes are minor and, it is hoped, contribute mostly to improved readability. The second change is more substantive. The new edition contains a total of 105 techniques, 35 more than the original. Although more is not necessarily better, this increase does improve the variety of potential problem-solving resources available. Third, I have reclassified many of the techniques, especially those originally intended for redefining and analyzing problems. Although these techniques can serve these functions, I have found the reclassified methods to be more useful for idea generation. For similar reasons, I also have reclassified some of the eclectic and miscellaneous approaches. The fourth change is the addition of a section in Chapter 4 on idea generation principles, an expanded discussion on brainstorming and brainwriting, new material on classifying techniques, and an analysis of the "anatomy" of idea generation methods. The final change concerns revisions I made to many of the previous techniques. These changes reflect my increased understanding of them as well as new insights provided by various researchers and practitioners.

The most important change, however, is the increased respect I have gained for the creative problem-solving process and its power to resolve a variety of ill-structured problems. This book never was intended to provide definitive answers for all the world's problems. Nor did I ever expect that users would follow the process without deviation. Problem solving, especially when ill-structured problems are concerned, should be approached as a flexible set of activities. The flowcharts and guidelines are only suggestions. We all need to decide how we best can solve problems. This book should be viewed as a resource with the potential to help you improve your problem-solving skills. How you integrate the material presented is up to you. For myself, creative problem solving has enabled me to approach life with more confidence in myself and my abilities.

Preface to First Edition

During the past 40 years, both academicians and practitioners have given considerable attention to creative thinking and its relation to the problem-solving process. A substantial portion of this attention has focused on the creative personality, a few of the more well-known idea generation methods, and various procedures for both individual and group problem solving. With only a few exceptions, relatively little attention has been given to research or use of approaches that combine both creativity and problem solving. Although many creative problem-solving techniques exist, only a few have been subject to intensive study by academicians or regular use by practitioners.

Such underutilization of a potentially valuable resource is difficult to explain. Although the common obstacles of lack of time, motivation, and money, and resistance to change are all plausible causes, there are at least two other factors that could be equally or more important. One factor could be a simple lack of awareness about the many techniques developed in the United States and abroad within the last 15 years. Another reason could be that many techniques were well known when first developed 20 or 30 years ago but then became more obscure as interests shifted elsewhere. Whatever the reason, this lack of attention is unfortunate since knowledge and/or use of only a few techniques will limit the number of options available for producing creative solutions.

A major purpose of this book is to increase awareness of the range of techniques available for assisting the creative problem-solving process. This is not a book on how to be a better problem solver nor is it a guide to instant creativity. It is, however, an inventory of a large proportion of the available problem-solving techniques, most of which emphasize achievement of creative solutions. Moreover, the applied aspects of creative problem solving are stressed. Although research and theory are important and a few of the techniques described have been studied intensively, the primary intent of this book is to serve as a resource guide for selecting and using techniques that, in most cases, can be immediately applied to everyday problems. Although some of the more complex techniques will require special training, they have been described in sufficient detail to permit evaluation of their usefulness and applicability. The majority of the techniques, however, require little in the way of special skills or training. Nevertheless, application of all the techniques will require some understanding about their appropriateness for different situations. It is hoped that the information provided in the chapters that follow will provide this understanding.

The book is divided into seven chapters. The first two chapters present general background information for using the techniques presented later on. Chapter 1 discusses the nature of problems and problem solving, possible responses to different types of problems, some benefits of using creative problem-solving techniques, and the basis for classifying the techniques. Chapter 2 provides guidelines for selecting techniques to use within the different problem-solving stages. The reader should find the flowcharts presented in this chapter to be especially helpful, particularly since many of the techniques will be appropriate for more then one problem-solving stage. Using a step-by-step format, the next five chapters present descriptions and evaluations of 105 different techniques. Four of these chapters have been organized to correspond roughly with different problem-solving stages. Chapter 3 contains descriptions of 10 techniques primarily useful for redefining and analyzing problems; Chapter 4 describes 61 individual and group idea generation methods; Chapter 5 presents 16 techniques for evaluating and selecting ideas; Chapter 6 describes four idea implementation approaches; and Chapter 7 includes 14 techniques categorized as either eclectic or miscellaneous.

As a final note, four possible shortcomings of this book should be mentioned. First, every effort has been made to accurately credit the originators of the techniques described. If any authors have been incorrectly credited or omitted, apologies are offered. Second, of the techniques described, there is a disproportionate emphasis upon idea generation methods and techniques designed for product development and technological innovation. This emphasis does not reflect any particular bias but, rather, indicates the previous and current "state of the art." Creative problem solving has been somewhat notoriously associated with generating ideas to the neglect of other problem-sovling stages. Furthermore, many of the techniques originated from a need to develop creative ideas in specific areas of industry; the same incentives have not always existed in the humanities or social sciences. Third, there is a noticeable lack of emphasis upon theoretical orientations or empirical research findings. This lack is both intentional and unintentional. It is intentional since the focus of this book is upon applied creative problem solving and, except for some of the technique evaluations, reports of research findings have been kept at a minimum to avoid detracting from the book's practical orientation; it is unintentional because of the absence of major research studies on most of the techniques—especially studies of a comparative nature. Finally, it should be noted that no pretense is made that problem solving will be greatly simplified or made easy as a result of consulting this book. Problem solving and creativity are hard work, and no book can provide easy solutions for doing this work. Thus, the structured format of the technique presentations can be deceptive. However, it is hoped that the number and variety of technique types and their step-by-step format can at least begin to take some of the mystery and uncertainty out of creative problem solving.

Acknowledgments

There are many people who should be thanked for their contributions toward the development of this book. I am particularly indebted to Horst Geschka for his descriptions and comments on many of the techniques used at the Battelle Institute in Frankfurt, Germany. For their comments or the literature they made accessible to me, I am most grateful to Charlie Clark of Kent, Ohio; Stan Gryskiewicz of the Center for Creative Leadership; Ron Hamilton of the Battelle Institute in Columbus, Ohio; William MacKinnon of the University of Arizona; Sidney Parnes of the Creative Education Foundation; Tudor Richards of the Manchester Business School; and Tom Wiggins of the University of Oklahoma. I would like to thank George Henderson of the University of Oklahoma for his moral support in helping me persevere during the many months of writing and the University of Oklahoma for its partial financial support. Also, I am most appreciative of the efforts of Barbara Kidwell, who did background research on several of the techniques, and Susan Matthews, who typed a substantial portion of the original manuscript. Finally, I am indebted to the many students, business clients, and users of this book who have provided me with numerous helpful comments and suggestions.

Contents

1
Introduction

Problem-solving activity pervades all aspects and levels of human life. There are economic, political, social, and technological problems, all of which can be found at individual, group, organizational, or societal levels. And, because of the interdependent nature of most problems, they can affect or be affected by other problems at any level of human activity. For instance, technological improvements in such fields as transportation or energy resources can drastically alter the nature of basic social structures at all levels. The opposite also can occur: Changes in patterns of human functioning can influence the nature of technological developments, creating new problems in this area. Little human activity takes place that does not involve the need for some tvpe of problem-solving effort.

Because problems are unavoidable, most persons spend a considerable portion of their time trying to solve them. Among other factors, the amount of time invested in problem-solving effort usually will vary with the perceived importance and complexity of a problem. Problems viewed as important and complex obviously will require more time and effort than those viewed as less important and complex. However, whether trivial or serious, simple or complex, all problems demand some attention. If nothing else, a decision must be made to ignore a problem and hope it goes away or to confront it directly and hope it can be solved.

The degree to which problem solving will be successful is determined by the nature of the problem and by the methods employed. Some problems are relatively routine and require little problem-solving effort since past experiences can be used as a guide. In such situations, there typically is certainty about what the problem is, how it should be solved, and whether it is likely to be solved. Other problems, however, are slightly more difficult to solve. These problems generally are characterized by less than adequate information and some uncertainty about what the problem is or how it can be solved. To deal with this type of problem, routine methods could be modified, although there might be less expectation of successfully solving the problem. Finally, there is a third type of problem that is the most difficult to solve. For this type of problem, nonroutine methods, which usually require a great deal more problem-solving effort, must be used. Because this third type of problem is relatively complex and ambiguous and provides little information but a lot of uncertainty, ready-made solutions or modifications no longer are adequate. Instead, custom-made solutions must be developed. However, even with a custom-made approach for structuring problem-solving procedures, there is still no guarantee of solution outcomes.

Many custom-made approaches are developed using a strategy of trial and error. Bits of available information are gathered and formed into some type of pattern to define a problem, and then attempts are made to develop solutions based upon this definition. The general procedure involved in such situations is usually hit-or-miss and less than systematic. Attempts might be made to introduce some structure, but they often lack any guiding theoretical base or logical consistency.

In addition to informal, trial-and-error approaches for solving nonroutine types of problems, there also are more formal, structured approaches that have been developed specifically to aid in solving such problems. These approaches are commonly referred to as creative problem-solving (CPS) techniques and are the primary concern of this book. Because other methods exist for routine-problem situations, CPS techniques will be most appropriate when custom-made solutions are required. Although these techniques might appear to operate without a guiding theoretical base or a logical pattern, the majority are based upon specific principles and assumptions about creative thinking and problem solving.

The major assumptions underlying the formal methods of CPS are specific to their intended purposes. Most techniques for analyzing and redefining problems, for example, assume that these functions can be best performed by factoring problems into their basic elements, examining the interrelatedness of these elements, and achieving perspectives that are remote from the original definition. Moreover, initial problem definitions may be either broadened in scope or made more narrow and specific. Most idea generation methods, in contrast, are patterned into forced-relationship or free-association processes and assume that deferring judgment and producing a large quantity of ideas are essential functions. However, many of the principles underlying one category of techniques often will apply to another. A more detailed description of these principles and assumptions will be provided later.

Before these techniques are discussed, the context surrounding their use needs to be detailed. In particular, the nature of problems and problem solving, use and benefits of CPS techniques, and classification of the techniques presented in this book will be discussed in the following sections. An understanding of these topics should help to increase the likelihood of selecting appropriate techniques and successfully applying them.

DEFINITION OF A PROBLEM

Obviously, CPS techniques should be used only when a problem exists. Investing time and other resources to resolve a situation in which there is no actual problem would be a fruitless exercise. Thus, the first step or precondition to effective problem solving is knowing the basic characteristics of a problem.

A problem can be defined as any situation in which a gap is perceived to exist between what is and what should be. If an actual and a desired state are viewed as identical, then no problem exists. However, all problems are relative since what might be a gap for some persons might not be for others. If a family has an income of $20,000 per year but believes that they need $50,000 to achieve their desired lifestyle, then they have a problem. Their neighbors, in contrast, might believe that their $20,000 a year income is adequate for their needs, so they do not have a problem.

In addition to being relative in magnitude, problem gaps are frequently dynamic in that either the actual or desired state of a problem, or both, are subject to change.[1] When the actual state remains constant but the desired state changes, the situation is one of "anticipated opportunities" since a change in goals will be required; when the actual state changes but the desired state remains constant, a situation of goal threat is created; when both states change, opportunistic developments might occur such as new-product ideas.

The degree to which problem gaps will be dynamic is entirely subjective. Gaps between current and desired states exist only as perceived by an observer. Consequently, the stability of problem states depends upon the stability of observer perceptions. If the "owner/perceiver" of a problem believes there has been a change in problem states or size of the gap, there will be a change; if no change is perceived, then no change will exist. In addition to the existence of a problem gap, four other "preconditions" must exist.[2] First, there must be some awareness that a gap exists. Without this knowledge, there can be no problem. Although this distinction appears obvious, it is an important one. If a production manager is unaware that productivity has declined below a desired level, then no problem exists since there is nothing to solve until awareness of this gap develops. Thus, it will be a problem *after* awareness develops but not before. Second, there must be a perceived need to solve the problem. If a chief executive officer (CEO) is aware of a toilet-paper shortage in company restrooms, the CEO might not be motivated enough to do anything about it. Of course, if the executive restroom is included in the shortage, then the CEO might quickly develop a perceived need! Third, the size of the gap should be measurable in some way. If the problem is low subordinate motivation, there must be a method to accurately measure motivation. Otherwise, there will be no way of knowing when the desired level of motivation is achieved. Finally, the skills and resources needed to solve a problem must be present or at least easily obtainable. If, for example, the director of a social-work agency sees a need to increase the number of in-home client visitations, the problem will be unsolvable unless the required number of people with the necessaryy skills are available. Thus, CPS techniques will only be as useful as the availability of resources needed to implement a problem solution.

In summary, the following preconditions are necessary in order to begin the problem-solving process:

1. The existence of a gap between what is and what should be
2. An awareness that a gap exists
3. The motivation to decrease the gap
4. An ability to measure the size of the gap
5. The abilities and resources required to close the gap

The absence of any one of these preconditions could indicate that problem-solving effort is not justified but that the existence of a problem should be reevaluated by examining the available information. Only by careful attention to problem identification can there be any hope of successfully using CPS techniques.

PROBLEM STRUCTURE AND TYPES OF RESPONSES

Most problems can be classified according to their degree of structure. Depending upon the amount of information available about a problem gap, problems can be classified as being well-structured, semi-structured, or ill-structured.[3] A *well-structured* problem is characterized by the availability of all the information needed to close a problem gap. As a problem solver, you are unfamiliar with either the current or desired states of how to go about closing the gap between them. Such a situation is typified by its routine, repetitive aspects and usually can be solved using standard operating procedures (SOPs) that provide ready-made solutions. A *semi-structured* problem falls between the other two types. Enough information is available to partially define the nature of the gap, but uncertainty about either the actual state or the desired state, or about how to close the gap precludes the exclusive use of routine procedures. Typically, a combination of SOPs and creative responses will be required to solve this type of problem. An *ill-structured* problem provides the problem solver with little or no information on the best way to develop a solution. Because no clear-cut procedures exist for closing a problem gap, the problem solver must improvise and use custom-made solutions. Thus, the information required to solve the problem must be generated during the problem-solving process. Creative problem-solving techniques will be most appropriate for problems of this type.

Classifying a problem in one of these three ways is an individual matter. Even if two people possess the same amount and quality of information, they are likely to perceive the problem in different ways. As a result, the type of response used to deal with each problem type will vary according to the amount of structure perceived to exist by an individual problem solver.

In general, responses to problem structure will be either algorithmic, heuristic, or creative. Well-structured problems often can be solved using *algorithms.*

An algorithm can be thought of as a "recipe" that guarantees a problem solution if the problem solver follows a prescribed series of steps.[4] For example, computation of compound interest is an algorithmic procedure. For solving semi-structured problems, *heuristics* can be used. Heuristics are rules of thumb or guidelines that increase the likelihood of successfully solving a problem. In contrast to algorithms that will guarantee a solution, heuristics will only increase the odds of achieving a satisfactory solution. For solving ill-structured problems, *creative responses* generally will be most effective. Since no precedent exists for solving ill-structured problems, the responses must be custom made. Although heuristics will be applicable to some well-structured and ill-structured problems and creative responses will be applicable to some semi-structured problems, the primary concern of this book is the use of CPS techniques to develop creative responses to ill-structured problems.

A GENERAL PROBLEM-SOLVING MODEL

Knowledge of problem types and responses is only the first step in determining the context in which CPS techniques are used. Perhaps more important is an understanding of the major phases or stages involved in problem solving. While routine responses are already structured, creative responses require the development of a program to provide the structuring needed to solve ill-structured problems. The development of this program is what the problem-solving process is all about.

Problem solving generally is considered to be a multistage process. Although many frameworks and models have been proposed, one of the most well known is Simon's[5] three-stage process of intelligence, design, and choice. In the intelligence stage, the problem is recognized and information gathered for formulating a problem definition; in the design stage, problem solutions are developed; in the choice stage, the solution alternatives are selected and implemented. Each of these stages has been modified and used to organize the techniques in this book in regard to problem analysis and redefinition (intelligence), idea generation (design), and idea evaluation and selection (choice).

These stages also are characterized by convergent and divergent processes. The convergent process involves a narrowing down of information to some manageable unit; divergent acts are just the opposite: Information is spread out in an ever-widening path. To illustrate the convergent and divergent processes, consider the problem-solving funnels shown in Fig. 1–1. Problem analysis and definition (intelligence) involves taking a large amount of information about a problem, analyzing it, and then narrowing down a number of definitions to achieve a working statement of the problem. After convergence on this statement, the idea generation stage (design) involves a divergent process of generating many different ideas. Finally, the idea evaluation and selection stage (choice)

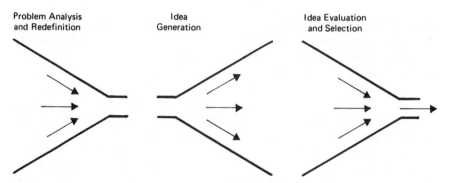

Fig. 1–1. Basic problem-solving funnels.

consists of reducing the pool of ideas to one or two that will be likely to solve the problem. The solution is then implemented and evaluated for its effect upon the problem.

For practical purposes, this model is limited in its ability to specify behaviors that should occur within each stage. A more useful approach would be to consider each of Simon's stages as a problem-solving stage in miniature. When the stages are divided into substages of intelligence, design, and choice, the necessary activities can be more clearly identified.[6]

Using an adaptation of a model developed by Brightman,[7] we present an expanded problem-solving model that incorporates CPS techniques in Fig. 1–2. The model begins when a problem situation is initiated by environmental stimuli. In the intelligence stage of the model, the initial problem definition is analyzed and a search is begun for collecting problem-relevant information. The design substage then is initiated in which alternative problem definitions are generated followed by selection of a working definition in the choice substage. This definition is stated in the form of a problem statement that is used to begin the intelligence substage of the design stage. The primary activity in this substage is the search for ready-made solutions that could be used in whole or modified form to solve the problem. If a solution is not available, possible CPS techniques are generated in the design substage and one or more techniques selected in the choice substage.[8] By use of these techniques, problem solutions are generated and the choice stage is entered. The intelligence substage of the choice stage is concerned with the search for information that can be used to evaluate the potential solutions. Possible solution consequences are then generated in the design substage followed by selection of a tentative solution in the choice substage. If no new information about the problem is received by the time a solution is needed, the solution is implemented and its success evaluated through the feedback loop to the environmental stimuli. If the solution is not implemented (due to new information or other factors), the process recycles to one of the

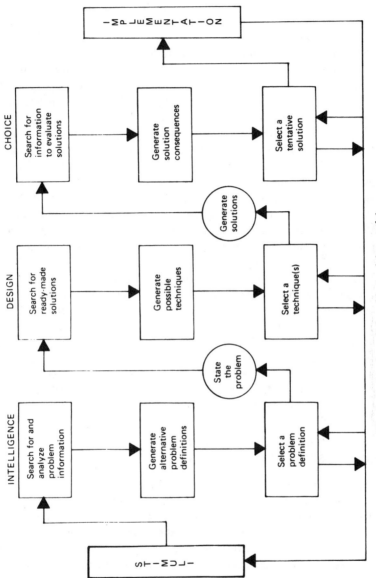

Fig. 1–2. An expanded problem-solving model.

three stages or the environmental stimuli. It also should be noted that events could cause the process to feedback to the starting point at the end of any one of the three stages.

Although the model in Fig. 1-2 is useful for describing basic CPS substages in relation to CPS techniques, it says little about the creative process itself. A considerable body of literature exists on this topic, the most well known represented by the work of Wallas.[9]   According to Wallas, the creative process consists of four stages: (1) preparation, (2) incubation, (3) illumination, and (4) verification.   Preparation involves gathering all available information about a problem and would correspond to the intelligence stage in Simon's model.   Incubation is not explicitly included in Simon's model but refers to the time at which conscious effort is suspended but attention is still given to the problem on a nonconscious level.   Illumination is the "aha" experience that often occurs when a feasible problem solution is recognized; it is likely to be present during all three of Simon's stages.   Finally, verification is testing the validity of an idea and making any necessary refinements.   Verification will be most evident during the choice stage.

Although all of these stages are important to the CPS process, not all of the techniques described in this book make full use of all four stages.   Most of the group idea generation techniques, in particular, are deficient in providing a period of incubation.[10]   Instead, these techniques sacrifice incubation for producing a large number of ideas within a relatively short period of time.   As a result, individual problem solvers must decide for themselves if a lack of incubation is justified by the quickness with which ideas can be generated with these methods.   Most of the individual techniques, of course, will provide greater opportunity for idea incubation.

THE USE (OR MISUSE) OF CREATIVE PROBLEM-SOLVING TECHNIQUES

Although it will not always be the case, CPS techniques have the potential to be misused if consideration is not given to the appropriateness of their application. When misuse of CPS techniques does occur, it often is due to a general misunderstanding about their purpose.   Perhaps the most common misperception about purpose is equating CPS with generating ideas.   Although many CPS techniques were developed for the purpose of idea generation, it is but one stage in the CPS process.   CPS is like any other problem-solving process except that primary attention is given to solving a specific type of problem.   In particular, CPS is concerned with solving problems characterized by inadequate information, indeterminacy of outcomes, and inadequacy of routine procedures.

There seem to be at least three ways in which CPS methods can be used (or misused).   For purposes of convenience, these approaches can be divided into the following categories: (1) the panacea approach, (2) the shotgun approach, and (3) the contingency approach.

The panacea approach is characterized by the universal application of a "tried and true" method without regard to its suitability for different problem situations. Persons who assume that there is one best way to solve a problem might reason that they have been successful in using their pet technique in the past and there is no reason why they should change now. A favorite technique of such persons is Classical Brainstorming, possibly because of its high visibility over the years. Frequently, people will persist in using the panacea approach because they have developed elaborate justifications for its use and, consequently, a strong sense of ownership. For such persons, the use of alternative approaches might be seen as involving too much risk.

The shotgun approach is based upon the assumption that even though there might be uncertainty about what the target is or how to get there, something is likely to be hit if you throw enough buckshot at it. Thus, it is assumed that the more techniques used, the greater will be the probability of solving the problem. Actually, this approach has some merit. The state of the art in problem solving is not sufficiently developed that it is possible to prescribe—with absolute certainty— a technique for every conceivable problem situation. A difficulty arises, however, when a number of techniques are indiscriminately applied to all problems encountered. When this occurs, the shotgun approach has little more to offer than the single-mindedness of the panacea approach. Nevertheless, users of the shotgun approach will be more open to trying a variety of different techniques.

The third approach, and the one upon which this book is based, assumes there is no one best way to solve nonroutine problems. Rather, it is assumed that the technique used will depend upon the nature of the problem and the conditions surrounding it. Persons using this approach typically will devote considerable effort to analyzing a problem and evaluating the appropriateness of a large number of techniques before attempting to solve the problem. The difficulty, of course, is knowing which techniques will be most effective in which situations.

All of these approaches will be subject to possible misuse: the panacea approach in emphasizing one best method; the shotgun approach in using a limited number of techniques without considering their appropriateness; and the contingency approach in failing to consider the specific features of a situation that will determine the likely success of a particular technique. The contingency approach, however, would seem to have the greatest potential for solving ill-structured problems.

BENEFITS OF USING CREATIVE
PROBLEM-SOLVING TECHNIQUES

Obviously, there will be many trade-offs involved in using most techniques. CPS techniques are by no means foolproof or immune from failure. Like many other products of the social and behavioral sciences, they are subject to the same limitations of human skills, abilities, and motivation; and, if inappropriately applied, they even could increase the severity of a problem.

There are, however, certain positive consequences that might be expected from using CPS techniques. According to Summers and White,[11] such benefits might include (1) a reduction in problem uncertainty, (2) an increase in the number of available solution alternatives, (3) an increase in competitive advantage, (4) a decrease in the number of solution revisions, and (5) a more efficient utilization of individual abilities.

Uncertainty Reduction

A major obstacle to solving many ill-structured problems is the initial uncertainty experienced about problem dimensions and likely outcomes. The existence of a problem might be recognized but its scope, number of dimensions and how they fit together might be totally unknown. Because of the emphasis upon generating problem data and possible solutions, most CPS techniques will decrease uncertainty by increasing the amount of problem-relevant information. Thus, the more information known about a problem and how to solve it, the less will be the uncertainty about eventual resolution of the problem.

Increased Alternatives

Perhaps the most widely recognized benefit of CPS methods is the possible increase in solution quality provided by the generation of a large number of alternatives. Based upon simple probability, a large number of alternatives will be more likely to yield a workable solution than the first one or two ideas that happen to emerge. If only a few alternatives are considered, the best possible solution might be overlooked.

Increased Competitive Advantage

This benefit applies to both profit- and nonprofit-oriented organizations. The expected benefits for the former will be increased profits; for the latter, benefits will be expected in improvements in services offered. The primary benefit for both types of organizations is derived from increased alternatives and new ways of looking at problems provided by many CPS techniques. If, for example, a company is concerned with expanding its market area or increasing the number of potential buyers in its present market, CPS techniques can provide the edge needed for survival or market dominance. In the case of expanding a market, CPS techniques can help in identifying new markets; in the case of increasing the number of potential buyers, new products or modifications of old ones might be more easily developed. In any event, CPS techniques can provide the unusual solution that might go beyond the capability of problem solvers using more conventional problem-solving methods.

Decreased Revisions

One frequently encountered difficulty is the need to revise a problem solution once it has been implemented. The need to revise a solution is usually a result of inadequate problem analysis or definition, or a lack of feasible alternatives from which to choose a solution. Regardless of the cause, revisions can be costly at any level of problem-solving activity. However, because of their emphasis upon analyzing problems and generating alternatives, creative methods can help to decrease the likelihood that many revisions will be required. When time is in short supply or revisions involve substantial investments in resources, this can be an important benefit.

Efficient Utilization of Individuals

Most persons use only a portion of their abilities in their personal and work lives. This underutilization of human resources is especially notable for persons who perform mainly routine types of tasks that require little in the way of creative approaches. CPS techniques can help improve human-resource efficiency by opening up new ways for solving problems. Although not all persons will have the opportunity to use CPS techniques, those who do have the opportunity and fail to take advantage of it could be wasting their abilities.

CLASSIFICATION OF THE TECHNIQUES

The 105 techniques described in this book have been classified with regard to their applicability to four problem-solving stages: (1) redefining and analyzing problems (Chapter 3), (2) generating ideas (Chapter 4), (3) evaluating and selecting ideas (Chapter 5), and (4) implementing ideas (Chapter 6). An additional chapter (Chapter 7) has been included for techniques that cannot be easily classified into any one of the other chapters. These techniques have been classified as being either eclectic or miscellaneous.

Although other classification schemes could have been used, this particular one was selected for two reasons. First, the use of a sequential process reinforces the need to use a structured approach for solving ill-structured problems. Second, a very basic framework was required since a majority of the techniques are too limited in their problem-solving scope to warrant a more expanded classification model. It must be noted, however, that this classification is not necessarily intended to be used as a guide for selecting techniques or for describing the problem-solving process. Many of the techniques will be appropriate for more than one stage, and the classification is intended only to indicate *primary* areas of appropriateness and not how problem-solving activity actually occurs.

Redefining and Analyzing Problems

A major obstacle to effective problem solving is development of an adequate problem definition. If a problem is inadequately defined at the outset of the problem-solving process, the probability of achieving an effective solution will be diminished. Since this initial perception of a problem often will determine how it will be approached during subsequent problem-solving stages, this stage is perhaps the most important of all the problem-solving stages.

For purposes of classification, the techniques for this stage have been organized into redefinitional and analytical methods. Although there is some overlap in the processes involved, the redefinitional methods serve to provide new problem perspectives while the analytical methods help to break down a problem into its major elements and identify any possible interrelationships between the elements.

The sequence in which these methods should be used is difficult to specify. For some problems, analytical methods might be best used when preceded by redefinitional methods; for other problems, the reverse might be true. In Chapter 3, the redefinitional techniques are described first although it could have been done the other way around (i.e., analytical before redefinitional techniques). The order of presentation is probably less important than devoting effort to collecting information about a problem and developing a new perspective on it. Chapter 3 describes five redefinitional and five analytical techniques, although many of the techniques described in other chapters also would be useful for achieving the objectives of this stage.

Generating Ideas

The idea generation methods are classified according to individual and group approaches, although the distinction will not always be clear-cut. That is, all of the individual approaches could be modified for use by groups but not all the group approaches could be used by individuals. The design of many of the group methods is premised upon a collective pooling of ideas that cannot be achieved with a single individual.

Although not done so in Chapter 4, the idea generation methods also could be classified in two additional ways: (1) as brainstorming or brainwriting procedures, and (2) free association or forced relationships. For descriptive purposes, brainstorming refers to verbal generation of ideas while brainwriting involves silent, written idea generation. Since the individual methods are essentially brainwriting methods (unless modified for group use), this distinction applies primarily to the group methods. Both individual and group methods, however, rely upon either free association, forced relationships, or some combination of both. Free association is a process by which ideas are generated without the benefit of any particular stimulus. However, each idea suggested is used as a stimulus to spark another. Forced relationships, in contrast, are highly dependent upon a specific stimulus as a source for ideas and function by "forcing" together two or more related or unrelated ideas. (A more detailed discussion of the classification of idea generation methods is presented in Chapter 4). In Chapter 4, individual and group techniques are described for the idea generation stage. In addition, many of the techniques described in Chapters 3 and 7 also are useful for this stage.

Evaluating and Selecting Ideas

The techniques described in Chapter 5 are useful for the decision-making (or choice) phase of the problem-solving process. In the classification of the techniques for this stage, no major distinctions have been made between evaluation and selection since most of the techniques incorporate elements of both. That is, most of these techniques provide structure for assessing a number of different potential problem solutions as well as for choosing from among these solutions. The only major exceptions would be several of the techniques that are voting procedures with no provisions for evaluation.

Implementing Ideas

Four techniques have been included to assist in putting ideas into action. Three of the techniques are primarily useful for systematically guiding implementation in moderate to complex problem situations. In particular, these techniques will be helpful when there is a clear need to coordinate the timing and sequence of different activities associated with a problem solution. The fourth technique also will be useful for idea implementation, but was designed specifically to assist in anticipating possible negative consequences of different solution alternatives. Although this technique (Potential-Problem Analysis) could have been classified as a method for evaluating or selecting ideas, it was judged to be primarily applicable to the implementation stage. Nevertheless, it probably is more of a transition technique required to bridge the gap between these two stages.

Eclectic and Miscellaneous Techniques

This class of techniques represents a "catch-all" category for techniques that cannot be easily classified in one of the other problem-solving stages. The eclectic techniques consist of methods made up of a portion or all of two or more different techniques. Four of the five techniques classified in this manner are structured using sequential problem-solving stages. The other three eclectic techniques are more "pure," consisting of combinations of different techniques but without regard to any particular problem-solving process. The miscellaneous techniques are primarily characterized by their use of two or more problem-solving stages but do not include combinations of different techniques. In addition, some of these techniques provide structured procedures for the social-interaction aspects of group problem solving—a neglected feature in most CPS techniques. Many of the eclectic and miscellaneous techniques also will be useful for redefining and analyzing problems as well as for generating ideas.

Before concluding this section, two possible unintended consequences of the classification system should be noted. First, the placing of techniques within specific categories could be interpreted as indicating that every technique within a given category will produce equal results. This is not the case, however, since very little comparative research exists on the majority of the techniques. A second possible unintended consequence would be a tendency to place too much emphasis upon the organization of the techniques within the different chapters. The chapter outlines are intended to serve as a convenient framework for presenting the techniques and not as a guide for selecting them. The evaluations that follow each technique as well as the guidelines presented in Chapter 2 should prove to have the most value for selecting techniques.

SUMMARY

All human activity involves problems that command the attention, time, and effort of those affected. Success in solving problems will be partially determined by the methods used. In general, structured approaches will be more effective for complex, ambiguous problems that require nonroutine procedures than will less systematic, unstructured approaches. Although a considerable body of literature exists on solving routine types of problems, the focus of this book is upon the development of custom-made, structured approaches for solving ill-structured problems.

A problem can be defined as a gap between "what is" and "what should be." In order for a problem to exist, there must be an identifiable gap, awareness of its existence, motivation to decrease it, ability to measure it, and the resources to close it. Problems can be classified as being well-structured, semi-structured, or ill-structured. Well-structured problems can be solved using algorithmic procedures ("recipes"); semi-structured problems can be best dealt with using heuristics ("rules of thumb"); and ill-structured problems will require the use of creative problem-solving procedures. The problem-solving process can be conceptualized as involving three stages of intelligence, design, and choice; each, in turn, can be divided into three like substages. The intelligence substages are concerned with searching for information; the design substages, with generating definitions, solutions, and solution consequences; and the choice substages, with selecting definitions, techniques, and solutions. The creative-thinking stages of preparation, incubation, illumination, and verification roughly correspond to the problem-solving stages, although the incubation stage is more implicit than explicit.

Creative problem-solving techniques must be appropriately used if they are to be effective. They can be misused by adopting one technique as a "favorite" and attempting to apply it to all problem situations, or by indiscriminately applying a large number of techniques to any situation. The preferred approach is to assume that the choice of technique will be contingent upon the particular characteristics of the problem situation—that is, no one technique is likely to be best for all problems. Although creative problem-solving techniques can be misused, certain benefits can be expected if they are appropriately applied. Included among these benefits are reduction in problem uncertainty, increase in the number of solution alternatives, increase in competitive advantage, decrease in required solution revisions, and a more efficient utilization of human resources.

The techniques in this book have been classified with regard to their primary usefulness in redefining and analyzing problems, generating ideas, evaluating and selecting ideas, or implementing ideas. Techniques not classifiable in this manner have been categorized as eclectic or miscellaneous. Not all of the techniques can be neatly classified, however, as there will be some overlap in the applicability of certain techniques for different problem-solving stages.

NOTES

1. MacCrimmon, K. R. "Managerial Decision Making." In J. W. McGuire, ed. *Contemporary Management, Issues and Viewpoints.* Englewood Cliffs, N.J.: Prentice-Hall, 1974.
2. MacCrimmon, K.R., and Taylor. R.N. "Decision Making and Problem Solving." In M.D. Dunnette, ed. *Handbook of Industrial and Organizational Psychology.* Chicago: Rand McNally, 1976. The requirement that the gap be measurable was added by the author.
3. *Ibid.*
4. It is important to note that most CPS techniques use a prescribed series of steps but that a problem solution cannot be guaranteed due to the ill-structured nature of the problems to which CPS techniques are applied.
5. Simon, H. A. *The New Science of Management Decision,* rev. ed. Englewood Cliffs, N.J.: Prentice-Hall, 1977.
6. The result of this division (shown in Fig. 1–2) is similar in both structure and process to the Osborn-Parnes five-step model of creative problem solving (see, e.g., Parnes, S. J., Noller, R. B., and Biondi, A. M. *Guide to Creative Action,* rev. ed. New York: Scribner, 1977; also see the description of the creative problem-solving process described in Chapter 7).
7. Brightman, H. J. "Differences in Ill-Structured Problem Solving Along the Organizational Hierarchy." *Decision Sciences* 9:1–18 (1978).
8. A detailed discussion on technique selection can be found in Chapter 2.

9. Wallas, G. *The Art of Thought*. New York: Harcourt, 1926.
10. Among the techniques appropriate only for group use, the two major exceptions would be the Collective Notebook and Delphi techniques.
11. Summers, I., and White, D. E. Creativity techniques: "Toward Improvement of the Decision Process." *Academy of Management Review* 1:99–107 (1976).

2
Guidelines for Selecting and Using the Techniques

Any attempt to propose selection guidelines for CPS techniques presents a dilemma in terms of the need to have such guidelines and the current lack of research evidence to support their adoption. On the one hand, CPS techniques are like other problem-solving tools in their requirement for cost-effective application. It would be a waste of time, for example, to use group methods if the same results could be obtained with individual methods in less time.[1] On the other hand, little research is available for suggesting which techniques are likely to work best in which situations. This lack of a supporting research base probably is due to disinterest in and/or a lack of awareness about the many available CPS techniques. As a consequence, most existing research has concentrated upon the effectiveness of only a few of the most well-known methods, and very little has been accomplished in the way of comparative research. To provide a sound research base, selection guidelines require extensive research of the comparative usefulness of different techniques in different problem-solving stages and situations.

Until more research is available, the guidelines that follow should be viewed as general rules of thumb and not as recipes that will guarantee appropriate technique selections. In this regard, the following discussion is based upon some empirical research evidence but is drawn mostly from anecdotal reports on the experiences of those who have used many of the techniques.

The guidelines are organized to loosely correspond with the expanded problem-solving model presented in Fig. 1–2. The substages of this model have been used to develop a series of flowcharts that are described in the following sections. Fig. 2–1 deals with pre-problem-solving considerations to determine if a problem exists; Fig. 2–2 considers the need to redefine and analyze a problem as well as the need for others to participate in the process; Fig. 2–3 presents a list of redefinitional and analytical techniques; Fig. 2–4 presents techniques for selecting problem definitions; Fig. 2–5 considers the need for idea generation methods; Fig. 2–6 lists individual and group idea generation techniques; Fig. 2–7 describes considerations involved in selecting idea generation techniques; Fig. 2–8 presents techniques for evaluating and selecting problem solutions; and Fig. 2–9 describes techniques for voting on solutions (if required) and for implementing the solutions finally selected. Three tables also are presented to assist in technique selection. Table 2–1 classifies the techniques with regard to problem scope, Table 2–2 classifies the techniques in terms of their special training requirements and implementation difficulty, and in Table 2–3 the author "goes out on a limb" and presents a list of the "top 40" most useful techniques.

PRE-PROBLEM-SOLVING

The decisions made before entering the major problem-solving stages are important in determining how successful problem-solving activities will be. If a problem does not really exist (i.e., does not have the potential to be solved), considerable time and effort can be wasted in trying to solve it. To determine if a potentially solvable problem exists, five pre-problem-solving questions are posed in Fig. 2–1.

Once awareness of a potential problem develops, the existence of an actual problem gap must be determined. The required question at this decision point is, What, if any, discrepancy exists between an actual and a desired state? A car manufacturer, for example, might be concerned about the discrepancy between current gas-mileage data on a particular make of car and those imposed by governmental regulations. The existence of a gap should be verified by seeking additional information, if necessary, to substantiate that a problem does exist. The rationale for seeking such verification is based upon the possible negative consequences of failing to seek any verification. Thus, the consequences of failing to solve an important problem could be more serious than trying to solve a problem where none exists.

Of course, the costs of seeking and obtaining verification must be weighed against the costs of not obtaining verification. Thus, it might be said that *if the costs of obtaining and verifying information about a problem gap are less than the costs associated with not solving a potential problem, assume that a problem gap exists.* For instance, assume that a manager is informed about a potential customer service problem. Obtaining and verifying information about this problem may be rather costly in time and money. Hiring a research firm or constructing and implementing an informal questionnaire will divert needed resources from primary tasks. However, if the customer service problem is not resolved, the results can be disastrous. The company might lose needed business because of dissatisfied customers. In this example, the costs of obtaining and verifying information are less than those associated with not attempting to deal with the problem. Therefore, a problem gap exists. However, if it is determined that no problem gap exists, the process can be terminated at this point.

If it is determined that a gap exists, then the size of the gap must be measured. Although it might be desirable to measure the gap in quantitative terms, this is not always possible. Many problem gaps cannot be quantified, and more subjective

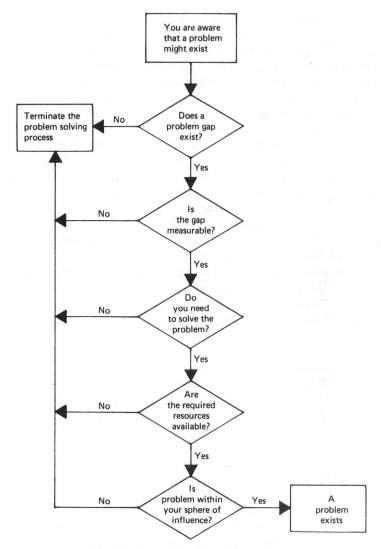

Fig. 2-1. Determining if a problem exists.

or qualitative measures must be used instead. Thus, a problem in machine tooling could be easily quantified, but a problem concerning the quality of working life would be more difficult to measure objectively. The use of either quantitative or qualitative measures, however, is probably less important than the ability to describe a current and desired state of a problem in precise, operational terms. That is, the measurement of a problem gap should be done using specific rather than general terms and with an understanding of how it will be known that the desired state of a problem has been achieved. A simple guideline at this point would be as follows: *If valid and reliable measurement criteria are available, assume that a problem gap exists.* If no technology exists for measuring a gap, the process should terminate since there will be no way of knowing if the problem was solved. When this occurs, you may want to select a new problem or redefine your current problem. If means are available to measure the gap, the next decision point in Figure 2-1 is encountered.

The next decision point is concerned with the problem solver's need to eliminate or narrow the gap. As discussed in Chapter 1, a problem will be present only when the motivation exists needed to close a problem gap. Furthermore, not all persons will be motivated equally by the same problem situations. Because of differences in values and needs among people, there can be considerable variability in the motivation that exists for any given problem situation. A basic guideline at this juncture would be this: *If closing a problem gap is likely to satisfy some personal need or value of one's self or significant others (e.g., friends, employers, coworkers), assume that a need exists to solve the problem.* Of course, such a determination will be subjective and not amenable to objective quantification. If no need exists, the process can terminate; if motivation to solve the problem does exist, the next step is to evaluate the availability of required resources.

A simple guideline exists for evaluating resource availability: *If the resources (time, information, money, personnel, etc.) required to solve the problem are not available and are not likely to be available in time to solve the problem, terminate the process.* A critical factor at this point is being able to predict if resources not needed at time X and not available then are likely to be available at time Y when they are needed. Of course, such a lack of information would, in itself, indicate an information resource deficiency. Furthermore, the seriousness of this deficiency must be weighed against the importance of solving the problem. If the problem is seen as important and uncertainty about the availability of resources can be tolerated, then a decision can be made to continue the problem-solving process. Nevertheless, if it can be assumed that adequate resources are or will be available, the last decision to be made in Fig. 2-1 is to determine if the problem is within the problem solver's "sphere of influence."

A problem will be within a problem solver's sphere of influence if actions can be taken without receiving authorization from superiors or others (e.g., peers, subordinates, experts) who might need to be involved. If the problem is not within this sphere of influence, superiors or relevant others must be consulted, their authorization or approval obtained, and their appropriate involvement determined. Should consultations with others reveal that a problem is totally outside of a problem solver's sphere of influence, the process will terminate unless approval to proceed is provided. Thus, a general guideline for this decision point would be as follows: *Consult with others whenever their authorization or approval is needed to solve a problem. If required authorization or approval cannot be obtained, terminate the process; otherwise, assume that the problem is within your sphere of influence.* If there is no need to consult with or rely upon others (i.e., the problem is within the problem solver's sphere of influence), and all of the preceding questions have been answered positively, then the pre-problem-solving activity can conclude with the assumption that a potentially solvable problem does exist.

REDEFINING AND ANALYZING PROBLEMS

Having concluded pre-problem-solving activity, the major problem-solving process can begin by entering the Intelligence stage (Fig. 1–2). As shown in Fig. 2–2, the first activity in this process is the search for and analysis of problem-relevant information. The major concern at this point is to collect information that can be used to determine the degree of problem structure. This is done by evaluating available information with regard to the current and desired problem states as well as the means for closing the gap between the states. Thus, the more that is known about the states and how to resolve the problem, the more structured the problem will be. Conversely, if little information is available about one or both problem states and how to close the gap, the problem will be more ill-structured.[2]

If available information indicates that the problem is *not* ill-structured, then routine procedures might exist for solving the problem and a search should be conducted to locate ready-made solutions. In this event, the problem solver would proceed to the Design stage where the applicability of ready-made solutions can be evaluated (see Fig. 2–5). CPS techniques would not be needed in this case, since the structure of the problem would provide the information needed to begin considering possible solutions. If the information about the problem states indicates that the problem is ill-structured, then CPS techniques can be used to analyze and redefine the problem. Before beginning this procedure, however, a decision must be made as to whether individual or group techniques would be more appropriate.

In most situations of this type, the decision to involve others will depend upon three factors:[3] (1) the need for a high-quality definition, (2) the need for others to accept the definition, and (3) the amount of time available. In most of the literature in this area,[4,5] the quality of a decision refers to the extent to which one solution (in this case, one definition) is likely to be more rational than another. Since rationality of definitions usually is not a major consideration when trying to solve ill-structured problems, this factor will be of little importance in formulating a guideline for involving others. The unknown characteristics of most ill-structured problems make it extremely difficult to say that one definition is likely to be better than another. In fact, the "best" definitions

Fig. 2-2. Selecting individual and group techniques for redefining and analyzing problems.

for problems that require creative responses usually are those that achieve a degree of remoteness from the problem area.[6] Thus, because the remoteness of one definition relative to another is a subjective matter, definition quality should not be a significant factor. The acceptance by others of the definitions and the available time, however, will be significant factors. Acceptance will be important if others are not likely to accept a unilateral decision on a definition or if others will be involved in proposing, evaluating, or implementing solutions. Time obviously will be an important factor since most group techniques will consume more time than individual methods.[7]

When the factors of acceptance and available time are used, the following guideline can be employed to help determine if individual or group methods will be better for formulating a problem definition: *If time is available and acceptance of others is critical, use group techniques; otherwise, use individual techniques.* This guideline should not be viewed as a hard and fast rule, however, since there are situations in which some flexibility might be desirable. For instance, if there is available time and acceptance of a definition is not critical, others might still be involved just for the sake of participation. This would be especially true in situations in which a manager might want to give subordinates an opportunity to practice their problem-solving skills. Another instance would be when an individual problem solver is dissatisfied with the definitions he or she has developed and wishes to receive additional stimulation from others. If time permits and acceptance is not critical, experts in the problem area also might be consulted to help analyze the problem. Nevertheless, the activity depicted in Fig. 2-2 would conclude with a decision to use either individual or group techniques.

With the need identified to select individual or group techniques, problem analysis and generation of alternative definitions can begin. The choice of one technique over another is difficult to specify since many of the techniques (shown in Fig. 2-3) are capable of producing similar results. The choice of a redefinitional technique is especially difficult since most of these methods use different means to produce the same result, that is, remoteness from the original definition. The analytical techniques, on the other hand, have a distinguishing feature that makes their choice somewhat easier. All of these techniques are designed to assist in breaking down a problem into its major elements or attributes. The result should be increased problem understanding.

Of the redefinitional techniques, three methods deserve special note because of their potential linking functions with other problem-solving activities. Two of these techniques, Boundary Examinations and Goal Orientation, can help in the transition between analysis and redefinition and will be particularly useful for testing initial assumptions about a problem and structuring the context for subsequent problem-solving effort. The third technique, Progressive Abstractions, has the potential to help in the transition between problem definition and the generation of problem solutions. This technique progressively enlarges a definition by moving through successively higher levels of problem abstraction. Repeated redefinition of a problem in this manner directs attention to the often changing nature of ill-structured problems that can occur throughout the problem-solving process.

Two useful redefinitional methods are the Five W's technique and the Why Method. The Five W's of Who? What? Where? When? and Why? help extract

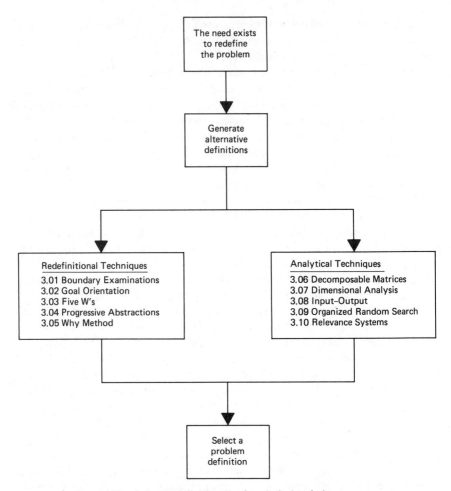

Fig. 2–3. Redefinitional and analytical techniques.

relevant problem information that can be used as stimulation for a variety of new definitions. The Why Method is relatively simple to use and a very powerful method for broadening an initial problem definition. It is similar to Boundary Examinations, but usually provides a greater number and variety of perspectives.

The analytical techniques, in contrast, can be more easily distinguished by their emphasis or lack of emphasis upon the interdependence of problem elements. Problems that exist as or can be conceptualized as systems can be analyzed by use of techniques that stress the interdependent nature of subsystems. Thus, these problems can be analyzed using Decomposable Matrices, Input-Output, or Relevance Systems. The other analytical techniques listed in Fig. 2–3 will be appropriate when there is little connection between problem elements and only a breakdown of the elements is desired.

Perhaps the best guideline for selecting redefinitional and analytical techniques is to use as many techniques as can be justified by the available time and the importance of the problem.[8] The more techniques used, the more thorough will be problem analysis and the greater the likelihood will be of achieving different problem viewpoints.

After analyzing the problem and generating alternative definitions, the next step in the process is to select a definition to use as a tentative problem statement. Although this decision can be made using intuition and personal judgment,

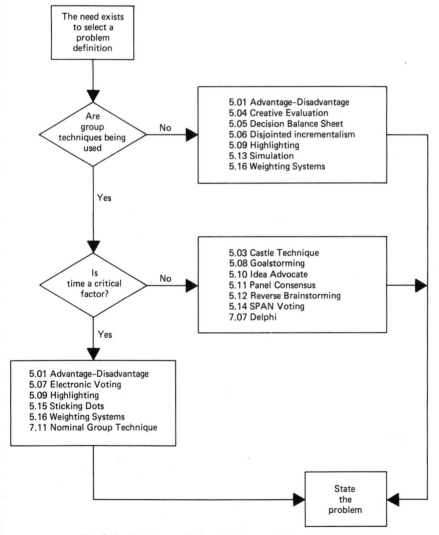

Fig. 2–4. Technique aids for selecting a problem definition.

there are situations in which more structured and systematic procedures might be desired. CPS techniques might be helpful, for example, in group problem-solving situations where there is likely to be conflict over preferred alternative definitions. Another situation might be when there is a large number of equally attractive definitions facing either an individual or a group. In either of these situations, the selection techniques listed in Fig. 2–4 might prove useful.

If individual methods are chosen, seven techniques are available as selection aids: Advantage-Disadvantage, Creative Evaluation, Decision Balance Sheet, Disjointed Incrementalism, Highlighting, Simulation, and Weighting Systems. Of these, Highlighting and Weighting Systems should prove to be the best all-around individual selection techniques.

If group methods are used, the amount of time available (or time willing to be committed) can be used as a criterion for choosing from among the group selection techniques. If time is available, there are nine techniques in the feasible set. All of these will be appropriate for evaluating and selecting definitions, with one exception. SPAN Voting makes no provision for group evaluation and will be useful only for purposes of voting. It also should be noted that the Delphi method is a group procedure appropriate for persons who are geographically distant from one another and should be used with this factor in mind. If little time is available, there are six potentially useful methods (which, of course, also could be used if time was not a critical factor). Of these, two are "pure" voting procedures (Technique 5.08 and 5.17) and one (Technique 7.10) includes a provision for explicit evaluation, as well as a voting procedure. Once a definition is selected and the problem is stated, the design stage of the problem-solving model can begin.

GENERATING IDEAS

As shown in Fig. 2–5, the first decision required in this stage is to determine if there are any ready-made solutions that can solve the problem. If no ready-made solutions (or ones that can be modified) are available, then CPS techniques can be used. If a ready-made solution is located, however, its applicability to the problems must be evaluated carefully. Depending upon the consequences of failing to solve a particular problem, a mistake in evaluating solution applicability could be disastrous. Solutions that worked in the past for an apparently similar problem might no longer be applicable to a present one. Thus, you must be certain that a previous solution can be transferred to a present problem. If you are not certain, then you must decide if transferring a previous solution will be worth the potential risk involved. Another consideration involved in evaluating the transferability of a ready-made solution is the amount of time available for problem-solving. Ready-made solutions typically will consume less time than custom-made solutions designed with the aid of CPS techniques. Thus, as a general guideline, the following can be said: *If time is available and a ready-made*

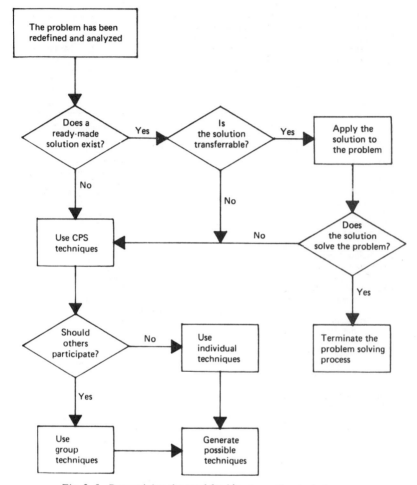

Fig. 2–5. Determining the need for idea generation techniques.

solution is not likely to solve the problem, use CPS techniques; otherwise, use ready-made solutions.

If it appears that a ready-made solution can be transferred to the problem, the solution can be applied and its effectiveness evaluated. If the problem is solved, the problem-solving process can be terminated; if the problem is not solved, the transferability of the solution can be reevaluated and the process continued until the problem is resolved or time runs out. However, if you decide to use CPS techniques, the use of individual or group procedures can be determined by using a previous guideline: *If time is available and acceptance of others is critical, use group techniques; otherwise, use individual techniques.* Once this decision is made, the next activity involves compiling a list of idea generation techniques.

Fig. 2–6 Idea generation techniques.

A list of such techniques is presented in Fig. 2–6 and is organized into either individual or group methods. As was true for the redefinitional and analytical techniques, all of the individual methods can be modified for use by groups, but the reverse would not necessarily be true.

Because of the large number of available idea generation methods, considerable difficulty might be encountered in selecting techniques to use. Although many of these techniques are capable of producing similar results, most problem solvers will be concerned about the cost-effectiveness of any methods they might employ. In addition to using the amount of time available and the acceptance of others to select individual or group methods, other important factors will be the scope of a problem, the implementation difficulty of a particular technique, and any special training requirements for using a technique. Other considerations involved in choosing idea generation techniques will be discussed in Chapter 4.

As an aid for screening the idea-generation methods, these latter three factors have been organized into a decision flowchart shown in Fig. 2–7. The first decision in evaluating a technique is to determine if the scope of the problem justifies the use of a particular technique. Using an overly complex method to generate ideas for a relatively simple problem might be a case of overkill; using a simple technique for a complex, wide-ranging problem, on the other hand, might be too limiting to generate solutions of sufficient breadth. Thus, a guideline would be as follows: *Select techniques that are proportionate in complexity to problem scope.* To illustrate, suppose that a problem exists on how to increase citizen participation in government—a rather broad-scope problem. To use relatively simple techniques such as Fresh Eye or Nonlogical Stimuli might be inadequate for the breadth of this problem. Instead, more appropriate methods might be the Collective Notebook, Delphi, or Nominal Group Technique.

In Table 2–1, the idea generation methods listed in Fig. 2–6 have been classified in regard to their estimated appropriateness for broad-, medium-, or narrow-scope problems. The techniques suitable for narrow- or medium-scope problems also might be suitable for broad-scope problems is used in combination to supplement one another. Personal experience in using the techniques, however, will be the best guide for problem scope decisions. If you decide that the scope of the problem does not justify the choice of a technique, consider another technique; if you decide that problem scope does justify the technique selected, the next decision is to evaluate the technique's implementation difficulty.

Implementation difficulty refers to such factors as the time, cost, and logistical considerations that might be encountered in using a technique. Obviously, most group techniques will present greater implementation difficulty than most individual techniques because of the effort involved in coordinating the activities of more than one person. The complexity of a technique, however, also will be a factor, regardless of the use of individual or group methods. For example, the Wildest Idea approach is a relatively simple group procedure that is slightly less complex than several of the individual procedures. Nevertheless, the need to solve the problem will be a major factor in justifying implementation difficulty. Thus, the following guideline might be used: *Select techniques that will be proportionate in implementation difficulty to the need to solve the problem.*

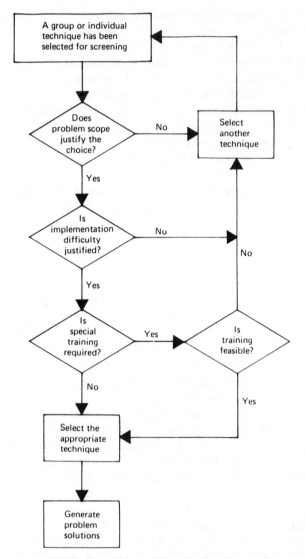

Fig. 2–7. Screening individual and group techniques for generating problem solutions.

At this point in the screening process, a technique that is justified by problem scope has been selected and a decision will have been made on whether or not its implementation difficulty justifies its selection. If its selection is not justified, another technique will have to be selected; if its selection is justified, the next decision concerns the need to obtain special training to use the technique.

Table 2-1. Classification of Idea Generation Techniques
According to Their Appropriateness for Problem Scope.

PROBLEM SCOPE			
BROAD	MEDIUM		NARROW
4.01	4.02	4.34	4.05
4.03	4.08	4.35	4.07
4.04	4.09	4.36	4.13
4.06	4.11	4.37	4.14
4.10	4.12	4.39	4.17
4.18	4.15	4.41	4.23
4.19	4.16	4.43	4.26
4.24	4.20	4.44	4.28
4.25	4.21	4.47	4.38
4.29	4.22	4.50	4.45
4.42	4.27	4.51	4.54
4.49	4.30	4.52	4.57
4.53	4.31	4.54	4.58
4.55	4.32	4.61	5.59
4.56	4.33		
4.57			
4.60			

Other than some practice in their use, most of the individual techniques do not require any special training. Many of the group techniques, however, do require a certain skill level on the part of a group leader and, in some cases, the group members. Because of these special requirements, caution must be used before selecting any of these methods unless the needed training can be obtained. For example, Synectics and Problem-Centered Leadership both rely upon a highly skilled group leader and probably should not be used unless such a leader is available. If training is important but it is not feasible to obtain it within the time available, another technique should be selected.

To evaluate training feasibility, the following factors should be considered: (1) the financial costs of the training program, (2) the availability of the program in relation to the urgency of the problem, and (3) the time the manager or others might be taken away from their jobs. If little time is available in which to solve the problem, techniques that involve substantial leader or member skill development should be avoided. A basic guideline for justifying the use of a technique that requires training is this: *Select techniques that will be proportionate in training importance to the need to solve the problem.* Thus, the greater the need is to solve the problem (and perhaps the more important it is), the greater will be the justification for using a technique that requires special training.

To aid in the selection decisions involving technique implementation difficulty and training importance, the group idea generation techniques have been

Table 2-2. Classification of Idea Generation Techniques According to Training Importance and Implementation Difficulty.

TRAINING IMPORTANCE

		HIGH	MEDIUM	LOW
IMPLEMENTATION DIFFICULTY	HIGH	4.31 4.55 4.57	4.54 4.56	4.37 4.58
	MEDIUM	4.35 4.42 4.60	4.36 4.43 4.47 4.49 4.51	4.32 4.33 4.38 4.40 4.45
	LOW		4.41 4.48 4.50 4.52 4.53	4.34 4.39 4.44 4.46 4.59 4.61

classified in Table 2-2 as being either high, medium, or low in these two dimensions. (The individual techniques have been excluded from this classification since, for the most part, implementation difficulty and training importance are not problematic for them.) As shown in Table 2-2, six (19%) of the 32 techniques have been estimated to be low on both dimensions while four (13%) have been estimated to be high on both dimensions. However, being either high or low on the dimensions is neither a positive nor a negative statement about the usefulness of the techniques classified. As noted previously, the amount of time available, urgency of the problem, and the feasibility of obtaining training also will be important determinants of whether one technique is selected over another.

After satisfactorily answering the questions in Fig. 2-7 and selecting a technique or combination of techniques, you should begin the Choice stage of the problem-solving process.

EVALUATING AND SELECTING IDEAS

Before beginning the Choice stage, you should reassess the need for others to participate.[9] Although either individual or group techniques will have been used prior to this point, their continued use might no longer be appropriate. For example, if previous activity has consumed more time than originally thought, the urgency of the problem also might increase requiring that a solution be selected in a short period of time. In addition, the need for others to accept a solution also might have changed, thus permitting an individual decision to be made when group procedures had been used before. Whatever the reason, the same participation guideline used previously should now be reassessed. This guideline stated: *If time is available and acceptance of others is critical, use group techniques; otherwise, use individual techniques.*

Fig. 2–8. Individual and group techniques for selecting and evaluating problem solutions.

The decision point for using this guideline is shown in Fig. 2-8 and immediately precedes the first activity of the Choice stage. After it has been decided whether or not individual or group procedures should continue to be used, the first Choice substage begins with a search for information to evaluate the solutions generated. This search involves comparing each solution with any solution criteria and evaluating the availability of any resources needed to implement a particular solution. One of the guidelines used to evaluate resource availability during the pre-problem-solving stage also can be used at this point. This guideline stated: *If the resources (time, information, money, personnel, etc.) required to solve the problem are not available and are not likely to be available in time to solve the problem, terminate the process.* In this case, if the resources are not available and are not likely to be available when needed, another solution can be selected instead of terminating the process. If resource availability is not a problem, then a technique can be selected to aid in further evaluation of the potential solutions.[10]   The choice of an evaluation and selection technique can be aided by considering the amount of time available for evaluation and selection. Other factors also could be important but were not included as a decision point. Perhaps the most important of these is technique implementation difficulty. In Fig. 2-8, the estimated implementation difficulty of the techniques is denoted in parentheses following each technique. If time is not critical (i.e., there is time available), techniques 5.02, 5.03, 5.05, 5.08, 5.10, 5.12, 5.13, or 5.16 can be used; if time is critical, then techniques 5.01, 5.07, 5.09, or 5.15 can be used. (Of course, these latter techniques also would be appropriate if time was not critical.)   Any further discriminations among these methods can be made after examining the individual descriptions and evaluations of the techniques.

Before one of the techniques is used to select a solution, however, one final issue must be considered, but only if group methods are used. If group methods are used, it often is difficult to achieve consensus on the one solution that would be most likely to solve the problem. Because of differences in individual values and needs, ownership of a particular solution, or other factors, most groups rarely achieve unanimous consent, especially when the stakes are high if the problem is not resolved. And, frequently, there might not be sufficient time for the group members to resolve their differences. In such situations, the following guideline could be used: *If there is likely to be an unresolvable conflict in regard to preferred solution alternatives, use voting procedures; otherwise, try to select a solution using consensus.*

There are six techniques described in this book that were designed to function in part or in whole as voting procedures. All of these methods are listed in Fig. 2-9, where they have been grouped in regard to their appropriateness for available time. If time is not critical, SPAN Voting or the Delphi method might be used, since both of these require a substantial amount of time to use relative to other techniques. If time is critical, the Castle Technique, Electronic

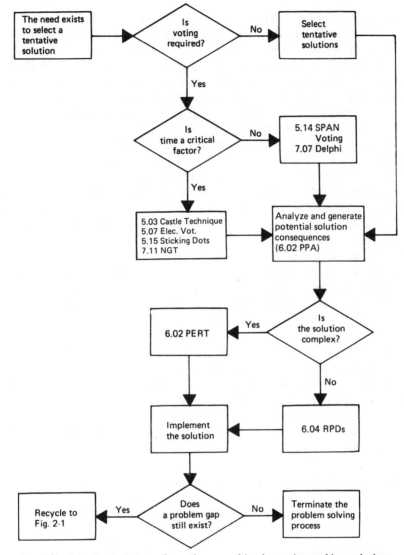

Fig. 2–9. Selecting techniques for voting on and implementing problem solutions.

Voting, Sticking Dots, or the Nominal Group Technique might be considered. If voting is not required, potential solutions will be selected and solution consequences analyzed.

By use of the selection techniques, several potential solutions should be chosen for final consideration. Prior to implementing any of these solutions, however, the potential consequences of each should be generated and analyzed.

Although this procedure can be done haphazardly and possibly be successful, the odds of successfully implementing a solution can be increased by using a more systematic procedure. One method would be to use one of the individual or group idea generation methods to develop a list of anticipated outcomes that might result from using the potential solutions. Then, a method such as Potential-Problem Analysis could be used to systematically guide consideration of the various possible solution consequences. Doing this should facilitate the selection of a final, tentative solution and result in less "postdecisional stress."[11]

The final solution should be considered tentative prior to implementation, since there is always the possibility that new information might become known that will alter the final solution choice. In this regard, the solution should not be implemented until it is absolutely necessary to do so. When it is time to implement the solution, one of two techniques may be used. The first, Program Evaluation and Review Technique (PERT), can be used with complex solutions requiring close monitoring of events and activities. The second implementation technique, Research Planning Diagrams (RPDs), can be used with less complex solutions and has the advantage of using feedback loops. Of course, not all solutions will require either of these techniques and all that might be needed is to consider who will do what, where, when, and how. As with any techniques, the costs of their use must be weighed against the potential advantages to be gained.

Following implementation of a chosen solution, the final activity in the problem-solving process is to determine if a problem gap still exists. If the gap between what is and what should be has been satisfactorily reduced or eliminated (using previously determined measurement criteria), the process can terminate. If, however, it is determined that a gap still might exist, the procedure should recycle to the pre-problem-solving activity described in Fig. 2–1. At this point, a decision would be made to begin the process again or to terminate it.

SUMMARY OF THE PROBLEM-SOLVING PROCESS

The problem-solving stages and guidelines can be summarized as follows:

Pre-Problem-Solving

1. Determine if a gap exists between what is and what should be.
   Guideline: If the costs of obtaining and verifying information about a problem gap are less than the costs associated with not solving a potential problem, assume that a problem gap exists.
2. Determine if the problem gap is measurable.
   Guideline: If valid and reliable measurement criteria are available, assume that a problem gap exists.

3. Determine if you need to solve the problem.
   Guideline: If closing a problem gap is likely to satisfy some personal need or value of one's self or significant others (e.g., friends, employers, coworkers), assume that a need exists to solve the problem.
4. Assess resource availability.
   Guideline: If the resources (time, information, money, personnel, etc.) required to solve the problem are not available and are not likely to be available in time to solve the problem, terminate the process.
5. Determine if the problem is within your sphere of influence.
   Guideline: Consult with others whenever their authorization or approval is needed to solve a problem. If required authorization or approval cannot be obtained, terminate the process; otherwise, assume that the problem is within your sphere of influence.

Problem Definition and Analysis

1. Search for and analyze problem information.
2. Determine if the problem is ill-structured.
   Guideline: The more information known about the problem states and how to resolve the problem, the more structured the problem will be.
3. If the problem is not ill-structured, search for and evaluate the adequacy of ready-made solutions.
4. If the problem is ill-structured, determine if individual or group procedures should be used to redefine and analyze the problem.
   Guideline: If time is available and acceptance of others is critical, use group techniques; otherwise use individual techniques. (Exceptions: If time is available and acceptance is not critical, others could be involved for their own personal development or to provide additional sources of stimulation.)
5. Select one or more redefinitional and analytical techniques.
   Guideline: Use as many techniques as possible that can be justified by available time and importance of the problem.
6. Generate alternative problem definitions.
7. Select a tentative problem definition.
   Guideline: Use CPS techniques in group situations if there is likely to be conflict over preferred definitions or in individual or group situations where there is a large number of equally attractive definitions.
8. State the problem definition decided upon.

Generating Ideas

1. Search for ready-made problem solutions.
2. If a ready-made solution exists, apply it to the problem and evaluate its success in eliminating the problem.

Guideline: If time is available and a ready-made solution is not likely to solve the problem, use CPS techniques; otherwise, use ready-made solutions.

3. If it is decided to use CPS techniques to generate problem solutions, determine if individual or group procedures should be used.

   Guideline: If time is available and acceptance of others is critical, use group techniques; otherwise use individual techniques.

4. Select an individual or group idea generation technique.

   a. Determine if the problem scope justifies the choice.

      Guideline: Select techniques that are proportionate in complexity to problem scope.

   b. Determine if implementation difficulty justifies the choice.

      Guideline: Select techniques that will be proportionate in implementation difficulty to the need to solve the problem.

   c. Determine if there are any special training requirements.

      Guideline: Select techniques that will be proportionate in training importance to the need to solve the problem.

Evaluating and Selecting Ideas

1. Determine if individual or group procedures should be used to evaluate and select ideas.

   Guideline: If time is available and acceptance of others is critical, use group techniques; otherwise, use individual techniques.

2. Search for information to evaluate the solutions.

   a. Evaluate resource availability.

      Guideline: If the resources (time, information, money, personnel, etc.) required to solve a problem are not available and are not likely to be available in time to solve the problem, select another solution.

   b. Compare solutions with solution criteria.

3. Select an individual or group evaluation and selection technique.

   a. Determine if time is a critical factor.

   b. Determine if implementation difficulty justifies the choice.

4. If individual procedures are being used, generate and analyze potential solution consequences; select a tentative solution for implementation.

5. If group procedures are being used, determine if voting procedures are required.

   Guideline: If there is likely to be an unresolvable conflict in regard to preferred solution alternatives, use voting procedures; otherwise, try to select a solution using consensus.

6. If voting procedures are required, use the amount of time available as one guideline for selecting voting techniques.

7. Generate and analyze solution consequences and select a tentative solution for implementation.

Implementation

1. Implement the solution, when appropriate, using implementation techniques. *Guideline:* If the solution is complex and requires close coordination of events and activities, use PERT; if the solution is less complex, use RPDs; if solution complexity does not justify the use of structured implementation techniques, use a less complex approach (e.g., who will do what, where, when, and how?).
2. Determine if a problem gap still exists.
3. If the gap has been eliminated or satisfactorily reduced, terminate the process.
4. If the gap still exists, recycle to the pre-problem-solving phase and begin the process again.

CONCLUDING COMMENTS

As mentioned at the beginning of this chapter, the development of technique selection guidelines is a difficult task. Even with such guidelines, there only can be a small reduction in the uncertainty over technique choice. The large number of techniques, lack of comparative research, and different intended purposes of the techniques make this choice all the more difficult. Yet, there must be some way to further reduce the number of techniques from which selections can be made.

One way to do this would be for an individual or group to read all of the technique descriptions and evaluations and apply a selection technique such as Weighting Systems to eliminate those methods that would not meet the needs of that individual or group. This procedure would be extremely time consuming, however, and require a high degree of motivation. Such motivation might be difficult to obtain since most people probably would rather expend their energy on the solution of current, "real life" problems.

Another alternative would be to present a list of "most useful" techniques. Although such a list would reduce the number of technique options, it could be an attractive alternative if used cautiously. To this end, I have developed my own list of the "top 40" techniques described in this book. The list, presented in Table 2–3, considerably reduces the number of available techniques described. As a result, conflict over technique choice will be reduced considerably, although the danger exists that a useful technique might be overlooked.

The techniques in Table 2–3 are not presented in any particular order of preference but are grouped according to their appropriateness for different problem-solving stages. In addition, no consideration was given to such factors as available time, problem scope, implementation difficulty, or training requirements. All of these factors still would be relevant for selecting the techniques. The list, however, does reflect my own judgment and biases and should be

Table 2–3. Suggested List of "Top 40" Techniques.

REDEFINING PROBLEMS	GENERATING IDEAS (GROUP TECHNIQUES)
3.01 Boundary Examinations	4.31 BBB
3.03 Five W's	4.35 Classical Brainstorming
3.05 Why Method	4.36 Component Detailing
	4.42 Gordon/Little
	4.43 Greeting Cards
	4.46 Pin Cards
	4.48 Rolestorming
	4.49 Sculptures
ANALYZING PROBLEMS	4.50 Semantic Intuition
	4.53 Stimulus Analysis
3.06 Decomposable Matrices	4.54 Storyboards
3.10 Relevance Systems	4.57 Synectics
	4.60 Visual Synectics
	7.07 Delphi Method
	7.11 Nominal Group Technique
GENERATING IDEAS (INDIVIDUAL TECHNIQUES)	**EVALUATING AND SELECTING IDEAS**
4.01 Analogies	5.02 Battelle Method
4.04 Attribute Association Chains	5.03 Castle Technique
4.13 Focused-Object	5.06 Decision Balance Sheet
4.20 Modifier Noun Associations	5.09 Highlighting
4.21 Morphological Analysis	5.10 Idea Advocate
4.22 Nonlogical Stimuli	5.15 Sticking Dots
4.23 Product Improvement CheckList (PICL)	5.16 Weighting Systems
4.24 Relational Algorithms	**IMPLEMENTING IDEAS**
4.29 Wishful Thinking	
4.30 Word Diamond	6.02 Potential Problem Analysis
	6.03 PERT
	6.04 Research Planning Diagrams

interpreted accordingly. Nevertheless, these 40 techniques do represent a wide range of technique alternatives that should be suitable for a variety of problem situations.

One notable omission in Table 2–3 is Creative Problem Solving. It was left out only because it does not conveniently fit into any one of the problem-solving stages. Otherwise, it could be considered a "top 40" technique across all of the stages.

Before concluding this chapter, one final comment should be made about the use of guidelines and flowcharts for selecting CPS techniques. It is not intended that such structured aids can substitute for individual creative processes. A lot of what can be termed creativity cannot be structured and packaged for use whenever needed. The techniques presented in the following chapters are only intended to serve as aids for adding structure—when it is needed—to the creative problem-solving process. In a like manner, the selection guidelines and flow-charts are not intended to imply that creativity can be structured. Instead, the primary intent of the guidelines and flowcharts is to provide a framework—when it is needed—that can help structure the *context* for using the techniques. The structure provided by the techniques and the context for their use will, it is hoped, help bring out more of the creative potential present in both individuals and groups.

NOTES

1. As will be discussed later, there are some occasions in which group involvement might offset the costs involved in expending more time for problem solving.
2. For a detailed discussion of problem structure, see my book: *Stalking the Wild Solution: A Problem-Finding Approach to Creative Problem Solving* (Buffalo, N.Y.: Bearly Limited, 1987). In it, I categorize problems into eight types, according to the degree of perceived familiarity with the initial and goal states and the transformations required to close the gap.
3. A complex model for prescribing subordinate participation in decision making has been developed by V. H. Vroom and P. W. Yetton (*Leadership and Decision Making,* Pittsburgh, Penn.: University of Pittsburgh Press, 1973). The model is based upon the formulations of N. R. F. Maier (*Problem Solving Discussions and Conferences: Leadership Methods and Skills,* New York: McGraw-Hill, 1963) and has been criticized for being unduly complex. For example, in an analysis of the Vroom-Yetton model, R. H. G. Field ("A Critique of the Vroom-Yetton Contingency Model of Leadership Behavior," *Academy of Management Review* 4:249–257 (1979) concludes that simpler models of participation can be equally valid. For this reason, a simpler model will be used in this discussion.
4. Maier, N. R. F., *op. cit.*
5. Vroom, V. H. and Yetton, P. W., *op. cit.*
6. de Bono, E. *Lateral Thinking: Creativity Step by Step.* New York: Harper & Row, 1970.
7. The outcomes of individual and group methods, however, can vary considerably due to differences in resources and the often inhibiting effects of social interaction.
8. The questions posed in Fig. 2–7 in regard to problem scope, implementation difficulty, and training importance might also be used to select the techniques, although the problem scope factor will be difficult to determine until more is known about the problem after analysis and redefinition.
9. There is some research evidence to suggest that groups of individuals writing alone (commonly known as nominal groups) are best used for generating ideas, but that verbally interacting groups are better for evaluating ideas (Van de Ven, A. H., and Delbecq, A. L. "Nominal Versus Interacting Group Processes for Committee Decision-Making Effectiveness." *Academy of Management Journal* 14:203–211 (1971)) Other research, however, casts some doubt on the validity of this finding. In a study by

T. T. Herbert and E. B. Yost ("A Comparison of Decision Quality Under Nominal and Interacting Consensus Group Formats: The Case of the Structured Problem," *Decision Sciences* 10:358–370 (1979)), it was found that nominal groups outperformed interacting groups on both idea generation and evaluation when the problem was structured.

10. The issue of resource availability is also likely to emerge when the evaluation techniques are used. However, because of its importance in implementing a solution, it was placed before technique selection to insure that it was considered.

11. Janis, I. L., and Mann, L. *Decision Making, A Psychological Analysis of Conflict, Choice, and Commitment.* New York: Free Press, 1977.

3
Redefining and Analyzing Problems

Although many of the methods discussed in the other chapters can be used to redefine and analyze problems, the techniques presented in this chapter have been selected for their special usefulness as problem redefinition/analysis methods. The ten techniques that follow have been grouped according to their applicability for either redefining or analyzing problems. For many problems, the distinction between these two processes will be blurred. The act of analyzing a problem often will involve analysis of major problem elements. The objective of both processes, however, is to develop a new way of looking at a problem.

In particular, the principles that underlie both redefinitional and analytical methods involve achieving a new perspective on the problem. The basic principle underlying the redefinitional techniques is one of developing a degree of remoteness from the original problem statement. By escaping from initial problem perceptions, the problem solver is forced to use divergent thinking that, in turn, should lead to more unique problem solutions. The analytical techniques, on the other hand, have as their underlying principle the factoring of a problem into its major dimensions or elements. The activities involved in breaking down a problem can help to organize the information available about a problem as well as to suggest new information that might not have been previously considered. Both processes are important, but neither one is capable of producing a "correct" problem definition. What should be produced, instead, is a better understanding of what the problem involves and a new way of viewing it.

As discussed in Chapter 2, the analysis and redefinition of a problem are the most important activities in the problem-solving process, since the produce of this stage largely will determine the nature and quality of any solutions that follow. However, once a problem has been analyzed and redefined, the new problem statement should be considered tentative. Next to failing to adequately analyze a problem, the largest error made by many problem solvers is rigidly sticking with the first new viewpoint that emerges. This error is especially significant for highly ill-structured problems where there can be considerable change in the amount and quality of information available. As new information is gained or new insights develop when ideas are generated or evaluated, many different revisions of a problem definition could be required. Thus, problem analysis and redefinition are not discrete functions to be separately carried out but, rather, activities that should occur simultaneously throughout the problem-solving process.

REDEFINITIONAL TECHNIQUES

3.01 Boundary Examinations

The act of defining a problem involves certain assumptions about problem boundaries. Boundaries determine how information is organized, how it is processed, and eventually how the problem itself is solved. Boundaries also make it easier to solve a problem by defining the amount of problem space available. If the boundaries initially are assumed to be closed and unchangeable, then it is not likely that they will be modified during subsequent problem-solving activity. Thus, if *A, B,* and *C* are assumed to represent problem boundaries at the outset of the problem-solving process, then they also will be assumed to be boundaries upon termination of the process. Although it is difficult to determine the correctness of such boundaries, there is no question that boundary rigidity will affect problem-solving success—especially when ill-structured problems are involved. Because ill-structured problems are open-ended, the initial analysis of their boundaries should be considered tentative since new information could arise that would require a restatement of a problem's boundaries. Thus, for the technique of Boundary Examinations to be effective, assumptions about problem boundaries must be examined throughout the course of problem-solving activity.

According to de Bono,[1] Boundary Examinations are based upon the assumption that a problem's boundaries are neither correct nor incorrect. It is not the assumptions underlying the boundaries that are examined. Rather, the objective of Boundary Examinations is to restructure the assumptions of a problem to provide a new way for looking at it. The basic steps for using Boundary Examinations are as follows:

1. Write down an initial statement of the problem.
2. Underline key words and phrases and examine them for any hidden assumptions.
3. Without considering the validity of these assumptions, identify any important implications they suggest.
4. Write down any new problem definitions suggested by the implications.

To illustrate this technique, consider the following problem of a pharmaceutical company: In what ways might *we encourage consumers to purchase* our medicine in caplet form? The boundaries of this problem can be examined by considering whether the locus of responsibility might be shifted from the company to the consumer or others; whether consumers might be rewarded rather than just encouraged to purchase the medicine (or, perhaps, punished in some way for not buying it); and whether the focus might be better applied to using rather than purchasing the medicine, since the purchasing decision is based more upon use than upon the act of purchasing. When these and other boundaries of this problem are examined, it might be restructured so that the problem-solving effort will take an entirely new and more productive direction.

Evaluation The major strengths of Boundary Examinations are their potential for (1) producing more provocative problem definitions, (2) clarifying often indistinguishable problem boundaries, (3) demonstrating the importance of formulating flexible problem definitions, and (4) coping with management teams that are overly precise in their problem definitions.[2] The major weakness of the technique is its lack of structure for specifying how boundary assumptions should be analyzed. In this regard, the technique is probably more a way of thinking about a problem than it is a step-by-step redefinitional procedure.

3.02 Goal Orientation

As described by Rickards,[3] Goal Orientation is a way of thinking about a problem for the purpose of clarifying its goals or objectives. It is implemented by considering the needs, obstacles, and constraints of a problem. The following steps are used:

1. Write down a general description of the problem, being sure to include all pertinent information.
2. Ask: What do I want to accomplish (needs)? What is preventing me from getting what I want (obstacles)? What restrictions must I accept to solve the problem (constraints)?
3. Using these questions as guidelines, write down possible redefinitions of the original problem statement.

As an example of this technique, consider the following general problem statement: I own a house located very near the ocean. The house is protected by an old sea wall that has settled and developed numerous cracks. I am concerned that the wall will collapse during a storm and damage or destroy my house.

Based upon the needs, obstacles, and constraints of this situation, the problem could be redefined as how to

1. Prevent the cracks from spreading (a need)
2. Keep the house away from the ocean (a need)

3. Keep the ocean away from the house (a need)
4. Continue relying upon the wall to protect the house (a constraint: the present wall must be retained for historical reasons)
5. Repair the wall (an obstacle: only limited funds are available)

By redefining the problem in this way, new possibilities might be suggested for solving the problem. Thus, one solution might be to raise the house on stilts and completely ignore the obstacle of high costs for repairing the wall.

Evaluation   According to Rickards, Goal Orientation is more an attitude than it is a technique, although it can be difficult to make a meaningful distinction between the two. In general, the process of applying the technique should help to create the attitude needed. Nevertheless, because it is a relatively unstructured approach for redefining problems, some practice will be needed to apply it effectively. Perhaps the most important consideration is to keep an open mind about exactly what the problem is and how it should be solved. Otherwise, the natural tendency will be to redefine and solve the problem using preconceived ideas—clearly an undesirable tactic, but especially so when dealing with ill-structured problems. When a problem has an unknown number of possible solutions, the initial definitions of the problem need to be as open-ended as possible.

Although there will be some individual differences in how well the technique is applied, it should be useful for forcing consideration of major problem needs, obstacles, and constraints—a consideration essential for all effective problem solving. The most fruitful application of the method, however, will be its use as a problem-broadening device at the outset of the problem analysis stage. Thus, Goal Orientation can be a critical problem-solving activity.

3.03 Five W's and H

The Five W's and H technique is a widely used redefinitional approach. It is a variation of the Who? What? Where? When? and Why? questions used in journalism, with a How? question added. In journalism, these questions help writers gather data about a story in a systematic manner. All the essential elements of a story are more likely to be included if their collection is structured.

In creative problem solving, fact gathering also is needed to stimulate problem redefinitions. As a result, the Five W's and H method has been used in a number of creative problem-solving models. Perhaps the most explicit use has been in the Osborn-Parnes CPS model.[4]   Although the Five W's and H approach is used primarily to collect problem information, it also can be used in other stages. For instance, the data generated by the questions might be used to develop criteria during idea evaluation and selection (Solution-Finding in the Osborn-Parnes model).

The primary purpose of the Five W's and H questions is to provide a framework for systematically gathering problem-relevant data. The data then can be used to generate new problem perspectives. From these perspectives, the most important one then would be selected and used as the basis for idea generation. Basic steps for the Five W's and H method are as follows:

1. State the problem using the format: In what ways might...? (IWWM ...?).
2. Write down separate lists of Who? What? Where? When? Why? and How? questions relevant to the general problem. Withhold all judgment during this activity.
3. Examine the responses to each question and use them as stimuli to generate problem redefinitions.
4. Write down any redefinitions suggested.
5. Select one redefinition that best captures the problem you are trying to resolve.

To illustrate this method, consider the problem, IWWM we motivate our employees to work harder? Possible questions and responses might be as follows:

Who are the employees? Blue-collar and white-collar workers; workers who are perceived as not working as hard as they should be.

Who doesn't work hard? Some employees with little direct supervision; employees who believe they are underpaid; employees who are physically sick on the job.

What is motivation? That which stimulates action and provides drive to accomplish a goal.

What does "work harder" mean? Accomplishing more with limited resources; being more efficient while maintaining quality.

What motivates most employees? Feelings of achievement; responsibility; recognition; money; sex; food; security; confidence that they know how to do their jobs.

Where are employees motivated to work hard? In their bosses' offices; in their work areas; at award ceremonies.

Where is employee motivation not a problem? Where basic personal and work needs are taken care of; where employees do a task from beginning to end; at companies *X*, *Y*, and *Z*.

When are employees not motivated to work hard? When they feel their contributions are not recognized and appreciated; when they don't have adequate resources to do their jobs; when their bosses are overbearing and exert too much direction and control; when their co-workers are uncooperative.

When do bosses try to motivate employees? During scheduled performance evaluations; when employees make a mistake; when employees do something well; when they are under pressure to increase productivity.

Why motivate employees to work harder? To increase productivity; to increase personal income due to employee participation in profit sharing; to become more competitive with other companies, to provide better customer service.

How can employees be motivated? With rewards; with punishment; by being told why they should work harder; through being asked what they want and need to do their jobs better.

After reviewing the responses to these questions, the following types of redefinitions might be generated:

IWWM we change perceptions about how hard employees work?
IWWM we provide certain employees with more direct supervision?
IWWM we obtain more money to reward hard-working employees?
IWWM we improve employee health benefits and services?
IWWM we establish more realistic employee work goals?
IWWM we better provide resources employees need to do their jobs?
IWWM we increase employee efficiency?
IWWM we better meet employees' basic needs?
IWWM we enrich employee jobs?
IWWM we involve employees in determining how to do their jobs?
IWWM we increase the company's overall productivity?
IWWM we increase cooperation among employees?
IWWM we improve customer service?

From this list, one redefinition would be selected for use during the idea generation stage. For example, the redefinition of better providing needed resources might be used as the problem statement. In this case, the focus then would shift from trying to change the employees to trying to change the situation.

In using this method, consider the following guidelines:

1. Do not include problem criteria in problem statements. For instance, an inappropriate statement would be: IWWM I reduce my inventory within three weeks at a cost of less than $1000? Using criteria "up front" this way often will limit potential perspectives and reduce the number of solution options.

2. Generate questions, responses, and redefinitions without regard to evaluation. Defer judgment until you have listed all the data. Then, converge and select the most useful items. Deferring evaluation usually will improve final quality of the redefinitions.

3. Remember that there is no such thing as a "correct" redefinition. The usefulness and importance of any redefinition depends upon the needs of each problem solver.

The latter solution then suggests a third problem definition: IWWM we move the tanks at the least possible cost? Since it is less costly to move a tank without disassembling it, this solution leads to a fourth definition: IWWM we to move a tank without disassembling it? Two solutions to this problem are to float the tank or roll the tank. Although it is possible that you might terminate the process at this level of abstraction, a final definition of the problem emerges: IWWM we float a large gasoline storage tank? Because this definition suggests one practical alternative (an air cushion) and one impractical alternative (construct a canal), the process is terminated, since further elaboration of the air cushion principle might be considered too abstract and thus impractical. This problem was actually solved by British army engineers who used the hovercraft principle to float 300,000-gallon gasoline storage tanks from one location to another. A rubber skirt was fitted around the base of a tank, inflated, and then towed to the desired site.

Another example of the Progressive Abstractions method is described by Rickards.[7] The problem in this case involved the development of a new machine for cutting grass. Two solutions were proposed: (1) develop a new lawn mower, and (2) develop new types of grass cutters. The grass cutter solution was used to suggest such possibilities as grass slicers, scrapers, or extractors. A manufacturer of grass-cutting machines might then select one of these possibilities for implementation. The solution selected, however, will depend upon the manufacturer's skill level. Thus, solutions involving mechanical operations would be within the feasible set of solutions while solutions that require biological treatment of grass, for example, would be rejected as too abstract.

Evaluation Progressive Abstractions is similar in principle to Relevance Systems and the Why Method, both of which also rely upon identifying connections among different problem elements. The major advantage of these approaches is the degree of structure provided the problem solver for systematically examining problem substructures and connections. However, when compared to less-structured redefinitional methods, such as Boundary Examinations, some loss in spontaneity and diversity might be expected. In addition, Progressive Abstractions has the potential disadvantage of requiring a decision on when the appropriate level of abstraction has been achieved (although this is also true with other similar methods). It is very easy to reject a definition as being too abstract when, in fact, further examination might reveal numerous practical applications. Conversely, it is just as easy to accept a definition as providing the best solution when a more abstract definition might produce a better solution. The type of problem, perceived problem importance, the problem solver's conceptual thinking ability, and the availability of necessary skills and resources all will help determine when the appropriate level of abstraction has been reached.

3.05 Why Method

Problems initially are defined at various levels of abstraction. Some problems are phrased in very specific terms, while others are more general with philosophical overtones. For example, a relatively concrete problem might be: In what ways might (IWWM) I improve the lighting in my office? An example of a more abstract problem would be: IWWM we increase compassion for our fellow humans?

Accepting the initial level of abstraction without further probing usually results in a limited problem perspective. The first definition formed may prove to be the least productive for idea generation. Therefore, it often is useful to explore a variety of abstraction levels. As each level is explored, a new problem definition is provided. One relatively easy way to do this is with the Why Method.

The following steps are used for the Why Method:[8]

1. State the problem as initially defined.
2. Ask why you want to do whatever is stated in the problem.
3. Answer the question asked in step 2.
4. Redefine the answer as a new problem question.
5. Repeat steps 2 and 3 until a high level of problem abstraction is achieved.

As an illustration of this method, consider the following problem: IWWM we reduce employee accidents?

Question: Why do we want to reduce employee accidents?
Answer: To protect employees from physical harm.
Redefine: IWWM we protect employees from physical harm?
Question: Why do we want to protect employees from physical harm?
Answer: So that they will be able to perform their jobs.
Redefine: IWWM we help workers perform their jobs?
Question: Why do we want to help workers perform their jobs?
Answer: To increase company profits.
Redefine: IWWM we increase company profits?
Question: Why do we want to increase company profits?
Answer: To improve the national economy.
Redefine: IWWM we improve the national economy?

In this illustration, the focus of the problem has moved from reducing employee accidents to improving the national economy. This last redefinition probably is beyond the scope of the company's resources and objectives. Thus, the best redefinition will be found at one of the lower levels of abstraction. However, it is possible that none of the redefinitions will be satisfactory. If so, the technique might be repeated using different answers for each of the questions.

It also might be useful to repeat the process even if one or more satisfactory redefinitions are produced. Additional perspectives will increase the number of options with a likely increase in redefinition quality.

Evaluation   The Why Method is similar to Boundary Examinations. However, it is perhaps even more useful for broadening a problem and exploring its various boundaries. It allows a problem to be pushed to its limits. In doing so, it can substantially increase the problem solver's understanding of the problem. The method also has a possible side benefit in allowing users to assess their basic goals and objectives. Choosing answers requires users to identify their value preferences, which usually are linked to goals and objectives. As a result, awareness will increase as to how the problem relates to broader concerns of an individual, group, or organization. Finally, the most basic strength of the Why Method is its ability to provide a variety of new problem perspectives.

A major weakness is the possibility that certain types of answers could limit the usefulness of the redefinitions. One inappropriate answer could affect all subsequent redefinitions. However, repeating the technique using different answers should overcome this weakness. Another difficulty might be trying to use the technique with a problem that initially exists at a relatively high abstraction level. The Why Method will work best with problems at low or moderate levels of abstraction. The best way to determine a problem's level is to use the technique and see how quickly the redefinitions become abstract.

ANALYTICAL TECHNIQUES

3.06 Decomposable Matrices

The method of using Decomposable Matrices to analyze problems has been drawn from the work of Herbert Simon,[9] who has extensively studied human problem-solving processes. Simon believes that complexity in the world has evolved from simple structures organized into progressively formal hierarchic systems. The human body, for example, consists of relatively simple, single cells organized into increasingly more complex patterns of functioning. The concept of a decomposable matrix is derived from Simon's view that hierarchic systems consist of successive, semi-independent subsystems, each of which is less complex than the preceding one (a box within a box within a box, etc.).

To understand complexity, complex hierarchic systems can be analyzed using a basic property of their structure: near decomposability. The concept of near decomposability refers to the fact that the subsystems of some hierarchic systems maintain some, although not total, interdependence upon other subsystems. For instance, in a formal organization, there generally will be less interaction between persons of different departments than between persons within the same department. In a totally decomposable system, in contrast, there will be no significant interaction among subsystems.

Simon's thinking in this area also can be extended to analyze complex, ill-structured problems. Problems that can be viewed as complex, hierarchic systems can be analyzed by breaking them down into their respective subsystems. The following steps are used for this process:

1. Determine if the problem is analyzable using subsystems.
2. List the major subsystems and the components of each.
3. Construct a matrix of the subsystems and their components.
4. Using a 1- to 5-point scale, weight the degree of relationship for each of the interactions between and within the subsystems.
5. Select the highest-weighted interactions for further analysis or generation of ideas.

To apply this technique, consider a problem of how to improve employee satisfaction within an organization. Since most organizations generally are viewed as complex social systems with hierarchic structures, this problem can be broken down into different subsystems. Three major subsystems related to this problem are shown in Fig. 3–2 and labelled, respectively, Organizational (A),

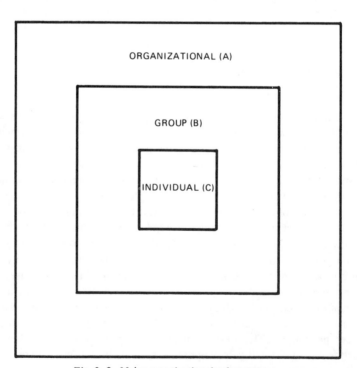

Fig. 3–2. Major organizational subsystems.

Group (B), and Individual (C). The components of each subsystem next are listed and arranged within a matrix as shown in Fig. 3–3. Weights then are assigned to each of the interactions, with higher numbers indicating greater frequencies of interaction or greater importance of the interactions. Based upon this matrix, the problem solver might want to concentrate upon all of the interactions *within* subsystems (the small triangles created by the diagonal line in Fig. 3–3) but pay particular attention to the interactions occurring between the group and individual subsystems, due to the higher weightings given these interactions. Relationships between specific components then could be selected as the focus for generation of problem solutions or additional analysis.

Evaluation This technique is similar to Relevance Systems in that there is a descending order of problem elements. The major difference is in the assignment of values and the consideration given to interactions between as well as within subsystems, both of which are not a part of Relevance Systems. There are, however, several factors that must be considered when using the Decomposable Matrices approach. First, not all problems can be analyzed into subsystem components or their scope might not justify such a breakdown. Second, the effectiveness of this technique will depend upon the problem solver's ability

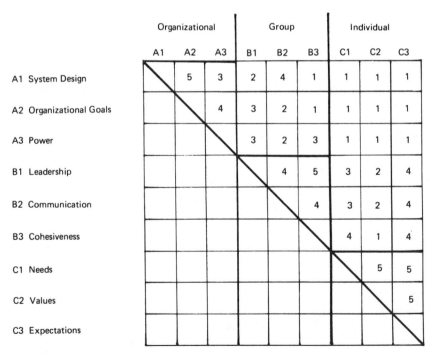

	Organizational			Group			Individual		
	A1	A2	A3	B1	B2	B3	C1	C2	C3
A1 System Design		5	3	2	4	1	1	1	1
A2 Organizational Goals			4	3	2	1	1	1	1
A3 Power				3	2	3	1	1	1
B1 Leadership					4	5	3	2	4
B2 Communication						4	3	2	4
B3 Cohesiveness							4	1	4
C1 Needs								5	5
C2 Values									5
C3 Expectations									

Fig. 3–3. A decomposable matrix of organizational subsystems and components.

to correctly identify all relevant subsystems and components and to accurately evaluate the strength or value of all their interactions. Third, the ratings are entirely subjective and should be interpreted cautiously. Finally, if there are a large number of interactions, problems of coordination might be created. On the other hand, Decomposable Matrices should be especially useful for highly system-based problems, such as those encountered in engineering and the social and biological sciences. Because this technique forces identification of problem subsystems, their components, and how they interact, it can cause a clearer picture of important problem elements to emerge.

3.07 Dimensional Analysis

An analytical method designed to clarify and explore the dimensions and limits of a problem has been developed by Jensen.[10] The technique, which will be referred to as Dimensional Analysis, examines five elements of a problem:

1. Substantive dimension
2. Spatial dimension
3. Temporal dimension
4. Quantitative dimension
5. Qualitative dimension

Each of these dimensions is directed toward answering, respectively, five fundamental questions: What? Where? When? How much? How serious? As shown in Table 3–1, the dimensions then are further analyzed by responding to a series of specific questions.

Although not described by Jensen as a step-by-step procedure, Dimensional Analysis could be used as follows:

1. State the problem.
2. Briefly write down separate descriptions of the problem in terms of What? Where? When? How Much? How Serious?
3. Using these descriptions, answer the questions listed for each of the dimensions (Table 3–1).
4. Evaluate the answers to these questions by considering the implications of each for solving the problem.
5. Select those areas most applicable to the problem for further analysis.

Substantive Dimension Commission or Omission? This question deals with whether something being done needs to be stopped or modified, or whether something not being done should be done. Employer-employee relationship problems, for example, might reflect mistreatment of an employee by the

Table 3–1. Dimensional Analysis.

SUBSTANTIVE	SPATIAL	TEMPORAL	QUANTITATIVE	QUALITATIVE
Commission or Omission?	1. Local or Distant?	1. Long-standing or Recent?	1. Singular or Multiple?	1. Philosophical or Surface?
Attitude or Deed?	2. Particular Location(s) Within a Location?	2. Present or Impending?	2. Many or Few People?	2. Survival or Enrichment
Ends or Means?	3. Isolated or Widespread?	3. Constant or Ebb-and-Flow?	3. General or Specific?	3. Primary or Secondary?
Active or Passive?			4. Simple or Complex?	4. What Values are Being Violated?
Visible or Invisible?			5. Affluence or Scarcity?	5. To What Degree are the Values Being Violated?
				6. Proper or Improper Values?

employer or a complete lack of attention on the part of the employer to the needs of an employee. Problems involving "sins" of commission are generally easier to detect and deal with than "sins" of omission, where the problem is less visible. Both types of behavior, however, deserve equal attention if the problem is to be adequately analyzed.

Attitude or Deed? It often is difficult to determine when a problem stems from an attitude or from observable behaviors. In many situations, problems can be solved best by changing attitudes rather than attempting to change behaviors. If a student's behavior is disrupting a class, the teacher should try to alter the attitude that led to the behavior. Of course, both attitudes and behaviors can be inseparable and, in some instances, attention would need to be directed toward the more urgent of the two.

Ends or Means? For some problems it is difficult to distinguish between cause and effect. What is observed or experienced might be only a symptom of the "real" problem. Jensen illustrates this situation by describing the frustration experienced by students in attempting to deal with an "inhumane" college administration. Although such frustrations might constitute a "problem" for the students, the actual problem could lie with an inadequate communication system.

Active or Passive? This question pertains to the type of threat posed by the problem. Some problems are threatening to the security and well-being of persons while other problems are just irritating obstacles that need to be over-come. In general, greater effort is needed to deal with active problems.

Visible or Invisible? Problem situations should be analyzed to determine if the "real" problem is readily apparent or if it is hidden and likely to be over-looked. Physical problems often tend to be visible while human-relations prob-lems tend to be more invisible. The problem associated with a damaged bridge, for example, can be more easily identified than human problems that often re-main hidden. The important thing is to recognize how visible the problem is.

Spatial Dimension   Local or Distant? The effects of some problems are limited to a local geographical area while the effects of other problems have more far-reaching implications. If the problem is local, such as an inadequate park system, then the information and the implications derived from the information will be local. On many occasions, however, local problems will have varying degrees of effect upon more-remote problems. What Jensen seems to be saying is that the problem boundaries need to be identified and examined.

Particular Location(s) Within a Location? The specific locations of a problem need to be isolated so that problem-solving activity can proceed without wasting efforts on irrelevant problem areas. A traffic congestion problem, for instance, might be restricted to only one or two areas of the city. Unless these areas can be pinpointed, attempts to solve the problem will be inefficient and wasteful.

Isolated or Widespread? The extent to which a problem is linked with prob-lems in other areas must be determined to insure successful problem solving. Student unrest, for example, might be associated with feelings about national politics, or limited to a specific campus and associated with local issues.

Temporal Dimension   Long-Standing or Recent? Some problems have been part of the world for centuries while others are a more recent phenomenon. Although many parent-child problems have been around for a long time, some of these problems can be attributed to modern technology. Television and the automobile, for example, have added a new dimension to parent-child relationships. Further-more, the solutions for some long-standing problems can become the causes for more recent problems. When a new highway is built to solve a long-standing traffic congestion problem for motorists, new problems are created for home-owners who are displaced by construction of the highway.

Present or Impending? This question involves determining if the problem exists now or if it is likely to occur if present trends continue. At the inter-national level, the domino theory would be an example of this type of situation. Thus, the problem might not be the destruction of one nation, but that the fall of this nation will lead to the destruction of others. Present problem situations need to be examined for their potential to develop into more serious problems.

Constant or Ebb-and-Flow? Some types of problems occur only in relation to certain cycles of time. In many cities, for example, traffic congestion is a problem only during certain hours of the day. Other types of problems might occur on a regular basis during a particular time of the week, month, or year. Problem occurrence, however, also might be more irregular. For instance, university enrollments began to decline during the 1960s just when the expansion of housing facilities had increased. Obviously, the more unexpected a problem is, the greater will be the difficulty involved in dealing with it.

Quantitative Dimension Singular or Multiple? A problem can exist because of a single item or because of many items in combination. Worker dissatisfaction, for example, might be caused by low wages or low wages plus working conditions plus supervisor attitudes. When considered by themselves, some items might not be a problem until they are combined with other items. Some people, for example, do not cause problems when alone but only when they interact with certain other people. Furthermore, the items that pertain to a problem often will not be equal in seriousness. For most problem situations, the relative seriousness of items requires the use of a weighting procedure.

Many or Few People? This question is related to the previous question but differs by emphasizing how many persons are affected by or are involved with a problem. Worker dissatisfaction might not be a problem unless a substantial number of workers are dissatisfied. The question, of course, is relative: What is small in one situation might not be so in another situation. The presence of key opinion leaders in a small group of dissatisfied workers, for example, can be as serious as a larger group of dissatisfied workers where no opinion leaders are present. Nevertheless, many problems cannot be adequately defined until the number of persons involved in the situation is determined.

General or Specific? The purpose of this question is to determine the most applicable area of the problem. Does it apply to a general category or only to specific subgroups within a category? Some forms of outdoor advertising, for example, might be a problem for metropolitan areas but not for interstate highways.

Simple or Complex? This question is intended to assess if the problem consists of only a single, isolated element or if it is made up of many interlocking elements. The energy crisis, for example, would be a complex problem since it involves more than a simple shortage of oil. The elements of international politics, profit motives of the oil companies, and various logistical considerations all interact to create a highly complex problem.

Affluence or Scarcity? A situation can be a problem due to either an abundance or a lack of something. A car dealer can have an inventory problem if there are too many cars in stock just when the new models are about to come out. The same dealer also might have a problem when demand is high but the inventory is low. The demand for fuel-efficient cars, for example, creates problems for some auto companies as well as dealers who are unable to reduce their inventory of larger, less fuel-efficient cars.

Qualitative Dimension Philosophical or Surface? This question is intended to determine if the intensity of the problem requires an examination of philosophical assumptions. A problem involving inadequate parking facilities obviously would be a surface issue, whereas the problem of nuclear escalation would be more philosophical. It is not difficult to see that analysis of philosophical assumptions would be especially critical for effective problem solving. Surface issues, in contrast, would require less intensive analysis.

Survival or Enrichment? A problem might be a matter of survival or merely bring into question the quality of a situation. A survival problem will require immediate action, while an enrichment problem can receive less immediate attention. Reductions in oil imports at increased cost might be a survival problem for persons on fixed incomes, but only a problem of the relative quality of life for persons who have no serious financial problems.

Primary or Secondary? The perceptions people have about the relative importance of a problem will determine how and when the problem is dealt with. Most persons are faced with several problems at the same time and a decision must be made on which problems should receive priority. Based upon individual perceptions of expected expenditures of time and energy as well as a problem's seriousness, some problems will be given primary importance while others will be classified as only secondary in importance.

What Values Are Being Violated? According to Jensen, this question represents one of the most crucial elements in problem analysis. While the previous questions have been concerned with obtaining facts about a problem (What is?), this question seeks to determine: What is wrong? As defined by Jensen, a problem exists whenever there is a violation of values. To analyze a problem it is necessary to determine which specific values are being violated. If a political candidate anonymously accuses an opponent of sexual impropriety and then is identified, the accuser might refer to the accusation as a harmless prank. Other persons, however, might not perceive the situation the same way. Therefore, to effectively analyze a problem, it is important to both identify values being violated and recognize that the importance of some values will vary from person to person.

To What Degree Are the Values Being Violated? Whenever a worthy value is violated, the implications for problem solving will be more important when the violation is serious than when it is trivial. If punctuality is considered to be a worthy value and someone is five minutes late for an appointment, the violation is much less serious than if the person had been 30 minutes late.

Proper or Improper Values? Another issue in the area of value violation is the question of whether a particular value should be honored. The worth of a given value is a complex, philosophical matter that cannot be easily resolved. Furthermore, the issue is complicated by the trade-offs in values that people often are required to make. For instance, someone might value being courteous to others but find that this is not possible in all situations.

Evaluation   One difficulty in using Dimensional Analysis stems from Jensen's definition of a problem as a violation of values. While it might be true that some problems involve value violations, the definition might have to be stretched a bit to accommodate all problem situations. Thus, a problem of how to redesign a toaster to be more efficient would seem to be quite different from a problem of how to reduce racial prejudice. Although the inefficiency of a toaster involves a value, a broader definition of a problem would seem to be more useful. On the other hand, Jensen's emphasis upon human-relations problems represents an area often neglected in many problem-solving techniques. Because of this focus upon social and psychological problems, some selectivity will need to be exercised in using Dimensional Analysis to analyze technical problems. In the area of new-product development, for example, the question of attitude or deed would need to be modified.

Another difficulty is that little guidance is provided on how to use the technique to analyze a problem. It should be noted, however, that Jensen does not refer to Dimensional Analysis as a technique. Rather, he has attempted to describe five areas to explore when analyzing a problem. Nevertheless, the description would have been more helpful if a systematic analysis procedure had been included. In particular, it would have been helpful to know *why* Jensen considers the different questions to be important, and *how* he would suggest that they be used. The step-by-step procedure described at the beginning of this section should be of some assistance in using Jensen's approach.

Aside from the lack of a systematic procedure, the technique should be useful in forcing a problem solver to consider the many implications associated with various problem dimensions. Also, once the dimensions and questions relevant to a problem are selected, problem-solving activity might proceed more smoothly than if no analysis was performed. The trick, of course, is knowing which dimensions and questions are relevant. Of the questions described by Jensen, the following would seem to have the broadest applicability:

Substantive Dimension:	Ends or Means? Active or Passive?
Spatial Dimension:	Local or Distant? Particular Location(s) Within a Location? Isolated or Widespread?
Temporal Dimension:	Present or Impending? Constant or Ebb-and-flow?
Quantitative Dimension:	Singular or Multiple? General or Specific? Simple or Complex?
Qualitative Dimension:	Philosophical or Surface? Primary or Secondary? What Values Are Being Violated? To What Degree Are the Values Being Violated?

In addition to problem analysis, Dimensional Analysis also might be useful for evaluating alternative solutions or for pre-problem-solving. After a problem has been analyzed and redefined (if necessary), and alternatives generated, the implications derived from the questions could help to bring forth possible problem areas associated with different alternatives. Perhaps the best use of the technique, however, would be as a checklist for use during pre-problem-solving activity, or as a general guideline preceding the use of some other analytical method. Such a checklist could help to provide a general perspective during the later stages of the problem-solving process.

3.08 Input-Output

The Input-Output technique was developed at the General Electric Company to aid in solving dynamic system-design problems involving various forms of energy.[11] That is, it was intended to assist in the design of physical devices that are functionally dependent upon different energy forms. As a problem analysis technique, however, it should prove useful for specifying connections between the elements of a variety of complex, dynamic problems. Thus, it should be suitable for problems in such areas as social planning, human relations, biology, and engineering.

The basic procedure for using the Input-Output method involves the following steps:

1. Establish the desired output (OP_D).
2. Establish the major input (IP_M) affecting the output.
3. Establish any limiting specifications (LS) that the output must meet.
4. Examine the connections between the inputs and outputs and determine how the inputs can be best used to achieve the desired output.

At its simplest level, this process can be represented as

$$IP_M \xrightarrow{\overset{LS}{\downarrow}} OP_D$$

Unfortunately, most problems do not lend themselves to such a simple analysis. Because many problems involve multiple combinations of inputs and outputs, a slightly more complex version of the procedure is often required. An example of a more complex model is shown in Fig. 3-4. In this case, the major input (IP_M) can produce multiple outputs (OP_1) that function as first-order inputs (IP_1) producing outputs (OP_2) that function as second-order inputs (IP_2), one of which might produce the desired output (OP_D). It should be apparent that more complex models could be developed with multiple input-output steps, each of which could branch out into progressively larger numbers of inputs and outputs.

It also should be apparent that the steps used in implementing the basic input-output model will not be adequate for dealing with more complex problems.

Fig. 3–4. Complex Input-Output analysis.

Steps will need to be added to sort out the different input-output transformations and to determine which branches will most likely lead to the desired output. A general procedure for more complex analyses might be described as follows:

1. Establish the desired output (OP_D).
2. Establish the major input (IP_M) affecting the output.
3. Establish any limiting specifications that the output must meet.
4. Determine which outputs (OP_1) are produced directly by the major input.
5. Considering the first-order outputs (OP_1) as inputs (IP_1), determine which outputs (OP_2) might be produced by each input (IP_1).
6. Considering the second-order outputs (OP_2) as inputs (IP_2), continue transforming inputs and outputs until the desired output (OP_D) is achieved.

An example described by Whiting[12] might help to clarify this procedure. Whiting describes a problem of how to develop a mechanical device capable of providing a warning in the event of fire. In this case, the desired output (OP_D) is the warning device, fire is the major input (IP_M), and the special requirements of the device are such factors as size, cost, and sensitivity level. The outputs (OP_1) associated with fire are: heat, light, various gases arising from combustion, and smoke (the first-order inputs). By redefining these outputs as inputs (IP_1, in Fig. 3–4), we can create new outputs (OP_2)—such as the expansion of metal subjected to heat, or chemical reactions caused by light and smoke. The task then is to select the outputs (OP_2)—transformed into inputs (IP_2)—that seem to be most capable of functioning as a fire-warning device (OP_D). For example, a smoke-sensitive chemical or a metal that melts below the boiling point of water could be used to trip a circuit that would sound an alarm.

Evaluation   This technique is similar to the redefinitional procedures since the transformations between inputs and outputs represent progressive redefinitions of the inputs. It was classified as an analytical procedure because of the required breakdown of problem subprocesses.

Analyzing a problem through the use of various input-output relationships can be a valuable exercise, especially for problems that involve some type of energy transformation. Furthermore, when multiple input-output steps are used, such a breakdown of problem aspects can help coordinate and clarify the idea generation process. A major weakness of this method, however, is that analysis of problems involving a large number of inputs and outputs can be a time-consuming and often confusing task. For this reason, the Input-Output method will be most suitable for only moderately complex problems that are considered to be important enough to justify using the procedures involved. Of course, computer programs exist that can overcome this weakness.

3.09 Organized Random Search

One method for systematically analyzing a problem is the Organized Random Search developed by Frank Williams.[13] Instead of randomly searching for ideas, Williams proposes that it is better to first break down the problem into its different subdivisions or parts. These then can be used to provide a direction for the generation of ideas. The steps are as follows:

1. Inspect the problem for possible subdivisions or ways of categorizing parts of the problem.
2. Write down the different subdivisions or parts and use them to generate ideas.

Williams provides an example of a problem involving recall of the names of all the U.S. states. If total random recall was used, it might be difficult to recall all the names except for the more popular ones or ones with some personal meaning attached to them. If, however, the search process was organized using geographical areas, the number of states recalled should substantially increase. Thus, the states could be clustered to include east and west coasts, central states, and so forth, and the names then recalled from within each area rather than from the entire United States. With such an analysis, the search for ideas still will be somewhat random, but at least it will be organized.

Another example, actually used by engineers in one company, was a problem of how to keep current in the problems and solutions within their areas of responsibility. Before attempting to generate ideas to solve this problem, the engineers broke it down into two areas: people and things. These areas were then further subdivided into internal and external aspects. The internal-people area contained items such as superiors, subordinates and staff while the external area listed customers, suppliers and competitors. Each of these breakdowns was then used as the starting point for generating ideas.

Evaluation   This method is similar in concept to Decomposable Matrices, Morphological Analysis, and Relevance Systems, all of which involve factoring a problem into its major elements to stimulate and clarify the idea generation process. These techniques, however, are somewhat more structured and systematic than the Organized Random Search method. In particular, Decomposable Matrices and Relevance Systems contain a degree of sophistication not present in the basic analytical procedures of Morphological Analysis and Organized Random Search. The use of binary systems, opportunity interfaces, and matrix weightings are elaborations that significantly increase the usefulness of these methods—especially for complex problems. Nevertheless, for problems containing few dimensions and having minimal interaction among the dimensions, the Organized Random Search method could be an appropriate choice.

3.10 Relevance Systems

Relevance Systems represent a method of organizing information about a problem through successive refinements of major problem elements. As each element is listed, other elements are identified and connected with the preceding ones until a pyramid-like structure results. A common example of Relevance Systems is the formal organization chart. Top-level managers are listed at the top and then connected by lines to progressively greater numbers of persons at lower organizational levels. This particular type of relevance system is comparatively easy to construct since the problem is essentially well-structured. It is more difficult, however, to construct a relevance system for ill-structured problems due to the often unknown qualities of problem elements and constraints.

According to Rickards,[14] there are two types of Relevance Systems: single and binary. A single system consists of all the elements related to a single problem; a binary system is comprised of two single systems that interact across the lower levels of the two systems (the opportunity interface). Thus, binary systems can be used to identify relationships between as well as within systems.

Relevance Systems can be constructed in two different ways: (1) starting with the highest-order elements and sequentially connecting elements in a downward direction, and (2) starting with clusters of lower-level elements and working upwards to the highest level. Although either method will produce a workable relevance system, better results generally will be produced if both methods are used. By working downward and upward, the validity of the elements included and their relationship to one another can be more easily assessed. The following basic steps are involved in constructing Relevance Systems:

1. Write down the highest-order element of the problem (the first-level element).
2. List the subelements that can be derived from the first level (the second-level elements).

3. Continue listing lower-level elements until all possible levels have been exhausted and the lowest level has been achieved. Achievement of the lowest level usually can be determined by looking for elements that answer the question: How? Higher level elements, in contrast, usually answer the question: Why?
4. After completing this system, assess the system's validity by working upward from the lower-level elements.
5. Use the lower-level elements to suggest possible problem solutions.
6. If the problem overlaps another area and needs to be integrated with it, extend the system by constructing a second system so that its lower-level elements interface with those of the first system. The result will be a binary relevance system.
7. Examine the interface to determine points of singular or mutual influence and/or to consider possible constraining factors that might affect the objectives expressed within either system.

An example of how a binary system could be used to improve a company's marketing strategy has been described by Rickards.[15] As shown in Fig. 3–5, a single system is constructed with the highest-order element being increasing the number of clients. Two lower-level elements are developed next (still asking the question: Why?), followed by the lowest level of elements, which are oriented toward the question: How? Then, if it is determined that the marketing strategy should be integrated with the overall policy decisions of the company, a second system could be constructed (also shown in Fig. 3–5). The resulting binary system allows both policy makers and marketing personnel to analyze any possible constraints that might influence potential problem solutions. For example, changing the company image could conflict with a policy alternative of increasing university contracts.

Evaluation   Because of its emphasis upon identifying connections among problem elements, the Relevance Systems method is very similar to Progressive Abstractions. Both techniques rely upon progressive breakdowns of problem elements and development of new problem definitions. The techniques differ slightly, however, in their use of problem elements. For Progressive Abstractions, increasingly abstract problem definitions are developed by synthesizing preceding problem solutions; for Relevance Systems, a problem is broken down so that *all* of its major elements and their connections can be examined. For some problems, the distinctions between the two techniques might be difficult to make. In such cases, the choice of technique might be made more on the basis of personal preference than any advantage of one technique over the other. Relevance Systems, however, are distinguished by taking into account the possible need to integrate one system with another. In addition to suggesting problem solutions

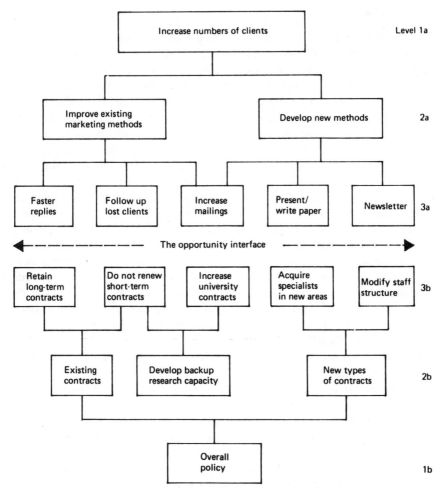

Fig. 3–5. A binary relevance system. Rickards, T., *Problem-Solving Through Creative Analysis,* published by Gower Press, Epping, 1974. Reprinted by permission.

that might not be considered with the Progressive Abstractions method, opportunity interfaces are an important strength of Relevance Systems. Because a problem solver is forced to consider potential-solution constraints, the likelihood of solution revisions should be reduced considerably. Another advantage of Relevance Systems over Progressive Abstractions is suggested by Rickards,[16] who indicates that the possible overlap of lower-level elements will increase the richness of problem solutions. When different combinations of problem elements are forced together, more unique solutions should be produced.

COMMENTS

Of the preceding techniques, no one method is likely to produce a "better" or very different problem perspective than another. All of the methods are capable of producing new problem viewpoints and/or factoring a problem into its essential elements. However, the two redefinitional techniques that are most versatile and useful are the Five W's and H and the Why Method. Both of these will be helpful for most types of problems. Moreover, with the exception of Boundary Examinations, they are the easiest to apply. Four of the ten techniques also have the added capability of showing how problem elements might be connected. These techniques are Progressive Abstractions, Decomposable Matrices, Input-Output, and Relevance Systems. This capability is especially important in complex problems where one element is likely to have a direct effect upon or relationship to one or more other elements. In particular, these four techniques will be especially useful for problems structured as systems—biological systems, social systems, mechanical systems, etc.—since a major characteristic of systems is subsystem interdependency. That is, a change in one part of a system is likely to affect one or more other parts in the system. For instance, a problem involving redesign of a car's ignition system (a subsystem of the engine) will affect the operation of other engine components. For such problems, it is essential that the interdependency of problem elements be considered.

Mention also should be made about termination of the analysis/redefinition stage. While it is true that this stage usually does not terminate until a solution has been implemented, there are occasions on which a decision must be made to terminate—at least temporarily—the redefinitional activity. Otherwise, this activity could continue to the neglect of the other problem-solving stages.

What then are the guidelines for ending one phase of the analysis/redefinition process? Perhaps the most useful guideline for redefinitions is to conclude this activity when a statement has been generated that best captures the essence of the problem situation. This so-called real problem is the one that is perceived to be the most important given the present situation. Of course, selecting the "real" problem is a subjective decision that will vary from one person to another. Another guideline is to stop redefining once a definition reaches a state of remoteness in which it would be difficult to bring the problem back down to reality. That is, when a definition becomes so abstract and philosophical that no further defining is likely to produce practical results, the process should be terminated. Again, it is not the correctness of definition that is being sought but, rather, a new way of looking at a problem.

The same guidelines also would have some effect upon termination of problem analysis. A specific guideline for this phase of the process is to discontinue breaking down a problem when the factors are judged to be too specific and/or irrelevant to the problem objectives. Such a decision is, of course, highly subjective, since there is always the danger of restricting the analysis to only a few elements and neglecting others that might prove to be essential later on. However, when a problem is broken down into too many elements, the processing demands on the problem solver will be increased and the problem can become unmanageable. Thus, a dilemma is created in trying to balance the need for factoring a problem against the demands required to process a large amount of information. One solution to this dilemma is to terminate analysis once the problem elements can be "chunked" or organized into clear-cut element groupings. One useful technique for organizing information in this manner is Morphological Analysis. Although it and other similar techniques can not substitute for individual ability in identifying problem elements, an advantage can be obtained by systematically organizing information about the problem.

NOTES

1. de Bono, E. *Lateral Thinking: Creativity Step By Step*. New York: Harper & Row, 1970.
2. Rickards, T. *Problem-Solving Through Creative Analysis*. Essex, U.K.: Gower Press, 1974.
3. *Ibid.*
4. Osborn, A. F. *Applied Imagination*, 3rd ed. New York: Scribner, 1963; Parnes, S. J., Noller, R. B., and Biondi, A. M. *Guide to Creative Action*, rev. ed. New York: Scribner, 1977. For an updated approach to Fact-Finding and Problem-Finding in the Osborn-Parnes model, see Isaksen, S. G., and Treffinger, D. J. *Creative Problem Solving: The Basic Course*. Buffalo, N.Y.: Bearly Limited, 1985.
5. When you are so familiar with a problem statement that a solution seems evident, I refer to the statement as a "problution" (VanGundy, A. B. *Stalking the Wild Solution: A Problem Finding Approach to Creative Problem Solving*. Buffalo, N.Y.: Bearly Limited, 1987). In essence, a problution is a cross between a problem and a solution. It is based upon the assumption that a clearly understood problem is a solved problem. Further extending this logic, it also could be argued that all creative problem solving—including idea generation—is a search for problem understanding.
6. Adapted from Geschka, H., Schaude, G. R., and Schlicksupp, H. "Modern Techniques for Solving Problems." *Chemical Engineering* 91–97 (August 1973).
7. Rickards, T., *op. cit.*
8. A variety of authors have described this technique. See, for example, Parnes, S. J. *The Magic of Your Mind*. Buffalo, N.Y.: The Creative Education Foundation in Association with Bearly Limited, 1981; and Isaksen, S. G., and Treffinger, D. J., *op. cit.*; VanGundy, A. B., *Managing Group Creativity: A Modular Approach to Problem Solving*. New York: AMACOM, 1984.
9. Simon, H. A. *The Science of the Artificial*. Cambridge, Mass.: MIT Press, 1969.
10. Jensen, J. V. "A Heuristic for the Analysis of the Nature and Extent of a Problem." *Journal of Creative Behavior* 12:168–180 (1978).
11. Whiting, C. S. *Creative Thinking*. New York: Van Nostrand Reinhold, 1958.
12. *Ibid.*

13. Williams, F. E. *Foundations of Creative Problem Solving.* Ann Arbor, Mich.: Edward Brothers, Inc., 1960.
14. Rickards, T., *op. cit.*
15. *Ibid.*
16. *Ibid.*

4
Generating Ideas

The creative problem-solving process often is inappropriately associated with and limited to idea generation methods. As a result, more techniques exist for generating ideas than for any of the problem-solving stages. Although this proliferation of techniques will be helpful for generating ideas, the availability and number of techniques might be construed to indicate that major emphasis should be placed upon generation of problem solutions. This statement, however, grossly misrepresents both the intent and function of creative problem solving. As noted previously, solution generation is important but not necessarily the most important problem-solving stage. Generating ideas, however, is vital to creative problem solving but not just as a procedure to be used for developing solution alternatives. Ideas also need to be generated for other aspects of the problem-solving process.

PRINCIPLES OF IDEA GENERATION

All of the techniques in this chapter are based upon divergent thinking—the process of generating many different types of ideas. There are several principles that will enhance this process when using idea generation techniques. Most of these principles are based upon Osborn's[1] brainstorming rules.

1. *Defer Judgment.* Most of us are conditioned by training and education to be analytical. Divergent idea generation, however, relies upon suspension of analysis and judgment. If each idea is criticized as it is proposed, only a limited number will be proposed. As a result, the odds of generating a unique solution will be reduced considerably. Thus, list every idea no matter how silly or impractical it may seem at first. Judgment and convergent thinking can be used later when you evaluate and select ideas.

2. *Quantity Breeds Quality.* This principle is dependent upon deferred judgment. More ideas can be generated when evaluation is put off. Moreover, the laws of probability favor increased quality when quantity also is increased. For instance, suppose there are five worthwhile, high-quality ideas out of a hypothetical pool of 100 ideas. If you devote all of your idea generation time to evaluating the first few ideas you list, the odds are against more than one of these ideas being of high quality. To increase these odds, always try to list as many ideas as you can.

3. *The Wilder the Idea, the Better.* Divergent thinking requires a certain amount of risk taking to be productive. "Breakthrough" ideas are unlikely to be produced if a cautious, conservative approach is used. Although a wild idea usually cannot be implemented as proposed, a modification often can be. The primary value of wild ideas lies in their ability to stimulate unique problem solutions. If you begin idea generation believing that you need to produce rational, logical ideas, that probably is the type of ideas you will get. Although such ideas frequently will be workable, they may not compare to the higher-quality ideas that can be stimulated by wild ideas.

4. *Combine and Improve Ideas.* Many creative ideas result from combinations or improvements of previous ideas. In workshops I sometimes use a 1912 magazine advertisement for an Oldsmobile automobile. In the ad, Mr. Olds touts the virtues of his "farewell car" and states: "I do not believe that a car materially better will ever be built." (Obviously, a few people have been able to combine ideas and improve upon existing designs to produce today's automobiles.) Most ideas can be combined with one or more other ideas or improved upon by modifying one or more attributes. Improvement, however, requires an attitude that changes are possible.

5. *Take a Break from the Problem.* We sometimes become so intensively involved in idea generation that our minds tire and inhibit our thinking. When we become tired, new perspectives and fresh ideas are unlikely. Therefore, it usually is wise to set a time limit to all idea generation sessions. In groups, 20 to 30 minutes typically is enough time for most idea generation techniques (although certain groups may require additional time). After this time period, a group should take a break or switch to another problem. For individuals, about 10 or 15 minutes would be ideal before taking a break.

The techniques presented in this chapter can be best characterized by their versatility and variety of application. They are versatile because they involve procedures that can be used to redefine and analyze problems, establish solution criteria, generate alternative solutions, and evaluate solutions. (Although the techniques presented in Chapters 3 and 7 also can be used to generate ideas, the ones in this chapter have been included because of their primary intent and frequent use as idea generation methods.) The techniques in this chapter are varied because of their applicability to either individuals or groups, use of brainstorming or brainwriting procedures, forced relationships or free association, and related or unrelated stimulation sources. Because of the implications involved for selecting and evaluating the techniques, some dimensions of this variety will be briefly discussed.

INDIVIDUALS OR GROUPS

About one-half of the techniques in this chapter were originally designed for use by individuals and have been classified as such; the group techniques, of course, were designed specifically for group idea generation sessions. Only some of the group methods can be used by individuals. However, all of the individual methods can be used by groups. By following the procedures for an individual technique, a group can pool the ideas they generate as individuals and then use the ideas to prompt additional ones. Furthermore, all of the individual techniques easily can be used as supplemental generation devices for most of the group techniques. The group techniques, on the other hand, are more limited in their applicability as individual techniques. Many of the group methods, however, can be easily applied by individuals, although some loss in the uniqueness and quantity of ideas might occur. The group techniques that easily can be adapted for use by individuals are Component Detailing, Games, Greeting Cards, Problem Inventory Analysis, Rolestorming, Sculptures, Semantic Intuition, Sequence-Attribute Modification Matrix, Stimulus Analysis, Storyboards, Synectics, Visual Synectics, and Wildest Idea.

BRAINSTORMING OR BRAINWRITING

Classification of the techniques as either brainstorming or brainwriting methods has been done in the broadest sense of the terms: Brainstorming is used to indicate verbal generation of ideas by a group, while brainwriting refers to group methods that emphasize the silent generation of ideas in writing. (Brainstorming, as a general procedure, can be vastly different from Classical Brainstorming, which uses specific principles to guide idea generation; the broader definition of brainstorming refers to any procedure in which verbal interaction is the primary method.) By definition, all of the individual techniques involve brainwriting, although a case could be made that it is inappropriate to classify individual methods in this manner. As originally conceived by their developers, both brainstorming and brainwriting techniques are intended for use in group situations.

After analyzing over 50 brainstorming and brainwriting techniques, VanGundy[2] developed a typology of the different variations. As shown in Table 4-1, there are five types of brainwriting techniques, two categories of brainstorming, and one category containing techniques that use both brainstorming and brainwriting.

Brainwriting techniques can be broadly categorized as being either nominal or interacting.[3]   In nominal brainwriting groups, the ideas generated are not seen by any of the other group members. Thus, no stimulation is received from the ideas of others—a major weakness of brainwriting procedures. In interacting brainwriting groups, each person's ideas are shared and used by the other members to stimulate new ideas.

Brainwriting I is included in the typology only to illustrate the "pure" form of brainwriting: individual idea production using formal idea generation techniques. Otherwise, brainwriting most commonly is viewed as a classification of group techniques. Brainwriting II uses participants who are not brought together.

Table 4-1. Typology of Brainwriting and Brainstorming Techniques.

	EXAMPLES
Brainwriting I	
An individual generates ideas alone and selects one to solve the problem.	Attribute Listing, Checklists, Exaggerated Objectives
Brainwriting II	
Written ideas are collected from persons who are physically separated. None of the ideas is shared.	Collective Notebook
Brainwriting III	
Written ideas are collected from persons who are physically separated. All of the ideas are shared.	Delphi Method
Brainwriting IV	
Written ideas are collected from persons in the same physical location. None of the ideas is shared and no discussion for stimulation takes place.	Crawford Slip Writing, Nominal Group Technique
Brainwriting V	
Written ideas are collected from persons in the same physical location. All of the ideas are shared, but none of the ideas is discussed.	Brainwriting Pool, Gallery Method, Method 6-3-5, Pin Cards
Brainstorming I	
A small, interacting group verbally generates ideas. No agreed-upon procedure is used by the group.	Unstructured group discussions
Brainstorming II	
A small, interacting group verbally generates ideas using an agreed-upon procedure.	Classical Brainstorming, Force-Fit Game, Phillips 66, Synectics
Brainwriting/Brainstorming I	
A small group generates ideas using agreed-upon written and verbal procedures.	Battelle-Bildmappen-Brainwriting, Brainwriting Game

They may be geographically dispersed, such as persons from different states, or they may be physically separated within the same organization. None of the participants sees the ideas of others. Brainwriting III is like Brainwriting II in that the participants are physically separated. However, ideas of Brainwriting III participants are shared and used for additional stimulation. With Brainwriting IV techniques, people are brought together (sometimes in very large groups of over 100) and silently generate their ideas without sharing them. In contrast, participants using Brainwriting V techniques are in the same physical setting and do share their ideas to obtain more stimulation. Except when participants cannot be brought together, Brainwriting V techniques usually will be the most useful and productive brainwriting procedures.

Most brainstorming techniques fall into two categories: unstructured and structured. Unstructured brainstorming (Brainstorming I) typically is used when a group convenes to "brainstorm some ideas." However, the process followed by the group is not guided by any agreed-upon set of procedures. Such groups also may lack a facilitator. The result often is an unproductive session with some grumbling about how meetings are a waste of time. In contrast, Brainstorming II techniques all use a relatively structured format to guide the group process. A common example would be Classical Brainstorming, which is based upon four major principles.

The need to distinguish between these procedures stems from their relative strengths and weaknesses. Brainstorming, for example, is most useful when there is only a small group of individuals, time is plentiful, status differences among group members are minimal, and a need exists to verbally discuss ideas with others. Brainwriting, on the other hand, is most useful for very large groups, when there is little time available, status differences need to be equalized, and there is no need for verbal interaction. In addition, brainwriting often will produce more ideas than brainstorming, although the uniqueness and quality of these ideas might or might not be superior to those produced by brainstorming. Brainwriting also will be useful when a large group (more than 30 persons, for example) is to be used but only a few group facilitators are available. In contrast to brainstorming, most brainwriting techniques can be used without having a facilitator for each group.

The only other caution to observe concerns the willingness of participants to express themselves orally or in writing. Some persons feel inhibited in group discussions because of a belief that they will be seen as inarticulate or suggest ideas that have little or no value; others might feel inhibited in writing their ideas because of a concern over their ability to express themselves in writing. If anonymity of responses is assured, however, most inhibitions associated with brainwriting should be minimal.

Many of the eclectic and miscellaneous techniques in Chapter 7 also can be classified with regard to their use of brainstorming or brainwriting. Bobele-Buchanan, Coca-Cola, Creative Problem Solving, and Phases of Integrated Problem Solving all have stages for generating ideas using the principles of Classical Brainstorming, while the Delphi method and the Nominal Group Technique are both based upon the general principles of brainwriting.

FORCED RELATIONSHIPS OR FREE ASSOCIATION

As a general procedure for producing ideas, forced relationships relies upon the forcing together of two or more objects, products, or ideas to produce new objects, products, or ideas. The elements that are combined may be related or unrelated to one another and may or may not be related to the problem in question. As a general guideline, elements that are related to each other and to the problem will be more likely to produce practical ideas than more unrelated elements. However, the ideas produced by using related elements are likely to be more mundane and less unique than ideas produced with unrelated elements.

Thus, when forced relationships are used, a balance must be sought in the relatedness of the elements. One way to help insure this balance is to use a mixture of related and unrelated elements. Another way would be to terminate idea generation activity when the most of the ideas produced are judged to be impractical. However, do not prematurely terminate this activity. To avoid overlooking a potentially useful idea, defer judgment on idea practicality as long as possible.

Free association often is viewed as a procedure for generating ideas without using any particular stimuli. This is not really the case, however, as ideas have to come from somewhere. Free association relies upon past experiences or the immediate physical, psychological, or social environment for idea stimulation. Furthermore, as will be described in the discussion on the Free Association method, previously developed ideas also can be used to prompt new ones or modifications of them. As a result, the stimulus elements used to prompt ideas will be either related or unrelated to the problem. The important point about free association, however, is that it relies more upon chance and incubation than deliberate and conscious attempts to produce ideas as is found in the forced-relationships procedure.

RELATED OR UNRELATED STIMULI

The idea generation techniques in this chapter rely upon related stimulus elements, unrelated elements, or a combination of both. In many of these techniques, the use of a related or unrelated stimulus element is not formally specified. Thus, when these techniques are used, the degree of stimulus relatedness is left to the discretion of the problem solver (i.e., a related element, an unrelated element, or both may be used). The other techniques, in contrast, have been specifically designed to use either related or unrelated stimuli. Some of the advantages and disadvantages associated with stimuli relatedness already have been discussed and will not be repeated here.

It should be emphasized that the relatedness of problem stimuli is a key determinant of idea uniqueness. Techniques that rely upon stimulus elements that are unrelated to the problem are more likely to produce novel ideas than techniques that use only related problem elements. (The superiority of unrelated stimuli probably can be attributed to their ability to provide new problem perspectives.) Nevertheless, the value of techniques using related stimuli should not be minimized. Not everyone can use unrelated stimuli productively, and many useful ideas can be prompted by related stimuli. Ideally, techniques using both types of stimuli should be used.

To help compare the techniques in this chapter, Tables 4-2 and 4-3 have been prepared. Both of these tables show how the techniques differ in regard to method (brainstorming or brainwriting), general procedure (forced relationships

Table 4-2. Classification of Individual Idea Generation Techniques.[a]

TECHNIQUE	PROCEDURE		STIMULUS	
	FR	FA	R	UR
4.01 Analogies	X			X
4.02 Assumption Reversals		X	X	
4.03 Attribute Analogy Chains	X		X	X
4.04 Attribute Association Chains	X	X	X	X
4.05 Attribute Listing		X	X	
4.06 Bionics	X			X
4.07 Catalog	X			X
4.08 Checklists		X	X	
4.09 Circumrelation	X		X	
4.10 Cliches, Proverbs, and Maxims	X			X
4.11 Creative Visualization	X	X		X
4.12 Exaggerated Objectives	X	X	X	
4.13 Focused-Object	X		X	X
4.14 Free Association		X	X	
4.15 Fresh Eye		X	X	
4.16 Heuristic Ideation Technique	X		X	
4.17 Hypothetical Situations	X			X
4.18 Listing	X		X	
4.19 Metaphors	X			X
4.20 Modifier-Noun Associations	X	X		X
4.21 Morphological Analysis	X		X	
4.22 Nonlogical Stimuli	X			X
4.23 Product Improvement CheckList	X			X
4.24 Relational Algorithms	X		X	
4.25 Reversals	X		X	
4.26 Storywriting	X	X	X	X
4.27 Symbolic Representations	X	X	X	X
4.28 Two Words	X		X	
4.29 Wishful Thinking		X	X	
4.30 Word Diamond	X		X	

[a]FR = forced relationships; FA = free association; R = related; UR = unrelated.

or free association), and stimulus elements (related or unrelated). Table 4-2 presents individual idea generation techniques and Table 4-3 presents group techniques.

As shown in Table 4-2, most of the individual techniques (60%) use forced relationships and differ somewhat in their use of related and unrelated stimuli (50% versus 36%). The situation is somewhat different when group idea generation techniques are analyzed. Table 4-3 demonstrates that most group approaches use free association only (55%) as the primary procedure, while related stimuli are clearly used in more group techniques than unrelated stimuli (71% versus 26%). A comparison of both individual and group techniques is provided in Table 4-4.

Table 4-3. Classification of Group Idea Generation Techniques.[a]

TECHNIQUE		METHOD		PROCEDURE		STIMULUS	
		BS	BW	FR	FA	R	UR
4.31	BBB	X	X	X	X	X	X
4.32	Brainsketching		X	X		X	
4.33	Brainwriting Game	X	X		X	X	
4.34	Brainwriting Pool		X		X	X	
4.35	Classical Brainstorming	X			X	X	
4.36	Component Detailing	X	X	X		X	
4.37	Collective Notebook		X		X	X	
4.38	Crawford Slip Writing		X		X	X	
4.39	Force-Fit Game	X		X			X
4.40	Gallery Method		X		X	X	
4.41	Games	X		X	X		X
4.42	Gordon/Little	X			X	X	
4.43	Greeting Cards	X		X			X
4.44	Method 6-3-5	X			X	X	
4.45	Phillips 66	X			X	X	
4.46	Pin Cards		X		X	X	
4.47	Problem Inventory Analysis	X			X	X	
4.48	Rolestorming	X			X	X	
4.49	Sculptures	X		X			X
4.50	Semantic Intuition	X		X		X	
4.51	S.A.M.M.	X		X		X	
4.52	SIL Method	X		X		X	
4.53	Stimulus Analysis	X		X			X
4.54	Storyboards	X			X	X	
4.55	Super Group®	X			X	X	
4.56	Super Heroes	X		X			X
4.57	Synectics	X		X	X		X
4.58	Systematized Directed Induction		X		X	X	
4.59	Trigger Method	X	X		X	X	
4.60	Visual Synectics	X		X			X
4.61	Wildest Idea	X			X	X	

[a]BS = brainstorming; BW = brainwriting; FR = forced relationships; FA = free association; R = related; UR = unrelated.

In Table 4-4, it is evident that most group methods in this book use brainstorming (65%), while brainwriting accounts for 23%, and combination techniques make up the remainder (13%). When looking at both individual and group methods, slightly more techniques use forced relationships than free association (48% and 38%, respectively). Related stimuli, however, are used more often than unrelated stimuli (61% versus 30%), while techniques using both account for only 10%.

Table 4–4. Comparison of Individual and Group Idea Generation Techniques.

	INDIVIDUAL (n = 30)		GROUP (n = 31)		TOTAL (n = 61)	
	No.	%	No.	%	No.	%
Method						
Brainstorming (BS) only	NA[a]	NA	20	65	20	65
Brainwriting (BW) only	NA	NA	7	23	8	23
BS and BW	NA	NA	4	13	4	13
Procedure						
Forced relationships (FR) only	18	60	11	35	29	48
Free association (FA) only	6	20	17	55	23	38
FR and FA	6	20	3	10	9	15
Stimulus						
Related only	15	50	22	71	37	61
Unrelated only	10	33	8	26	18	30
Related and unrelated	5	17	1	3	6	10

[a]NA = Not applicable (only group techniques qualify as brainwriting).

There are several implications and conclusions that might be drawn from these data. First, there probably are an adequate number of brainstorming techniques from which to choose. Although underrepresented, more brainwriting methods probably are not needed. Second, there is a balanced representation of techniques that use forced relationships and free association. However, forced relationships are more likely to be found with individual methods. Finally, techniques using unrelated problem stimuli are grossly underrepresented. Group methods are much more likely to use related than unrelated stimuli (71% versus 26%). Also, almost two-thirds (61%) of the 61 idea generation methods in this book use related stimuli, while about one-third (30%) use unrelated stimuli. Because unrelated stimuli are more likely to help prompt unique ideas, groups should avoid using only techniques with related stimuli. Instead, groups might consider adapting individual techniques that use unrelated stimuli.

ANATOMY OF IDEA GENERATION TECHNIQUES

As discussed, idea generation techniques are designed for either individuals or groups. The group methods use either brainstorming or brainwriting. Both individual and group approaches are based upon forced relationships or free association, and related or unrelated problem stimuli. Because of the way these elements are related to one another, a certain "natural" order seems to exist. That is, when these elements are combined in a hierarchy, a specific form and structure is produced. Such a hierarchy can be used to analyze existing techniques or produce new ones.

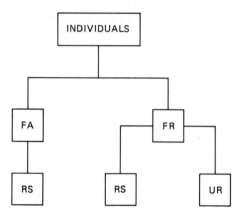

Fig. 4–1. Classification hierarchy of individual techniques. Note: FA = free association, FR = forced relationships; RS = related stimuli, UR = unrelated stimuli.

For example, a relatively simple structure appears to exist for individual techniques. As shown in Fig. 4–1, individual methods are based upon either free association or forced relationships. Techniques that use forced relationships receive stimulation from either related or unrelated stimuli; techniques that use free association, however, rely upon only related stimuli. Since there is no forcing together of elements and each association is used to prompt a new one, all the stimuli will be related.[4]

Adding the category of brainstorming versus brainwriting substantially increases the complexity of the hierarchy for group techniques. Structured and unstructured varieties of brainstorming and nominal and interacting varieties of brainwriting further complicate the structure of group methods. As shown in Fig. 4–2, structured brainstorming and interacting brainwriting can be categorized the same as individual techniques (Fig. 4–1). That is, both of these categories contain techniques that use related and unrelated stimuli with forced relationships, but only related stimuli with free association. Moreover, unstructured brainstorming and nominal brainwriting both are restricted to techniques that use related stimuli with free association.

Upon inspection of these two hierarchical structures, it should be evident that the potential for variety should be greater among group techniques. In contrast, only three combinations of elements are possible with individual techniques: free association and related stimuli, forced relationships and related stimuli, and forced relationships and unrelated stimuli. However, eight combinations are possible with group techniques. Of course, even more possibilities exist for both

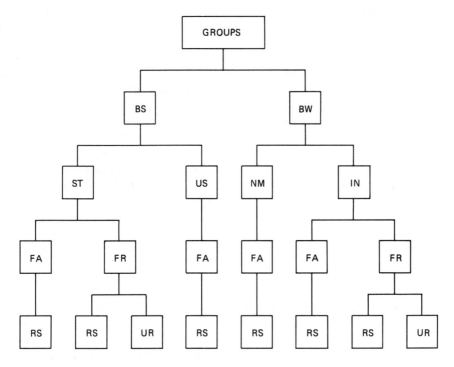

Fig. 4–2. Classification hierarchy of group techniques. Note: BS = brainstorming, BW = brainwriting; ST = structured; US = unstructured; NM = nominal, IN = interacting; FA = free association; FR = forced relationships; RS = related stimuli, UR = unrelated stimuli.

individual and group structures by using combination approaches (e.g., free association and forced relationships).

One implication for developing new idea generation techniques should be obvious. A developer could build a technique by starting at either the top or bottom of a hierarchy. A group approach, for example, might be designed by selecting a brainwriting format in which group members interact in some way when sharing their ideas. The ideas could be stimulated using forced relationships that rely upon unrelated stimuli. Conversely, problem elements (related stimuli) might be selected, free-association ideas generated in writing for each, and then the associations used to stimulate additional written ideas (a combination approach). Finally, all the ideas could be collected for later evaluation (a nominal brainwriting approach).

INDIVIDUAL TECHNIQUES

4.01 Analogies

An analogy is a statement about how objects, persons, situations, or actions are similar in process or relationship to one another. Analogies are reflected in statements of comparison such as these: This organization operates like the military; the engine of this car runs like a fine Swiss watch.

The major value of analogies during idea generation is to create new problem perspectives. When attention is temporarily directed away from the focal problem, self-imposed constraints often can be overcome and new insights generated. This new perspective then is related to the original problem and a new idea is generated. According to de Bono, the best analogies are those that create movement and appear to take on a life of their own.[5]

One way to generate ideas with analogies is to think of something similar to the problem. Then, use this similarity as a stimulus for suggesting new ideas. Although such an approach can be useful, a more structured and elaborated approach should yield better results.

The following is a somewhat more productive way to use analogies:

1. Withholding all evaluation, generate a list of objects, persons, situations, or actions that are similar, but unrelated to the problem. Think of the major principle that underlies the problem and use it to guide generating analogies that are similar in concept. For example, if the problem is preventing school vandalism, think of things in life that involve the concept of prevention (birth control, spraying a car to prevent rust, etc.). In general, use inanimate analogies with problems involving living things and animate analogies with problems involving nonliving things.[6]
2. Select one of the analogies and describe it in detail. List all of the parts, functions, or uses. Be sure to include a variety of action-oriented phrases. While completing this step, try to forget about the problem.
3. Examine each description listed and write down any new ideas suggested.[7] Use the similarities in the descriptions as stimuli for new ideas.
4. Select another analogy and repeat steps 2 and 3 until a satisfactory idea is suggested or available time runs out.

To illustrate using analogies to generate ideas, consider the following problem: In what ways might we improve a common household flashlight?

The first step is to think of things that involve the concept of improvement. Because the problem is inanimate, most of the analogies should involve living things. For instance, things in life that involve improvement might include

a. A facelift
b. Sessions with a psychiatrist

c. A heart transplant
d. Piano lessons
e. Attending college
f. A professional development conference
g. Exercising
h. Skin grafts
i. Gene splicing
j. Dog obedience classes
k. Learning brain surgery with a correspondence course[8]

The second step is to look over all the analogies and select one that looks interesting. The amount of knowledge you have about an analogy also can be used to guide selection. However, you don't have to be an expert. In this example, the analogy of the brain surgery correspondence course might be selected, simply because it is an intriguing concept. Elaborations of this analogy could include the following:

a. You will need a detailed instruction manual, especially one with a lot of pictures.
b. You will need to have frequent contact with your instructors.
c. It might be difficult to find patients to practice on.
d. Your lesson plans will be graded and returned to you.
e. You will have to buy your own surgical instruments.
f. A room in your house will have to do as a practice operating room.
g. Your brother-in-law might be able to help as an anesthesiologist.
h. You will need to increase your current liability insurance.
i. You may have trouble getting certified to practice surgery.
j. You may want to add insulation to your house so the screams will not bother your neighbors.

Using these descriptors as stimuli, you might have some of these ideas:

a. Enclose first-aid manuals inside each flashlight (from "instruction manual").
b. Devise a place to put personal, backlit pictures on the outside surface of the flashlight (from "pictures" in the manual).
c. Install small radio transmitters and receivers for emergencies or for children to play with (from "frequent contact with instructors").
d. Build in an emergency repair kit of small tools (from "surgical instruments").
e. Design a rechargeable flashlight that looks like an electrical outlet in a wall. It would serve for everyday and emergency lighting needs, yet blend in with the other electrical outlets (from "practice operating room").
f. Build in a mace spray for self defense (from "anesthesiologist").

g. Market flashlights by awarding lifesaving certificates to heroes who save lives in situations involving flashlights (from "getting certified to practice).

h. Insulate flashlights to protect the batteries from temperature extremes (from "add insulation to your house").

Evaluation   The usefulness of the Analogies technique in solving problems has been fairly well documented in experimental research using contrived problems.[9] Moreover, analogies have been used with much success in formal techniques such as Synectics,[10] as well as in informal problem-solving efforts by numerous practitioners.   It is a powerful technique that has the potential to generate unique ideas.   By using unrelated stimuli, Analogies helps overcome perceptual constraints and provides new problem perspectives.   For difficult-to-solve problems that require innovative approaches, Analogies would be highly recommended.

A major disadvantage of analogies is that many people have trouble using them as a formal idea generation technique.   Although we all use analogies everyday (either implicitly or explicitly), they can be difficult to use in a structured format.   However, with practice and adherence to a few guidelines, they can be successful for solving many types of problems.   Important considerations to bear in mind are (a) use the "essence" of the problem to suggest analogies (e.g., prevention, change, improvement), (b) use animate analogies for inanimate problems and vice versa, (c) withhold all judgment when generating analogies and their elaborations, and (d) try to include as many action-oriented descriptions as possible when describing a chosen analogy in detail.

4.02 Assumption Reversals

Creativity consultant Stephen Grossman developed Assumption Reversals[11] to overcome the logical paradox that often hinders problem solvers.   A logical paradox exists when a contradiction is perceived between the current and desired states of a problem.   Take the example of a manager who is instructed to reduce expenditures by 10% but to increase productivity by 15%. The apparent contradiction involved in doing more with less presents a major problem-solving obstacle.

One way to overcome this obstacle is to alter one or more basic problem assumptions to create a more productive viewpoint.   Making this alteration is known as an assumption reversal.   There are three primary steps:

1. List all the major assumptions about the problem.   Include even the "obvious" assumptions that might be taken for granted.
2. Reverse each assumption in any way possible. (There is no such thing as a "correct" reversal.)
3. Using the reversals as stimuli, generate any ideas suggested.

To illustrate Assumption Reversals, Grossman uses the problem of improving restaurants. Some basic assumptions about restaurants are that they serve food, are located outside the home, serve people food, people pay for the food, and the food is prepared by the restaurants. Reversing one of these assumptions results in the statement: "Restaurants don't serve food to people." This statement then can be used as a stimulus to suggest such ideas as a restaurant in which people cook their own food, where pets rather than people are served, and a cooperative restaurant run by local residents.

Evaluation Assumption Reversals is similar to the Reversals technique. The major difference is that assumptions of a problem are reversed rather than the actual problem statement. As such, it shares many of the strengths and weaknesses of Reversals. The major advantage of Assumption Reversals is that it is relatively easy to use and readily provokes many new problem perspectives. The major disadvantage is that many people will have difficulty listing all the major assumptions. Because it is so easy to overlook basic assumptions, the most productive aspect of the technique may be underused. Thus, maximum benefit of this method will be achieved only when all of the most basic problem assumptions are revealed.

4.03 Attribute Analogy Chains

Attribute Analogy Chains is a combination of Attribute Listing and Analogies. Analogies help generate ideas by examining problems that are similar in principle. For instance, analogies for improving a flashlight might involve such problems as improving yourself by enrolling in a course or having cosmetic surgery (analogies involving living things generally are used with problems involving nonliving things). However, unlike Analogies, Attribute Analogy Chains generates ideas by developing analogies for each major problem attribute. The steps are as follows:[12]

1. List all of the major problem attributes.
2. List subattributes for each major attribute.
3. Write down one or more analogies for each subattribute.
4. Using the analogies as stimuli, generate ideas.

The problem of improving a garden hose will be used to illustrate this technique. Major attributes are listed first, followed by subattributes for each:

Name: Garden hose
Form: Cylindrical, round
Parts: Hose, connectors

Material: Rubber, steel threads, brass
Function: Transferring water, spraying, filling swimming pools

Next, analogies are developed for each subattribute:

Name: Water transmitter
Form: A slithering snake in the grass; a flexible tube
Parts: Tube, straw, blood vessel; closures, joiners, attachments
Material: Springy matter, stretchable fabric; spiraling bands; shining hardness
Function: Siphoning gasoline; dispersing insecticide; filling a drinking glass.

Finally, each analogy is used to prompt ideas for improving a garden hose. Some possible ideas include the following:

1. Electronically monitor water dispersal rate and ground coverage
2. Put holes in hose and program it to slowly roll across the ground
3. Reinforce hose so that it can be bent into any shape
4. Put reflective material on hose for easy nighttime identification
5. Make a hose telescopic for easy storage

Evaluation A major strength of the Analogies technique is that the analogies often develop a "life of their own" which can help stimulate ideas.[13] Furthermore, analogies usually will be more provocative when they involve movement rather than being limited to object similarities. Because it is based upon problem attributes, a potential weakness of Attribute Analogy Chains is the overuse of object analogies. Because movement and elaboration are not specified, ideas generated by the analogies in this technique may have less stimulation value. On the other hand, Attribute Analogy Chains is an interesting use of related and unrelated stimuli. It clearly possesses more idea generation potential than Attribute Listing alone (where ideas are generated simply by examining different problem attributes). In addition, the activity involved in developing the analogies would transfer easily to group problem-solving sessions.

4.04 Attribute Association Chains

Attribute Association Chains was developed by VanGundy.[14] It was modeled after Attribute Analogy Chains and shares elements of Free Association and Attribute Listing. However, unlike Attribute Analogy Chains, which uses analogies for stimulation, this technique uses free associations as stimuli.

The steps for using Attribute Association Chains are as follows:

1. List all of the major problem attributes.
2. List subattributes for each major attribute.

3. Look at one of the subattributes and write down the first word suggested. This word may or may not be related to the problem.
4. Using this word as a stimulus, list the next word suggested and so on until four or five associations have been written down.
5. Repeat steps 3 and 4.
6. Using the free associations as stimuli, write down any new ideas suggested.

To illustrate this technique, consider the problem of improving a vacuum cleaner. The first steps are to list the major attributes and subattributes:

Name: Vacuum cleaner
Parts: Brushes, bag, motor, handle, belt, cord
Shapes: Circular, oblong
Functions: Picks up dirt, stands up carpet, lights floor, cleans
Material: Fabric, metal, rubber, plastic

The next step is to free associate using several of the attributes. For instance:

Vacuum cleaner: Dirt machine, motorcycle, race, track
Bag: Collect, deposit, bottles, glass, cleans
Motor: Engine, start, run, idle, lazy
Cord: Electricity, shock, volts, battery, charge
Stands up carpet: Sits down, squats, exercises, breathe, air
Fabric: Cloth, thread, needle, sew
Plastic: Melt, wax, impression, painting

Finally, the free associations are used to stimulate ideas. For instance, "track" suggests installing a track guide under the carpet to guide a self-propelled vacuum cleaner. Other ideas are to build in a reusable dirt collector (from "collect" and "deposit"), to use sound waves to loosen dirt (from "shock" and "charge"), to install a thread/string collector or cutter on the bottom of the vacuum (from "thread"), and to build in resistance to pushing as an arm exerciser for people who don't get enough exercise vacuuming (from "exercises").

One elaboration of this technique is Cross Attribute Comparisons.[15] Instead of using associations from within a category, Cross Attribute Comparisons combines two or more associations from different categories. For example, instead of using "collect" and "deposit" as stimuli from the bag category, you might select "cleans" from the bag category and "shock" from the cord category. The combination "cleans-shock" then might suggest such ideas as using compressed air for automatic height adjustment when cleaning surfaces at different heights. Another idea would be to build in a heavy-duty dust filter for people with severe dust allergies (from the combination "engine-air").

Evaluation   As mentioned, Attribute Association Chains was patterned after Attribute Analogy Chains. The latter technique probably has a slight edge in its potential to stimulate unique ideas. This is because it relies upon analogies as the primary stimulus, while Attribute Association Chains uses free associations. Analogies usually will provoke more unique ideas if used appropriately.

The Attribute Association Chains technique shares many of the same strengths and weaknesses of Free Associations, Nonlogical Stimuli, Attribute Listing, and the Product Improvement CheckList. All of these techniques except Attribute Listing use unrelated stimuli. This alone can prompt many unique ideas—especially if a positive creative climate exists. Attribute Association Chains also is somewhat easier to use than Attribute Analogy Chains. Most people experience less difficulty generating free associations than they do analogies. On the other hand, both techniques can encourage a playful attitude, especially when they are used by groups.

4.05 Attribute Listing

Attribute Listing, one of the oldest of the formal idea generation methods, was developed by Robert Crawford[16] in the early 1930s. Its basic premise is that all ideas originate from previous ideas that have been modified in some way. The ratchet screwdriver, for example, evolved by changing one of the attributes of the traditional screwdriver—pushing rather than turning the handle. There are three major steps involved in Attribute Listing:[17]

1. State the problem and its objectives.
2. List all of the parts and characteristics of a product, object, or idea related to the problem.
3. Withholding all evaluation, systematically modify the characteristics or attributes to meet the objectives of the problem.

To develop a better hammer, for example, the following parts could be listed: (1) straight, wooden, varnished handle; (2) metal head with round striking surface on one end and a claw on the other; and (3) metal wedge in the top of the handle to secure the head to the handle. Of these parts, the basic attributes of handle shape/composition and the metal wedge could be selected for possible modification. The handle could be constructed of fiberglass, wrapped with a shock-absorbing material, and shaped to better fit the human hand; the metal wedge could be modified by replacing it with a synthetic, pressure-treated bonding. These modified attributes then would need to be evaluated against the specific objectives of designing a better hammer—for example, a handle that would not split and a head that would not loosen.

There is also a variation of Attribute Listing, described by Goldner[18] as attribute shifting. This variation uses the same steps as in Crawford's procedure but with one exception: Step 2 is altered by shifting the attributes to a product, idea, or object that does not use the attributes. To illustrate, Goldner describes a problem where a client wished to build a 50,000 square-foot building on a 10,000 square-foot location that was zoned for only one-story buildings. The dominant attribute in this case is area, as measured in square feet. Goldner suggests solving this problem by shifting the attribute of area to the attribute of height, and then building a five-story building with four floors underground.

Evaluation   Two aspects of Attribute Listing must be considered when using the technique. First, it is very easy to become wrapped up in attributes that are really not essential to the product, object, or idea under consideration. It probably would be wise to focus upon only those attributes related to primary functions. In the example of the hammer, the color of the hammer would be a nonessential attribute, but the handle and the striking face would be essential. Second, there is probably a limit to the number of attributes that can be considered for any one product, object, or idea. A useful guideline would be to use no more than seven attributes at any one time. Otherwise, the number of relations between attributes can become too large and unmanageable. The one exception, of course, might be when attributes can be quantitatively described and analyzed using computer technology. It also should be noted that Attribute Listing can be restrictive in the sense that some new ideas often will be very similar to the original attributes. For this reason, a technique involving fantasy might be considered if more unique ideas are desired.

4.06 Bionics

Bionics is a specific application of Analogies. Like Analogies, Bionics involves searching for idea stimulation in similar objects, functions, products, and processes. However, Bionics differs by restricting the search for stimulation to biological and botanical systems. Nature already has solved many of the technical problems that humans have been trying to solve (as well as many undiscovered problems).

Bionics has been widely used in industry and private research labs to solve a variety of electronic, thermal, hydraulic, mechanical, and chemical problems.[19] For instance, characteristics of the human ear helped Alexander Bell produce the telephone, the eye of a beetle was used to develop an aircraft ground-speed altitude indicator, the eye of a frog led to development of a type of electronic filter and radar displays, rattlesnake temperature-sensing organs were used to create the Sidewinder heat-seeking missile, and Velcro was invented after observing the hook closures on cockleburs.

The steps for using Bionics are as follows:

1. Clearly state the problem.
2. Describe the problem in terms of its major, underlying principle or process. (For instance, the underlying principle of a telephone receiver problem might be transmission or communication.)
3. Search for similar principles or processes in animal or plant life.
4. Using any similarities identified, generate new ideas.

Evaluation As has been demonstrated in numerous practical and theoretical inventions, Bionics is a valuable approach for stimulating problem solutions. Like Analogies, it helps provide new problem perspectives. And, it has the potential to provoke unique ideas through the use of unrelated stimuli. A major weakness of Bionics is that it requires knowledge of biology and botany to be applied most effectively. For some problems, it can be difficult to locate an appropriate analogy in nature and apply the analogy without expert knowledge. However, interdisciplinary teams can overcome this weakness. For engineers and other technical specialists, Bionics can be difficult to use due to problems of developing mathematical models. Nevertheless, such models are not required in all situations. The act of searching for stimuli in nature often can prompt useful solutions.

4.07 Catalog

The Catalog method, one of the simplest idea generation techniques, generates ideas by forcing together two apparently unrelated words, objects, or ideas and examining the product for possible solutions. As described by Taylor,[20] the following steps are used:

1. Write down a statement of the problem.
2. Consult a catalog, magazine, or dictionary and randomly select two words, objects, or ideas.
3. "Force" the two selections together and evaluate the product for its applicability to the problem.
4. If the two selections do not result in a practical combination, randomly select two new words, objects, or ideas and repeat step 3 until a satisfactory solution is produced.

As a simple example, a problem of how to create a new packaging material might be solved by forcing together the words *cardboard* and *plastic*. This combination might then be used to develop a cardboard container that would be both strengthened and made waterproof by the addition of a plastic coating.

Evaluation   The procedure for randomly selecting the stimulus elements can be both a strength and a weakness of the Catalog technique. Random stimulation can be a strength because of the degree of problem remoteness created and the likelihood that solutions will be innovative and unique; it is a weakness because of the possible difficulty involved in trying to apply random elements to certain types of problems. In particular, the technique would not be suitable for problems that are both well structured and narrow in scope. For ill-structured, broad-scope problems, however, the Catalog method could provide the stimulation needed to develop creative solutions. The only other caution is to use several different stimulus element combinations before concluding the idea generation activity. The more combinations considered, the more likely it is that a useful solution will be found.

4.08 Checklists

The Checklists technique generates ideas by preparing a list of items related to a problem and "checking" the items against certain aspects of the problem. Although Checklists can be used in many different ways, Taylor[21] describes two major uses: (1) as a problem-delineation list, and (2) as a possible-solution list. The purpose of a problem-delineation list is to provide a direction for the idea search, to make sure that no ideas have been overlooked, and to evaluate the applicability of ideas borrowed from a previous problem. Checklists used for possible solutions are concerned with developing new ideas. The problem-delineation list typically is used as follows:

1. List all of the major characteristics of the problem.
2. Check each item on the list to determine how similar it is to a previous, similar problem.
3. Evaluate the applicability of the similar items to the present problem.

Perhaps the most common use of Checklists involves new-product development. A simple problem-delineation list in this area might be developed as follows:

I. Physical Characteristics
   a. Size?
   b. Shape?
   c. Color?
   d. Weight?
II. Marketing Characteristics
   a. Likely consumers?
   b. Competitors?

     c. Retail support?
     d. Distribution plan?
  III. Packaging Characteristics
     a. Type of material?
     b. Availability of material?
     c. Structural adequacy?
  IV. Production Characteristics
     a. Adequacy of existing equipment?
     b. Suitable labor force?
     c. Quality control?

In contrast to the more general nature of the problem-delineation list, a possible-solution list focuses specifically upon new uses for a product, idea, or object. For example, a new product might be developed by altering an old one. A typical possible-solution checklist has been constructed by Osborn[22] and involves asking such questions as the following:

1. What other product is like this one (adapt)?
2. How could I change this product (modify)?
3. How could I add to this product (magnify)?
4. What could I take away from this product (minify)?
5. What could I use instead of this product or a portion of it (substitute)?
6. How could I alter this product's composition (rearrange)?
7. How could I turn this problem around (reverse)?
8. What could I put together to make a new product (combine)?

This list also can be used in conjunction with a problem-delineation list. The physical characteristics of a new product, for example, can be modified by changing the color, magnified by making it larger, or altered in some similar way.

As described by Davis and Scott,[23] another possible solution checklist is a variation on Osborn's list. This list, developed by Davis et al.[24] for product improvement, uses seven items to stimulate ideas:

1. Add and/or subtract something
2. Change color
3. Vary materials
4. Rearrange parts
5. Vary shape
6. Change size
7. Modify design or style

According to Davis and Scott, college students who used this checklist to change or improve a thumbtack and a kitchen sink generated significantly more ideas than a control group of students who did not use the list. Other possible-solution checklists include Eberle's[25] SCAMPER acronym (substitute, combine, adapt, magnify or minify, put to other uses, eliminate or elaborate, and rearrange or reverse) and Shore's[26] CREATIVITY acronym (combine, reverse, enlarge, adapt, tinier, instead of, viewpoint change, in other ways, to other uses, yes! yes!). VanGundy's[27] Product Improvement CheckList (PICL) is a more specialized checklist that is described elsewhere in this chapter.

Evaluation   Although the results obtained in the Davis et al. study are encouraging, it must be noted that the results are generalizable only to a specific population of college students who used a problem that, presumably, had little meaning or relevance to them. This caution does not mean that this or any checklist is incapable of stimulating ideas in more applied areas; it only means that results of such studies must be interpreted cautiously.[28]

The major advantages of possible-solution checklists seem to be that they are simple to use, help prevent overlooking "obvious" solutions, and are useful for adapting previous solutions to current problems. Problem-delineation checklists, however, probably should not be used as the sole method for generating ideas. Because the type of ideas generated will be limited by the specific items listed, the problem-delineation checklist should be used primarily as a supplement to more open-ended techniques.

4.09 Circumrelation

Circumrelation is a forced-relationship method developed by Frank Laverty[29] for individual idea generation. The technique uses a circular instrument known as a circumrelator, which consists of three concentric cardboard or plastic disks. The disks are 3, 5, and 7 inches in diameter and are divided, respectively, into 8, 12, and 16 sections. Each section on a disk contains one factor; there is thus a total of 1536 different factor combinations. A fourth disk with a segmented opening can also be added as a cover to permit uncluttered viewing of only three factors at any one time. As described by Laverty, the steps in applying Circumrelation are as follows:

1. Write down a general definition of the problem.
2. Determine the three major problem areas (divisions).
3. Generate a list of all possible factors for each problem area.
4. Reduce the number of factors until the problem areas contain 8, 12, and 16, factors, respectively.
5. For each section on the circumrelator, write in one of the factors corresponding to the appropriate problem divisions.
6. Hold two of the divisional circles steady while rotating, in turn, the other circle.

7. Evaluate the relationships produced by each set of factors, and write down any ideas suggested for future consideration.
8. Evaluate the potential of each idea for solving the problem.

If the factor combinations do not seem to produce satisfactory ideas, an additional disk that contains factors completely unrelated to the problem can be added.

As an example of how the procedure can be used, Laverty describes construction of a circumrelator using factors from the recreational field. On the top disk are listed recreational facilities; on the middle disk, activities; and on the bottom disk, different types of recreation. When the three disks are rotated and the alignment of any three factors is examined, new ideas are suggested. For example, alignment of snowmobiling (types), group competition (activities), and club rooms (facilities) can suggest an idea for various contests located at snowmobile lodges. Or, to use another example, gliding and water skiing (a combination factor) can be combined with rentals (a facility) to suggest development of a rental business using water skis and hang gliders. Obviously, not all combinations will produce useful ideas. The large number of combination possibilities, however, should increase the chances of producing at least one workable idea.

Evaluation   Although not acknowledged by Laverty, the procedure of forcing together factors from different problem dimensions is the same concept used in Morphological Analysis. Circumrelation simply alters the principle of the Allen Morphologizer[30] by moving disks instead of vertical strips containing problem factors. Furthermore, the use of disks is not unique, also having been proposed by Rickards.[31]

It is not surprising then that Circumrelation has the same advantages and disadvantages as Morphological Analysis. For example, it provides a quick, structured procedure for generating ideas, is inexpensive to develop and use in terms of time and resource requirements, and does not require any special training. In addition, the circumrelator is somewhat easier to manipulate than the Allen Morphologizer since the circumrelator is constructed as a single unit. On the other hand, Circumrelation has such disadvantages as being limited in the number of dimensions and factors that can be included, relying upon individual perceptions of what dimensions and factors should be included, and producing slightly less unique solutions than might be obtained with other methods in which remote problem elements have been included in the procedure, for example, Focused-Object. Of course, this latter disadvantage must be weighed against the structured, systematic procedure provided by Morphological Analysis and Circumrelation.

4.10 Cliches, Proverbs, and Maxims

A variation of the Checklists approach involves using a list of cliches, proverbs, and maxims as unrelated idea stimuli. The approach described here was developed by VanGundy,[32] who observed how some people misuse Analogies by substituting cliches. The technique is relatively simple to use. The steps are as follows:

1. Select a cliche, proverb, or maxim that appears interesting and is unrelated to the problem.
2. Without thinking of the problem, write down any implications and interpretations of the cliche, proverb, or maxim.
3. Using the implications and interpretations as stimuli, write down any ideas suggested.
4. Select another cliche, proverb, or maxim and repeat steps 2 and 3 until a satisfactory solution is achieved.

To guide selection of the cliches, proverbs, and maxims, the criteria of familiarity and visual imagery can be used. Higbee and Millard[33] asked undergraduate psychology students to rate 203 proverbs and other sayings according to their familiarity with them and their ability to arouse visual images. The author analyzed the Higbee and Millard results and rank ordered the ratings according to their average ratings in familiarity and visual imagery (the highest-rated item was ranked 1, the second highest was ranked 2, and so forth). The 25 items that were most familiar to the study's participants were the following:

1. Practice makes perfect.
2. Better late than never.
3. If at first you don't succeed, try, try, again.
4. Like father, like son.
5. A place for everything and everything in its place.
6. Two wrongs do not make a right.
7. Two's company, three's a crowd.
8. Where there's a will, there's a way.
9. Don't count your chickens before they're hatched.
10. Easier said than done.
11. All's well that ends well.
12. Practice what you preach.
13. You can't tell a book by its cover.
14. An apple a day keeps the doctor away.
15. A penny saved is a penny earned.
16. Cleanliness is next to godliness.
17. Mind your own business.
18. Beggars can't be choosers.
19. Easy come, easy go.
20. Beauty is only skin deep.
21. Beauty is in the eye of the beholder.
22. You can't teach an old dog new tricks.

23. Better safe than sorry.
24. Two heads are better than one.
25. Actions speak louder than words.

The 25 top-rated items according to their perceived ability to evoke visual images were as follows:

1. When the cat's away, the mice will play.
2. The early bird catches the worm.
3. Like father, like son.
4. Kill two birds with one stone.
5. Don't count your chickens before they're hatched.
6. If the shoe fits, wear it.
7. Monkey see, monkey do.
8. A man's home is his castle.
9. The bigger they are, the harder they fall.
10. Birds of a feather flock together.
11. Two's company, three's a crowd.
12. You can lead a horse to water, but you can't make it drink.
13. Don't cry over spilt milk.
14. Two heads are better than one.
15. We're all in the same boat.
16. Never bite off more than you can chew.
17. One bad apple spoils the barrel.
18. Put on your thinking cap.
19. You can't teach an old dog new tricks.
20. You can't tell a book by its cover.
21. When it rains, it pours.
22. Don't rock the boat.
23. Too many cooks spoil the broth.
24. Look before you leap.
25. A penny saved is a penny earned.

Six of the sayings ranked were included in both lists. The familiarity sayings that also were included in the visual imagery list were numbers 4, 9, 13, 15, 22, and 24. Thus, these sayings are most likely to arouse images and be familiar.

To illustrate this technique, consider this problem: In what ways might we encourage drug-dependent employees to seek treatment?

The first step is to select an interesting cliche, proverb, or maxim that appears to be unrelated to the problem. In this case, "Too many cooks spoil the broth" is selected.

Next, write down any implications and interpretations suggested. For instance: (1) Some tasks require a minimum number of people—anything beyond that will be counterproductive; (2) completing a single, clear-cut task requires coordinated effort; (3) if physical facilities limit the number of people who can work on a task at any one time, they should take turns; and (4) when each person working on a group task has a different opinion, the task may not be completed.

Finally, use these statements as stimuli and record any new ideas. For example: (1) Form employee support groups of people with drug problems, (2) assign drug-dependent employees the task of developing a company-wide drug education program, and (3) have drug-dependent employees take turns role-playing a counselor.

Evaluation   Like Checklists, Analogies, and similar approaches, this technique is well suited for stimulating unique ideas using unrelated stimuli. The variety of cliches, proverbs, and maxims available provides a varied array of stimulators. This technique also is easily adapted for use by groups, where it can promote a playful atmosphere conducive to creativity. Furthermore, even if the interpretations are not accurate, useful stimulation still can be produced. One disadvantage is familiarity. If the cliches, proverbs, and maxims are too familiar to the user, idea uniqueness may be retarded. The Higbee and Millard study lends some support to this notion, since less than one-fourth of the top-rated familiar sayings also were rated high in visual imagery potential. This approach also shares a disadvantage with other techniques that use unrelated stimuli: Some people may have trouble using unrelated stimuli and making the "force fit" required to produce a workable idea.

4.11 Creative Visualization

Most of us use images in our day-to-day thinking and problem solving. Some of these images are fleeting and of short duration, while others are more stable and long-lasting. Once images are harnessed, they can help solve many types of problems. Unfortunately, we often are not aware of our images and how to use them.

To take advantage of images, a targeted approach should be used. The images we recall from memory must be consciously constructed to make full use of their problem-solving potential. Like many creative problem-solving techniques, success is based upon a rather interesting paradox: Creativity must be both structured and unstructured. Images must be allowed to flow freely, but they also must be shaped and used in a more or less structured format.

There are a variety of approaches for using images to generate ideas.[34] Because no single approach is likely to work best, each person should experiment with different approaches. The goal is to become so proficient in using visualization that it becomes a natural way of thinking and solving problems.

A typical approach to Creative Visualization would involve the following steps:

1. Try to become physically and mentally relaxed. If possible, use relaxation exercises (e.g., tense and relax different muscle groups or practice controlled breathing by inhaling through the nose and exhaling through the mouth).
2. Use a warm-up exercise to practice visualizing a variety of images. For instance, pretend your mind is a blank screen and allow images to flow across it. Select one of the images and examine it in detail. Then, select another image and examine it. Repeat this exercise using four or five images. During this time, write down any ideas that might emerge. However, do not consciously look for ideas during this exercise.
3. Using a partner or tape recording, follow a visualization script. This script should require you to visualize yourself doing a variety of activities in several different settings. The script should direct you to examine everything you encounter in detail. You also should experience the images using more than one sense. At some point in the script, you should discuss your problem with someone you visualize.
4. After visualizing for about 10 or 15 minutes, terminate the exercise. Immediately write down any problem ideas you can think of.

An example of a typical visualization script is described by VanGundy.[35] It begins by visualizing yourself standing in front of a large, carved wooden door and examining it in detail. Observe every detail and feel its surface. Next, open the door and walk into a room and visualize it in detail. Several people in the room discuss your problem and share some of their ideas with you. In the center of the room is a computer. Turn it on and watch the images that appear on the screen's monitor. Each image suggests a problem solution. Then, before you leave the room, someone comes up to you and gives you at least one more idea. Finally, after you leave the room and close the door, sit down on a couch beside someone. Describe your new ideas in detail to this person.

Evaluation   Creative Visualization can be a useful procedure for generating a variety of unique ideas. When used with relaxation exercises, the technique can prompt a fairly large number of ideas. The visualization process usually is an interesting experience that also can be fun. On the other hand, visualization probably is not well suited for everyone. It requires an open mind and an ability to generate images easily. Although practice can improve the ability to play around with images, existing mental blocks must be removed first. For most people, however, some training in using visualization is enough to get them started on their own.

4.12 Exaggerated Objectives

Techniques such as Analogies and Reversals require that you "stretch" a problem to produce new perspectives and stimulate ideas. Exaggerated Objectives is similar to these techniques in that it stretches a problem by exaggerating major problem criteria or objectives. These exaggerations then are used to stimulate new ideas.

The steps for using Exaggerated Objectives are as follows:[36]

1. List the major problem objectives (i.e., the major requirements a solution needs to satisfy).
2. Exaggerate or stretch each objective in any way possible. There is no "correct" way to do this.
3. Using each exaggerated objective as a stimulus, write down whatever ideas might be suggested. The ideas do not need to be logically related to the objectives.

This technique can be illustrated using the problem, in what ways might a hotel attract more customers? Exaggerated Objectives could be set up as follows:

Original Objectives	*Exaggerated Objectives*	*Possible Solutions*
Low cost	Costs $5 million	Have a contest and give away money to guests
Requires no new personnel	Hire 10,000 people	Offer free rooms to employees who recruit customers; have singles weekend package deals
Rooms occupied on weekends	Rooms never occupied	Offer two rooms for the price of one
Involves no new maintenance	Each room has a maintenance engineer	Place discount coupons and coupons for free rooms in selected rooms

Evaluation   A primary advantage of Exaggerated Objectives is that new perspectives can be created easily. By simply playing around with problem objectives, the problem solver can gain new sources of idea stimulation. Moreover, the problem objectives can be used as criteria to evaluate ideas once they have been generated. One disadvantage of this technique stems from the use of related problem stimuli. Because the technique relies upon elements related to the problem, idea uniqueness may suffer slightly. However, if the objectives are stretched sufficiently, this may not be a major difficulty.

4.13 Focused-Object

The Focused-Object technique, developed by Whiting,[37] generates ideas by examining the relationships produced by forcing together fixed and randomly selected elements. The following steps are used:

1. Select a fixed element (usually related to a part or all of the problem).
2. Select a random element (usually an object from the immediate physical environment that seems to be unrelated to the problem).
3. Using these two elements, free-associate on different ways they could be combined to produce a new object or idea (first-level ideas).
4. Using the first-level ideas (step 3), try to think of new ideas (second-level ideas).
5. Continue free-associating until all possible ideas have been generated.
6. After all ideas have been exhausted using the fixed and random elements, select a new random element and repeat the process using the original fixed element.
7. Terminate the process once a useful pool of ideas has been generated.

To illustrate this technique, Whiting describes a problem of how to develop ideas for a new chair design. A chair is selected as the fixed element and a light bulb is selected as the random element. Free-associating with these elements produces ideas such as a glass chair or a bulb-shaped chair (first-order ideas). Using these ideas and other similar ones, second-order ideas are generated. For example, the idea of a bulb-shaped chair could suggest an idea involving flowers (or floral designs) and something shaped to fit the human body—ideas produced by free-associating with the words *bulb* and *shape*. Another random element, such as a table, could then be introduced and the procedure started again.

Evaluation   By using a fixed element that is related to the problem, this technique has a potential advantage over other forced-relationship techniques: The solutions generated should be more practical than those derived from mehtods that rely entirely upon random elements. Moreover, the use of random elements should help ensure solution uniqueness. By combining related and unrelated stimuli, Focused-Object is a well-balanced approach that should be useful for dealing with many types of problems.

4.14 Free Association

The Free Association technique is the most basic of all the idea generation techniques. Ideas have to come from somewhere, and Free Association is the method generally used to draw ideas from the mind's "stream of consciousness." In contrast to forced-relationship techniques, pure Free Association does not rely upon a fitting together of two objects to produce ideas. Instead, one idea is used to generate another, which is then used to generate a third idea, and so forth until a useful idea is found.

According to Taylor,[38] there are two different versions of the Free Association technique: (1) pure, or unstructured free association, and (2) mixed, or structured free association. In unstructured free association, ideas are listed as they naturally occur, with one idea usually building upon another. This approach is typified by Classical Brainstorming and its variations, where ideas often are generated out of the "clear blue sky." Structured free association, in contrast, attempts to increase the relevance of ideas to the problem. To do this, the following steps are used:

1. Write down a symbol (word, number, object, condition) that seems to be directly related to the problem or some aspect of it.
2. Write down whatever is suggested by the first step, withholding all concern for its relevance to the problem.
3. Continue step 2 until all possible associations have been listed (try to develop at least 20 different associations).
4. Review the list of associations and select those that seem to have special implications for the problem.
5. Using the associations selected in step 4, develop ideas that seem capable of solving the problem. If none of the ideas seem useful, go back to step 1 and repeat the process, using a new symbol.

As an example of this procedure, Taylor describes the problem of developing a product name for a soap or detergent cleaning agent. A symbol, such as the word *clean,* could be written down and a list of associations developed, such as *sunny* or *bright.* After reviewing these and similar associations, *sunny* then might be selected as one of several associations that could be used to suggest a new name. In this case, the name Sunny Suds might be selected as the new name for the product.

Evaluation The structured version of Free Association is referred to as mixed, because it relies upon a specific stimulus to generate ideas but also allows the mind to consider more random thoughts. By using a stimulus that presumably is related to the problem, the structured approach has the advantage of increasing the likelihood of generating practical ideas. On the other hand, the structured version also could create more "logical" or inflexible ideas than might otherwise be desired. A combination of both versions would probably be more advisable.

4.15 Fresh Eye

For many types of problems, it is often difficult to generate unique ideas when there has been close and constant contact with a problem. One way of overcoming this obstacle is to introduce a "fresh eye" or new perspective on the problem. When this is done, the tendency to become locked in or functionally fixed on a problem can be reduced. There are two variations of this technique:[39]

Variation One

1. State the problem as clearly as possible.
2. Closely concentrate upon the problem with the goal of finding something positive about it.
3. Write down any previously overlooked ideas brought on by this close examination.

Variation Two

1. State the problem as clearly as possible in written form.
2. Present the written statement to a person or persons who have had little or no direct experience with the problem and have them write down their ideas.
3. Collect the ideas and evaluate their potential for solving the problem.

Evaluation   The Fresh Eye technique provides little in the way of a structured, systematic approach for generating ideas. Its potential for providing a fresh viewpoint on a problem, however, should not be overlooked. Children or novices in an area often are capable of developing many unique solutions, primarily due to their lack of exposure to or training in the background of the problem. Partly for this reason, variation two would seem to be more likely to produce innovative solutions. Variation one does not offer the same opportunity of developing a "fresh eye" on a problem. Nevertheless, the usefulness of this technique will be limited by the number of times a problem is examined and the number and variety of other people who are consulted. For this reason, it will be most suitable as a supplemental idea generation method.

4.16 Heuristic Ideation Technique (HIT)

The Heuristic Ideation Technique (HIT) was developed by Edward Tauber[40] to provide a systematic procedure for developing new-product ideas. It is patterned after Attribute Listing and Morphological Analysis. However, it differs slightly in using large, complex grids of product factors and in relying upon "heuristics" to structure the idea search.

Unlike some approaches, where a broad search for ideas is conducted, HIT shifts the focus to discovering heuristics first. Heuristics, or rules of thumb, then are used to structure the idea generation process by helping the problem solver systematically search for optimal combinations of product factors.

Instead of combining factors to produce a product idea, HIT decomposes existing products into lists of factors. For example, brownies might be decomposed into such factors as: brownie, chocolate, walnuts, mix, box, mixing, baking, pan, and so on. Then, another product would be decomposed and the two lists arrayed in a grid. Finally, different combinations would be examined for possible stimulation.

According to Tauber, heuristics are an efficient way to eliminate potentially poor solutions and retain more nearly optimal solutions. By reducing the number of factor combinations considered, HIT helps ensure that only the best solution candidates will be considered.

To reduce the number of idea combinations considered, HIT is based upon two major heuristics. First, the "heart" of most product ideas can be described using a two-word combination. For instance, the combination "toaster/tart" is a basic combination that might suggest a practical idea, such as the breakfast food currently on the market. A second heuristic is that some combinations of factors will be more interesting than others. In particular, combinations from different categories are more likely to prompt unique ideas than combinations from similar categories. Thus, the combination "vegetables/fruits" might be considered less interesting than the combination "breakfast/milkshake" or "ice cream/cereal."

The steps for using HIT are as follows:

1. Develop an idea generation grid consisting of factors that make up two product areas. Thus, a grid might contain packaging formats (e.g., aerosol, bag, boil in bag, box, can, jar, pan, tube) and food forms (e.g., biscuit, bread, burger, cookie, crust, dip, dressing, fish, juice). Assign a number to each possible combination. Thus, the combination of aerosol and biscuit might be assigned a 1, bag and bread a 2, and so forth.
2. Review all of the factors and cross out any two-word combinations that already exist on the market.
3. Circle the number of any combination that appears to have market potential.
4. Develop a brief statement for each combination. This statement should describe why the combination is interesting, why it has market potential, how it might be used, and so forth.
5. Transform the best two-word combinations into more workable ideas.

Evaluation   Like Morphological Analysis, the Heuristic Ideation Technique is a systematic way to generate a relatively large number of possible ideas. It helps remove some randomness and uncertainty from the idea search process. It also has the potential to increase the number of product ideas that are considered. Thus, solution quality should be enhanced. Finally, no special training is required. HIT can be used easily by almost anyone.

A major weakness of HIT is that all relevant product factors may not be included in the grid. Care needs to be taken to extend the search for product factors so that the most important ones are included. Like similar methods, HIT relies upon related stimuli and forced relationships to generate ideas. As a result, idea uniqueness may not be as high as is possible with unrelated stimuli. In addition, some people may have difficulty transforming the two-word combinations into more workable ideas. This technique (like most others) provides no heuristics for making such transformations. Nevertheless, it should prove to be a valuable tool for new-product developers as well as for others in less tangible problem areas.

4.17 Hypothetical Situations

Another way to redefine a problem is to construct a hypothetical situation using the question: What would happen if . . .? This technique was developed by John Arnold,[41] who used it to increase the creative problem-solving abilities of engineering students. Arnold developed a mythical planet named Arcturus IV and detailed its particular characteristics—for example, volatile atmospheric conditions, a gravitational pull 11 times that of the earth's, and birdlike creatures with three fingers on each hand who were the planet's inhabitants. He then instructed his students to design cars, appliances, and other devices that the birdlike creatures could use. The intent of such an exercise was to remove a problem from its normal environment and create a new problem perspective that could lead to more novel solutions.

There are three basic steps involved in using Hypothetical Situations:

1. State the problem.
2. Develop a hypothetical situation related to the problem. The situation should not be too remote from the problem, and it should be within the problem solver's area of competence and availability of required resources.
3. Use the hypothetical situation as a stimulation source for generating ideas.

Another example of using this technique might involve a problem of how to develop a more gas-efficient automobile. If a hypothetical situation was developed in which there was no more oil in the world, the problem must be redefined to compensate for this new constraint. Thus, ideas might be suggested for developing a solar- or electric-powered car.

Evaluation   The basic mechanism of this technique is similar to that used for Wishful Thinking and Synectics, in that both make use of fantasy (Synectics, in particular, makes use of an operational mechanism known as fantasy analogy). The primary effect of fantasy is to remove the problem solver from the immediate situation and force consideration of new problem constraints. The problem solver then can use these new constraints to consider alternative problem perspectives. The Hypothetical Situation approach differs slightly from Wishful Thinking and Synectics, however, in it s use of a situation that has some direct relation to the general problem area. As a result, there is more immediate force fit between fantasy and reality. In contrast, other fantasy methods use a more gradual and indirect forcing together of fantasy and reality. Such a difference in process does not necessarily make one approach better than another, since both have their advantages. The indirect approach is more likely to produce highly unique problem perspectives, while the more direct approach will make it easier to apply the perspectives to reality. The direct approach, however, might result in slightly less unique perspectives.

When the Hypothetical Situations technique is used, the important considerations are to construct situations that are (1) directly related to the problem, (2) realistic in terms of known laws of nature, and (3) suitable for your level of expertise and available technological resources.

4.18 Listing

The Listing technique is a systematic, forced-relationship method typically used for new-product development, although other topics also would be suitable. The steps for implementing this technique are as follows:

1. State the problem.
2. Think of a general subject area and then list all of the objects, products, or ideas that are related to the subject area.
3. Assign a consecutive number to each object, product, or idea.
4. Compare #1 with #2, #1 with #3, and so forth, until all possible combinations have been compared.
5. For each pair compared, free-associate on possible ideas suggested by the combination.
6. Select the best of the combinations for further evaluation.

To illustrate the use of the Listing technique, Whiting[42] describes a problem of an office equipment manufacturer who wishes to introduce a new line of products. To solve this problem, the general subject area of office furniture is used to generate a list of five items: (1) desk, (2) chair, (3) desk lamp, (4) filing cabinet, and (5) bookcase. The ten possible combinations of these items are then compared and free associations made for each pair. Thus, a desk is compared with a chair, a desk lamp, a filing cabinet, and a bookcase; a chair is compared with a desk lamp, a filing cabinet, and a bookcase, and so on until all possible comparisons are made. When a desk and a bookcase are compared, for example, the idea might be suggested to construct a desk with a built-in or detachable bookcase. Each suggested idea then would be written down and evaluated later.

Evaluation   A potential disadvantage of the Listing technique is listing more items than can be conveniently handled. To avoid having to deal with an unmanageable number of item combinations, the number of items in a list should be limited to about seven, and certainly no more than ten. Another potential disadvantage is that the technique might be too restrictive in the number of ideas that can be generated. Other sources or methods for stimulating ideas probably should be used to increase the richness of problem solutions. On the other hand, a major strength of the procedure is its focus upon elements directly related to a problem. Nevertheless, when unique solutions are desired, a balance between related and unrelated elements should be sought. For example, combining the Listing technique with the Focused-Object approach would help by introducing a random element with the potential for prompting innovative ideas.

4.19 Metaphors

A metaphor is a figure of speech applied to something that is not literally applicable. To say that someone has "muscles of steel," for example, is a metaphorical statement since the words are used to provide a special effect in describing someone's strength. Metaphors are very similar to Analogies and, like Analogies, can be used to create a fantasy situation for gaining new problem perspectives.

Jensen[43] has described five different categories of metaphors (see Table 4-5) that can be used to help redefine problem statements: (1) metaphors of restoration, (2) the journey metaphor, (3) metaphors of unification, (4) creational metaphors, and (5) nature metaphors. Other metaphors also could be used, and Jensen's categories are presented only as representative examples. In using Jensen's categories, ideas can be generated as follows:

1. Write down a general statement of the problem.
2. Select a category presented in Table 4-5 and examine the examples given for each subcategory.
3. Using these examples as stimuli, try to generate new ideas.
4. Repeat steps 2 and 3.

To illustrate this procedure, consider a problem of how to improve communication methods within an organization. Journey metaphors, for example, might be examined and clogged channels selected as a stimulus for new ideas. Thus, ideas might be generated on how to unclog channels of communication. These ideas might then lead to looking at ways to speed up the flow of information, reduce communication bottlenecks, and break up information into manageable chunks.

Evaluation Like analogies, metaphors are useful for developing unusual ideas. Development of a practical metaphor, however, can be difficult. Not all individuals will be able to create metaphoric relationships that are both unique and practical. The fantasy element needed for metaphoric thinking is foreign to many persons and requires some practice to master. On the other hand, once the process of developing metaphors is learned, the resulting ideas can be well worth the effort.

Table 4-5. Categories of Metaphors.

MAJOR CATEGORY	SUBCATEGORY	EXAMPLES
Restoration	Medical	Ills, Rash, Cancer
	Theft	Stolen, Robbed
	Repairman	Repair, Broken down
	Cleansing	Clean up, Dirty
Journey	On Land	Barriers, Maze, Clogged channels
Unification	Family	Home, Offspring
	Shepherd	Flock
	Sports	Team, Out of bounds
Creational	Edifice	Foundation, Planks
	Weaver	Fabric, Weaving
	Musical composer	Disharmony, Symphony
Nature	Light-Dark	Sheds light, Eclipse, Dull, Bright
	Physical phenomena	Whirlwind, Oasis
	Biology	Cobra, Monster

4.20 Modifier-Noun Associations

This technique was developed by VanGundy[44] as a way to combine free associations, forced relationships, and unrelated stimuli to develop new-product ideas. The idea stimuli are produced by selecting a noun and a modifier that are unrelated to the problem. Free associations are generated from this modifier-noun combination. The associations then are used as idea stimuli. The following steps are used:

1. Select a noun and a modifier. Appropriate examples would be, for example, running geese, glowing apples, heavy light bulbs, corrosive bed sheets, and silent springs. The resulting combination should be unrelated to the problem.
2. Using this combination as a starting point, free-associate additional combinations of modifiers and nouns.
3. Using the original combination and the free associations as stimuli, generate new ideas.
4. If desired, select another noun and modifier and repeat steps 2 and 3.

If your problem involves improving a flashlight, for example, you first would select a noun and modifier. For purposes of illustration, consider the combination "exploding manure." Next, you would free-associate, starting with this combination. In this case, you might think of flying output, floating programs, bouncy boats, and so on. Finally, you should use all the combinations as stimuli and generate any ideas that might be suggested. In this illustration, the following ideas might come to mind: adjustable-size batteries (from exploding manure), use foam that would enable a flashlight to float if dropped into the water (from floating programs), and programmable flashes for emergency messages (from bouncy boats).

Evaluation   A primary advantage of this technique is the combined use of free associations, forced relationships, and unrelated stimuli. With such a combination, unique ideas should result. The diversity of stimuli possible with Modifier-Noun Associations also helps ensure that a large number of ideas will be produced. A disadvantage is that some people may have difficulty using unrelated stimuli and making the force fit between an unrelated stimulus and a practical idea. As with similar techniques, a playful attitude is required when the stimuli are unrelated to the problem.

4.21 Morphological Analysis

Morphological Analysis (also known as Matrix Analysis or the Morphological Box) was originally proposed by Zwicky[45] and later expanded upon by Allen.[46] The technique has been widely used in a variety of areas including product design, technological innovation, market research, and social-problem analysis. It is an eclectic, forced-relationship approach that consists of dividing a problem into its major parameters or dimensions and then subdividing these into different forms of the original dimensions. Various combinations of the subdivisions then are forced together and examined for possible solutions to the problem. In doing this, the method combines elements of both Attribute Listing and the Listing method.

Although any number of major problem dimensions can be used, a typical approach is to break down a problem into two or three dimensions. For problems involving four or more dimensions, a special version of Morphological Analysis, known as the Allen Morphologizers, has been devised by Allen. In addition, more general versions of multidimensional Morphological Analysis exist.[47]

Regardless of the approach used, however, the basic procedure of subdividing a problem is the same. The only difference between morphological approaches is in the number of problem dimensions used and the specific procedures involved in constructing and sorting problem subdivisions.

Two- and Three-Dimensional Morphological Analysis   The following steps are used for both two- and three-dimensional problems:

1. State the problem and its objectives.
2. Identify two or three major problem dimensions.
3. List all of the relevant subdivisions for each dimension.

4. Using either a matrix (two dimensions) or a cube (three dimensions), write in the subdivisions listed for each dimension.
5. Take a subdivision from the first dimension and compare it with a subdivision from the other dimension(s).
6. Evaluate every combination of subdivisions for its potential to provide a problem solution.
7. Eliminate any combinations that are inconsistent with the problem's objectives or too impractical to implement.
8. Based upon preestablished criteria, select the combination that will be likely to solve the problem.

To illustrate the use of Morphological Analysis for a two-dimensional problem, consider a situation where the problem is to develop an innovation program within a company. The two dimensions identified for this problem are organizational level and areas of application. The subdivisions listed for level include individual, group, intergroup, and organizational. For areas of application, the following subdivisions are listed: technical, structural, people, and process. By repeated combination and evaluation of pairs of subdivisions, one from each dimension, a variety of program formats are suggested. As shown in Fig. 4-3, the program could involve group technical innovations or intergroup methods for stimulating innovation by individuals. In addition, combinations of subdivisions also might be used, such as a program that would focus upon technical and

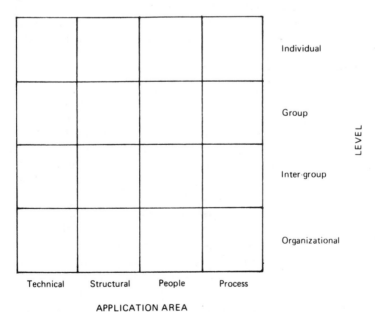

APPLICATION AREA

Fig. 4-3. Two-dimensional morphological analysis.

structural innovations involving individuals and intergroup relationships. For this company, organization-wide technical innovations might be rejected as being too costly.

As an example of a three-dimensional problem, suppose that someone in a product-design department wants to develop a new cookie package. The objectives of this problem are to develop a package that will be durable and can be easily opened and closed by the consumer, yet retain the freshness of the product. The Three major dimensions identified for this problem are material, shape, and closure. For each of these dimensions, four subdivisions are listed as follows:

Material	Shape	Closure
cellophane	square	adhesive
wax paper	rectangular	snaps
aluminum foil	round	tabs
cardboard	cylindrical	clips

As shown in Fig. 4–4, a cube is constructed and the dimensions and their subdivisions listed on each of the cube's three axes. (A total of 64 different solutions are produced by this approach in contrast to the two-dimensional problem that only produced 16 different combinations.) The different combinations then can be evaluated for their potential to solve the problem. A square, aluminum-foil package using snaps, for example, might be considered as a potential solution, while a round, cardboard container with clips might be eliminated as being unsatisfactory. Obviously, as the number of subdivisions is increased, there will be a geometric increase in the number of possible combinations that must be evaluated. Thus, if the number of subdivisions in each dimension of the cube in Fig. 4–4 were doubled, a total of 512 different combinations would be produced ($8 \times 8 \times 8$).

Cubes are not the only forms that can be used to construct morphological matrices made up of three or more dimensions. Geschka, von Reibnitz, and Storvik[48] describe a two-dimensional grid that can be used to analyze several problem parts. Problem parameters are listed in a column on the left-hand side of a chart. Solution options for each parameter then are listed, extending to the right. Different solution option combinations (one from each parameter category) then are examined to suggest new ideas.

As an example, Geschka et al. describe a problem of designing garbage separation equipment. Major parameters are listed first: garbage collection, methods for determining composition, transportation alternatives, separation devices, and so on. Next, solution options are listed for each parameter. Thus, garbage might be collected using conveyor belts, hoppers, or stationary containers; composition determined using optical, chemical, or mechanical analyses; the garbage transported using gravity, chutes, or cranes; and separation devices employed such as magnets, shaking actions, air separation, or flotation. Finally,

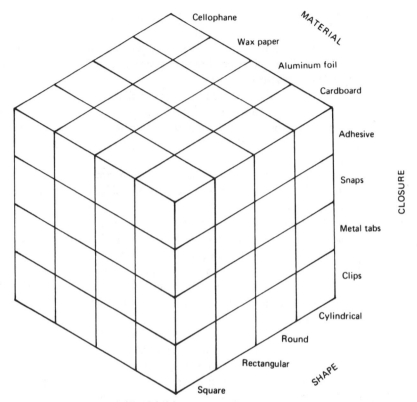

Fig. 4–4. Three-dimensional morphological analysis.

various combinations of these options are examined to suggest new ideas. In this illustration, such an idea might consist of a system that uses stationary containers, chutes, and magnetic separation. Other ideas also could be formed using other combinations.

The Allen Morphologizer Allen's approach to Morphological Analysis was greatly influenced by Zwicky. However, in addition to forming his own ideas on creative thinking and problem solving, Allen is probably best known for the technical refinements he developed for using morphological problem solving. The most notable of these refinements is the Allen Morphologizer, a technique used to organize and sort problem dimensions and their subdivisions. (Allen refers to dimensions as parameters and to subdivisions as components.) The following steps are suggested by Allen[49] for using the Allen Morphologizer:

1. Collect all information that possibly could be related to the problem, without considering its importance.

2. Record the information on 2½-by-3-inch cards, with the 3-inch side horizontal.

3. Organize the cards into groups of 12, without regard to any particular order. The cards in each group should be placed so that they are three cards wide by four cards high.

4. Quickly read over all of the cards four or five times.

5. Leave the cards and engage in a different activity for about 30 minutes.

6. Return to the cards, carefully study them, and arrange them into general categories so that all of the cards in one category appear to be related to one another.

7. Think of a descriptive title for each category, write the titles down on separate cards (using a different ink color), and place the title cards next to each card group.

8. Reduce the number of groups by repeating steps 3 through 6, treating the groups as units. Continue synthesizing and reducing the groups until at least four but no more than seven groups remain. Each one of these groups is now considered to be a problem parameter (dimension).

9. Study the factors within each parameter and reduce their number to seven. These seven factors are called components (subdivisions).

10. Construct a chart, recording the parameters across the top of a page, with the seven components listed below. Thus, the parameters will define the columns of the chart and the components, the rows.

11. Paste the chart on a piece of cardboard (or use poster board to begin with), and cut it into the same number of vertical strips as there are parameters.

12. Place the strips side by side, slowly move each one up and down, and observe the combinations produced by different arrangements of the components across the parameters.

13. Reduce the number of irrelevant or minor combinations by using Zwicky's concept of a King Value. That is, determine what one problem objective needs the most attention and, if achieved, will solve the problem.

To illustrate what the parameters and components might look like when placed on cardboard strips, an example of a morphological chart is shown in Fig. 4-5. The problem represented is how to put together an eclectic technique to help develop a new product. Five parameters are used to indicate five different elements of the problem-solving process. After the number of available techniques is examined, the total is reduced to four within each parameter. The strips then are manipulated until the solution depicted in Fig. 4-5 is produced. The method selected will combine the Five W's and H technique for redefining the problem, Dimensional Analysis for analyzing the problem, Synectics for idea generation, the Battelle Method for selecting an idea, and Research Planning Diagrams for implementing the final solution. Thus, a total of 1024 different combinations were hypothetically evaluated to yield the five techniques to be

REDEFINING PROBLEMS	ANALYZING PROBLEMS	GENERATING IDEAS	SELECTING IDEAS	IMPLEMENTING IDEAS
Boundary Examinations	Decomposable Matrices	Attribute Listing	Battelle Method	Gnatt Chart
Progressive Abstractions	Input-Output	Focused-Object	Reverse Brainstorming	Potential Problem Analysis
Five W's and H	Organized Random Search	Brainwriting Pool	Simulation	Program Evaluation Review Technique
Why Method	Dimensional Analysis	Synectics	Weighting Systems	Research Planning Diagrams

Fig. 4–5. Illustration of the Allen Morphologizer. Adapted from the Allen Morphologizer, from the book, *Morphological Creativity: The Miracle of Your Hidden Brain Power* by Myron S. Allen. © 1962 by Prentice-Hall, Inc. Reprinted by permission of the Publisher, Prentice-Hall, Inc., Englewood Cliffs, New Jersey 07632.

used for solving the problem. (This might be described as using a problem-solving technique involving other problem-solving techniques to solve a problem!)

Evaluation   Based upon the procedures used to solve problems with Morphological Analysis, the technique would seem to have the following advantages and disadvantages:

Advantages

1. The development of problem dimensions and their respective subdivisions introduces considerable structure into the problem-solving process. Because of the systematic nature of the method, trial-and-error problem solving is avoided. In addition, ideas will be considered that might have been overlooked using a less systematic method.
2. The method can be applied either individually or in groups. According to Geschka, Schaude, and Schlicksupp,[50] groups are best used when identifying problem dimensions and constructing the morphological chart.
3. The use of matrices and boxes illustrates all the possible idea combinations and promotes identification of any subdivisions and dimensions that might need to be added, changed, or deleted.
4. Although Morphological Analysis can be used with any problem-solving stage, it would seem to be especially suitable for analyzing problems, generating ideas, and perhaps implementing solutions.
5. The approach is easily adapted for use by computers in evaluating different solution combinations against preestablished criteria.
6. The structure of the process forces separation of information-gathering, idea-generating, and idea-evaluating stages.
7. Although certain intellectual abilities are required to use the technique, there is no need for any form of special training. Constructing a morphological chart for matrix is relatively easy; evaluation of the possible solutions is more difficult.

Disadvantages

1. As the number of problem dimensions and subdivisions increases, there will be a geometrically corresponding increase in the difficulty involved in evaluating solution combinations. For most morphological charts, no more than about seven major dimensions should be used.
2. The relative ease involved in constructing a morphological chart might lead some persons to use the technique to the exclusion of other methods. Morphological Analysis probably has been most successful with technical innovations and design problems and is perhaps even more useful when used to complement another technique, such as Synectics. Unfortunately, there is little research available to document this supposition.

3. Because of the highly structured nature of Morphological Analysis and its reliance upon related stimuli, many of the solutions produced will not be as original as those produced by other, less structured techniques that use unrelated stimuli.

4. Identifying the major problem dimensions can be a difficult task for some problems and some persons. Certain cognitive and information-processing skills are required that might not be possessed by all persons. According to Zwicky, the method is most appropriate for problems with a known number of problem dimensions, although the technique could be useful for structuring the search for problem dimensions when the total number is unknown. Nevertheless, users should include only important factors as major problem parameters or dimensions.[51] Including nonessential attributes (e.g., color for some problems) may result in a less useful matrix. However, it should be cautioned that attribute importance will vary from problem to problem.

5. To be successfully applied to most problems, the technique requires extensive knowledge of the problem area. This is particularly true for the activity of identifying the problem dimensions and subdivisions and in selecting possible solution combinations.

6. Methods currently available for solution evaluation do not seem to be entirely satisfactory. Zwicky's King Value concept is of some value, but it can be difficult to sort out factors that are most pertinent to the problem's objective—especially when a large number of subdivisions are involved. Tarr[52] describes guidelines for reducing a matrix to about six dimensions with an average of 20 subdivisions per dimension. Tarr's guidelines are (a) exclude obviously inferior subdivision factors; (b) evaluate different combinations for contradictory relationships (be especially concerned with factors in one dimension that, if combined with factors in another dimension, might make any resulting combinations impractical); (c) assign specific criteria to each dimension so that any subdivisions that exceed the criteria can be rejected; (d) eliminate any subdivision that is not directly related to the problem's primary objective; and (e) discuss the range of possible solution combinations with the decision maker and determine the extent to which he or she is willing to consider different possibilities.

7. The final combination or set of combinations should be considered tentative, subject to additional refinement and development to make the solution(s) workable. The apparent simplicity involved in producing solution combinations might tempt some persons to accept the solution as presented, without bothering to analyze further factors needed for solution implementation.

4.22 Nonlogical Stimuli

As described by Rickards,[53] the Nonlogical Stimuli method is a more general application of a variety of other idea generation methods. It is based upon de Bono's[54] use of random stimulation to promote thinking patterns characteristic of his Lateral Thinking approach. The major premise of the Nonlogical Stimuli method is that new directions for generating ideas can be developed by introducing an unrelated or random element. From this, it is hoped, an idea or solution not previously considered will emerge. Although not a systematic procedure, this method uses three steps:

1. Expose yourself to a variety of experiences that are entirely unrelated to the problem.
2. Examine the experiences for possible applicability to the problem.
3. Using the experiences as stimuli, write down any ideas suggested.

For example, conversing with persons unfamiliar with the problem (the Fresh Eye technique), using a dictionary (the Catalog technique), or using out-of-focus slides (similar to Visual Synectics) all could be used to prompt unusual problem solutions. The most important thing to remember when using this method is that the more remote from the problem that an experience or stimulus is, the more likely it is that a unique solution will be produced.

Evaluation   Nonlogical Stimuli is not so much a structured technique as it is something to be aware of when trying to solve a problem. Although not highly structured, it does require some deliberate effort. In particular, a conscious attempt must be made to be aware of nonlogical sources of stimulation. For problems in which a highly unusual solution is desired, this technique can be of some value—although it probably is most useful as a supplemental procedure.

4.23 Product Improvement CheckList™ (PICL)

The Product Improvement CheckList™ or PICL (pronounced "pickle") was developed by VanGundy[55] as an unrelated, forced-relationship aid for improving products. Although it originally was intended for use with tangible products such as toasters, tires, and telescopes, it also has proven useful for a variety of less tangible problems. For example, it has been used to generate ways to market a new product and to improve customer satisfaction.

PICL is available as a 27-by-22-inch worksheet and in disk form for IBM and Apple Macintosh personal computers. It can be used by either individuals or groups, although the computer versions are best suited for individuals.

PICL consists of two different formats: BASIC PICL and PICL JUICE. Each format can be used independently of the other. No particular sequence is required.

BASIC PICL   BASIC PICL uses 91 idea-stimulating questions to prompt ideas. These questions are organized into categories of Who? What? Where? When? and Why? Some sample product questions are as follows:

- Who does it make happy?
- What other name could describe it?
- Where is it first tried by the consumer?
- When is it altered by the consumer?
- Why is it designed the way it is?

BASIC PICL uses the following steps:

1. State the primary problem objective.
2. Read each question and write down any responses.
3. Review the responses and use them as stimuli for suggesting new product ideas or improvements.

To illustrate, suppose you manufacture a breakfast cereal known as Greenies. One of the questions that interested you was, "When does it make people sad or angry?" Your response was that some people are upset by a packaging weakness. The wax paper lining apparently tears easily and makes it difficult to re-seal the product to retain its freshness. Based upon this response, you might redesign the package or substitute another lining material.

PICL JUICE Most of the PICL worksheet is made up of 576 idea stimulators contained in PICL JUICE. These stimulators are organized into four major word groupings: TRY TO, MAKE IT, THINK OF, and TAKE AWAY OR ADD. Each of these groups contains 144 words or phrases preceded by the four major prompting categories. Below are examples of words and phrases in each of the categories:

TRY TO:	sketch it, wipe it, tighten it, twist it, build it up, do it backwards, whip it, inflate it
MAKE IT:	soft, transparent, magnetic, portable, disposable, vacillate, zigzag, adjustable
THINK OF:	escalators, Sir Lancelot, oatmeal, stethoscopes, time bombs, eggshells, disappearing ink
TAKE AWAY OR ADD:	layers, sex appeal, friction, rhythm, sand, pathos, moxie, energy, turbulence, anticipation

The primary stimulators are formed by combining the category prompters (TRY TO, MAKE IT, THINK OF, TAKE AWAY OR ADD) with the words and phrases contained within each respective list. For instance, the stimulators for the first category would be read as: Try to sketch it, wipe it, and so forth.

PICL JUICE can be used as follows:

1. State the problem objective.
2. Select a category and review the words or phrases listed.

3. Try to relate each word or phrase to the problem.
4. Write down any new ideas or product improvements suggested.

The problem of improving the Greenies breakfast cereal also can be used to illustrate PICL JUICE. Phrases such as "sprinkle it," "bag it," "twist it," "stack it," and "squeeze it" might suggest several ideas. For example, the cereal might be crushed and repackaged as a salad topping (from "sprinkle it"), sold in small bags as a snack food (from "bag it"), or twisted to offer a novel shape (from "twist it"); the flakes might be enlarged, flattened, and sold in a cylindrical container like a well-known potato chip (from "stack it") or reconstituted as a hot cereal and squeezed out of a plastic container (from "squeeze it").

It also is possible to use PICL JUICE in a variety of other ways. One way is to select two words or phrases from within or between categories, force them together, and see what ideas might be suggested. For instance, you might arbitrarily select "divide it" from the TRY TO list and "in cans" from the MAKE IT list. The combination of "divide it in cans" suggests a way to market cereal for travelers and others for whom conventional packages might be crushed easily. In addition, several different cereals could be sold in one can containing interior partitions.

Another variation involves selecting a word or phrase from one list and combining it with the product. Next, combine the word or phrase with one from another category. Then, select a word or phrase from another list and use it to modify the two combinations. For example, if the product is a briefcase, you might select "concentrated" from the MAKE IT list and produce the combination "concentrated briefcase." Next, you might combine "concentrated" with "adhesion" from the TAKE AWAY OR ADD list to form the combination "concentrated adhesion." Finally, a phrase such as "protect it" might be chosen from the TRY TO list and used to modify one or both of the combinations. In this case, an idea for briefcase security might be suggested such as using a heat-sealed closure that requires a certain chemical to reopen.

A third variation would be to select a phrase from the TRY TO list and force it together with a word from the MAKE IT list. Write down any ideas suggested by this combination. Then, combine this idea with a word from the TAKE AWAY OR ADD list and write down any ideas prompted by this combination. For instance, you might select "inject it" from the TRY TO list and combine it with "bubbles" from the MAKE IT list. For the breakfast cereal problem, the combination of "inject it/bubbles" might suggest injecting flakes with air to produce "bubble flakes." You then could combine this idea with a word such as "frost" from the TAKE AWAY OR ADD list. This combination might lead to an idea such as coating the bubble flakes with sugar.

Although many other individual uses are possible, there also are numerous ways to use PICL in groups. For instance, employees of a technical company in the Northeast placed PICLs in glass frames and hung them on a wall. To choose the words and phrases randomly, they took turns shooting darts at the PICL charts. Whatever word or phrase was under a dart was used for stimulation. Another group places a PICL on the floor and has group members sit in chairs around it. Each member is given a penny, a nickel, or a dime and takes turns tossing one of the coins onto the PICL worksheet. The spot where the coin lands determines the word or phrase used for stimulation; the particular coin tossed determines the minimum number of ideas that must be generated. Thus, if a nickel is tossed, at least five ideas must be generated.

Evaluation   In general, PICL is a handy resource for generating ideas. A major advantage is the number and variety of stimulators and the flexibility possible in using them in different combinations. The use of different categories adds further variety, which should enhance the quality of potential solutions. The use of unrelated problem stimuli also contributes to the technique's strength by increasing the odds for generating unique ideas. As a result, it should be hypothetically possible to stimulate large numbers of ideas. Moreover, the size of the PICL worksheet makes it ideal for use with groups. A major disadvantage of PICL is one shared by other methods that rely upon unrelated problem stimuli. Many people have trouble using forced relationships when the stimuli are not related to the problem. Thus, PICL probably works best with people who have a positive internal creative climate. In particular, it is appropriate for people who have the ability to play around with ideas and see connections among ideas where none may be immediately apparent.

4.24 Relational Algorithms

A major assumption of many idea generation methods is that combining problem elements often can suggest new problem perspectives. For example, the Listing technique systematically compares all major problem components in an attempt to spark ideas.

A weakness of the Listing procedure is that it is limited to those ideas suggested by the combination of two elements. For instance, if the problem involves improving a filing cabinet, two elements such as handle and drawer might be combined. Then, this combination would be examined to see if any improvements or new ideas might be suggested. However, there are only two ways the elements can be combined. In this case, the combination is either handle/drawer or drawer/handle.

Relational Algorithms partially overcomes this weakness and adds an action element as well. Problem elements still are forced together to provide stimulation, but relational words are inserted between the elements to increase the stimulation value of the combination. This procedure was developed by Crovitz,[56] who suggests using the following list of 42 relational words:

about	at	for	of	round	to
across	because	from	off	still	under
after	before	if	on	so	up
against	between	in	opposite	then	when
among	but	near	or	though	where
and	by	not	out	through	while
as	down	now	over	till	with

Using these words, the technique can be applied as follows:

1. List the major elements of the problem.
2. Insert each of the relational words between each pair of problem elements.
3. Examine each set of elements and relational words for possible ideas and suggestions.
4. Select those combinations most likely to solve the problem.

For an example of how this technique can be used, Crovitz has borrowed the hanging-ropes problem described by Duncker.[57]   In this problem, there are two ropes at some distance from each other hanging from a ceiling. A small hook is on the end of one rope and a small ring on the other rope. The object is to fasten the two ropes together. The problem is complicated, however, by the fact that the distance separating the ropes makes it impossible to reach both ropes at the same time. Using the major elements of rope and hand, the relational words are inserted for two sets of possible problem-element combinations: rope-rope and rope-hand. The rope-rope set produces combinations such as: take a rope across a rope, take a rope under a rope, and take a rope to a rope. The second set could then be used to produce such combinations as: take a rope against a hand, or take a rope in a hand. After considering these and other combinations, a final solution is suggested from: take a rope to a rope, and take a rope in a hand. Specifically, the solution is to hold one rope in one hand while swinging the other rope so that it can be caught with the other hand.

Evaluation   Although somewhat tedious to apply, the Relational Algorithms method can help to increase solution possibilities by forcing a problem solver to consider associations that otherwise might have been overlooked. The number of possible problem elements that can be conveniently dealt with at any one time, however, will be limited by one's attention span. Nevertheless, there are at least four things that can be done to insure that useful associations are not overlooked due to fatigue or temporary attention lapses: (1) do not try to use all 42 words at one time—break the list up into units of six or seven words, (2) go through the list more than once, (3) take periodic breaks, and (4) have at least one other person go over the list and try to develop associations to compare with yours.

In addition to the words included in Crovitz's list, the author has found the following list of prepositions to be helpful:

above	below	except	toward
along	beneath	into	upon
amid	beside	past	within
around	beyond	since	without
behind	during	throughout	

The addition of these words obviously increases the time required to apply the technique. However, if only one or two problem elements are involved, the additional 20 words should not be too difficult to incorporate and the range of possible solutions will be greatly expanded.

4.25 Reversals

For many problem situations, the initial problem definition limits our ability to generate ideas. The meaning of the words used or their order may not be stimulating enough to provoke unique ideas. However, if a few simple alterations are made, a more productive viewpoint often can be created. In particular, new perspectives might be generated by reversing the direction of a problem. Such a reversal should lead, in turn, to a more innovative solution.

For example, a university was able to solve a parking problem for its commuter students by applying the Reversals method. As originally stated, the problem was, how to provide parking spaces for commuter students on an already overcrowded campus. Reversing this problem produced a new definition: how to provide commuter students for parking spaces. This definition led to the solution of developing parking lots on the outside edges of town. The commuter students would drive to these lots and then board buses that would take them directly to campus. Had the parking planners spent time in trying to solve the problem as originally defined, a less than satisfactory solution might have resulted. Constructing a parking garage, for example, obviously would have been a high-cost alternative. Fortunately, in this case, the commuter lots provided the lowest-cost solution.

A more well-known example is the "sting" operations used by many law enforcement agencies. In a typical operation, the police notify selected criminals that they have won a prize and are invited to attend a party for a grand prize drawing. Once the unsuspecting "guests" show up, they are apprehended—many still disbelieving that they have been duped. In this situation, the police reverse the problem of how to go out and catch the criminals. Instead, they define the situation in terms of how they might get the criminals to come to them—a nice reversal of perspective.

The following are the basic steps for using the Reversals technique:[58]

1. State the problem as originally defined.
2. Reverse the direction of the problem in any way possible. (The type of reversal is not as important as rearranging the information about the problem situation.)
3. State the new definition of the problem and examine its practical implications.
4. If practical solutions are not likely to be produced, reverse the problem in a different way.
5. Continue reversing the problem until a satisfactory solution is produced.

Evaluation   One problem with the Reversals method is that not all reversals will produce practical solutions. When a particular reversal is not judged to be useful, a different slant on the reversal should be attempted. In the example of the commuter-student parking problem, a new slant might have been achieved by redefining the problem as: how to eliminate parking spaces for commuter students. This definition then might suggest the alternative of allocating all campus spaces without regard to status within the university. It is possible, of course, that turning a problem upside down will be a fruitless exercise. Given the low costs involved in using this method, however, there is little to be lost in trying it since the potential gains can more than justify its use.

4.26 Storywriting

Solving ill-structured problems involves gathering information to increase problem familiarity. The more information that exists about a problem, the easier it will be to solve.[59] Although many direct methods exist for gathering problem information (e.g., the Five W's and H technique), they usually are associated with problem redefinition and analysis. Indirect methods often are included as a part of idea generation techniques so that information is gathered and then used for idea stimulation. The Storywriting technique uses this approach. Basically, ideas are generated by writing a brief story that is somewhat related to the problem. Information in the story is examined and then is used as idea stimulation. There are three major steps:[60]

1. Write a brief (under 1000 words) fictional story about the problem. Avoid writing directly about the problem. Instead, allow your imagination to wander and write whatever seems appropriate. Don't be afraid to be a little playful and whimsical in your approach, if that is your style.
2. Carefully read over your story and list any major principles, actions, characters, events, themes, expressions, objects, and so on that seem interesting.
3. Using these data, write down any problem solutions they might suggest.

To illustrate this method, consider the following problem: In what ways might people reduce their nervousness when giving public speeches?   A brief version of a story for this problem might be written as follows.

Billy Joe Bob (BJB) fidgeted nervously with his tie. It was his first clandestine meeting and he was apprehensive.   Beads of perspiration wound their way down his face like rivulets of hot fudge melting on a three-scoop ice cream sundae.   Taking out his handerkerchief, he made a futile effort to mop his brow.

He glanced around to make sure there were no suspicious characters lurking about.   Since joining the super-secret spy agency, he had been dreading this day. If anything went wrong, it could be the end of his career. However, from what he could see, everyone in sight appeared to be functioning normally.   The usual assortment of weirdos were frolicking in front of a pawn shop. And people too busy to be busy bustled by him on the sidewalk.

Suddenly, out of the corner of his eye, he spotted a man wearing a bright red, plaid sport coat.   His contact!   He was dressed exactly as BJB had been told he would.   BJB began walking toward Mr. Plaid and tried to remain cool. He didn't want to show how nervous he was.

As he got to within about three feet of Mr. Plaid, BJB extended his hand in greeting.   As they drew closer together, BJB noticed that there was no sign of recognition in Mr. Plaid's eyes.   In fact, Mr. Plaid ignored BJB's outstretched hand and continued walking by him!

BJB was stunned.   His first assignment had been a bust. However, if that wasn't bad enough, there was more.   He just had been ignored by his own brother.

The next step in using this technique is to look over the story and extract different principles, observations, themes, facts, phrases, and so on.   In this case, the following list might be developed:

1. Fidgeting nervously with a tie
2. Clandestine meeting
3. Beads of perspiration
4. Rivulets of hot fudge
5. Futile effort
6. Suspicious characters lurking about
7. Dreading something
8. The end of his career
9. Functioning normally
10. Usual assortment of weirdos
11. People too busy to be busy
12. Bright red, plaid sport coat
13. Hiding nervousness

14. Shaking hands
15. One-way visual recognition
16. Being surprised by lack of recognition
17. A busted assignment
18. Brotherly love

The final step for the Storywriting technique is to look over all of the information listed and used it as a source of idea stimulation. Write down, without evaluation, whatever ideas might be suggested by each item. For instance, in this illustration, the following ideas might be generated:

1. Wear a tie made of a material that is soothing to the touch.
2. Before the speech, meet with as many audience members as possible. It usually is easier to talk to people you have met at least casually.
3. Carry worry beads in one of your hands.
4. Say something "sweet" about the audience to help get them on your side.
5. Before the speech, take a survey of audience members to find out specifically what they would like to hear and how they would like you to present the material.
6. Think of the worst possible thing that could happen during your speech. The chances are, even if it does happen, it won't be as bad as you might imagine. Often, such situations are excellent sources of tension release and can add a human element to the speech.
7. Use relaxation exercises before the speech.
8. Pretend that everyone in the audience is a complete weirdo and that you are superior to them in every way.
9. Involve the audience in experiential exercises.
10. Avoid wearing clothing that would be distracting visually.
11. If you are standing behind a podium, gently shake your legs in an exaggerated fashion. This should reduce any noticeable shaking in other parts of your body.
12. Pretend that you are looking at the audience from behind a one-way mirror: You can see them, but they can't see you.
13. Before you begin the speech, tell a joke with a surprise ending. This should help warm up the audience.
14. Pretend that everyone in the audience is a close relative who likes you a lot.

As another variation of this technique, you could ask someone else to write a story and use it as your stimulation source. This would be especially useful if you don't consider yourself a good writer. You also might consider this option if you think you are too familiar with the problem and would have trouble writing a story with enough useful stimulation.

Evaluation Storywriting has the potential to be a rich source of idea stimulation. With most stories, the stimuli will be unrelated enough to provoke unique ideas. On the other hand, a tinge of similarity in some stories can suggest practical solutions. The story used in the illustration was similar to the problem of giving a speech, but not identical. However, there was enough similarity in the topics of nervousness and dealing with people that some practical ideas were prompted. Beyond these considerations, a major advantage of Storywriting is that it may help draw out problem insights that might have been overlooked using more straightforward techniques. A primary weakness is that it requires a minimal ability to express yourself in writing. However, as mentioned, stories written by other people also can be used.

4.27 Symbolic Representations

The Symbolic Representations technique uses abstract symbols related to a problem to generate ideas. Production of the symbols, however, is largely intuitive. No direct relationship to the problem is used. As a result, the unrelated stimuli produced can lead to unique ideas. However, some people may have trouble dealing with the amount of abstractness involved.

Symbolic representations essentially are "doodles" related in an abstract way to a problem. After the doodles are drawn, they are used as the primary stimulation source. The steps are as follows:[61]

1. Write down a statement of the problem.
2. Restate this problem in terms of the essential, underlying principle involved. For example, does the problem involve increasing, decreasing, changing, preventing, reversing? To illustrate, a problem of improving a lawn mower might be restated in terms of how to eliminate things; a problem of increasing parking spaces might be redefined in terms of how to stack or store things.
3. Write down an abstract symbol (a "doodle") that generally represents this principle.
4. Using this symbol as a starting point, free-associate and draw another symbol suggested by the first one.
5. Draw a third symbol suggested by the second one and continue free-association in this manner until four or five symbols have been drawn.
6. Using each symbol as a stimulus, write down any ideas they might suggest.

Evaluation The potential ambiguity and lack of structure involved in this technique could make it difficult to use. Some people may have trouble relating the symbols to the problem. As a result, their stimulation value will be zero. Another potential problem with Symbolic Representations is that some people may have

difficulty stating their problems abstractly. However, a little practice in searching for the underlying principle should overcome this obstacle. On the plus side,
this approach may stimulate unique ideas that might have been overlooked using
a more direct approach. Moreover, drawing the doodles can be a fun exercise in
creative self-expression.

4.28 Two Words

The Two Words technique uses forced relationships and related problem stimuli
to generate ideas. The problem stimuli are derived from examining different
combinations of alternative descriptions of two "key words" in the problem
statement. The rationale behind this approach is that the words initially chosen
to represent a problem may be limited in their ability to provoke certain types
of ideas. By restating the problem using alternative meanings, the technique will
provide new perspectives that might stimulate new ideas. As described by
Olson,[62] the following basic steps are used:

1. Select two key words from the problem statement. Usually these words
   are a verb and a noun.
2. List alternate meanings for each of the key words. A thesaurus will be
   helpful for this task.
3. Select the first word from the first list and combine it with the first word
   from the second list.
4. Using this combination as a stimulus, write down any ideas suggested.
5. Combine the first word from the first list with the second word from the
   second list, and write down any ideas suggested by this combination.
6. Continue combining words in this manner until all possible combinations
   have been examined for stimulation.

To illustrate this technique, consider this problem: In what ways might I
better organize my work? First, two key words are selected, such as "organize"
and "work." Next, alternate meanings are generated for each word as follows:

Organize	*Work*
arrange	labor
plan	job
design	task
prepare	performance
distribute	assignments
allocate	duties
sort	effort

Finally, different two-word combinations are examined for possible idea stimulation. For instance, different combinations might prompt the following types of ideas: (1) develop a list of priorities (from "arrange-labor"), (2) demonstrate how I work to someone else and ask them for suggestions (from "arrange-performance"), (3) delegate time-consuming responsibilities (from "arrange-assignments"), (4) do the most difficult tasks first (from "arrange-effort"), (5) do a time-motion study (from "design-job"), (6) assemble all necessary equipment and information before starting a task (from "prepare-labor"), and (7) develop contingency plans and anticipate things that could go wrong and how to circumvent them (from "prepare-effort").

Evaluation   The major strength of the Two Words technique lies in its ability to provide a variety of new problem perspectives—any one of which might prompt a high-quality solution. It also is relatively easy to use, is systematic in its approach, and requires minimal time. On the other hand, its reliance upon related problem stimuli might restrict the uniqueness of the ideas generated. Nevertheless, its ease of use makes it an attractive choice for either tangible or intangible types of problems.

4.29 Wishful Thinking

Wishful Thinking is frequently overlooked by many pragmatic-minded individuals. Such persons often assume that alternative problem perspectives must be based upon logical and rational modes of analysis. Although this type of analysis is especially useful for well-structured problems, it will not work as well with most ill-structured problems.

When a problem is open-ended, some degree of fantasy can provide the degree of loosening needed to produce many unique ideas. For instance, the process of manufacturing bread might be reconceptualized by looking for ideal characteristics such as a short rising time, long shelf life, minimal packaging costs, and a high yield in proportion to the quantity of ingredients used. Thinking about what might be provides a goal to be attained, increases motivation, and helps create a new and different thinking pattern.

The basic steps for using the Wishful Thinking technique are as follows:

1. State the problem.
2. Assume that anything is possible.
3. Using fantasy, make statements such as: What I really need to do is. . . . What really needs to happen to solve this problem is. . . . The only way this problem can be solved would be if. . . .
4. Examine each fantasy statement and, using it as stimulation, return to reality and make statements such as: Although I really cannot do that, I can. . . . It might be possible to do that, but first I would have to. . . .
5. If necessary, repeat steps 3 and 4.

As an example of Wishful Thinking, Rickards[63] cites a problem in Great Britain involving road deaths caused by automobile collisions with streetlight columns. The Road Research Laboratory had been studying this problem and experimenting with new materials without much success. Eventually, a senior research engineer was assigned to the project and decided that an entirely new approach was needed. After giving much thought to this problem, the engineer fantasized that the problem was actually one of how to construct a column that would disappear on impact. Based upon this perspective of the problem, a second engineer designed a column based on the principle of a shear joint. When struck by a car at high speed, the upper portion of the column breaks away and lands out of danger away from the car. The column does not actually disappear, of course, but the suggestion of a disappearing column led to a practical solution.

Evaluation   Wishful Thinking is similar in principle to Hypothetical Situations and Metaphors in that all three are based on fantasy. By getting away from the problem, useful perspectives can be produced that typically would not be considered when using a more logic-based approach. The major difficulty with such approaches, however, is that some perspectives might be unrealistic and incapable of provoking practical solutions. In addition, there probably will be some differences among individuals in their ability to develop a fantasy and then bring it back down to reality. When Wishful Thinking does not appear to yield useful solutions, it might be wise to consult with persons from diverse backgrounds (as in the Fresh Eye method) for aid in fantasy development. Experts in the problem area also might be consulted to help deal with the practical implications of the fantasies.

4.30 Word Diamond

The Word Diamond technique was developed by VanGundy[64] as a variation of the Two Words technique. Like Two Words, it uses forced relationships and related problem stimuli to prompt ideas. However, instead of using different word meanings, the Word Diamond approach uses different combinations of words or phrases in the problem statement. Because at least four words are required, complex problem statements will be most appropriate.[65]

The following steps are involved in constructing a Word Diamond and using it to generate ideas:

1. Select four key words or phrases from the problem statement.
2. Arrange the words or phrases in the shape of a diamond, with one word or phrase at each point.
3. Select one of the words or phrases, combine it with another one, and write down any ideas suggested.

4. Combine the selected word or phrase with the other two and write down any ideas suggested by these combinations.
5. Select another word or phrase and combine it with the others. Continue this process until each word or phrase has been combined with the other ones and all possible ideas have been written down.

A problem of motivating employees to clean up their work areas will be used to illustrate this approach. In this case, the problem is, In what ways might the employees be motivated to clean up their work areas? Four key words or phrases are selected from this statement and arranged in a diamond shape as shown in Fig. 4–6. Finally, different combinations of these words and phrases are formed to see if any might prompt ideas.

In this example, the following types of ideas might be suggested: (1) Make the surroundings pleasant with accessible trash receptacles (from "motivate/work areas"), (2) provide financial rewards to employees who cooperate (from "motivate/employees"), (3) pay employees a piece rate for the amount of scrap waste they pick up (from "motivate/clean up"), (4) instill a sense of ownership in the employees so that they will be less likely to "dirty their own nests" (from "employees/work areas"), (5) sponsor a contest and award prizes to the cleanest department (from "employees/clean up"), (6) form employee discussion groups such as quality circles and hope that they learn how to motivate themselves (from "employees/motivate"), and (7) institute dress codes and hope that enforcing dress standards will carry over to cleaning the work areas (from "clean up/employees").

Evaluation   The Word Diamond approach is easy to set up and implement and is capable of sparking workable problem solutions. It requires very little time to use and, therefore, is a relatively low-cost technique. There is very little to lose from trying it. On the other hand, it shares the weaknesses of other methods

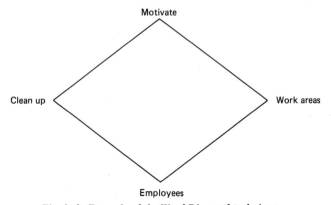

Fig. 4–6. Example of the Word Diamond technique.

that rely upon forced relationships and related problem stimuli. For instance, its potential to prompt unique ideas may be less than an approach that uses unrelated problem stimuli. Despite this potential weakness, it should not be overlooked due to its simplicity of use.

GROUP TECHNIQUES

4.31   Battelle-Bildmappen-Brainwriting (BBB)

The BBB technique (also known as "picture folder brainwriting"[66]) was developed by the Battelle Institute research unit on innovation and creativity in Frankfurt, Germany. Although it combines elements of both Classical Brainstorming and Visual Synectics, it generally is considered to be a brainwriting variation. BBB starts with Classical Brainstorming, is followed by idea stimulation from a picture portfolio (the bildmappen), and then ends with a second round of idea generation using the basic brainwriting method. Six steps are involved in using this technique:[67]

1. A problem is read to a group of from five to eight persons.
2. The group verbally brainstorms to develop known or trivial solutions to the problem.
3. Each group member is given a folder containing eight to ten pictures that are unrelated to the problem.
4. Each person writes down any new ideas or modifications of old ideas suggested by the pictures.
5. The solutions of each group member are read to the entire group.
6. The group discusses the ideas with the goal of developing additional variations.

As an example of how the BBB method is used, Geschka, von Reibnitz, and Storvik[68] use the problem of inventing a new way to bind paper without staples. After an initial brainstorming session, the participants were given individual picture folders. For example, one of the pictures showed fire fighters working on a burning airplane. The use of extinguishing chemicals suggested the ideas of impregnating the binding edge of paper with an adhesive or using microcapsules that are crushed under pressure to release an adhesive. Another aspect of the picture involved using foam from a pipe nozzle. This concept suggested the idea of punching the sheets of paper and then injecting adhesive.

Evaluation   A major advantage of the BBB method is that the individual writing of ideas stimulated by the pictures can help overcome the personal inhibitions often found during face-to-face idea generation sessions. Furthermore, the use of pictures provides an additional source of idea stimulation not normally present in a Classical Brainstorming group.[69]   Thus, when the BBB method is is used, ideas are generated by individual free association, by stimulation from the ideas of others, and by stimulation from pictures. Idea uniqueness should be high. The method does not, however, totally control for the possibility that some individuals might feel inhibited about suggesting ideas after the picture-generated solutions are read. An optional procedure might be to extend the process by allowing for additional individual ideation and evaluation of ideas following the group discussion (i.e., after step 6).

4.32 Brainsketching

The mental images we develop about problems usually are fleeting and some-what obscure. However, such images can be valuable aids for conceptualizing and understanding problems. One way to make these images more permanent is to represent them with rough sketches.

Most people probably draw pictures to represent some types of problems. At one time or another we all have used sketching as a problem-solving tool. Thus, there is no reason why the same process would not work equally well in groups. In fact, the outcome might be enhanced considerably by the joint input and stimulation received from others.

Brainsketching originally was developed as a variation of the Pin Cards tech-nique by students enrolled in one of the author's classes.[70] The author sub-sequently made slight modifications. There are six steps:

1. A small group discusses the problem for purposes of clarification. No solutions should be suggested.
2. Each group member individually draws a sketch of how the problem might be solved. No talking is permitted during this activity, and the drawings should not be shared at this time.
3. After 5 to 10 minutes, the group members pass their drawings to the per-son on their right.
4. The person receiving a sketch modifies it if desired. Brief, written nota-tions also may be added.
5. After about 20 minutes of this activity, the sketches are collected and evaluated.
6. The group members then may select a final solution from the existing sketches or discuss how a solution might be constructed from elements of different sketches.

Evaluation   As a variation of the Pin Cards technique, Brainsketching adds a unique dimension. By replacing written idea generation with visual sketches, Brainsketching provides a creative outlet for people who prefer visual means of expression. And, as Adams[71] has noted, an important element of problem solv-ing is using the most appropriate problem-solving language. Thus, for some people, Brainsketching may be the best approach to use for certain types of problems. In general, this technique can be used most easily with concrete, tangible types of problems (e.g., developing ways to improve a vacuum cleaner). However, it also will work with more intangible, abstract problems. For these problems, the sketches can be used to symbolically represent direct aspects of the problem. The result can be an enjoyable experience as a group exercise.

In some respects, Brainsketching is similar to Symbolic Representations. A major difference is that the Brainsketching drawings should be less abstract than those typically used in Symbolic Representations. Brainsketching also shares most of the advantages of brainwriting in general. Specifically, interpersonal conflict, status differences, and effects of a dominating group member are minimized. In addition, sharing the sketches provides additional stimulation that can improve overall solution quality.

The weaknesses of Brainsketching are the same as those shared by most other brainwriting methods. For instance, some people find it difficult to be silent when generating ideas and social interactions are reduced considerably. However, the provisions for discussion in the first and last steps should help overcome this limitation.

4.33 Brainwriting Game

The Brainwriting Game was developed by Woods as an alternative to Classical Brainstorming and Synectics.[72] In particular, Woods wanted a technique that was fun for participants and did not require a high level of leader or participant skill. Brainwriting and its variations fits these requirements well. The steps for the Brainwriting Game follow:

1. A problem statement and objective of the exercise are read to a group. The objective of the game is that the most improbable idea wins the game.
2. The group members buy a specified number of blank, numbered cards from a facilitator at one cent each. The initials of the purchaser are written on a sheet of paper containing numbered spaces corresponding to the card numbers.
3. On each card purchased, the participants write down the most improbable problem solution they can imagine.
4. The cards are displayed for the entire group to review.
5. The participants individually study each idea and attempt to convert it into a more practical idea to reduce that individual's chances of winning. No talking or criticism is permitted during this activity.
6. After about 20 minutes of modifying the ideas, each member is given two votes and instructed to vote—as an individual—for the two most improbable ideas. The person whose idea receives the most votes is awarded the money.

7. The group is divided into two subgroups. Each group is given one-half of the cards.

8. The groups are instructed to use the ideas on the cards to develop six practical problem solutions. After 20 minutes of discussion, each group attempts to "sell" their ideas to the other group. Both groups then try to agree upon a final list of the best ideas.

Evaluation   A major strength of the Brainwriting Game is that it combines the advantages of both brainwriting and brainstorming. The brainwriting portion reduces the effects of any dominating individuals and insures that all participants have an equal opportunity to participate; the brainstorming portion helps insure that needs for social interaction and verbal idea generation are satisfied. Another positive feature is the friendly competitive atmosphere provided by the game format. Such an approach should be motivating for most participants. In addition, no particular training is required for either the group facilitator or the members. Once the steps are understood, the technique can be implemented easily. A potential weakness of the Brainwriting Game is its competitive aspect. If hostility surfaces and the competition is taken too seriously, the game may be counterproductive. Another related difficulty is that not all groups may be interested in using a game format. Finally, if little time is available, another brainwriting approach—such as Pin Cards—might be a better choice.

4.34 Brainwriting Pool

Another of the brainwriting variations from the Battelle Institute at Frankfurt is the Brainwriting Pool.[73] It is very similar to the Pin Cards technique. However, instead of passing cards around a small group, the participants exchange pieces of paper in a "pool" located in the center of a table. It is relatively simple to implement and uses the following steps:

1. Five to eight people are seated around a table.
2. A group leader presents a problem to the group.
3. The participants silently write down their ideas on a sheet of paper.
4. As soon as an individual has listed four ideas, the sheet is placed in the middle of the table (the pool) and exchanged for another sheet. A schematic representation of this procedure is shown in Fig. 4-7. (An optional procedure is to create the pool from ideas that have been generated previously. The pool then will be ready-made and there will be no need to require an initial listing of four ideas.)
5. The participants then continue to add ideas to the sheet taken from the pool, exchanging it for a new sheet whenever additional stimulation is needed.
6. After 20 to 30 minutes, the process is terminated and the idea sheets are collected for later evaluation.

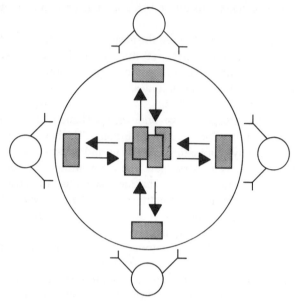

Fig. 4–7. Example of the Brainwriting Pool technique.

Evaluation   Due to the complete lack of verbal interaction, the Brainwriting Pool (like most brainwriting methods) is immune from the negative consequences that often accompany group discussions. This lack of discussion and the absence of any direct activity among the participants insure that individuals are not likely to disturb or be disturbed by others. Furthermore, a greater sense of anonymity is more likely to be maintained than is found in other brainwriting methods (especially if the initial pool is ready-made). Pin Cards and Method 6-3-5, for example, involve direct exchanges of ideas with other group members. Although such exchanges are not a major weakness of these methods, they could cause some persons to feel inhibited in their responses. The Brainwriting Pool, in contrast, completely eliminates this possibility since ideas are exchanged with an anonymous pool. In addition to these advantages, Geschka[74] reports that this method also is more likely to produce higher quality and more diverse ideas than those found in some other brainwriting variations—especially Method 6-3-5. The primary weakness of the Brainwriting Pool (common with other brainwriting methods) is that there might be some loss of idea spontaneity. When brainwriting methods are used, stimulation for new ideas or improvements upon old ones is usually derived from the written ideas of others. If more diversity in idea content is desired, additional stimulation aids should be used.

4.35 Classical Brainstorming

Classical Brainstorming is the forerunner of many of the current group idea generation methods. Since it was originally developed in the late 1930s by Alex Osborn,[75] it probably has become one of the most widely known and used group methods and has spurred the development of many related techniques and variations.

Contrary to what some people might believe, Osborn was not just concerned with developing an organized idea generation method. In the books he subsequently wrote on the topic of creativity, it is clear that he also considered idea evaluation to be an essential element of the problem-solving process. As he conceptualized creative problem solving, there are three major procedures involved: (1) fact finding, (2) idea finding, and (3) solution finding. Fact finding contains two substages: problem definition and preparation. In the problem-definition substage, problems are defined by breaking them down into their different parts. Only problems capable of eliciting a large number of ideas should be considered. The preparation substage primarily consists of gathering and analyzing any information that might be related to the problem. Idea finding uses the brainstorming method to initially generate ideas and then further refines them through modification, combination, or other idea development procedures that might be helpful. Solution finding, the third component of the process, involves evaluating and selecting an idea or ideas for further development or implementation.

Classical Brainstorming is based upon two principles and four basic rules. The first principle is that of *deferred judgment*. According to Osborn, the human mind uses both judgmental and creative thinking. Because of training and various background experiences, judgmental thinking often emerges as the dominant force when a problem situation is encountered. The purpose of deferred judgment, then, is to enable the creative part of the mind to generate ideas by overcoming judgmental thinking. All considerations of an idea's worth, importance, practicality, and so on, must be put aside. This does not mean, however, that ideas are never judged. On the contrary, the ideas are judged later, *after* all idea generation has taken place.

The second brainstorming principle states that *quantity breeds quality*. The rationale behind this principle is that the greater the number of ideas generated, the greater is the possibility that one of them will provide a solution for the problem. In other words, an idea can never be a solution to the problem unless it is openly stated as a possible solution. Another, related reason behind this principle is based upon the associations that develop when many ideas are considered. One idea often leads to another and so on until a desired solution is reached. However, the initial ideas seldom turn out to be the best ones. Thus, the more ideas that are generated, the greater the probability that the best ideas will be uncovered.

Four basic rules are used to guide a brainstorming session:

1. Criticism is ruled out. This is perhaps the most important rule. Unless the evaluation of ideas is withheld until later, the principle of deferred judgment will not have an opportunity to operate. The failure of a group to abide by this rule is often a major reason why some brainstorming sessions do not produce the expected results. This rule is what primarily differentiates Classical Brainstorming from traditional conference methods.

2. Freewheeling is welcomed. This rule is intended to encourage participants to suggest any idea that comes to mind, without fear that it will be evaluated immediately. The most desirable ideas are those that might initially seem to be wild and far out. Whether they are or not is not important at this stage. The important thing is that all inhibitions are to be relaxed while ideas are being generated. This rule has the dual purpose of increasing the number of ideas while, at the same time, establishing an appropriate climate for idea finding.

3. Quantity is wanted. The more ideas generated, the greater the odds a successful solution will be found. This rule restates the principle of quantity breeds quality.

4. Combination and improvement are sought. The purpose of this rule is to encourage the generation of additional, better ideas by building upon the ideas of others. This activity is commonly referred to as hitchhiking or piggy-backing.

Although there are no universally accepted guidelines for the specific steps to use in implementing a brainstorming session, the following leader activities are fairly typical:

1. Develop a statement of the problem.
2. Select a group of six to twelve participants.
3. Send a one- to two-page memorandum to the participants at least two days and not more than seven days before the meeting. The memorandum should contain the statement of the problem, the general background of the problem, examples of possible solutions, the four brainstorming rules, and the time and place for the meeting.
4. Conduct an orientation meeting with the participants immediately before the actual brainstorming session. The activities of this meeting should include an explanation of the format the brainstorming session will use, a review of brainstorming principles and rules, a warm-up exercise unrelated to the problem, and if necessary, redefinition of the problem.
5. Begin the brainstorming session by writing the problem on a chalkboard or chart visible to the entire group.
6. Restate the four brainstorming rules.
7. Request ideas by asking that hands be raised whenever a participant wishes to suggest an idea. Only one idea should be suggested at a time.

8. Have a recording secretary write down all ideas.
9. After 30 minutes of generating ideas (never more than 45 minutes), terminate the idea-finding process.
10. Select an evaluation group of five persons.
11. Present this group with the list of ideas and instruct them to select the best ideas.
12. Provide the original group with a report on the ideas selected by the evaluation group and request that they submit any additional ideas stimulated by this list.
13. Present the selected ideas to the persons responsible for implementing them, using persuasion to "sell" the ideas if necessary.

Along with these steps, there are also several other factors that must be considered to insure the success of a brainstorming session. These factors pertain to the composition of the group, the problem statement, the way the process is handled by the leader, and the evaluation group.

Group Composition Most brainstorming groups consist of three elements: group members, a leader and an optional associate leader, and a recording secretary. If at all possible, the members of a brainstorming group should never be randomly selected. Ideally, only persons who have some knowledge of or experience with the problem should be chosen. Osborn also suggests that only persons of equal status be invited to participate. If superiors and subordinates are mixed together, the free wheeling essential for the success of the session will be reduced. In addition, if the same group is to be used repeatedly for different problems, outsiders might be invited in periodically to provide a fresh perspective. Finally, persons who have been overtrained in the usual types of noncreative conferences probably should be avoided.

The selection of a group leader should be made with great care. The most important features to look for are a person's ability to maintain a relaxed and friendly atmosphere, knowledge and experience with the problem, and knowledge and experience with the brainstorming process. In some cases, an associate leader also might be selected, especially with somewhat larger groups. This person should possess the same qualities as the leader.

The primary function of the recording secretary is to provide a numbered, written list of all suggested ideas. This way, the leader can tell the group how many ideas they have come up with and prompt them to develop even more. In addition, the leader also can use the numbered list as the basis for a specified number of ideas to achieve in the remaining time. When ideas are suggested, the secretary should write down the meaning of the idea but does not have to be concerned with obtaining a verbatim statement. The name of the person who suggested an idea, however, should not be noted since knowledge of anonymity will encourage free wheeling. Two secretaries also can be used if greater accuracy is desired, but in no case should a secretary participate in the group process.

The Problem Statement   Not all problems are suitable for brainstorming sessions. A problem involving the potential marketability of a new product, for example, would not be appropriate. Brainstorming was designed primarily to find ideas, not to judge existing ideas. Thus, it would be suitable for developing new-product ideas but not for evaluating those already developed. A brainstorming problem also should have many different possible solutions. Furthermore, the problem should be stated in specific terms so that specific ideas can be developed. And, complex problems should be avoided or broken down into their separate parts. A separate brainstorming session then should be conducted to deal with each part.

The Brainstorming Process   The basic steps involved in conducting a brainstorming session already have been presented. In addition to these steps, there are also a few tips that a leader might find helpful. First, if the members brought a list of ideas with them to the meeting, the leader should collect the lists before the meeting and read them aloud during the course of the meeting. Second, when members wish to hitchhike on an idea, Osborn suggests that the leader instruct them to snap their fingers to signify to the leader that they have a hitchhike. This way, the leader can give priority to the idea before it becomes lost in the stream of new ideas. Finally, the leader should not become overly concerned during brief periods of silence. This generally indicates that the members are thinking up new ideas or digesting one just suggested. If the group begins to run out of ideas, the leader can suggest ideas, set a goal for a final number of ideas, or suggest other possible use or ways that an idea might be changed.

The Evaluation Group   While a typical brainstorming group may contain anywhere from six to twelve persons, the evaluation group should contain exactly five persons. The reason for this is that an odd number eliminates the possibility of ties when making a decision on an idea. The membership composition of this group may vary. It may consist of only persons from the idea generation group, a combination of persons from this group and outsiders, or a completely new group of individuals. Using the same persons has the advantage of insuring problem familiarity, while using a group of outsiders has the possible benefit of greater objectivity. Osborn prefers using different persons, although not everyone agrees with him on this matter.

The task of this group is to evaluate all the ideas and select the best ones for possible implementation or additional study. After the leader of this group receives the idea list from the recording secretary, the ideas are edited to make sure they all are expressed clearly and concisely. The ideas are then sorted into logical categories (usually five to ten different categories) and presented to the evaluation group for review. The process can be facilitated by using a checklist of criteria pertaining to an idea's simplicity, timeliness, feasibility, or other similar items. This group, or others more directly responsible for the ideas, should then attempt to verify the best ideas by subjecting them to practical tests.

A classroom exercise conducted by the author can be used to illustrate the number and variety of ideas that are typically produced in brainstorming sessions. Six groups of about six graduate students each were asked to use the rules of Classical Brainstorming to generate as many uses as possible for a wire coat hanger. Because of time constraints, only 12 minutes were allowed for this activity. The following is a sample from the list of ideas produced, after all duplicate ideas had been eliminated:

1. hose clamp	26. to turn on lights
2. tow rope	27. sewing needle
3. opening locked car door	28. knife
4. tie-downs for a truck tarp	29. spoon
	30. fork
5. key rings	31. pipe cleaner
6. door holder/opener	32. car muffler repair
7. edging for shrubbery	33. Christmas wreath
8. plant climber pole	34. bucket handle
9. fish stringer	35. splint for broken bones
10. extra tire chain link	36. film dryer
11. plant hanger	37. heat and melt holes in plastic
12. tent tie-down	38. heavy picture hanger
13. meat hook	39. magnetize and pick up small metal objects
14. gluing clamps	40. back scratcher
15. car trunk lid tie-down	41. tip for an arrow
16. fish hook	42. car antenna
17. hot dog roaster	43. pants suspenders
18. cooking grill	44. tie hanger
19. electric fence	45. letters for a sign
20. cattle prod	46. window shade opener
21. toilet unplugger	47. toothpick
22. a pointer for briefings	48. repair lawn chairs
23. trap material	49. hole puncher
24. darts	50. nail
25. to stir paint	

Given the artificiality of the problem, the short time limit imposed, and the lack of any practice in using brainstorming, the ideas exhibit exceptional variety.

Evaluation   Classical Brainstorming has stimulated more research studies about its effectiveness, procedures, and assumptions than any other creative problem-solving technique. Most of this research is probably justified given the popularity of Osborn's major book on the subject, *Applied Imagination*,[76] and its widespread use in many situations. In 1965, the eighteenth printing of his book had sold over 150,000 copies. Yet, since the late 1950s, the research results have generated considerable controversy. Most of the studies conducted in experimental settings have produced rather negative findings while, at the same time, positive anecdotal accounts of the method have piled up. It appears that brainstorming proponents find supportive results, while its opponents do not.

To be realistic, no simple conclusions can be drawn. There simply has not been enough research to conclusively determine how and under what conditions brainstorming works best. The issue is further complicated by methodological differences across studies. The type of problem, sex and personality of subjects, group size, and other factors have all varied considerably. Perhaps most important, however, is the fact the majority of studies have been conducted in rather artificial situations, with less than real problems, using college students as subjects.

On the surface, the disadvantages and weaknesses of the technique appear to outweigh the advantages and strengths. A superficial examination of the brainstorming process suggests four major advantages:

1. Produces a large number of ideas in a relatively short period of time
2. Provides a stimulating and ego-satisfying environment for some persons
3. Satisfies individual social-emotional needs
4. Includes an idea evaluation component

The surface-level disadvantages and weaknesses are more numerous:

1. It is limited to relatively simple problems. For more complex problems, separate brainstorming sessions must be held for each problem part. This limitation makes it difficult to consider complex problems as a whole.
2. The free-wheeling climate can be difficult to control and could result in many superficial ideas.
3. It is unnatural for most persons to defer judgment on an idea.
4. It requires persons who have a basic familiarity with the problem.
5. Because of the method's apparent simplicity, it will often be used where individual methods might be more appropriate, thus wasting valuable resources.
6. It fails to provide an adequate incubation period for the digestion of ideas, possibly limiting the quality of any hitchhiked ideas.
7. Unless a highly skilled leader is used, some group members could monopolize the session.

8. Stating of the brainstorming principles and rules might not be sufficient to make up for the inhibitions of some persons in a group setting.
9, It fails to provide individual recognition for ideas generated.

Although many of these comments could be made about quite a few other group methods, the actual research evidence on Classical Brainstorming is damaging. Before this evidence is discussed, however, it must be noted that the large number of research studies conducted on brainstorming has made it a highly visible technique. Because less research has been conducted on other group methods, it would be unfair to conclude that Classical Brainstorming is less useful than all of the other group methods. Some of these other methods could be better or worse; they just have not received the same amount of attention that has been given to brainstorming.

Due to the different approaches used to study brainstorming, sifting through the evidence to come up with a clear picture is a difficult task. Furthermore, the majority of this evidence would probably be of little interest to the intended audience of this book. For the reader who is interested in a comprehensive (although technical) review of this literature, Stein[77] has made an excellent contribution to the second of his two-volume set, entitled *Stimulating Creativity*. The following represents a distillation of Stein's work as well as some evidence gathered from more recent sources.[78] In no respect, however, should this summary of findings be viewed as comprehensive.

1. Instructing persons to defer judgment will produce a greater number of ideas than methods that stress idea evaluation. Deferring judgment, however, does not produce higher quality ideas than simply asking persons to come up with high-quality ideas.
2. The principle that quantity breeds quality appears to be valid. There is some evidence, however, that quality might be related more to personality characteristics than to receiving instructions on this principle.
3. The overall effectiveness of Classical Brainstorming might not be attributable solely to the principle of deferred judgment. The separation of idea generation from idea evaluation might be equally responsible.
4. Brainstorming groups are not necessarily any more cohesive, better motivated, or more satisfied with their procedures than groups that use a more judgmental method.
5. The upper limit on the number of persons to include in a brainstorming group might be unrealistic. Better results might be obtained if the maximum number of participants is set at five to nine.
6. Nominal groups (groups in name only) consistently outperform brainstorming groups in the number of ideas produced and sometimes in the quality of ideas.

This last finding is perhaps the most damaging of all. The fact that a group of individuals working in isolation can produce a greater number of ideas than a brainstorming group (containing the same number of people) is a surprising finding. An essential feature of the brainstorming method is that individuals will be stimulated by the ideas of others. To the proponents of brainstorming, such a result presents a basic inconsistency. The reasons behind it, however, are somewhat ambiguous and several explanations have been advanced.

One view is that individuals working alone will have a lower standard of evaluation when considering their own ideas. In contrast, the same individuals might be more inhibited and thus more judgmental when placed in a group situation. (This would suggest that simply instructing persons to defer judgment might not be sufficient.) A second explanation is that the period of time used to compare nominal and brainstorming groups could have influenced the results. In an examination conducted by the author of nine different comparative studies, the average time for idea generation was 17.6 minutes. If the average time period had been longer (e.g., 30–40 minutes), the brainstorming groups might have produced more. That is, at some point in the idea generation process, individuals might begin to run out of ideas on their own and rely more upon the ideas of others for stimulation. It must be remembered, however, that the results pertaining to the quality of ideas are less conclusive. Had longer time periods been used, the issue of idea quality might be better established. Nevertheless, the fact remains that the majority of these studies were conducted in artificial settings using problems with little or no personal relevance to the participants. Caution must be used when applying these findings to more realistic situations.

Based upon these findings (tentative though they might be) and others not previously discussed, the following recommendations are made for anyone considering using Classical Brainstorming:

1. If possible, provide the participants with both training and practice in brainstorming procedures.
2. Select persons who are likely to be cohesive with others and who exhibit interpersonal effectiveness.
3. Use a brainstorming procedural variation known as sequencing. As developed by Bouchard,[79] sequencing involves a round-robin verbal presentation of ideas: Group members individually present their ideas in order and say "pass" when they have nothing to offer. This procedure insures that no one person can monopolize the session.
4. Better yet, use sequencing plus personal analogy. This latter procedural variation was borrowed from Synectics and involves an individual behaving like or acting out an idea or object—for example, physically coiling like a spring. In research for her doctoral dissertation, Burns[80] found that

brainstorming plus analogies significantly increased the number of original ideas produced.

5. At the outset of the session, establish a goal for a specific number of ideas to be attained. This often will increase participant motivation.
6. If you are still determined to use a group session, have the participants individually generate their ideas and then evaluate them as a group.

4.36 Component Detailing

A number of idea generation methods stimulate ideas using related problem elements that are either forced together or used as a springboard for free association. Most of these methods rely upon some degree of imagery to develop new ideas. That is, the problem solver is required to visualize an aspect of the problem and either combine it with another visualized problem element or use it to free-associate. Because not everyone can use imagery equally well and because related stimuli do not always provoke unique ideas, these mehtods often are unsatisfactory.

Component Detailing compensates for some of these weaknesses and provides a stimulating group exercise as well. As developed by Wakin,[81] this technique combines features of Attribute Listing, Morphological Analysis, and Brain-sketching. It is relatively easy to implement and usually results in an enjoyable group experience. There are seven major steps:

1. As a group, the participants list the major components of the problem.
2. The group lists the attributes of each component.
3. Each group member is given a different problem component. Ideally, the members will be given an actual part of a product.
4. The group members study the component and its attributes, being careful to note all details.
5. Each member draws a picture of his or her assigned component. The picture should include as much detail as possible.
6. The drawings are collected and pinned to a bulletin board or placed on a large table. They are assembled in such a way that their placement approximates their location in the product.
7. The resulting collage is examined for possible stimulation. Because the drawings most likely will vary in size, new perspectives will be created. These perspectives should be discussed and elaborated with the goal of generating improvements or entirely new products.

As an illustration of this approach, Wakin has used a common door lock. The group first lists all components, such as knobs, latch, pins, tumblers, keys, bolts, springs, striking plate, and so on. The attributes of these components then are listed. For example, a spring might be described as being a spiral, under tension, capable of being stretched, and varying in size depending upon the size of the lock. Next, the group members draw pictures of their components. Finally, the pcitures are placed together to represent the product and examined for idea stimulation. For instance, the knob might be changed in size or shape and the bolt might be made larger and interlock with a mechanism in the doorjamb.

Evaluation Component Detailing is a useful way to help a group analyze a problem. It also helps participants see a problem from new perspectives by using component drawings that vary in size. The viewing of an assembly of pictures derived from different drawing styles and problem perspectives probably is the most unique and useful feature of this technique. Moreover, this feature also will encourage group member involvement. It clearly promotes active participation which, in turn, should enhance motivation. The primary weakness of Component Detailing is that it probably will work best with tangible problems— those that involve actual products. However, people who are skilled in abstract thinking also should benefit from this technique. Of course, their pictures will be abstract depictions of the components and therefore more subjective. Nevertheless, such drawings should provide interesting stimulus material for people who are comfortable with ambiguity. The only other weakness is that the use of related stimuli could limit the uniqueness of the ideas. Although this weakness is shared by other similar techniques, it may be lessened somewhat by the use of drawings and the varying sizes and perspectives of the components.

4.37 Collective Notebook (CNB)

The Collective Notebook technique was developed by John Haefele,[82] of the Procter & Gamble Company, as a method for individuals within an organization to independently generate ideas. Although not originally recognized as such, CNB can be classified as a brainwriting variation: Ideas are developed through free association and recorded in writing without any verbal interaction among participants. The procedure for implementing CNB is as follows:

1. The participants are each given a notebook containing a broad statement of a problem and directions for using the technique.
2. For one month, participants write down at least one new idea every day.
3. At the end of the one-month period, the participants develop a written summary containing (a) their best idea, (b) their ideas for possible directions that might be researched to solve the problem, and (c) any new ideas that might be unrelated to the original problem.
4. The notebooks are given to the person assigned to be the coordinator.
5. The coordinator reviews the notebooks, categorizes the ideas, and prepares a detailed summary of all the ideas generated.

6. The participants are notified that, after the summary statement is prepared, they may have access to all of the notebooks for study.
7. If desired, a group discussion is conducted to discuss the ideas generated.

Haefele suggests that the process of recording ideas can be facilitated through the use of different formats such as (1) direct solutions, (2) related or unrelated ideas, (3) interesting facts or material read, or (4) new symbolizations (e.g., analogies). He also recommends using specific stimulation aids to help prompt ideas. For example, Haefele suggests (1) simple and direct changes (reverse, expand, or reduce the problem); (2) enforced broad exploration (a list of a specific number of problem characteristics or things similar to the problem); (3) "off-trail" hints (use the five senses to stimulate ideas); and (4) rousing remote associations (look for unusual properties of other substances). In addition to these aids, priming also can be used to further stimulate ideas. Priming involves providing the participants (at regular intervals during the month) with related material gathered from the literature or prepared by company personnel or experts.

Although there are few published descriptions of how the CNB method has been used in practice, a rather interesting variation of the technique is reported by Pearson.[83]   During a workshop on creativity held in England in 1978, the participants decided to conduct a postworkshop exercise using a modified CNB approach. The purpose of this exercise was to examine the applicability of the CNB method when the participants are geographically dispersed. That is, notebooks would be given to persons working in a variety of organizations throughout Great Britain rather than just to persons from within a single organization.

The design of this exercise varied considerably from the format described by Haefele. In addition to the use of geographically remote participants, there were five other major differences in the procedure used by the Pearson group. First, the participants were given three instead of four weeks to record their ideas. Second, three coordinators instead of one were used to process and organize the data. It was thought that the crucial role of coordinator might be better fulfilled by spreading it out and thereby reducing the workload and dependence upon a single individual. Third, the task was to generate elements of a future scenario. Specifically, the participants were asked to list the major factors which could affect managers and their work over the next 20 years; indicate whether the factors are likely to occur within five years (short-term), five to ten years (medium-term), or more than ten years (long-term); and to describe possible consequences associated with each factor. Haefele's procedure, in contrast, only requires participants to list ideas and not to make predictions. Fourth, the participants were not instructed to develop written summaries of their best ideas, additional research directions, or any ideas unrelated to the problem (step 3 of Haefele's procedure). Finally, the fifth and perhaps most significant major difference was in the method used to stimulate ideas. After receiving their notebooks, the participants spent two weeks recording ideas in the manner described by Haefele. However, instead of turning the notebooks in to the coordinator, the participants exchanged their notebooks with one of the other participants (who were preassigned as recipients). They then read over the other participants' ideas and recorded any ideas of their own triggered by these new ideas. After one week, all notebooks were turned in to the coordinators for processing.

Because of these modifications, it would be inaccurate to describe this exercise as an example of the CNB method. The procedure, instead, seems to lie somewhere between the Delphi approach, CNB, and Method 6-3-5. Prediction of the future and the use of geographically dispersed participants is characteristic of the Delphi technique, while the written exchange of ideas is similar to the procedure used in Method 6-3-5. As a result, the procedure is more eclectic than it is representative of the CNB method described by Haefele. However, since only portions of different methods were borrowed, it cannot be assumed that the same strengths and weaknesses would apply to the procedure described by Pearson. For example, the Delphi approach encourages convergence of ideas while the modified CNB method is more likely to produce divergence of ideas; Method 6-3-5 involves repeated exchanges of ideas with all members of a group in one location in contrast to only one exchange with persons geographically dispersed. Thus, a rather nice blending of procedures resulted in an approach tailored specifically for a particular problem.

In the modified CNB exercise, notebooks were given to 12 persons and returned to the coordinators. Each coordinator received four notebooks and was instructed to locate and underline key ideas. Based upon a preliminary analysis of the data, the responses were categorized according to statements of issues and their logical consequences. The 400 responses categorized in this manner then were recorded on index cards. Next, the cards containing consequences were sorted into major groupings of political, social, technical, economic, personal, and resources. Statements within these grouping were analyzed and a scenario constructed in a narrative format. An alternative grouping also was developed in which new categories were analyzed with respect to short-, medium-, and long-term futures. From this analysis, a different composite scenario was constructed. The two scenarios were compared, discussed by the coordinators and with other persons (nonparticipants), and then new ideas generated.

As a result of conducting this exercise, the following conclusions and recommendations were made about the modified CNB approach:[84]

1. Very little time is required on the part of the participants.
2. Some participants reported problems in maintaining their motivation. The lack of interaction among the participants might have contributed to this feeling, although day-to-day work pressures and lack of involvement in the problem also could have been factors.
3. The problem statement and description of the task need to be clearly outlined; too much structure, however, could be counterproductive.

4. The use of multiple coordinators might make it difficult to achieve consensus on how to interpret the results. On the other hand, the administrative burden involved in processing the data is considerably reduced.
5. The exchange of notebooks seemed to produce a narrowing of idea scope. Increasing the number and/or frequency of exchanges might help to alter this situation. In addition, the use of a checklist of stimulus words (similar to what Haefele suggested) might help to increase idea variety.
6. The method might be most profitably used as a tool to stimulate further discussion on a topic, rather than as an all-inclusive technique.
7. The flexibility of the technique permits examination of different alternative scenarios.
8. The method would be suitable for use with a relatively large number of participants. When used with important, long-term problems and a large number of participants, computer storage and retrieval of the data might be considered.
9. Analyzing, sorting, and categorizing the results is a highly motivating activity, especially if all of the participants work together as a group. In addition, such involvement can increase the variety of ideas generated, when followed by a discussion of the results.
10. Additional research is needed to assess the relative value of the modified CNB approach—as a scenario generation device—against other methods designed to generate ideas.

Evaluation*   A major advantage of the CNB method over other techniques is its built-in provision for a period of idea incubation. While most idea generation methods require spontaneous production of ideas, CNB allows participants to mull over an idea for an extended period of time so that its good and bad points can be more fully digested. In addition, the extended time period provides an opportunity for participants to be exposed to a number of different stimuli or experiences that can be used as sources for possible ideas. It is possible, of course, that the participants could become "stale" during this period. Some form of regular stimulation, such as the priming suggested by Haefele, would seem to be necessary for the method to work effectively. As with other brainwriting techniques, the use of written-idea recording also can help to minimize problems often encountered in methods using face-to-face formats.

The major disadvantages of the CNB method are more procedural than substantive. Specifically, the technique might be improved in two areas. First, the exact duties of the coordinator should be more carefully spelled out, especially with respect to how the ideas should be categorized. This might be a monumental

---

*Although the comments that follow might apply equally well to the modified CNB approach, they are directed primarily at the method described by Haefele.

task if a large number of notebooks is involved. The use of multiple coordinators should be seriously considered. Second, and most important, a procedure for evaluating the generated ideas would make the technique much more useful. Haefele suggests the use of a "final creative discussion" but only "if desired." The manner in which the ideas are sorted and then applied, however, is just as important as how they are generated. This, of course, is a weakness also shared by many other idea generation methods.

In summary, it would seem that Pearson is correct in recommending that CNB not be viewed as an end in itself; additional procedures should be added to assist in evaluating, selecting, and implementing ideas.

4.38 Crawford Slip Writing

Most of the brainwriting methods described in this book were developed in Europe in the late 1960s and early 1970s. One brainwriting procedure that has received increasing attention in recent years uses slips of paper to generate ideas. The most well-known procedure of this type was developed in the United States by C. C. Crawford in the 1920s.[85]   Dr. Crawford refers to his procedure as the "Crawford Slip Method."   In addition to general applications of the method, Crawford and his associates also have extended its use in such areas as productivity improvement, teaching, and managerial supervision.[86]

One of the current proponents of the general method of using slips of paper to generate ideas is Charles H. Clark,[87] who has published a do-it-yourself manual describing the method, its benefits, and several procedural variations. Clark reports that he has used the slip method successfully to help a variety of organizations generate a large number of ideas in a relatively short time. The description that follows is based upon Clark's version of writing upon paper slips.   It should not be considered representative of Crawford's procedure. According to Clark, the basic steps for his version are as follows:

1. Each person in a group of up to 5000 or more people is given a pad or stack of at least 25 3-by-5-inch slips of paper.
2. A problem statement is read to the group using words such as: How can we. . . ? or How to . . . ?
3. The group is instructed to begin writing one idea on each slip of paper. The ideas should be recorded without thought given to their priority or importance.
4. After five to ten minutes, the group is instructed to stop writing and the slips are collected.
5. An evaluation task force is appointed and its members evaluate the ideas by sorting them into piles according to their frequency of occurrence or degree of usability.
6. Once the ideas are sorted, the best ones are developed into workable proposals.

There also are several variations to this basic procedure. For example, Clark suggests using idea trigger sheets, in the form of graphics, to produce stimulation for additional ideas. One graphic used by Clark to help organizations attract new members shows a pattern of dots organized into a square, with a series of randomly placed dots trailing out from one side. Another variation involves using dyads for the slip-writing procedure, with one member of the dyad recording the ideas for both persons. In a third variation, problem statements instead of problem solutions are generated. Finally, Classical Brainstorming groups, for example, can use the slip writing method to establish problem priorities.

Evaluation   According to Clark, there are at least seven major advantages of the Crawford Slip Writing Method: (1) It generates a large quantity of ideas—90% of most group members will list five or more ideas; (2) it generates this large number of ideas in less than ten minutes; (3) when ideas are sorted into categories immediately after they have been generated, action planning will be speeded up considerably—planning delays caused by many committees are eliminated; (4) the technique can be used with almost any size group; (5) seating arrangements, such as rooms with fixed seats, are not an obstacle to using the method; (6) group participation is maximized and involvement in the process is likely to create more commitment to implementing the ideas; and (7) the possibility of accidentally discovering previously unthought-of ideas (serendipity) is increased.

Perhaps the most important advantage is the ability of the slip method to generate a large number of ideas using a group of almost unlimited size. This advantage, however, has certain potential disadvantages associated with it. One disadvantage is the amount of coordinating effort required to process and sort a large number of idea slips. For particularly large groups, the evaluation task force might be tempted to sort the ideas quickly to provide the participants with immediate feedback. If this process is accomplished too quickly, superficial categories might result. In such situations, it might be better to defer the feedback until more time can be spent evaluating the ideas. Of course, if the ideas fall into clear-cut categories and specific problem priorities can be easily identified, then this information might be shared immediately with the group. Another potential disadvantage is that stimulation for the ideas relies primarily upon individual ideation. Although this factor is not necessarily a major disadvantage, the quality and diversity of ideas produced might be less than could be obtained if external sources of idea stimulation were used. Finally, some resentment on the part of the participants might develop if they are not informed of the outcome of any actions taken as a result of using the slip method. While this might also be a factor with most group idea generation methods, its effects would be magnified greatly in a group of several hundred or more people.

The little time required for implementation makes this technique an ideal choice for both small- and large-group situations. In small groups, it will be better to combine it with another brainwriting procedure that uses shared ideas for stimulation (e.g., Pin Cards or the Brainwriting Pool). The slip-writing approach also will be a good choice for small groups when there are physical obstacles such as fixed chairs and no tables. However, the slip-writing process probably is best suited for large groups when practical considerations (e.g., lack of tables, absence of facilitators) preclude the use of other brainwriting techniques. (Except for the table requirement, Systematized Directed Induction and the Phillips 66 method also are appropriate for large groups.)

4.39 Force-Fit Game

This technique, developed at the Battelle Institute in Frankfurt, Germany, by Helmut Schlicksupp, was designed to stimulate ideas by involving participants in an idea game. The Force-Fit Game is based upon the general principle of forced relationships and involves the following steps:[88]

1. Two groups of from two to eight persons each are formed.
2. One person, who is not a member of either group, is assigned the role of referee/recorder.
3. A problem statement is written on a chalkboard or flip chart and is read aloud to the participants.
4. One of the groups begins the game by suggesting an idea that is remote from the problem.
5. The second group is given two minutes to develop a practical solution from the idea suggested by the first group.
6. If the referee/recorder believes that the second group was successful in developing a practical solution, they are awarded one point; if they are judged unsuccessful, the first group is given the point.
7. The referee/recorder writes down each solution as it is proposed.
8. After 30 minutes, the group with the most points is declared the winner and the ideas are evaluated later.

Evaluation   By introducing an element of competition, the Force-Fit Game will be appropriate for groups that (1) need stimulation and motivation to begin the idea generation process, (2) tend to run out of ideas quickly, and (3) produce ideas that are less than unique. The competition, however, might not be as important as the use of another group to provide idea stimulation. In this regard, the technique is similar to other forced-relationship techniques except that other people instead of pictures, objects, or words are used as idea sources.

Although the technique is relatively easy to implement and requires little in the way of group-process skills on the part of the referee/recorder, it does have one major disadvantage. Because the referee/recorder is given responsibility for judging the problem solutions, too much reliance can be placed upon this individual's judgmental abilities. Since the primary intent of the technique is to generate and not to evaluate ideas, an understanding might be reached with the group members that the ideas will be subjected to a more intense evaluation following conclusion of the game. Unless this or a similar understanding is presented to the group, some members might feel inhibited in their responses if their ideas are continually judged to be impractical by the referee/recorder. Uniqueness and diversity of response are likely to be increased if the judgments are seen as just a part of the game. Of course, there is also the possibility that reducing the significance of the judgments will reduce participant motivation. If a reduction in motivation is likely and the participants do not feel they could be stimulated under this condition, then another technique should be sought.

In addition to clarifying the referee/recorder's role, there are at least three ways to increase the potential effectiveness of the Force-Fit Game. The first would be to have the groups reverse their roles and conduct another 30-minute session. Second, attention might be given to the composition of the group membership. Persons with diverse backgrounds and abstract minds probably would produce the best solutions. Finally, the group that suggests the remote ideas might benefit from using a tangible stimulation aid, such as pictures (e.g., Visual Synectics, graphic designs, text from a book or catalog).

4.40 Gallery Method

This brainwriting variation is used at the Battelle Institute in Frankfurt, Germany, by reversing the procedure used in the Pin-Cards method. In the Pin-Cards technique, individuals write down ideas on cards and pass them around to other group members to provide additional stimulation. The Gallery Method, in contrast, reverses this procedure. That is, instead of moving ideas among people, the people move among the ideas (much in the same way that people might browse in an art gallery). The following steps are used for this technique:[89]

1. Sheets of flip-chart paper are pinned to the walls of a room (or flip charts on stands are placed around the room).
2. A problem statement is written on a location visible to a small group (from five to seven persons).
3. The group discusses the problem statement to make sure that all group members clearly understand it.
4. The group members silently write down their ideas on the sheets of paper.
5. After 20 to 30 minutes of writing, a break is taken and the participants are given 15 minutes to walk around, look at the other idea sheets, and take notes.
6. A second round of silent writing is conducted in which the group is instructed to generate new ideas or make improvements on the ideas of others.
7. After the terminal round is completed, the group examines the ideas and selects those deserving further attention or implementation.

Evaluation   This technique shares the advantages characteristic of most brain-writing methods—persons who have difficulty communicating ideas verbally find writing to be much easier, and a larger number of ideas is usually produced. In contrast to other brainwriting procedures, however, the Gallery Method is distinctive in that the participants are permitted to move about during the break period. Whether this movement contributes to creativity remains to be seen, although Parnes, Noller, and Biondi[90] report that a combination of physical and mental activity is conducive to idea generation. Controlled studies will need to be conducted to verify this assumption. The weaknesses of the Gallery Method also are similar to those found in other brainwriting procedures—participants often feel hurried and distracted by the presence of others, and there is little opportunity for idea incubation. In addition to these considerations, some persons using the technique might be distracted if other group members begin to move around before the end of the writing period. Because this is an unanticipated distraction, it might be interesting to experiment and permit the participants to move around at any time (or at least after the first round of silent writing).

4.41 Games

The Games technique was developed by VanGundy[91] as a way to promote a playful climate during the idea generation process. The challenges of a game are combined with a creative-thinking exercise to produce an idea generation method capable of stimulating unique ideas. In this case, the stimuli are unrelated to the problem and arise from the game itself. A group facilitator follows eight steps:

1. Discuss the problem to insure understanding.
2. Select three categories for the game (e.g., sports, technology, school subjects).
3. Ask the members of the group (at least four people are required to play) to list four or five examples for each of the categories.
4. Divide the group evenly into two teams.
5. Instruct each team to select one example from each category and list things that the examples have in common. For instance, baseball, lasers, and English might be selected as examples of the categories sports, technology, and school subjects, respectively.
6. Instruct each team to select one of the commonalities and elaborate upon it as much as possible. Thus, baseball, lasers, and English might be identified as having rules as a common factor. Elaborations for rules might include the following: They need to be revised periodically, they are not followed by everyone all the time, and certain rules of nature cannot be broken. Impose a time limit of 10 minutes for this activity.
7. Have the teams use the elaborations as stimuli for generating as many ideas as possible within 15 minutes.

8. Tally the number of elaborations and ideas generated by each group. The group that has generated the most elaborations and ideas is declared the winner.

Evaluation   Two positive features of the Games technique are that it can be both an enjoyable and a productive exercise. The mild competitive aspect can be emotionally stimulating and several workable ideas may be produced. Like the Force-Fit Game, participants' motivation often is increased when an element of competition is introduced. And, when idea generation is added, a double benefit is provided. Moreover, looking for commonalities among the category examples and generating elaborations for each are instructive creative-thinking exercises. On the negative side, some people may have difficulty identifying similarities and thinking of elaborations. If so, the technique is not likely to be successful. Although it is important for any idea generation approach, a creative atmosphere (within both individuals and the group) is especially important for the Games technique. In addition, using unrelated stimuli to generate ideas requires abilities and attitudes not possessed by everyone.

4.42 Gordon/Little

William Gordon, who for many years was associated with the Arthur D. Little consulting firm in Cambridge, Massachusetts, developed a brainstorming variation intended to overcome a possible disadvantage of Classical Brainstorming. When brainstorming on a problem, people often propose what they consider to be an ideal or obvious solution and then slow down in their creative efforts or withdraw from further discussion. To counter this tendency, Gordon developed a procedure that initially avoids presentation of the problem to be solved. Instead, the leader guides the group in focusing upon the underlying concept or principle of the problem, gradually revealing more and more information as different ideas are developed. The steps involved in implementing the Gordon/ Little technique are as follows:[92]

1. The leader introduces a general, abstract problem and instructs the group to think of different ideas for resolving this problem.
2. As the group produces ideas, the leader gradually reveals key bits of information associated with the problem and redefines it at a less abstract level.
3. The group continues to generate ideas with the leader providing increasing amounts of information until all idea possibilities have been explored.
4. The leader reveals the original problem to the group.
5. Using the previous ideas as stimuli, the group generates ideas specifically related to the original problem.

In one frequently cited example of the technique, group members are instructed to devise ways for stacking things. As various ideas are suggested, the leader directs the group to become more and more specific. Then, the leader redefines the problem at a less abstract level. For instance, the leader next might ask the group to think of ways to store a large object weighing over a ton. Finally, the leader reveals that the problem involves devising a new way to park cars. The group then attempts to modify and apply their ideas or develop new ones based upon their previous ideas.

Evaluation   The major advantage of the Gordon/Little technique is its ability to avoid locking in on an obvious solution. As a result, it helps prevent premature problem closure. Because of this feature, the technique often can produce unique or commonly overlooked solutions. Furthermore, because the leader holds back on revealing the problem, individuals are less likely to become personally attached to a favorite solution. On the other hand, there are also certain disadvantages. Unique solutions are not likely to be produced unless the group leader is skilled in guiding group processes and the members are selected carefully for specific attributes.[93]   The group members should be flexible and open in their thinking, tolerant of ambiguity, compatible with each other, and generally knowledgeable about the problem area. This technique can be frustrating to participants who are used to working on highly structured problems, but the final product can be well worth the effort. Because the Gordon/Little technique focuses upon underlying problem principles, it also can be useful for redefining problems.

4.43 Greeting Cards

Greeting Cards was developed by Pickens[94] as part of a course he taught on creative problem solving. It originally was designed to illustrate the importance of a playful attitude during idea generation. The steps for using this technique were borrowed from Pickens and modified slightly by VanGundy:[95]

1. A group is given general instructions about the technique. The problem is not presented until the greeting cards have been produced.
2. Each group of about four or five people is given a small stack of general catalogs or magazines.
3. Group members look through the catalogs or magazines and cut out pictures that look interesting. At least ten pictures should be cut out.
4. Either as individuals or as a group, members paste the pictures onto folded sheets of paper to form greeting cards. The cards should be based upon some theme such as birthdays, holidays, friendship, get well, and other special occasions.

5. Once all the cards have been constructed, the problem is revealed and discussed.
6. Using the themes and pictures as stimuli, the group members attempt to generate ideas to resolve the problem.
7. If time is available and more than one group is involved, the groups can exchange cards and repeat step 6.

During a seminar on idea generation techniques, the author facilitated a Greeting Cards session involving the problem of increasing international airline passenger satisfaction. One group designed a card with the theme that concerned a male friend who recently had been divorced. The front of the card read: "True . . . the judge may have awarded her the alimony. . . ." On the inside of the card was a picture of a man's lower torso with underwear. The concluding caption read: "So we're awarding you the SUPPORT!" Another card had a picture of a first-aid kit on the front and, on the inside, the message: "Let's patch things up!" These pictures and themes, as well as those from several other cards, then were used as stimuli to suggest ideas. Some of the ideas suggested were to design seats with more back support and to provide each passenger with a small sewing kit.

Evaluation   Greeting Cards, like similar methods, combines idea generation with a built-in procedure for promoting the playful attitude needed for creative thinking. (This attitude will be enhanced if the groups are instructed to develop cards with humorous themes.) The lively atmosphere it often produces can result in many unique ideas. In addition, the use of unrelated problem stimuli also insures that unique ideas are more likely to be generated. Unlike many other techniques, the Greeting Cards approach uses both themes and pictures to provide a double-barreled stimulation source. A possible weakness of this method is one it shares with similar methods. Some individuals will be reluctant to engage in the minimal playful behavior required. Typically, such individuals prefer direct, literal approaches to their problems. The cards and the unrelated stimuli associated with them may be viewed as inappropriate and of little use. Thus, Greeting Cards probably will work best with individuals who are tolerant of ambiguity and who can maintain a playful attitude in groups.

4.44 Method 6-3-5

This technique is another brainwriting variation that uses a structured procedure for generating and developing ideas in writing. Three versions of Method 6-3-5 have been developed and are distinguished primarily by minor procedural variations. In the first version, described by Warfield et al.,[96] "6" refers to the number of participants in a group, "3" refers to the number of ideas initially generated by each participant, and "5" is the number of minutes spent on each round. The following steps are used for this version:

1. Six persons are seated around a table and a problem is presented by the group leader.
2. Each participant writes down three ideas related to the problem.
3. At the end of five minutes, the participants pass their papers to the person sitting next to them.
4. The ideas received by each person are further developed and/or new ideas added.
5. The process continues with rounds of five minutes until each member receives his or her original paper.
6. The group leader collects the papers and the ideas are evaluated later.

The second version is a slight modification of the first procedure. In particular, the participants are given three ideas to begin developing instead of generating their own ideas at the outset. Other than this alteration, the procedure is basically the same as that used in the first version. As described by Geschka,[97] the steps for this altered version are as follows:

1. Six persons are seated around a table and a problem is presented by the group leader.
2. Each person is given a sheet of paper on which three columns have been drawn. At the top of each column is listed one basic idea.
3. The participants write down an idea that improves upon the one listed in each column. If the preceding idea cannot be improved, a new idea is written down.
4. At the end of five minutes, the participants pass their papers to the person sitting next to them.
5. The process continues with rounds of five minutes until each member receives his or her original paper.
6. The group leader collects the papers and the ideas are evaluated later.

Rickards[98] describes yet another version that he attributes to practitioners in Germany and Holland. Also known as the recorded round-robin technique, the major differences between this version and the others are the use of a highly structured procedure for exchanging ideas and the lack of a time limit for the rounds. This version has seven steps:

1. Six persons are seated around a table and a problem is presented by the group leader.
2. Each person is given three cards and asked to write the problem on each card.

3. The participants write one different idea on each card.

4. The cards are passed to another group member who has been previously designated to receive the cards from a particular individual. For example, person #1 might be assigned to give his or her cards to person #6; person #2 might give his or her cards to person #1, and so forth.

5. As the cards are received, new ideas are added or improvements made on existing ones.

6. The cards are passed to the next person designated to receive them and the process continues until each idea has been improved upon or added to, five different times.

7. The group leader collects the cards and the ideas are evaluated later.

Evaluation   Of the three different versions of Method 6-3-5, the first one probably is the most practical. The second version is limited by prior specification of only three ideas that may be worked on; the third version is made unnecessarily complex by imposing a random sequence for passing the cards. The second version, however, can be practical when a large number of ideas can be narrowed down to just three and further refinements are desired.

Regardless of which version is used, there are some difficulties involved in the basic 6-3-5 procedure. First, some duplication of ideas is inevitable, although this problem is usually offset by the large number of ideas produced. Another problem is that five minutes typically will not be enough time to come up with ideas during the later rounds. During this time, the participants often begin to run out of new ideas or improvements upon old ones. This problem, of course, will not exist in the third version, where there is no prescribed time limit. Other disadvantages include a possible loss of idea spontaneity, lack of opportunity for verbal clarification of ideas, and production of solutions that tend to be rather mundane or less than unique. On the other hand, Method 6-3-5 does eliminate group process dysfunctions such as destructive interpersonal conflicts and dominance of a discussion by one or more group members. Like other brainwriting variations, it also eliminates the need for a recorder and minimizes the need for a skilled group facilitator. In addition, Geschka[99] reports that the procedure produces the best results in areas such as advertising where one or a few ideas need to be progressively developed.

4.45 Phillips 66

The Phillips 66 technique (or Phillips 66 "buzz" session, as it is often known) is *not* a method for dealing with gasoline problems, nor is it associated with the Phillips Petroleum Company. Instead, this technique was developed by Donald Phillips,[100] a past president of Hillsdale College, as a method for encouraging audience participation in submitting ideas or questions to a speaker or panel. It is especially applicable for large groups when some of the benefits of small-group discussions are desired. The basic steps for applying this technique follow:

1. A conference leader subdivides a large group into smaller groups of six persons each.
2. The groups isolate themselves from one another and elect a discussion leader and a secretary-spokesperson who records and reports the group's ideas.
3. A carefully worded problem or issue is presented to the group for discussion. (In some applications of the method, the groups are given different parts of a problem to discuss if it is especially complex.)
4. The groups spend six minutes discussing the problem and/or suggesting ideas.
5. After all group members have expressed their opinions or ideas, each group evaluates the results of their discussion and selects the most valuable ideas for presentation to the large group.
6. The groups return to their original location and the conference leader records the ideas reported by the secretary-spokesperson of each group.
7. The entire set of ideas is either (a) presented to an individual or committee for additional evaluation or discussion, or (b) discussed by the larger group at the time they are presented.

According to Maier,[101] there are six factors that need to be skillfully applied to achieve the best results with this method: (1) choice of problem, (2) clear assignments, (3) size of group, (4) proximity of groups, (5) time limit, and (6) informal climate. The *problem* to be discussed should be suitable for the group's experience and interests, relevant to the program, capable of producing differences of opinion, and limited in scope so that all group members will be discussing the same topic. The *assignment* given to the groups should be as specific as possible to force the groups to achieve consensus. The final product of the groups should not be limited to a summary of opinions but should represent a resolution of differences of opinion. Since originally developed by Phillips, the Phillips 66 method has not always been restricted to six-person groups. *Group size* should be guided by the flexibility of seating arrangements and the size of the audience. When an audience contains around 25 persons, a group size of three or four persons would be appropriate; for audiences of about 100 persons, eight- to twelve-person groups would be best. The *proximity* of the groups is another factor that should be considered. In general, the small discussion groups should remain together in the same room since the activity level can promote greater interaction among group members. (However, too many people crowded into a small room can be disruptive.) Although Phillips originally limited the groups to six minutes of discussion time, the *time limit* set for most groups should be determined by the topic and the size of the groups. When the topic is likely to generate considerable differences of opinion and the groups have more than three or four members, six minutes will not be enough time. As a general rule of thumb, most groups should be given at least 20 to 30 minutes to discuss the topic. Finally, an *informal structure* can help to insure the success of the method. The conference leader should indicate the approximate size of the groups and then let the audience divide itself up. In addition, Maier believes that the groups should not be required to elect either a discussion leader or a secretary-spokesperson. Too much structure might detract from the groups' primary purpose and should be avoided if at all possible.

Evaluation   The major advantage of the Phillips 66 method is that it allows a large number of people to participate in a group discussion. In most large groups, the amount of participation is limited. However, by dividing a group into small ones, the method gives everyone an opportunity to make a contribution. In addition, this technique creates a situation in which differences of opinion can be resolved—a feature also not possible in many large groups. A possible limitation of the method, however, might be its emphasis upon unstructured discussions. Although Maier[102] reports that groups are more likely to reach consensus when the leader does not structure the discussion activity, the quality of the ideas produced might not be as high. If consensus is the goal and the leaders have no special discussion skills, then Phillips 66 is likely to be effective. On the other hand, if solution quality is desired, then a more structured approach might be needed. Another limitation is the reliance upon verbal interaction to produce ideas. As discussed in the description on Classical Brainstorming, verbal procedures often inhibit some group members, thereby reducing idea spontaneity. Finally, the procedure for evaluating all of the ideas when the groups reconvene can be difficult to coordinate, especially when a large number of groups is involved.

4.46 Pin-Cards

As described by Geschka,[103] the Pin-Card technique is a brainwriting variation in which individuals write ideas on different-colored cards and pin them on a board for group examination. Stimulation for ideas is derived from examining the ideas of other group members. In this regard, it is identical to the Brainwriting Pool. However, instead of idea sheets being exchanged in the center of a table, idea cards are passed directly from one person to the next. There are nine steps for the Pin-Card technique:[104]

1. A problem statement is written on a chalkboard or chart visible to a group of from five to seven persons.
2. The group discusses the problem statement to make sure that all group members clearly understand it.
3. Stacks of colored computer cards are distributed among the group members, with each person receiving a different-colored stack.
4. The group members silently write down one idea on each card and pass it to the person on their immediate right (see Fig. 4–8).

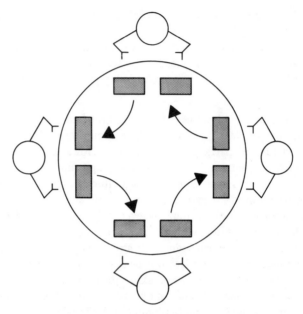

Fig. 4–8. Example of the Pin Cards technique.

5. When group members need stimulation for generating additional ideas, they pick up a card passed on from the person on their left and read it. Then, they write down on a new card any new ideas stimulated by it and pass the new-idea card on to the person on their right (the stimulation card may be either retained or passed on at the same time).

6. After 20 to 30 minutes of this activity, a group moderator announces that the idea generation period is over.

7. The group members collect the cards on their right and begin pinning them on a large pinboard. The cards usually are sorted into idea categories, using title cards as headings for the different columns.

8. The group members read over all of the cards and, if necessary, move some cards to different categories and eliminate duplications.

9. The group moderator points to each card and asks for comments or questions to help clarify idea meanings. Because the ideas are color-coded, the originator of a particular idea can be easily determined and, if necessary, questions asked of this individual.

Evaluation   The Pin-Card technique possesses basically the same advantages as other brainwriting methods. In particular, it reduces anxiety for persons who have trouble verbalizing ideas in group situations, and a larger quantity of ideas can be generated than typically is found with most brainstorming procedures. There are, however, certain difficulties that must be considered when using the technique. A major problem is that bottlenecks often will develop when a group member receives more cards than he or she passes on. To avoid such situations, the moderator should encourage (or require) group members to pass on stimulation cards as soon as they have been used. A second difficulty is a feeling of time pressure to generate as many ideas as possible. Such feelings will be particularly evident in groups with highly competitive members. A related difficulty is that the hurried pace virtually eliminates any idea incubation. This loss of incubation, however, must be weighed against the possible benefits of idea spontaneity. Finally, the use of color-coded cards to identify idea originators might cause some persons to be inhibited in their responses. Such identification methods should be used only when an open group climate exists. Otherwise, the ideas generated might be more conservative and less diverse than when anonymity is assured.

A possible extension of the Pin-Card technique also should be noted. Because the cards are arranged in columns corresponding to idea categories, a natural format for Morphological Analysis is created. To take advantage of this format, the cards can be taped to sheets of flip-chart paper which, in turn, can be pinned to the board. With each sheet representing a category of ideas, the sheets then may be moved up and down to allow the group to examine possible combinations produced by forcing together ideas across the rows. If any new ideas are produced by this examination, they then can be listed separately and evaluated along with other categories using a procedure such as the Sticking Dots technique.

4.47 Problem Inventory Analysis (PIA)

A common marketing procedure in new-product development is to start with a consumer need and then develop a product to fit that need. However, identifying and measuring needs is not an exact science. As a result, many companies generate new ideas and then assess consumer reaction.

Since Osborn[105] popularized brainstorming, more and more companies have relied upon a variety of creative problem-solving techniques to assist in new-product idea generation. According to Tauber,[106] these techniques are fine, but they do little to discover well-defined consumer problems. Although focus groups are widely used to identify consumer needs, the unstructured nature of these groups makes them fairly unreliable. Tauber suggests that Problem Inventory Analysis (PIA) be used instead.

PIA alters the procedure typically used in new-product development. Rather than asking consumers to identify problems associated with various products, PIA asks consumers to look at problems and describe problems that come to mind. These problems then are used as stimuli to suggest new-product ideas. As described by Tauber, the primary steps involved in using PIA are as follows:

1. Develop a list of consumer-related problems.
2. Prepare a list of statements that mention a problem, but omit reference to a specific product. For example, "Preparing _____ leaves so many pans to clean."
3. Administer the questionnaire and tabulate the responses.
4. Study the problems in depth and identify those that represent the most important problems for the general population.
5. Apply creative problem-solving techniques to help generate new-product ideas based upon these problems.

To help construct the problem inventory questionnaire, Tauber suggests developing a matrix of problem types in a particular product area. For instance, in the area of food products, problems might be categorized as (a) physiological (e.g., weight, hunger), (b) sensory (e.g., taste, appearance), (c) activities (e.g., meal planning, storage), (d) buying and usage (e.g., portability, portion control), and (e) psychological/social (e.g., serve to company, eat alone). Examples of potential statements that might be developed from these categories include: "Packaged _____ doesn't dissolve fast enough," "_____ makes a mess in the oven," and "It's difficult to get _____ to pour easily."

Tauber originally developed Problem Inventory Analysis to help discover potential consumer problems that might be translated profitably into new products. However, because consumers are required to project themselves into a sentence completion task, PIA also can serve as an idea stimulator.

In particular, the responses themselves can be direct sources of stimulation. Combinations of responses within or between categories also might suggest many potential new products. For instance, if a large number of consumers respond that pie makes a mess in the oven, a new design for a pie plate or splatter protector might be suggested.

Evaluation   It is relatively easy to find fault with PIA as an idea generator since it was not designed for this task. In addition, its primary focus is upon new-product development. It may not be as suitable for other areas. Nevertheless, PIA does have the potential to suggest ideas. However, because the stimuli are related directly to the problem, it is unlikely that many unique ideas will result. On the other hand, modifying PIA slightly by forcing together responses from different categories could provide the unrelated stimuli needed to prompt idea uniqueness. Another strength of this approach is its direct reliance upon consumer marketing to target high-potential new-product areas. The major weakness of PIA stems from its strength in market analysis. Surveying large numbers of people can be costly and time consuming.

4.48 Rolestorming

Rolestorming was developed by Griggs[107] as a brainstorming variation. According to Griggs, most people are inhibited in traditional brainstorming sessions. Rolestorming overcomes this weakness by allowing group members to assume someone else's identity. There are three steps:

1. Using the four brainstorming principles, group members generate 20 to 30 ideas.
2. Each member selects someone not present (but known to the member) and assumes his or her role. The selected person may be someone else in the organization, a typical consumer, a great leader, or other people.
3. Based upon the selected person's attitudes, preferences, and opinions, group members pretend that they have a stake in the problem. When generating ideas, they might use such phrases as, "My person would try to. . ." or My person would favor. . . ."

Evaluation   By combining role-playing with Classical Brainstorming, Rolestorming compensates for some brainstorming weaknesses not dealt with by brainwriting. Specifically, Rolestorming still satisfies social interaction needs while providing new perspectives and minimizing the effects of inhibition. In this respect, it is similar to the Super Heroes technique; unlike Super Heroes, the roles are not fantasy figures. As a result, the ideas may not be as unique. However, assuming another role should increase the likelihood of generating new perspectives that could lead to some unique ideas. Moreover, if the roles are not limited to people known personally, idea uniqueness might be even greater.

According to Griggs, Rolestorming produces at least 60% to 70% more ideas beyond those generated during a typical brainstorming session. Although this may be a subjective opinion, it is highly plausible. For one thing, simply switching to another technique following brainstorming often can increase idea quality. In addition, the new perspectives provided can increase quantity which, in turn, can improve idea quality. Because it is relatively easy to use, Rolestorming can be recommended strongly as a supplemental brainstorming approach. It also should generate a fun, positive atmosphere conducive to creativity.

4.49 Sculptures

Symbolic Representations uses abstract symbols as idea stimuli. The Sculptures technique uses unrelated stimuli in a similar way. However, instead of relying upon sketches or doodles, the Sculptures approach relies upon the actual physical construction of an abstract work. Variations of this process have been used for years by management trainers as group exercises. The version presented here is based upon the approach developed by creativity consultant Ole Faafeng[108] of the Norwegian Management Institute. The following are the basic steps:

1. Discuss the problem as a group.
2. Collect enough varied and unrelated items to construct an abstract sculpture. For instance, the following types of things might be used: string, rope, wire, blocks of wood, small chairs, books, colored paper, tape, paper clips, modeling clay, cardboard, scissors, and gluesticks.
3. Spend a few minutes looking at and examining the resources available for the sculpture.
4. Begin constructing a sculpture (as a group) that in some way represents some aspect of the problem. (An optional approach is to use an unrelated sculpture.)
5. Discuss the sculpture, its parts, and their relationship to one another.
6. Using the sculpture as a stimulation source, brainstorm ideas.

In one application of this method described by Faafeng, a group was trying to resolve a problem involving communication channels within an organization. A string stretched across a portion of their sculpture reminded one of the group members about the problem. He suggested that the problem be dealt with by altering a line of communication in a way that had not been considered previously. Other group members joined in and they soon had generated a number of ideas.

Evaluation   The Sculptures technique shares many of the strengths of similar approaches such as Symbolic Representations, Games, Greeting Cards, and Super Heroes. It uses unrelated stimuli to generate ideas and its format helps promote a playful atmosphere conducive to creativity. As a result, many unique ideas should be possible with this technique. Another positive feature of Sculptures (also shared by Greeting Cards and Super Heroes) is its emphasis upon physical movement. As noted in the discussion of the Gallery method, physical movement may influence idea generation positively.[109] Some weaknesses of this technique are (a) certain resources are required to build the sculptures, (b) not everyone will be motivated to participate in what may appear to be a silly exercise, (c) conflict may develop as to what form the sculpture should take, and (d) some group members may have difficulty using unrelated stimuli to generate ideas. Of course, all of these weaknesses are shared by similar techniques and should be considered during technique selection.

4.50 Semantic Intuition

Semantic Intuition is another of the idea generation methods developed by the Battelle Institute in Frankfurt.[110]   It is suitable for use by individuals or with groups of from five to seven persons. The technique was developed by reversing the naming procedure typically used when a new invention has been created. That is, most inventions are given names after they have been developed. Semantic Intuition, in contrast, proceeds by first developing names and then attempting to find inventions that will be suitable for the names. The following steps are used:

1. Using the principles of Classical Brainstorming, an individual or a group generates two sets of words related to the problem area.
2. A word from one set is combined with a word from the other set to create a new name.
3. An attempt is then made to develop an invention that will fit this name.
4. The process continues until all possible names have been created and inventions sought for each.

A problem of developing new devices for painting a house can help to illustrate this technique. First, two sets of words are produced. The first set of words is derived from objects within the problem area, while the second set consists of words involving tasks associated with the problem. The two sets of words produced are

Set One	Set Two
wall	paint
ceiling	scrape
window	sand
trim	brush
ladder	clean
eaves	roll

Next, different combinations of the words from each set are produced. Examples of such combinations include wall-scraper, window-cleaner, trim-sander, ceiling-roller, and ladder-roller. Of these, window-cleaner and trim-sander are selected for consideration of any inventions that might be suggested. Window-cleaner, for example, could suggest a product that would easily remove paint from glass but not affect the wooden- or metal-painted parts of a window. Trim-sander could lead to a device designed specifically for sanding small areas and curved surfaces.

Evaluation Semantic Intuition is almost identical to the forced-relationship method of manipulating nouns and verbs that is used as part of the Creative Problem Solving technique. To a lesser extent, there also is some similarity between Semantic Intuition and Morphological Analysis. While the latter is more suited for a wider variety of problems, Semantic Intuition seems best suited for product design problems. This does not necessarily detract from

Semantic Intuition but, rather, emphasizes the parallel development of creativity methods in different fields and in different countries.

One difficulty in using Semantic Intuition involves identification of words in two related problem areas that will lead to innovative ideas. The words should not be too remote or practical inventions might be overlooked in the process of moving from the abstract to the concrete. The problem, then, is to produce words that will be balanced in remoteness. A major difficulty with the technique, however, is the imaginative leap required between the word combinations and the name of a new invention. Structure is provided for generating the word combinations but not for naming the inventions, since the latter activity requires more intuition. As a result, the uniqueness of the final product can very well be determined solely by individual differences in intuition.

There are, however, two minor modifications that can facilitate using the technique. First, multiple combinations of words from one set might increase the range of possible inventions. In the illustration used, for example, a combination such as trim-scraper-sander might suggest a device that would combine trim scraping and sanding functions into one tool. When only two-word combinations are considered, such possibilities might be overlooked. Second, a modification of the Relational Algorithm technique can be used for generating words for the two sets in the illustration. To do this, the individual or group generates some of the words in the two sets by applying the 42 relational words to, for example, the word "house." Thus, combinations such as the following are provided: across a house, against a house, and on a house. The combination of against a house might suggest using the word "ladder," while the combination on a house might suggest the word "trim." The relational words can be used in a similar manner for other types of problems.

4.51 Sequence-Attribute Modifications Matrix (SAMM)

The SAMM approach to idea generation was developed by Brooks[111] for use with problems that involve a sequence of steps. It combines elements of Attribute Listing, Checklists, and Morphological Analysis and uses forced relationships and related stimuli to prompt ideas. As described by Souder and Ziegler[112] and Souder and O'Keefe,[113] the steps are as follows:

1. List the primary steps involved in the problem process.
2. List generic ways that any process could be modified (e.g., eliminate, substitute, rearrange).
3. Construct a two-dimensional matrix with the steps on the left side and the modifications listed along the top.
4. Examine each cell of the matrix and identify modifications that look promising or require in-depth analysis.

5. If necessary, use other idea generation methods to suggest ideas for making the modifications.

As an example of SAMM, Souder and Ziegler describe a problem involving a hot steel slab rolling operation. Some of the key steps in the process are (a) heating steel slag to a pliable state, (b) transferring the material from a heating furnace, (c) positioning the rolls at a desired setting, (d) passing the slab through the rolls (elongation), (e) checking the slag gauge, (f) shearing the slab to a desired length, and (g) transferring the sheared product. Potential modifications then are listed, for example: eliminate, substitute, rearrange, combine, enlarge, reduce, and separate. Finally cells in the matrix are checked where priority modifications seem possible. In this example, the positioning and passing activities are checked as two steps that can be combined and rearranged. The SAMM matrix does not suggest how this might be accomplished, however.

Another illustration of SAMM can be described with a less tangible problem. In this instance, the problem is one of improving a staff meeting. A possible matrix for this problem is shown in Fig. 4–9. In this matrix, calling the roll and approving the minutes from the previous meeting have been marked as having potential for elimination. Discussing new business has been marked for rearranging. In this case, the new business might be placed before the old business. And, announcements have been designated for enlargement. Experience may suggest that more time needs to be set aside for this activity.

Potential Modifications

Process Activities	Eliminate	Substitute	Rearrange	Combine	Increase	Decrease
1. Call the roll	X					
2. Approve minutes	X					
3. Make announcements					X	
4. Discuss old business						
5. Discuss new business			X			
6. Adjournment						

Fig. 4–9. Example of the SAMM technique.

Evaluation   Because it is so similar to Attribute Listing, Checklists, and Morphological Analysis, the SAMM approach shares all of their advantages and disadvantages.   For example, SAMM relies upon related stimuli, which may limit idea uniqueness.   Also, the ideas generated may be limited to the particular attributes included in the matrix.   In addition to these, SAMM also has a unique disadvantage.   Because it was designed for use with problems involving a logical sequence of steps, SAMM's applicability will be restricted. However, this weakness also is a strength in that problem processes often are overlooked during problem solving.   Thus, SAMM will be especially useful for problems in which a clear-cut process is evident. The use of specific ways to modify a process is another strength of this technique.   However, many different modifications should be considered.

4.52 SIL Method

The SIL Method (or Successive Integration of Problem Elements, as translated from the German) is a brainstorming[114] variation developed by Helmut Schlicksupp of the Battelle Institute in Frankfurt, Germany.   It combines elements of both free association and forced relationships in progressively integrating ideas until a final problem solution is accepted by a group.   According to Warfield et al.,[115] the following steps are used for the SIL Method:

1. A group of four to seven persons individually generates ideas in writing to a previously stated problem.
2. Two members of the group read one of their ideas.
3. The rest of the group attempts to find ways of integrating the two ideas just read.
4. A third member reads an idea and the group attempts to integrate all three ideas into one solution.
5. This procedure continues until all of the ideas have been read and attempts made to integrate them.
6. The procedure is terminated when an integrated solution is accepted by the group.

Evaluation   One potential weakness of this technique is the difficulty sometimes experienced in trying to integrate two ideas that will lead to a useful solution. Ideas with totally different characteristics, for example, can be especially difficult to integrate and a certain amount of individual skill is required to do this. Another potential weakness is the restrictive nature of the procedure. Because the final solutions will be limited to those built upon previous ideas, many unique solutions might be overlooked. The use of different idea stimulation aids can help to overcome this problem. On the other hand, the manner in which the ideas are used is a potential advantage. Because the process is structured so that each person's ideas must be considered, status differences or the influences of a dominant personality are less likely to determine which ideas are considered. In addition to this advantage, the SIL Method can be superior to Classical Brainstorming by generating the initial ideas in writing instead of verbally. These two techniques differ, however, in the type of solution that is produced. Classical Brainstorming is basically a divergent type of thinking process, while SIL combines both convergent and divergent thinking. The latter technique produces one very specific solution while the former produces many solutions, most of which require further refinement. Although the SIL Method has a built-in refinement procedure, some idea spontaneity might be lost by repeatedly diverging and converging. The totally divergent nature of Classical Brainstorming, in contrast, encourages spontaneous idea development but does not structure idea refinement. To help insure against loss of idea spontaneity during the integrative phase of the SIL Method, the group members should be encouraged to defer evaluation of a possible solution and consider many different types of solutions.

4.53 Stimulus Analysis

This technique is one of the many idea generation methods developed by H. Geschka and G. Schaude of the Battelle Institute in Frankfurt, Germany. It is appropriate for either individuals or groups and, when used in groups of from five to seven persons, will take about 45 minutes to implement. The basic procedure consists of developing a series of stimulus objects, analyzing the characteristics of the objects, and, from this analysis, attempting to derive a problem solution. The following steps are involved:[116]

1. A list of ten concrete objects (unrelated to the problem) is generated.
2. One of the objects is selected and then broken down into its descriptive characteristics (structures, basic principles, specific details).
3. Each characteristic is analyzed separately for stimulation and a solution is sought based upon the outcome of the analysis.
4. When all possible solutions have been exhausted, another object is selected and the process is repeated.
5. This activity continues until all ten objects have been analyzed and solutions generated.
6. The solutions are studied and the ones with the most potential for solving the problem are selected for further analysis.

To illustrate how the technique is used, consider a situation in a factory where many workers have injured their hands while operating a metal stamping press. The problem, as defined, is to develop a method to warn the workers when their hands are in danger of being caught in the press as it closes downward. Ten objects are generated by a group. The first one, table lamp, is analyzed by describing its characteristics. Corresponding solutions then are developed for each of the characteristics. This analysis is shown in Table 4–6. The group then selects another object and repeats the process until all possible solutions have been developed for the characteristics associated with each object.

Evaluation Stimulus Analysis is relatively easy to implement and provides a stimulating experience for most individuals and groups. Furthermore, in analyzing the stimulus characteristics and developing solutions, the participants are required to fully exercise their creative abilities. In this regard, the technique also could be used as a device for training in creative thinking. The success of the method, however, would seem to depend upon two factors. First, the types of objects generated in step 1 will determine the types of solutions developed later on. To be effective in developing a variety of solutions, it is important that the objects only be related remotely to one another. If both table lamp and desk lamp were generated, for example, one might be deleted so as to increase the range of possible solutions. The second factor pertains to the background of the participants. In order to develop practical solutions from analysis of the stimulus objects, at least one of the group members should have some familiarity with the problem.

Table 4–6. Example of Stimulus Analysis.

PROBLEM: To develop a warning device that will help prevent workers' hands from becoming caught in a metal stamping press.
STIMULUS: Table lamp

ANALYSIS	SOLUTION
1. Uses electricity	An electrical field produces a mild shock whenever hands remain in the press too long.
2. Emits light	When hands pass in front of a photoelectric cell, a switch is tripped shutting off the press.
3. Generates heat	Temperature-sensing cells are installed that cause the press to shut down when heat from human hands is sensed.
4. Clicks when turned on	When the arm of the press reaches a certain point, a clicking sound is emitted to warn the workers to withdraw their hands.

4.54 Story Boards

Development of the Story Board technique usually is attributed to Walt Disney, although its origins probably go back much further.[117] For example, DaVinci apparently drew rough sketches on walls before committing them to canvas. Walt Disney began using Story Boards as a way to avoid meetings required to discuss the thousands of drawings required for animation. To remedy this problem, he had his artists pin their drawings (in sequence) on walls. As a result, the process proceeded much more smoothly. Advertising agencies and many other organizations now use Story Boards as a guide for problem solving, planning, and idea generation, to name just a few areas.

Vance usually is credited with adapting the Story Boards approach for idea generation.[118] He refers to his approach as the Storybook technique. In addition, many other variations and elaborations also exist. Two of these additions are the approach used by the Creative Thinking Center (5100 Darrow Road, Hudson, Ohio 44236) and the FASTTRACK system developed by Bauer & Associates (210 East Huron, Ann Arbor, Michigan 48104). They are similar in their use of notecards and headings and subheadings which are pinned to a board and examined by a group; they differ in refinements and modifications that have been developed for special purposes and applications.

The Storybook Technique   The Story Boards version developed by Vance requires a flip chart, corkboard, thumbtacks, and several stacks of 5-by-7-inch cards. The steps are as follows:

1. The group leader presents the problem.
2. Participants verbally generate solution categories. Each category is written down on a card and pinned across the top of the corkboard.
3. The group leader asks idea-prompting questions about each category. Participants write down their responses on the cards and pass them to the leader.
4. The leader groups the cards according to themes and pins them up under the appropriate category.
5. The leader asks additional idea-prompting questions, based upon the initial answers.
6. Steps 3 and 4 are repeated until a sufficient number of ideas have been generated.
7. The groups within categories are ranked by group consensus or vote.
8. The three most popular idea groups within each category are discussed further; the leader asks idea-prompting questions as appropriate.
9. The final ideas are ranked again (if necessary) and implementation teams are formed.

Fig. 4-10. Example of the original Story Board technique.

An illustration of the Storybook version is shown in Fig. 4-10. The problem concerns what to do with personnel who work in an area being phased out. Possible idea categories are generated, such as training, punishment, rewards, and peer pressure. These are written down on cards and pinned to the corkboard as header cards. The group leader next asks questions about the categories. Examples of these questions would be (a) "How else might the company use these employees?" and (b) "In what ways might peers be used to help relocate or counsel these employees?" Using these and other questions as stimuli, the participants write down their ideas on cards and pass them to the leader. The leader reads the ideas aloud (without criticism), groups them, and pins them on the board under the proper headings (ideas #1, #2, and #3 are examples in Fig. 4-10). The leader then asks more questions to stimulate ideas, conducts a vote to determine the top three groups within each category, asks for additional ideas about these groups, and records them on a flip chart. Finally, the idea groups are ranked by vote and implementation plans are developed.

The Creative Thinking System   The Creative Thinking Center uses Story Boards for idea generation, planning, organization (implementation), and communications. Only the Idea Story Board will be described here. It uses the following major steps:

1. The leader describes the topic, pins a topic card to a board, and checks to insure that everyone understands the topic.
2. The leader reviews the four rules of brainstorming (no criticism; the more ideas generated, the better; the wilder the ideas, the better; hitchhike and combine ideas whenever possible) and asks the group to generate ideas for a warm-up problem (e.g., foods that begin with the letter "B").
3. The leader assigns one group member each to perform the roles of pinner and writer. Pinners pin cards to the board and writers write down on cards the data generated.
4. The word "purpose" is written on a card and pinned to the top, upper left-hand corner of the board. Participants generate purpose statements, which are written down and pinned beneath the purpose card.
5. The purpose statements are discussed to determine the basic reasons for doing the board. Statements are added or deleted as desired and the statements are rearranged.
6. "Headers" (cards with main headings written on them) are developed and pinned across the top of the board.
7. The headers are discussed to determine if any should be added, deleted, changed, or combined. The headers are rearranged if desired.
8. "Subbers" (subheadings or subtopics) are generated for each of the headers.
9. The subbers that require clarification or additional understanding are discussed. The subbers are rearranged if desired and the subbers are combined whenever feasible.

As an example of this approach, Smithers[119] describes how a group dealt with the problem of designing a unique restaurant (the topic). Purpose statements first were pinned to the board. Examples included (a) make money, (b) satisfy own desire, (c) change of pace, (d) entertain, (e) nutrition, (f) serve customer, and (g) fulfill need. After discussing these statements, the group decided to eliminate all except a, c, f, and g. Next, Headers were pinned to the board. These included such topics as entertainment (deleted as a purpose and moved to the header category), theme, atmosphere, employees, seating, parking, location, pricing, and a miscellaneous category. The group then started to discuss the headers. However, it was suggested that the theme needed to be analyzed before any other headers could be discussed. Thus, subbers were generated (e.g., underwater, Alice in Wonderland) and discussed for the theme header. After this discussion, subbers were generated for the other headers and they too were discussed. The result was the final product for the restaurant concept.

FASTTRACK   The FASTTRACK approach to Story Boards is somewhat more refined and elaborated than the other versions. The basic process is similar, but more guidance is provided for participants and the group leader. In addition to idea generation, FASTTRACK includes a separate Story Board approach to problem solving. The facilitator's steps for the FASTTRACK idea development story board are as follows:[120]

1. Describe the process to the group. Clarify roles and responsibilities. The primary roles are a group leader who conducts the session, a facilitator with final authority who sees that things progress as intended, the participants, and a pinner who works with the cards on the board.
2. Select a warm-up topic and have the group generate ideas, following the four brainstorming rules.
3. Describe and discuss the problem topic to be investigated. Once the topic is understood, write it down on a card (5 by 7 inches) and pin it at the top center of the board.
4. Generate a "why" heading card (4 by 6 inches) and list subpoints on cards (3 by 5 inches) that then are pinned below the heading card. (Subpoints are the group's perceptions of the purpose of the session for dealing with the topic.)
5. Generate other heading cards that deal with the major issues or points that need to be considered. The facilitator might ask, "What are all the ideas, thoughts, or issues we need to consider in order to fully develop the topic?"
6. Evaluate the heading cards and remove duplicates or add cards as necessary. Save rearranging and combining until the next step. Deleted cards should be placed under a "wild cards" heading. If members disagree about placement of a heading, put it under a "miscellaneous" heading. Periodically review wild cards and miscellaneous cards as possible sources of stimulation for headings or subpoints.
7. Combine and rearrange the heading cards as required.
8. Generate subpoints for each heading. Pin the subpoint cards under the appropriate heading card. Use "bullet" cards (2 by 2 inches) to add information or detail and to prevent afterthoughts from being lost.
9. Evaluate the subpoints in the same manner the heading cards were evaluated (steps 5, 6, and 7).
10. Develop implementation plans and review the session.

An arrangement of cards for a sample FASTTRACK session is shown in Fig. 4–11. In this simplified depiction, only one major heading is included in addition to the why, miscellaneous and wild card headings. In practice, several more heading cards would be used. Also note the bullet card attached to one of the subpoints under the "invitations" heading.

In addition to idea development, it also is possible to use FASTTRACK for more complex problems. Such problems typically will require a structured problem-solving process. The FASTTRACK approach to problem solving is

Fig. 4–11. Example of the FASTTRACK Story Board technique. Reprinted with permission from *The Participant's Guide to FASTTRACK.* Ann Arbor, Michigan: Bauer & Associates, 1985.

similar to the basic Story Board versions described previously. It also uses headings and subpoints. The major difference is that the headings are predetermined categories representing different problem-solving stages. The FASTTRACK approach has eight stages:

1. State the problem clearly.
2. Define the essential criteria a solution must meet to be satisfactory.

3. Use creative brainstorming to search for solutions.
4. Check the selected solution(s) against the problem and its underlying causes.
5. Develop an action plan for implementing the solution.
6. Develop an assessment plan to determine how effectively the solution is being implemented.
7. Implement the solution(s).
8. Follow through on the assessment steps.

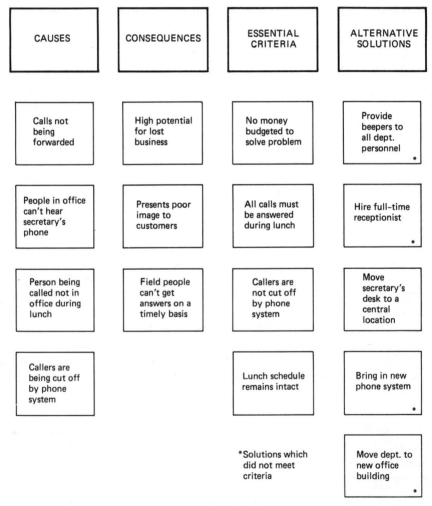

Fig. 4–12. Example of a FASTTRACK problem solving board. Reprinted with permission from *The Participant's Guide to FASTTRACK*. Ann Arbor, Michigan: Bauer & Associates, 1985.

A sample FASTTRACK problem-solving board is shown in Fig. 4–12. The problem/topic (not shown) is that telephones are not answered during the lunch period. The first step involves creating a topic card, a why card (the "causes" card in the figure), and a consequences card (a heading for a listing of what is to be gained or lost from solving or not solving the problem). If it is decided to proceed after this analysis, "essential criteria" are generated. This step is followed by generation and selection of solutions, devising action steps for implementation and, finally, follow-up by assessing implementation.

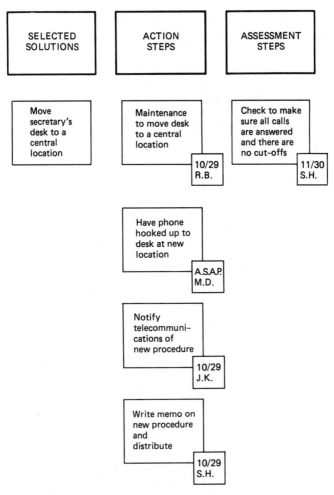

Fig. 4–12. (con't.)

In addition to the materials and guidelines already described, there are additional hints and materials that can enhance the FASTTRACK process. For instance, 3M Post-It^{TM} notes can be used in place of cards, yarn or ribbon can be used to show connections among ideas, colored dots can be used to highlight priority ideas. Further information on FASTTRACK is provided in the Leader's Kit marketed by Bauer & Associates.

Evaluation   The Story Board approach is a brainstorming variation that uses some elements of brainwriting in one of its versions. Its major strengths lie in its visual presentation, flexibility and ease of making alterations, high level of participant involvement, broad range of applicability, emphasis upon cooperation and teamwork, results orientation, tendency to automatically organize the process so that progress can be evaluated easily, and provision for a written record of the session.

Its major weaknesses are that some versions require a high level of facilitator skill (the Vance version); one approach establishes criteria before idea generation (FASTTRACK), thus placing possible constraints upon the creative process (although this occurs only in the broader problem-solving model); and a certain amount of time must be available to coordinate the required activities. Story Boards in general also share most of the weaknesses associated with brainstorming techniques. For example, interpersonal conflict may arise and a dominant member might disrupt the process. However, a skilled facilitator can overcome most of these disadvantages. It also is possible to modify these versions to compensate for some weaknesses. For instance, the Vance version could be altered to minimize the leader's role. Thus, the leader could spend more time facilitating idea generation without relying upon idea-prompting questions.

Another major problem concerns the use of related problem stimuli. Story Boards have a clear advantage over brainwriting techniques that rely upon nominal groups with no external stimulation. Persons using Story Boards at least receive idea stimulation from others. Nevertheless, the stimuli still are related generally to the problem. The technique could be improved by adding unrelated stimuli. One interesting approach would be to supplement Story Boards with techniques such as Stimulus Analysis or Visual Synectics. Moreover, computer applications of the technique also should be explored. Software currently exists that can combine graphics and text on a large screen or as part of a network on individual computers.

4.55 Super Group®

The Super Group® approach to idea generation and concept development was begun in 1977 by Foy Conway, CEO of Conway/Milliken & Associates (Corporation for Marketing Research, John Hancock Center, 875 N. Michigan Avenue,

Chicago, Illinois 60611).[121]   It was developed to assist in the new-product idea generation process. However, it differs markedly from the focus group approach widely used in the new-product field. Typically, such groups bring together consumers and probe for opinions using a highly judgmental research process. Such a rational approach usually is counterproductive for creative thinking. As a result, not many unique ideas are likely to be generated. The Super Group® technique, in contrast, is designed to bring out the creative potential of the participants. Moreover, the process goes beyond simple ideation by moving core ideas to more fully developed, test-ready concepts.

Super Group® is implemented using one of three formats: (a) creative consumers, (b) target market consumers, and (c) creative clients. Groups using creative consumers consist of persons who have been screened and selected based upon their creative ability.[122]   In addition, they are given formal training in idea generation methods. Target market consumers also are recruited on the basis of their creative ability. However, these consumers also are selected to fit a set of specific marketing characteristics (e.g., male beer drinkers between the ages of 18 and 34). The third type of Super Group®, creative clients, is formed by bringing together client personnel representing a variety of backgrounds and positions (e.g., marketing, marketing research, research and development, public relations, and agency people).

A typical Super Group® process uses the following steps:

1. Specify the creative objectives and prepare a comprehensive session plan for the ideation phase.
2. Using the principles of "interactive association" (similar to the four brainstorming rules), generate ideas. Several other idea stimulation aids also are used, including the Product Improvement CheckList[TM] .
3. Compile an inventory of the core ideas. Evaluate the most useful ideas and combine ideas where required.
4. Rework and refine the final ideas to transform them into finished product concepts.

Among the ideas generated by Super Group® are low- and no-alcohol beer, carbonated soft drinks with real fruit juice, and high-fiber products. Beyond new-product work, the approach also has been used successfully to generate brand and flavor names, for advertising positioning, and for various promotional activities.

Evaluation   Because of its emphasis upon idea generation and creativity linked directly to consumers' experience, Super Group® nicely bridges the gap between focus groups and general idea generation methods. It combines the positive features of both rational and intuitive approaches. As a result, the Super Group®

concept has much to recommend it as an all-around idea generation and concept development technique—especially in the new-product area. Its use of skilled facilitators and unrelated stimuli as supplemental idea generation aids also are noteworthy. The most distinguishing feature of this technique, however, is its use of varied groups and, most significantly, its use of specific selection criteria for group membership. Having a group of persons with "natural" creative ability and knowledge of the problem area probably is more important than the techniques used. Idea generation methods are used most efficiently when they can compensate for weaknesses in individual creative thinking and losses due to group process dysfunctions. Unlike most other techniques, the Super Group® is truly "super" in specifying the composition of the group. About the only shortcoming of the method is that it requires a certain amount of financial resources and professional skills to implement.

4.56 Super Heroes

The Super Heroes technique was designed by Grossman and Catlin[123] to provide a playful group atmosphere during idea generation. Group members assume the identity of different Super Hero characters and then use the characters as stimuli for sparking ideas. The steps are as follows:

1. Descriptions of various Super Hero characters are distributed to group members.
2. Group members select one of the characters and assume its identity. If desired, costumes can be used to elaborate upon the characterization. At a minimum, members should be provided with signs to wear stating the name of the hero they selected.
3. Each group member, in turn, describes his or her character in as much detail as possible. This description should include such things as special powers, strengths, weaknesses, and habits.
4. After each hero is described, group members use the information as stimuli for generating ideas. For example, Spiderman's web might suggest a network concept for solving some problem.

Any number and type of Super Heroes can be used for this technique. If possible, there should be more characters than group members to select from. Below are some common heroes and their major characteristics.

Superman has X-ray vision, superhearing, can fly, and is the strongest man on earth. When not on duty, he is disguised as mild-mannered newspaper reporter, Clark Kent. He can be weakened only by Kryptonite, a leftover rock from his birth planet. Superman is faster than a speeding bullet and is able to leap tall buildings in a single bound.

Batman and his sidekick Robin, The Boy Wonder, are first-rate detectives who always manage to outwit the most sinister criminals. They have at their disposal an assortment of "Bat" paraphernalia, such as a Batmobile, Batplane, Batcycle, Batrollerskates, Batrope, ad nauseum. Batman's alter ego is millionaire Bruce Wayne.

Wonder Woman is a truly liberated woman. With extraordinary strength, agility, and all-around athletic ability, she easily can overpower the most macho man. With her magic bracelets, she even can deflect bullets shot at her. And, with her magic lasso, she can rope almost anything. When wrapped around someone, her lasso always causes that person to tell the truth. On occasion, she flies her own airplane, which is invisible.

Captain America represents the ultimate in All-American ideals (truth, justice, apple pie, and mom). With his winning personality he usually has no trouble persuading others to see his viewpoint. The captain also is known for his positive outlook on life and his great strength and athletic skills. If all of these attributes are not enough protection, he also has a Captain America shield that can protect him from any harm.

Dr. Strange tries to live up to his name. As a skilled magician and sorcerer, he can create numerous illusions. He also is able to cure sicknesses, control people and situations, and change one thing into something else. Another strange thing about Dr. Strange is that he is afflicted with temporary lapses of concentration.

E-Man, whose most distinctive feature is his unlimited supply of energy, can take on any form he wishes. However, once he assumes a form, he is affected by its weaknesses. His favorite sleeping place is a toaster.

Nova Kane is the female counterpart to E-Man. She previously worked as an exotic dancer.

Spiderman, or "Spidey," as he is affectionately known by his fans, can walk on ceilings and walls. With his ever-present web, he can swing through the air as well as capture bad guys. Spiderman also has a unique ability to detect any dangerous situation before it affects him.

Mr. Fantastic is the smartest man in the world and, although no logical correlation is involved, he can stretch his body to any length. He is a very flexible person.

Invisible Girl, as her name implies, can make herself and other people and things invisible. She also can make people and things reappear. When in danger, she creates an invisible shield which protects her from all harm.

The Human Torch is said to be a short-tempered hothead. He has the power to emit and control fire. Heat never bothers him. He also can fly whenever the mood strikes.

Evaluation If the group members possess a playful attitude, the Super Heroes method can work well. It is similar to Games, Greeting Cards, and Rolestorming in that it has a built-in mechanism for generating ideas and helping insure an atmosphere conducive to creative thinking. Discussing the various characters often is sufficient for loosening up the group. As a result, the ideas may flow easily. Super Heroes also is likely to produce unique ideas because of its use of unrelated stimuli. In addition to the usual weaknesses of any brainstorming approach, Super Heroes has one major disadvantage. The playful attitude required may not exist in all groups and some members may be reluctant to participate. On the other hand, requiring members to assume different roles may be just the thing needed to liven up some groups.

4.57 Synectics

Synectics was originally developed by William Gordon[124] who, in 1944, began observing individual problem-solving activity and inferring from it the psychological processes involved. Gordon later was joined by George Prince[125] at the Arthur D. Little Company and together they established Synectics, Inc. in Cambridge, Massachusetts, in 1960. Gordon subsequently left Synectics, Inc., and both Gordon and Prince developed their own versions of the Synectics process.

There is enough similarity between the two approaches, however, to permit combining them into one presentation. The major differences lie in the terminology used to describe similar activities. To avoid confusion, only one set of terms will be used. Most of these will be taken from Gordon, although a few specific distinctions will be made. Thus, the need to switch back and forth from one approach to the other will be avoided. In doing this, little of the flavor of Synectics should be lost. The reader interested in a more precise differentiation in terminology can consult the references cited for both Gordon and Prince.

The word synectics comes from Greek and means the joining together of different and apparently irrelevant elements.[126] Synectics uses analogies and metaphors to both analyze a problem and develop possible solutions. Two operational mechanisms are used to accomplish these activities. The first, making the strange familiar, is designed to let the user better understand the problem by viewing it in a new way; the second, making the familiar strange, attempts to pull the problem solver away from the problem so that more creative solutions can be developed. The purpose of these mechanisms is to create five psychological states that are necessary to achieve creative responses: (1) involvement and detachment, (2) deferment, (3) speculation, (4) autonomy of object, and (5) hedonic response. Only when these states are reached can the unconscious and irrational aspects of the mind be merged with the conscious and rational for attaining greater creative efficiency.

The effective use of Synectics also requires that close attention be given to the problem-solving process and the roles that the participants play in using the method. Synectics, as a problem-solving technique, is relatively structured in its approach. A trained leader is essential for guiding the group through the different stages and for integrating the comments of the original problem poser. Unless the problem-solving activity is carefully orchestrated, the psychological states are not likely to be attained and a high-quality, creative solution is less likely to result. For this reason, Synectics should not be considered a do-it-yourself technique.

Any organization seriously considering the use of Synectics would be wise to write directly to Synectics, Inc., in Cambridge, Massachusetts, or its sister organization founded by William Gordon, Synectics Education Systems at 121 Brattle Street in the same city. Both organizations offer a variety of training programs and materials designed to provide a better understanding of both the theory and practice of the Synectics method.

The objective of the following sections is to present a broad overview of the key elements involved in Synectics and how they are used to develop creative solutions. The intended psychological states will be presented first, followed by the operational mechanisms, group-member roles and characteristics, the basic stages of the Synectics problem-solving process, "Mindspring" theory, and a general evaluation.

Psychological States   As mentioned previously, the psychological states are considered to be a prerequisite for the development of creative thinking. They are interrelated and, except for the state of hedonic response, are brought about by using the operational mechanisms. Hedonic response was added after the other four had been developed and as yet no operational mechanism exists for this state. The five psychological states are described below.

1. Involvement and Detachment.   This state involves the feeling people experience about their relationship with a problem. When involvement is experienced, there is a feeling of being tied to a problem to such an extent that it cannot be avoided. Gordon describes the feeling of a person trying to invent a spring mechanism for a dial, stating that he is unable to get away from his own "springiness." A person involved with a problem experiences the sensations needed to really understand the problem. Detachment is an opposite feeling. When feeling detached, problem solvers sense a distance between themselves and the problem. That is, they feel that they are on the outside looking in. Both feelings are necessary to develop creative solutions: Involvement provides the sense of closeness needed to understand a problem, while detachment provides the separation needed to view a problem objectively.

2. Deferment.   Development of this psychological state helps a problem solver avoid premature solutions. A danger exists in applying the obvious and immediately available solution, since better solutions might be overlooked. Such solutions must be temporarily put aside until additional solutions are presented (or present themselves).

3. Speculation. This state reflects the capacity of a group and its members to allow their minds to run free, without being hindered by traditional constraints. Thus, persons should feel free to consider: What would happen if. . . ? or If there was such a thing as. . . ? Development of such an attitude indicates receptiveness to considering the impossible or nearly impossible.

4. Autonomy of Object. As a problem solver moves closer to a final solution, a feeling develops that the solution is "outside" of the problem solver. The solution begins to appear as if it has an identity of its own and is no longer in the control of the problem solver. As with all of the psychological states, this feeling should not be suppressed but, rather, should be encouraged to develop and grow.

5. Hedonic Response. When a feeling develops of being on the right track, without having validating evidence, it may be said that hedonic response is being experienced. Hedonic response is generally accompanied by a pleasurable sensation similar to that which accompanies tuition or inspiration—the "aha" experience. Although no operational mechanism exists to develop this feeling, it is obviously of major significance to the creative problem-solving process.[127] If it were possible to recognize such a sensation, then much wasted effort could be avoided in pursuing unfruitful, tentative solutions. Instead, effort could be directed toward those areas suggested by the hedonic response. Unfortunately, there is no way to verify the operation of this state.

Operational Mechanisms   The operational mechanisms are the working tools of the Synectics process. They are primarily responsible for making the familiar strange and, when used appropriately, can create the sense of distance needed to avoid looking at a problem in conventional and familiar ways. Each one of the mechanisms is capable of producing a different degree of separation from a problem, depending upon the requirements of the individual problem-solving stages. In this regard, it is the responsibility of the leader to select the appropriate mechanism and guide the group in its use. Although the operational mechanisms are not involved in the entire Synectics process, they do play an important role and probably can be considered to constitute the central core of Synectics. The operational mechanisms are listed below.

1. Personal Analogy. To use a personal analogy is to lose one's self in trying to become an object, thing, person, or idea. An individual must imagine that he or she actually is the object under study. If the problem is to design a better door hinge, then the problem solver must assume the identity of a door hinge and actually try to experience (through imagination) what it feels like to be a door hinge. For example, what does a hinge "think" or "feel" as it is being moved back and forth?

For practical purposes, the greater the degree of personal submersion into an object, the more effective the analogy is likely to be in producing the desired psychological state. If a person is deeply involved in becoming an object, then the familiar is more likely to become strange, thus creating the necessary distance between the person and the object. That is, through involvement, the object is experienced in a way not normally seen or felt. There are at least four possible degrees of involvement that use personal analogy:

First-person description of fact. The object under study is described by simply listing its basic characteristics. A common door hinge, for example, can be described as being hard, made of metal, and consisting of two plates, securing screws, and a connecting pin. At this level, the degree of involvement is minimal and very little distance is likely to be achieved.

First-person description of emotions. Using the door hinge example again, an analogy at this level might involve someone describing how tired he or she gets from opening and closing all the time. Such a description is typically too general and of limited usefulness since many different types of objects can experience the same emotion.

Empathetic identification with a living thing. This type of analogy involves both physical movement and emotional feelings. Although the door hinge itself can not be used directly as an example, the perspective of a person using a door hinge can. For instance, the problem solver might try to imagine what a person is thinking when using a door. Thus, does the person tire easily when opening the door? Does the person get frustrated from pulling on the door when the hinge is too tight? This type of analogy is more useful than the two previous ones.

Empathetic identification with a nonliving thing. The deepest level of involvement should be experienced at this level. The door hinge, for example, might describe how sore it gets from all the opening and closing. In addition, it might wish that there was some way it could better support the weight of the door.

Although all four types of personal analogy permit some degree of involvement, the third and fourth types probably will be of most value in making the familiar strange. The first two, while of less value for this purpose, could be useful as practice devices for the operational mechanisms and also could help the group to work together more effectively.

2. Direct Analogy. Of all the operational mechanisms, direct analogy is generally considered to be the most basic and the most valuable. In contrast to the other analogies, direct analogies attempt to describe a clear and straightforward relationship between the problem and some object, thing, or idea. The opening and closing of a door hinge, for example, can be likened to a similar feature of a clam shell. In fact, biological organisms have been found to be the richest source of direct analogies. This does not mean, however, that only biological analogies should be sought. Any source that can provide a direct relationship between the problem and an object can be used. There are, nevertheless, two guidelines that are thought to increase the usefulness of direct analogies. First, biological analogies are probably best used with nonbiological problems, while nonbiological analogies are better for biological problems.

Second, when a problem is being studied for the first time, analogies with only a small psychological distance from the problem should be used; when the problem has been studied more extensively, analogies that are more irrelevant (i.e., of greater psychological distance) should be used.

3. Symbolic Analogy. According to Gordon,[128] this analogy "uses objective and impersonal images to describe the problem." Although the resulting relationship might be flawed technically, it should be pleasing to observe, and even poetic in nature. That is, practicality is not so important as is the strangeness of the relationship. Quite often, however, the strangest relationships will produce the most psychological strain. As the analogy takes the problem solver further and further away from the problem, it becomes increasingly difficult to relate cognitively to it, thus producing strain. It is in the attempts to resolve this strain that the most productive insights will be produced.

As an example of symbolic analogy, Gordon describes a problem of how to design a jacking mechanism that will fit into a 4" X 4" box and yet extend three feet upward and support four tons. In the course of the group discussion on the problem, one of the members suggested that the problem is "like the Indian rope trick." Using this suggestion as a stimulus (once the familiar had been made strange) the group then proceeded to develop a practical application of the Indian rope trick and solved the problem. (The problem was solved by adopting the mechanics of a bicycle chain, which only unfolds in one direction. The linking together of two chainlike mechanisms creates a jack that is both flexible and strong enough to support a heavy object.)

4. Fantasy Analogy. This operational mechanism is based upon Freud's notion that creative thinking and wish fulfillment are strongly related. An artist, for example, has certain creative needs that are satisfied only by wishing for something that is eventually translated into a work of art. Synectics has borrowed this idea and operationalized it. One Synectics group used fantasy analogy to develop a vapor-proof closure for space suits. After some discussion, they devised a rubber and steel spring mechanism that solved the problem. This was accomplished by asking the question, How do we in our wildest fantasy desire the closure to operate? Gordon believes that this analogy is of limited value because of a tendency of people to quickly run out of suitable analogies. It is probably of greatest value if used in the initial stages of making the familiar strange. In this manner, it can serve as a link between problem stating and problem solving, thus providing a stimulus for the use of other operational mechanisms.

Group-Member Roles   There are three basic roles that make up a typical Synectics group: (1) the leader, (2) the group members, and (3) the client-expert. The success of the problem-solving process will be highly dependent upon how effectively these different individuals can work together. In contrast to traditional (i.e., unstructured) meetings where the roles often are not clearly defined, participants in a Synectics meeting must clearly understand the roles played by the other participants. The following discussion is based upon the work of Prince.[129]

The Leader. Leaders of both traditional and Synectics meetings use certain behaviors to control other group members. The difference between the two types of leaders lies in the ultimate purpose of such controlling behavior. In a traditional meeting, the leader often is concerned with controlling a group to encourage development of a particular or personal point of view; in a Synectics meeting, in contrast, the leader acts to control the behavior of the group members without having any particular viewpoint in mind. The traditional leader often is more self-oriented; the Synectics leader, more others-oriented. According to Prince, an effective Synectics leader should abide by eight major principles:

1. Never go into competition with your group. This principle is intended to encourage full participation in the problem-solving process. The leader should be concerned primarily with supporting and facilitating the contributions of others more than his or her own contributions. Only when the group seems to be having difficulty in coming up with ideas should the leader attempt making a contribution.

2. Be a 200 percent listener to your team members. To encourage a climate of openness and self-worth, the leader and other members must fully understand the meaning of each individual's contributions. To do this, the leader may paraphrase a comment but should avoid any form of evaluation. All of the group members should feel that their ideas are worthy of being heard by the others.

3. Do not permit anyone to be put on the defensive. If an open climate is to be achieved, members of the group should feel free to contribute an idea without fearing that they must justify its merit. The leader should actively seek opposing viewpoints and discourage negative comments. If negative comments are made about an idea, the leader should ask for comments about its positive aspects.

4. Keep the energy level high. Ideas are likely to be more spontaneous and generated more quickly if the group senses a high energy level among its members. The leader can encourage this feeling by physically moving around, maintaining a high pace of activity, challenging assumptions, and making use of humor.

5. Use every member of your team. The leader should reinforce responses made by shy members and subtly discourage responses from highly verbal members who attempt to dominate the discussion. The final outcome is likely to be better if all members participate equally in the Synectics process.

6. Do not manipulate your team. One of the major errors a Synectics leader can make is to attempt pushing the group in the direction of a particular solution. Although the leader does manipulate the group—in the sense of guiding it in the appropriate use of Synectics—manipulation is used only to help the group develop new problem solutions. If the leader has a favorite solution, it should be suppressed at all times.

7. Keep your eye on the expert. The ultimate objective of a Synectics meeting is to provide the problem expert (who is often the client or problem poser)

with as many different solutions as possible. Since this individual will be more knowledgeable about the problem area than the other group members, the leader should constantly be aware of how this person is reacting to different aspects of the discussion. If the expert seems to be particularly interested in a possible solution, the leader should encourage the group to further develop and elaborate upon this solution. In cases of extensive expert involvement, the leader could even suggest that the expert temporarily assume the leader's role.

8. Keep in mind that you are not permanent. To avoid the assumption of excessive power and authority, leaders of Synectics meetings should be rotated periodically among the other group members. Leader rotation increases members' motivation to participate fully while, at the same time, it gives them an opportunity to gain a persepctive on the advantages and disadvantages of both roles.

Group-Member Roles and Characteristics. The primary responsibility of the participants is to develop an understanding of what the appropriate behaviors and attitudes of a Synectics meeting should be. The members should (1) be aware of their own uniqueness and individuality so that they can contribute fully in their own way, (2) avoid prejudging any ideas they or others might have, (3) try to look for the positive aspects of an idea, and (4) observe the leader's behavior and their reactions to it so that they might better fulfill their own role as the leader. Among the characteristics that group members should have, Gordon suggests (1) high energy level, (2) the ability to generalize, (3) entrepreneurial ability, (4) diverse job backgrounds, (5) a record of having shifted fields of educational interest, (6) a mediocre work record (the process could "liberate" their productive potential), (7) metaphoric capacity, (8) a need to take risks, (9) emotional maturity, and (10) a lack of interest in status differences.

The Client-Expert. This is the person who is generally responsible for solving the problem and who will be held accountable for developing a solution. However, because some of this responsibility is delegated to a group, the expert must consider how to behave appropriately during the meeting. The role of this individual can be best fulfilled by (1) not becoming defensive in using the assistance of a group to solve the problem, (2) setting a good example in openly and freely suggesting possible solutions, (3) not pushing for acceptance of a specific solution, (4) fully participating in the discussion, (5) looking for the positive aspects of ideas receiving negative criticism, (6) building upon the ideas of others, (7) being realistic in pointing out the advantages and disadvantages of an idea, and (8) demonstrating to the group a willingness to seriously and constructively consider all ideas generated.

Stages of the Synectics Process When using the operational mechanisms and other aspects of the method, a Synectics group often will appear to be quite disorganized. To the casual observer, the group might seem to bounce from one unrelated topic to another, with little apparent sense of direction. Such an observation, however, would be inaccurate. If guided by a skilled leader, a Synectics meeting is actually a highly structured activity. Based upon the members' familiarity with the process and the guidance provided by the leader, a Synectics group will work sequentially through about eight different stages. Although not all groups will spend the same amount of time on each stage, nor rigidly stick to the prescribed format, there will be evidence of continuity as the group progresses from one state to another.

A typical Synectics meeting will consist of three major parts. The first part involves defining and analyzing the problem to increase the members' understanding of it (making the strange familiar). The second part is where the operational mechanisms are applied to the problem (making the familiar strange). Finally, in the third part, the group attempts to integrate (force fit) the results of applying the operational mechanisms with the problem. If this integration produces an acceptable solution or an idea that might lead to one, then the process is concluded; if this is not the case, then the process can be repeated, building upon the understanding of the problem already achieved. The major stages of the Synectics process are as follows:

1. Problem as Given (PAG)
2. Short Analysis of the PAG
3. Purge
4. Problem as Understood (PAU)
5. Excursion
6. Fantasy Force Fit (FFF) or Force Fit (FF)
7. Practical Force Fit (PFF)
8. Viewpoint or New Problem as Understood

1. Problem as Given (PAG). A general statement of the problem is read to the group. The problem can come from someone external to the group or from one of the group members.

2. Short Analysis of the PAG. The primary purpose of this stage is to make the strange familiar. This can be accomplished in a number of ways. The group can use metaphors and analogies, the Gordon/Little technique can be applied, the client-expert can present an analysis, or some combination of these methods can be used. If the client-expert presents an analysis, only enough detail should be described to insure that the group has a good understanding of the problem. Because the expert will also function as a participant, there is no need for the group to possess the expert's complete knowledge about the problem. For example, the expert might generally describe the major constraints of the problem but avoid discussing technical details.

3. Purge. The major objective of this stage is to eliminate the rigid and super-ficial solutions often suggested as a result of mulling over the problem during the first two stages. The early verbalization of these ideas allows more innovative solutions to be explored later on. The purging activity also helps to clarify further the original problem statement (PAG). Because the expert is also a group participant, these early solutions can be criticized, thereby providing additional information on problem constraints as well as the types of solutions that are not likely to work.

4. Problem as Understood (PAU). This stage begins with the selection of a part of the problem to work on. To do this, each participant describes how he or she sees the problem using, if possible, a fantasy analogy or wishful thinking. The leader then writes down each of the viewpoints. After recording the view-points, the leader consults with the expert and selects, for further analysis, one of the ways of looking at the problem.

5. Excursion. This stage of the process has been described by Prince as an "artificial vacation" or a "holiday from the problem." The group leader asks the participants to shut out all conscious thinking about the problem and to concentrate on the task at hand. The leader directs the group in further examination of the problem with the goal of making the familiar strange. It is during this stage that the operational mechanisms are used. The leader proceeds by asking questions that require or will evoke an analogical answer. After a number of analogies have been generated, the leader then might select one for detailed analysis and elaboration. Typically, the leader will select an analogy on the basis of its irrelevance to the problem and the group's knowledge and/or interest in the analogy. Once the analogy is fully understood, the excursion is terminated and the group moves on to the next stage.

6. Fantasy Force Fit (FFF). It is at this stage that the greatest divergence occurs between the approaches of Gordon and Prince. Gordon's approach is to force a fit between the last analogy used in the Excursion stage and the problem as understood. For Gordon, the use of fantasy during this activity helps produce more creative responses. Prince, in contrast, uses a somewhat more structured approach to develop a force fit. One of his methods is to use a "forced meta-phor" in which the group considers the two elements to be forced and tries to make a connection by speculating wildly. Another method, referred to as the "get-fired technique," is designed to break up the logical thinking patterns often found during this stage. The leader instructs the participants to individually write down a force fit. The force fit, however, must be written in such an illogi-cal, outrageous way that it would result in the writer being fired if it were made known to his or her boss. Whatever approach is used, the group must play with the problem and the analogies until a new way of looking at the problem is achieved.

7. Practical Force Fit (PFF). The PFF involves developing a practical appli-cation of the analogy developed in the FFF stage. Gordon uses an example of a

problem of how to invent a better mousetrap. The analogy of the Trojan horse is used first to develop a fantasy force fit. In this case, the analogy involves "leaving something about which the mice will covet so much that they will pull it into their nests." The next step is to remove the fantasy force fit and develop more practical applications. Thus, one practical solution might be to treat lint with a chemical so that when it is heated by the bodies of the mice, it would give off a lethal gas. The line would be left around for the mice as nest-building material. Once they pulled it into their nests, they would be killed.

8. Viewpoint or New Problem as Understood. The Synectics process should end with the production of a viewpoint (a new way of looking at the problem) that can lead to a solution, or to a problem as understood. If a viewpoint is produced, then it should be considered tentative until a solution has been developed, implemented, and evaluated; if a new problem as understood (PAU) is the end result, then the process should be repeated using the PAU to develop a viewpoint.

At the end of the process, several different viewpoints typically will have been developed from which only one will be selected to apply to the problem. Some caution must be used at this time to insure that the most promising viewpoint is selected. According to Prince, the leader should ask the expert to make the final choice from among the available viewpoints. Once a viewpoint is selected, the expert should provide the structure needed to transform it into a solution. At this stage, either the client-expert or the group can begin to develop plans for implementing the solution.

Since his original work, Prince has reinterpreted his perceptions about the thinking processes involved in Synectics.[130] He proposes that "Mindspring" theory be used to describe the creative problem-solving process. Mindspring theory posits that all thinking involves six major elements: (1) wishing, (2) retrieving, (3) comparing, (4) transforming, (5) storing, and (6) imaging. Problem-solving effectiveness using these elements will be determined by the ability to switch back and forth between a "tolerance for approximation and a wish for precision."

To illustrate Mindspring theory and the role of alternation, Prince describes a problem involving the design of a new type of thermos bottle closure. To solve this problem, most people probably would think of other types of closures. Then they would try to see how each type might be adapted to suit the problem. For instance, the slide on a spice can might suggest only an approximate solution. However, after several solution attempts, a more precise solution might be identified with the potential to solve the problem.

To apply this basic principle of alternation in thinking, Prince describes how each Mindspring element relates to the thermos problem. Wishing would be used first in expressing a desire for a new type of closure. Information retrieval might follow next while observing that a spice can lid has a unique closure system.

However, comparing the spice can lid with the thermos bottle would show that the solution was not precise enough. Thus, the size of the slide might need to be modified or a new material substituted in order to satisfy the requirements of the thermos bottle (a transformation activity). After the possible transformation is considered, it must be stored for future reference. Finally, it can be noted that imaging was used with each Mindspring element.

Evaluation   There is relatively little research available on the major assumptions employed in Synectics and its problem-solving process. The research that is available is mostly anecdotal, although there have been some attempts to study the operational mechanisms.

Although research on the use of analogies in Synectics is rather sparse, there is at least one study that sought to investigate the frequency of use of the different analogies. In a 1972 study, Khatena[131] investigated the verbal images produced by 141 male and female college students preselected for their high scores on a test of originality (the Adult Version of Onomatopoeia and Images[132]). The test instructs persons to produce unusual verbal responses based upon "the sound and connotations" of a word. According to Khatena, this activity approximates making the familiar strange, as used in Synectics. The responses of the students were then categorized into the four operational mechanisms. Of a total of 5640 different analogies produced, 5545, or 98.8% were direct analogies. The other three analogies combined produced only 1.2% of the total number produced (results that achieved a high level of statistical significance). This finding is interesting in light of the fact that Gordon and others suggest that direct analogies are the most productive of all the mechanisms. It may be that this productivity derives from greater familiarity with direct analogies, based upon prior training and general learning experiences. If this is plausible, then efforts might be directed toward more intensive training and encouragement of Synectics participants in the use of the other three operational mechanisms. Such an effort conceivably could increase the richness of the solutions produced by Synectics.

Although the Khatena study is useful in describing how often innovative people make use of the different analogies, it sheds little light on the effectiveness of analogies in producing ideas. At least three studies can provide more insight into this area.

In one study, Bouchard[133] investigated the relative effectiveness of two brainstorming procedures. The first procedure used Classical Brainstorming rules plus Bouchard's sequencing procedure (participants verbalize ideas one at a time in sequence); the second involved the addition of personal analogy to the first procedure. The subjects were instructed to produce different ideas for nine different problems (e.g., brand names for a cigar). His results indicated that the subjects who used the second procedure (Classical Brainstorming plus sequencing plus personal analogy) generated more ideas than subjects using the first procedure (where personal analogy was not included). On four of the problems, the differences between the groups attained statistical significance (i.e., the differences were not likely due to chance alone). To account for the difference made by using personal analogy, Bouchard speculates that this mechanism might have involved the participants more in the problem and focused their thoughts and suggestions in a direction more relevant to the problem.

A second study, conducted by Klimoski and Karol,[134] used Classical Brainstorming and personal analogies to examine the effect of different levels of intermember trust upon the number of ideas generated. The authors hypothesized that using analogies should improve performance in groups with an initially low level of trust. Although the study participants using personal analogy reported that they experienced more ease and a greater sense of freedom in their groups, they did not perform significantly better or worse than the Classical Brainstorming participants. This result is not consistent with Bouchard's finding that there was a difference between groups. It must be noted, however, that Bouchard made use of a sequencing procedure not used in this second study. To account for the difference between the two group procedures, Klimoski and Karol suggest that personal analogy might not have as powerful an effect upon group performance as one of the other three operational mechanisms. Together, these two studies present an obvious direction for future research—comparing the effectiveness of the different types of analogies.

Finally, a third study investigated Synectics in general, but did not look specifically at analogies. Thamia and Woods[135] compared the long-term effectiveness of a number of creative problem-solving techniques used by a multinational corporation in the United Kingdom. Among the techniques studied were Synectics, Classical Brainstorming, Attribute Listing, Morphological Analysis, Structured Discussions, Checklists, Value Analysis, Role Playing, and Relevance Tree. Effectiveness of the techniques was determined by subjective ratings involving a six-point scale (1 = excellent, 6 = failure).

Synectics was used 28 times, or in 19% of the total number of sessions conducted. The majority of the Synectic's sessions were given a rating of 3 (good). This ranked Synectics in third place, behind Potential Problem Analysis and Attribute Listing. In spite of this success, however, Synectics gradually was replaced by structured discussions as a favorite problem-solving technique. According to the authors, many senior managers were uncomfortable with the fantasy aspects of Synectics. These managers also considered the ideas that resulted from Synectics to be out of line with "normal logical thinking." Moreover, such ideas were seen as high risks for implementation success.

The following advantages and disadvantages of the Synectics technique are based partly upon anecdotal reports, but mostly upon pure supposition. Until more hard research evidence is available, any conclusions must remain tentative. There is no question that Synectics can produce new ways of looking at a problem and, in most cases, novel solutions to some types of problems. As with most group creativity techniques, however, the major difficulty is knowing under what conditions and with what types of problems Synectics is likely to prove most effective.

Advantages

1. The psychological states appear to be valid representations of the states thought to exist during creative-thinking activities. In particular, the states seem to correspond roughly to those described by others working in the creativity area.
2. The operational mechanisms seem to be capable of unlocking rigid thinking patterns for many individuals. Although the mechanisms have not been exhaustively studied using scientific methods, they do provide structure for an activity that often is unstructured.
3. Synectics has proven useful (although unscientifically) for problems requiring a new design, or when a new operational principle is needed. Since its development, Synectics has been shown to be especially valuable for producing highly imaginative solutions to technical problems.
4. The Synectics process provides the structure needed by many persons to develop creative solutions.
5. The Excursion stage encourages the use of the subconscious mind in the creative process.
6. The operational mechanisms and the stages involved in the Synectics process could be easily adopted for use with other group methods.
7. The analogical methods should be especially valuable for redefining ill-structured problems.
8. The Purge stage helps to insure that commonplace, conventional solutions will be avoided in favor of more innovative responses.
9. Rotation of group leaders provides an opportunity for all members to more fully participate in the process.

Disadvantages

1. To attain optimal effectiveness, Synectics requires the use of a highly trained leader who is knowledgeable about the technique and its use. The suggestion to rotate group leaders must be weighed against the possible disadvantages of having to adjust to a new leader. Unless the group is composed of persons selected on the basis of uniform selection criteria, there is likely to be considerable variability in skills among the group leaders.
2. If persons in the group do not possess the characteristics thought to be needed for a successful meeting, then the results are likely to be of lower quality than if the "right" types of persons were included. This, of course,

assumes that the relevant characteristics are well known. There is little evidence to justify selecting the group members according to the characteristics prescribed by Gordon. One fairly well-established guideline is to try to include persons with moderately diverse backgrounds in terms of their work and educational experiences. If the group is too similar, it will be less likely to produce highly innovative solutions; if it is too different, dysfunctional conflict among the members might develop.

3. As previously mentioned, there is little hard research evidence to attest to the validity of the assumptions, procedures, and outcomes of Synectics.

4. Instead of relying upon free associations to produce analogical and metaphorical comparisons, an alternate procedure might be to use a list of specific stimulus objects, words, or pictures. The use of Visual Synectics, for example, could provide a richer source of possible comparisons.

5. There is some evidence to suggest that it is difficult to use a Synectics group on a long-term basis within a formal organization. Factors such as time pressure, lack of receptivity to new ideas, absence of commitment to the process, and unavailability of trained leaders make it difficult for a Synectics group to last very long in many organizations. Again, the same comment also could be made about many group techniques designed to promote creative thinking.

6. A major disadvantage of the Synectics method (and one it shares with other methods) is that it does not provide the structure needed to implement and follow up on solutions. This stage of the problem-solving process is left up to the client-expert or the group.

4.58 Systematized Direct Induction (SDI)

Systematized Directed Induction (SDI) is a problem identification and solution generation technique described by Bosticco,[136] an English management consultant. According to Bosticco, SDI was developed in the United States during the 1950s and has been used since then under a variety of names in different companies. She learned of the method while working as a consultant in California but does not identify the technique's originator (if he or she is known).

SDI is based on four principles: (1) Creativity is present in everyone; experts on a subject are not the only persons who can have useful, creative ideas. (2) The more persons involved in generating ideas and solutions, the better the product is likely to be. (3) All persons are willing to offer their ideas and advice; to do so is a satisfying experience. (4) Most persons are creatures of habit and dislike change; yet, change is inevitable and will be implemented more successfully if persons participate in the process using their own ideas.

As described by Bosticco, SDI is especially suited for problems involving people. Such problems as increasing sales and productivity, reducing costs, and cutting down employee turnover are all appropriate applications of the method. Furthermore, the technique can be used with either very small or very large groups as well as with personnel from the same or different organizational levels. The steps involved in using SDI follow:

1. A targeting session is conducted with management to determine the purpose of the SDI workshop.
2. The consultant and management jointly agree upon the specific company personnel that should be involved.
3. The participants are assigned to four-person groups, each seated at a different table.
4. The consultant describes the reason for conducting the workshop.
5. The target is written on a chalkboard visible to all participants.
6. With the use of yellow slips of paper previously placed on each table, a warm-up exercise is conducted in which the participants are asked to write down the greatest problem in their daily work.
7. The yellow slips are collected and replaced with pink slips that have the words "How to. . ." written across the top.
8. The participants are instructed to complete the sentence in the form of a problem preventing the achievement of the target.
9. A five-minute "buzz session" is conducted at each table. During this session, the participants discuss the problems they have recorded.
10. The sessions are terminated and the participants resume recording problem statements. At least one but no more than five statements should be written.
11. The problem slips are ranked in order of importance by writing a "1" on the slip with the most important problem, a "2" on the slip with the second most important problem, and so forth, until all problem statements have been ranked.
12. While the participants take a coffee break, piles of green paper slips are placed on each table.
13. Using the green slips, the participants write down a solution to their number-one problem.
14. A second buzz session is held in which the participants at each table discuss the different problems and their proposed solutions.
15. The participants write down a solution to their number-two problem and a buzz session is conducted as was done in step 14. This activity continues until all of the problems and solutions have been discussed.
16. Based upon the suggestions of others, new solutions might be recorded for some or all of the problem statements.
17. The workshop is terminated by having the participants clip each of the problem statements (pink slips) together with the solution statements

(green slips) and putting a rubber band around them to produce a separate bundle for each participant.

18. The bundles are collected and given to a consultant whose task is to organize, analyze, and synthesize all of the data.

19. A report is written by the consultant and given to management for implementation. Depending upon the nature of the original target, the report can be organized to contain a separate analysis of each major subproblem category.

To illustrate the use of SDI, Bosticco describes how one company successfully applied the technique to solve a major problem facing it. The "XYZ Potato Crisp Company" was experiencing organizational problems after acquiring a smaller competitor which retained its original name. The parent company also was being severely pressed by one of its larger competitors; in addition, it was soon to move to a new location and employee morale seemed to be extremely low. Consultants were called in and a targeting session was held. The outcome of this session was a decision that the target would be: How to improve operations and increase company prosperity. Because the target involved the entire company, representatives from all departments and supervisory levels were selected to participate in the workshop. The company's general manager invited to 80 persons selected and explained to them that their advice was being solicited to help the company during its current period of expansion.

On the day the workshop was conducted, the participants gathered in a large room, were seated four to a table, and were greeted by the consultant. The consultant explained the purpose of the meeting and wrote the target statement on a chalkboard. The target was described as being what the XYZ company wanted to achieve but that there were several obstacles in the way. The participants were told that, as individuals, they were aware of some of the obstacles and that by pooling resources they could form an overall picture of the major obstacles.

After conducting the warm-up exercise, the participants began to write down their problem statements and then conducted the first buzz session. According to Bosticco, these sessions provide an opportunity for participants to learn (1) how their behavior creates problems for other departments, (2) the nature of problems facing other company personnel, and (3) how their jobs dovetail with others. The most important function of the buzz sessions, however, is crossfertilization of ideas: Interaction with others can help to clarify poorly defined ideas and help to stimulate new ideas. This buzz session was terminated, new problem statements written and ranked, solutions written, and then the second round of buzz sessions was conducted. Finally, the workshop was concluded and the slips were collected by the consultant.

In the final report prepared by the consultant, separate chapters were included on the topics of general management, field operations, office work, communications, marketing, sales operations, and the move. After reviewing this report, management instituted a formal sales training program, developed a sales manual using suggestions gathered from the workshop, and put together a new organization chart based upon clarification and redefinition of job responsibilities. Bosticco also reports that management received information on such matters as quality control, customer relations, and personnel management. In addition, a by-product of the workshop was increased staff morale.

Evaluation   Through its use of written responses and verbal interaction, SDI combines features of both brainwriting and brainstorming. Although some of the benefits associated with these approaches also are present in SDI, there are some benefits specific to the SDI technique. First, one of the major benefits of SDI is its ability to accommodate a large number of persons from within an organization. The number of participants is limited only by the availability and ability of persons to process the data. Second, because persons from different organizational levels are included (if required by the target), both large and small problems can be brought out. As an example, Bosticco cites problems listed by the XYZ company director and a production worker. To the company director, the most important problem was obtaining more financing; to the production worker, reducing the number of broken potato chips was the number-one problem. Although different types of problems will be identified with the technique, this is not necessarily its most distinctive feature. What is distinctive is that the persons who identify problems are usually the ones most likely to know how to solve them. A third benefit of SDI is its emphasis upon worker participation in problem solving. Soliciting opinions and showing workers that their ideas and suggestions are valued help maintain employee morale at a relatively high level. Fourth, the use of a large number of persons helps to insure that a large number of diverse problems and solutions will be generated. As shown in studies on creative methods, idea quality is likely (although not always) to be directly tied to idea quantity and the background diversity of participants. Finally, the method of recording problems and solutions insures that all responses will remain anonymous. Once the paper slips are turned in for processing, there is no way that individual responses can be identified.

Although there are many positive aspects associated with the technique, there are also certain features that can be improved upon. These features will be discussed in the approximate order in which they appear during the SDI process. First, it is noteworthy that only management and consultants are involved in selecting the target. Worker motivation might be increased substantially if more persons were to participate in this activity. If the persons involved in the general area were allowed to participate, a greater sense of "ownership" in the target should result. Second, Bosticco does not mention how representatives were selected from the different departments. While the actual method used is probably not that important, it is important that the procedure be perceived as equitable. If, for example, employees were selected on the basis of their work performance, less high-performing employees might be resentful. Third, ownership in the target might be increased further by having management introduce the workshop and set the climate instead of having a consultant perform this task. The employees should view the exercise as a company workshop and not something being done to them by an outside person. Fourth, Bosticco does not specify how persons should be assigned to the groups. It would seem to be important, for example, that supervisors and subordinates not be placed in the same group. A subordinate's major problem might be his or her supervisor, and a fear of reprisals could inhibit the openness of discussions. Another factor to consider when assigning persons to groups is whether or not persons from the same department should be placed in the same group. Obviously, if the target area is limited to a single department, this will not be a problem. If, however, the target concerns an entire company or a major division within it, then it might be wise to systematically mix persons from different departments so that no more than one person from the same department is in any one group. Fifth, the five-minute time period allotted for the buzz sessions might not be adequate to discuss the problems and solutions. A ten-minute period would be more realistic. Sixth, although the participants are assured that their responses will remain anonymous, a perception of a supportive, trusting climate is essential to insure confidence in the anonymity of responses. In this regard, the initial selection of participants and description of the workshop's purpose can be crucial to the success of the entire exercise. Seventh, when a large number of participants are used, processing of the resulting data might be a cumbersome task for one individual. More than one person should be assigned this job. In addition, Bosticco makes no mention of how the problem rankings are consolidated. The nature of this task needs to be clearly specified. Eighth, the evaluation of the problem solutions apparently is left up to the consultant. If management is expected to be committed to implementing the solutions, then provision should be made for them to be included in the data analysis and evaluation process. There are too many examples in the literature of consultants writing a report, handing it to management, and then leaving it up to the company to interpret the results and develop or implement an action plan. In addition, some procedure should be included for providing the workshop participants with a summary of results and an opportunity to be involved in deciding how to implement solutions.

4.59 Trigger Method

The Trigger Method is a brainstorming variation that, according to Bujake,[137] was developed by George Muller of the Ford Motor Company. It has been frequently used with Classical Brainstorming, but requires adherence to certain guidelines if it is to be effective. Otherwise, the process can be disorganized and too cumbersome to be of much practical value. The following steps are used to conduct a Trigger Method session:

1. A problem statement is read to a group of from five to nine persons.
2. Each member of the group silently writes down ideas for about five minutes.
3. One member reads his or her ideas aloud to the rest of the group.
4. These ideas are discussed for ten minutes with the goal of developing idea variations or totally new ideas (all evaluation is suspended during this time).
5. The process continues until all ideas are read and discussed (duplicate ideas are eliminated and previously discussed ideas are not repeated).
6. New ideas or variations triggered by the original ideas then can be used to start a new trigger session.

There is also a variation on the Trigger Method that can help provide a fresh perspective on a problem. In this variation, a second group observes the trigger group and writes down any ideas stimulated by the reading of the individual ideas or by the group discussion of the ideas. These ideas then can be discussed along with those generated by the trigger group. The possibility exists, of course, that the second group will inhibit the first one. Thus, before a second group is used, the permission of the trigger group should be obtained.

Evaluation   By having participants write down their initial ideas, the Trigger Method has an advantage over Classical Brainstorming in that the group members will not feel inhibited in developing their own ideas. However, the fact that the ideas will not remain anonymous might counteract this advantage to some extent.   A better procedure might be to collect the ideas, mix them together, and select one idea at a time for discussion. In addition, the role of the group leader can be important in insuring that the time limits are followed for writing and discussing ideas.   This individual should try to see that each idea receives equal consideration.   Beyond these responsibilities, no special skills are required for the group leader unless, of course, personality conflicts develop over preferred solutions.   In that event, conflict resolution skills will be needed.

The Trigger Method is similar to the SIL Method except that in the SIL Method, there is a deliberate forcing together of two ideas to produce one new idea.   Both of these techniques have their own advantages and disadvantages and the choice of either will be a matter of personal preference.

4.60 Visual Synectics

Visual Synectics was developed by Geschka, Schaude, and Schlicksupp at the Battelle Institute in Frankfurt, Germany.   Although originally designed as an aid for suggesting analogies during a Synectics meeting, it also can be used by itself as an idea generation method and is appropriate for use by either individuals or groups. The basic mechanism involved is the use of pictures (e.g., posters, color slides, almanac pages) to stimulate problem solutions. The following procedure is used for group sessions:[138]

1. The statement of the problem is written down on a chalkboard or flip chart.
2. By use of a large poster or projector, a picture unrelated to the problem is shown to a group of five to seven persons.[139]
3. Each group member verbally describes what he or she sees in the picture.
4. The picture descriptions are written down on the chalkboard or flip chart.
5. The group attempts to relate elements from the picture descriptions to the problem.
6. When the group runs out of solutions, another picture is shown and the process is repeated (ten pictures are generally shown in any one session).

As an example of how Visual Synectics is used, Schaude[140] describes a problem of developing a warning device to awaken miners who have fallen asleep on a conveyor belt. A group is shown a picture of a waterfall in Norway and describes the following elements in the picture: (1) stones, (2) valley narrowing in the distance, (3) waterfall, (4) sheep and rocks, and (5) sound of the waterfall. These descriptions are written down on a flip chart and attempts are made to relate each element to the problem. For example, the waterfall might suggest blowing cold, humid air across the conveyor belt, or the differences in weight between the sheep and the rocks could stimulate the development of a sensor that would scan for weight differences between the human body and coal. Additional pictures then would be shown and the ideas generated written down and evaluated later.

Evaluation Visual Synectics is almost identical to Stimulus Analysis. They share the same structured procedure and most strengths and weaknesses. There is, however, an important difference in the procedure used to prompt problem solutions. Stimulus Analysis uses specific terms generated by free association while Visual Synectics relies upon preselected pictures to generate solutions. Because of this difference, an advantage could be gained by using both techniques in tandem. In this way, a richer variety of solutions might be produced than could be obtained using either words or pictures alone.

The effectiveness of Visual Synectics will be determined largely by the type of pictures selected and the characteristics of the person or persons using them. Therefore, some care must be taken in the selection of both persons and pictures. When persons are selected, a group with diverse backgrounds should be chosen; when pictures are selected, an attempt should be made to avoid pictures that are likely to provoke negative emotions, are too abstract and difficult to understand, or are very similar to the problem.[141] In addition, the best pictures are probably those that either show or imply motion, without emphasizing human figures.

4.61 Wildest Idea

Brainstorming groups often become stale when generating ideas for a particular problem; the range and uniqueness of ideas considered can decrease sharply after a period of time. One way a group leader might try to remedy this situation is to introduce the Wildest Idea technique. Three steps are involved:

1. The leader selects a wild idea (or asks the group to do so).
2. Using this idea as a starting point, the group then continues to generate ideas.
3. If no practical ideas emerge, another wild idea is used and the process continues until an acceptable idea is found.

As an example of using this technique, Rickards[142] describes a brainstorming problem involving different ways a company could use waste material. After brainstorming for some time, most of the ideas seemed to deal with various recycling methods. One of the group members happened to mention that the company recently had acquired another firm with an interest in lighters. This comment then gave rise to the idea of using the waste to heat the factory—a previously overlooked solution. The point is, in most discussions involving development of a specific solution, seemingly irrelevant comments or ideas will be passed by in order to focus upon the stated task. Instead, such ideas should be given at least minimal consideration by incorporating them into the brainstorming process.

Evaluation One major problem with the Wildest Idea technique is that no specific guidance is given on how wild ideas should be generated. The procedure is thus somewhat hit-or-miss in its appraoch: Free association is used to generate ideas that might or might not be useful for stimulating practical ideas. Although this technique is capable of producing highly creative solutions, it should be used when the group clearly seems to be bogged down in one particular, nonproductive line of thought. In many instances, the need for using the method might stem from a failure to adequately analyze the problem as originally stated. If, however, this is not the case, then the Wildest Idea technique might be considered along with some of the individual idea generation methods, for example, Focused-Object or Listing, as additional sources of stimulation.

COMMENTS

One of the most interesting characteristics of most group techniques in this chapter is the lack of provision for a period of incubation. The implicit assumption underlying these techniques seems to be that rapid, spontaneous idea production will lead to unique ideas while more deliberate consideration of a problem will lead to less unique ideas. (Although most of the individual techniques also do not have a built-in incubation period, the problem is less severe given the nature of individual problem solving.)

It can be argued that the minimal time requirements of most of the group techniques justify omission of a digestion period and that the large number of ideas produced will more than offset any losses due to a lack of incubation. On the other hand, a short time period for idea generation can reduce the pool of potentially useful ideas by limiting the sources of idea stimulation. When ideas are generated in a group situation, stimulation will be limited to previous experiences, the immediate environment, interaction with others (i.e., the cross-fertilization that occurs during brainstorming sessions), and specific stimulation aids included in some of the techniques (especially those that rely upon forced relationships). An extended incubation period, however, has the advantage of increasing the number and variety of stimulation sources. The method of Nonlogical Stimuli, for example, relies upon chance encounters in everyday life. Of the group techniques, only the Collective Notebook method and the Delphi method described in Chapter 7 make explicit provisions for idea incubation.

Nevertheless, neither the absence nor the presence of an incubation period is likely to be the sole determiner of idea quality or uniqueness. The use of related or unrelated problem stimuli and the conduciveness of individuals or groups to creative thinking are more likely to influence idea quality.

Perhaps the best approach would be to avoid having too little or too much time to generate ideas. This suggests using individual techniques in conjunction with group techniques and also providing for specific periods of incubation either before or after using the group techniques (and possibly both before and after). In addition, methods that do include an incubation period also might be combined with those that rely more upon spontaneous idea production. Such combinations of methods and procedures will be more likely to increase both the number and variety of ideas.

NOTES

1. Osborn, A. F. *Applied Imagination,* 3rd ed. New York: Scribner, 1963.
2. VanGundy, A. B. "A Typology of Techniques for New Product Idea Generation." Paper presented at the Sixth Annual Conference of the Product Development and Management Association, Philadelphia, Pennsylvania, 1981.
3. VanGundy, A. B. *Managing Group Creativity: A Modular Approach to Problem Solving.* New York: AMACOM, 1984.
4. As can be seen in Table 4–3, many of the techniques that use unrelated stimuli use free association. However, in all cases, these techniques also use forced relationships as an idea stimulation procedure. Thus, unrelated stimuli are listed in the classification only where a procedure is based upon forced relationships.

5. de Bono, E. *Lateral Thinking: Creativity Step by Step.* New York: Harper & Row, 1970.
6. This is not an absolute rule. However, it probably should be observed as much as possible.
7. The basic procedure involved in this step is known as a "force fit." The unrelated stimulus element generated from the analogy is force fitted with a related aspect of the problem. Formal use of the force-fit mechanism has been polularized in the Synectics technique.
8. Not all analogies have to be serious and practical. In fact, some of the most useful analogies are those that involve some element of fantasy or playfulness. This is especially important in groups where playfulness often is the key to unique ideas.
9. Dreistadt, R., "The Use of Analogies and Incubation in Obtaining Insights in Creative Problem Solving," *Journal of Psychology* 71:159–175 (1969); Gick, M. L., and Holyoak, K. J., "Analogical Problem Solving," *Cognitive Psychology* 12:306–355 (1980); Holyoak, K. J., Junn, E. N., and Billman, D. O., "Development of Analogical Problem-Solving Skill," *Child Development* 55:2042–2055 (1984); Keane, M., "On Drawing Analogies When Solving Problems: A Theory and Test of Solution Generation in an Analogical Problem-Solving Task," *British Journal of Psychology* 76:449–458 (1985).
10. Gordon, W. J. J. *Synectics.* New York: Harper & Row, 1961.
11. Grossman, S. R. "Releasing Problem Solving Energies." *Training and Development Journal* 38:94–98 (1984).
12. Koberg, D., and Bagnall, J. *The Universal Traveler.* Los Altos, Calif.: William Kaufmann, Inc., 1976.
13. de Bono, E., *op. cit.*
14. Van Gundy, A. B. "How to Get the Idea that Leads to the Product." The National New-Products Conference, Chicago, Illinois, May 8–9, 1984.
15. *Ibid.*
16. Crawford, R. P. *The Techniques of Creative Thinking.* Englewood Cliffs, N.J.: Prentice-Hall, 1954.
17. Whiting, C. S. *Creative Thinking.* New York: Van Nostrand Reinhold, 1958.
18. Goldner, B. B. *The Strategy of Creative Thinking.* Englewood Cliffs, N.J.: Prentice-Hall, 1962.
19. The Advanced Technology Staff, "Bionics," in G. A. Davis and J. A. Scott, eds., *Training Creative Thinking,* Huntington, N.Y.: Krieger, 1978; Gordon, W. J. J., *op. cit.;* Hallacy, D. S., Jr., *Bionics: The Science of "Living" Machines,* New York: Holiday House, 1965; Papanek, V. J., "Tree of Life: Bionics," in S. J. Parnes, R. B. Noller, and A. M. Biondi, *Guide to Creative Action,* rev. ed., New York: Scribner, 1977; Papanek, V. J., *Design for the Real World,* New York: Pantheon, 1972.
20. Taylor, J. W. *How to Create Ideas.* Englewood Cliffs, N.J.: Prentice-Hall, 1961.
21. *Ibid.*
22. Osborn, A. F., *op. cit.*
23. Davis, G. A., and Scott, J. A., eds., *op. cit.*
24. Davis, G. A., Roweton, W. E., Train, A. J., Warren, T. F., and Houtman, S. E. *Laboratory Studies of Creative Thinking Techniques: The Checklist and Morphological Synthesis Methods.* Technical Report No. 94, Wisconsin Research and Development Center for Cognitive Learning, University of Wisconsin, 1969.
25. Eberle, R. *Scamper: Games for Imagination Development.* Buffalo, N.Y.: D.O.K. Press, 1972.
26. Shore, S. *Creativity in Action* (monthly newsletter). Sharon, Conn.

27. VanGundy, A. B. *Product Improvement CheckList* (PICL). Point Pleasant, N.J.: Point Publishing Co., 1985a.
28. A follow-up study to the Davis et al. research reinforces this conclusion. T. F. Warren and G. A. Davis ("Techniques for Creative Thinking: An Empirical Comparison of Three Methods," *Psychological Reports* 25:207–214 (1969)) found that Morphological Synthesis (Morphological Analysis) stimulated more ideas than either short or long checklists for a problem involving improvements to a doorknob. Groups using Morphological Analysis and the short checklist produced more ideas than groups using Osborn's checklist and a control group using no specified technique.
29. Laverty, F. "Creative Idea Through Circumrelation." *Journal of Creative Behavior* 8:40–46 (1974).
30. Allen, M. S. *Morphological Creativity.* Englewood Cliffs, N.J.: Prentice-Hall, 1962.
31. Rickards, T. *Problem-Solving Through Creative Analysis.* Essex, U.K.: Gower Press, 1974.
32. VanGundy, A. B. *108 Ways to Get a Bright Idea.* Englewood Cliffs, N.J.: Prentice-Hall, 1983.
33. Higbee, K. L., and Millard, R. J. "Visual Imagery and Familiarity Ratings for 203 Sayings." *American Journal of Psychology* 96:211–222 (1983).
34. See, for example, Bry, A., with Bair, M., *Visualization: Directing the Movies of Your Mind,* New York: Barnes & Noble, 1978; Gawain, S., *Creative Visualization,* Mill Valley, Calif.: Whatever Publishing, 1978; McKim, R. H., *Experiences in Visual Thinking,* Monterey, Calif.: Brooks/Cole, 1972.
35. VanGundy, A. B., *op. cit.,* 1983.
36. See, for example, Olson, R. W., *The Art of Creative Thinking,* New York: Barnes & Noble, 1980; VanGundy, A. B., *op. cit.,* 1983, 1984.
37. Whiting, C. S., *op. cit.*
38. Taylor, J. W., *op. cit.*
39. *Ibid.*
40. Tauber, E. M. "HIT: Heuristic Ideation Technique–A Systematic Procedure for New Product Search." *Journal of Marketing* 36:58–61 (1972).
41. Arnold, J. E. "The Creative Engineer." *Yale Scientific Magazine,* 12–23 (March 1956).
42. Whiting, C. S., *op. cit.*
43. Jensen, J. V. "A Heuristic for the Analysis of the Nature and Extent of a Problem." *Journal of Creative Behavior* 12:168–180 (1978).
44. VanGundy, A. B. "The New Product Creative Process." *The National New-Products Conference,* Chicago, Illinois, May 1–2, 1985b.
45. Zwicky, F. *Discovery, Invention, Research Through the Morphological Approach.* New York: Macmillan, 1969.
46. Allen, M. S., *op. cit.*
47. Geschka, H., von Reibnitz, U., and Storvik, K. *Idea Generation Methods: Creative Solutions to Business and Technical Problems.* Columbus, Ohio: Battelle Memorial Institute, 1981.
48. *Ibid.*
49. Allen, M. S., *op. cit.*
50. Geschka, H., Schaude, G. R., and Schlicksupp, H. "Modern Techniques for Solving Problems." *Chemical Engineering,* 91–97 (August 1973).
51. Geschka, H., von Reibnitz, U., and Storvik, K., *op. cit.*
52. Tarr, G. *The Management of Problem Solving.* New York: Wiley, 1973.
53. Rickards, T., *op. cit.*
54. de Bono, E., *op. cit.*
55. VanGundy, A. B., *op. cit.,* 1985a.

56. Crovitz, H. F. *Galton's Walk*. New York: Harper & Row, 1970.
57. Duncker, K. "On Problem Solving." Translated by L. S. Lees. *Psychological Monographs* 58:No. 5 (1945).
58. de Bono, E., *op. cit.*
59. VanGundy, A. B. *Stalking the Wild Solution: A Problem-Finding Approach to Creative Problem Solving*. Buffalo, N.Y.: Bearly Limited, 1987.
60. VanGundy, A. B., *op. cit.*, 1983.
61. Modified from VanGundy, A. B. *Ibid.*
62. Olson, R. W., *op. cit.*
63. Rickards, T., *op. cit.*
64. VanGundy, A. B., *op. cit.*, 1983.
65. A "word triangle" can be used if only three key words or phrases are available. Of course, a five-sided figure also can be constructed.
66. Geschka, H., von Reibnitz, U., and Storvik, K., *op. cit.*
67. *Ibid.*; Warfield, J. N., with Geschka, H., and Hamilton, R., *Methods of Idea Management*, Columbus, Ohio: The Academy for Contemporary Problems, 1975.
68. Geschka, H., von Reibnitz, U., and Storvik, K., *op. cit.*
69. Some support for the stimulus value of pictures in idea generation has been found in a recent study (Rothenberg, A., "Artistic Creation as Stimulated by Superimposed Versus Combined-Composite Visual Images," *Journal of Personality and Social Psychology* 50:370–381 (1986).
70. VanGundy, A. B. From a course taught on creative problem solving, University of Oklahoma, Norman, Oklahoma, 1980.
71. Adams, J. L. *Conceptual Blockbusting: A Guide to Better Ideas,* 2nd ed. New York: Norton, 1979.
72. Woods, M. "The Brainwriting Game." *Creativity Network* 5:7–12 (1979).
73. Geschka, H., Schaude, G. R., and Schlicksupp, H., *op. cit.*; Warfield, J. N., Geschka, H., and Hamilton, R., *op. cit.*
74. Geschka, H. *Methods and Organization of Idea Generation.* Paper presented at Creativity Development Week II, Center for Creative Leadership, Greensboro, North Carolina, September 1979.
75. Osborn, A. F., *op. cit.*
76. *Ibid.*
77. Stein, M. I. *Stimulating Creativity, Volume 2, Group Procedures.* New York: Academic Press, 1975. Studies drawn upon by Stein include Bouchard, T. J., Jr., "A Comparison of Two Group Brainstorming Procedures," *Journal of Applied Psychology* 56:418–421 (1972); Campbell, J. P., "Individual Versus Group Problem Solving in an Industrial Sample," *Journal of Applied Psychology* 52:205–210 (1968); Dunnette, M. D., Campbell, J. P., and Jaastad, O., "The Effects of Group Participation on Brainstorming Effectiveness for Two Industrial Samples," *Journal of Applied Psychology* 47: 10–37 (1963); Parnes, S. J., and Meadow, A., "Development of Individual Creativity Talent," in C. W. Taylor, and F. Barron, eds., *Scientific Creativity: Its Recognition and Development,* New York: Wiley, 1963; Taylor, D. W., Berry, P. C., and Block, C. H., "Does Group Participation When Using Brainstorming Facilitate or Inhibit Creative Thinking?" *Administrative Science Quarterly* 3:23–47 (1958).
78. Much of the research since Stein's analysis has resulted in essentially the same conclusions. Examples of these more recent studies include Jablin, F. M., "Cultivating Imagination: Factors That Enhance and Inhibit Creativity in Brainstorming Groups," *Human Communication Research* 7:245–258 (1981); Madsen, D. B., and Finger, S. R., Jr., "Comparison of Written Feedback Procedure, Group Brainstorming, and Individual

Brainstorming," *Journal of Applied Psychology* 63:120–123 (1978); Maginn, B. K., and Harris, R. J., "Effects of Anticipated Evaluation on Individual Brainstorming Performance," *Journal of Applied Psychology* 65:219–225 (1980); Street, W. R., "Brainstorming by Individuals, Coacting and Interacting Groups." *Journal of Applied Psychology* 59:433–436 (1974).

79. Bouchard, T. J. Jr. "Training, Motivation, and Personality as Determinants of the Effectiveness of Brainstorming Groups and Individuals." *Journal of Applied Psychology* 56:324–331 (1972).

80. Burns, M. G. "A Comparison of Three Creative Problem-Solving Methodologies." *Dissertation Abstracts International* 45:341A (1984).

81. Wakin, E. "Component Detailing." Presentation at the 31st Annual Creative Problem Solving Institute, Buffalo, New York, June 1985.

82. Haefele, J. W. *Creativity and Innovation.* New York: Van Nostrand Reinhold, 1962.

83. Pearson, A. W. "Communication, Creativity, and Commitment: A Look at the Collective Notebook Approach." In S. S. Gryskiewicz, ed. *Proceedings of Creativity Week I, 1978.* Greensboro, N.C.: Center for Creative Leadership, 1979.

84. *Ibid.*

85. Crawford, C., and Demidovich, J. *Crawford Slip Writing Method: How to Mobilize Brainpower by Think Tank Technology.* Los Angeles, Calif.: School of Public Administration, University of Southern California, 1983. For another description, see Whiting, C. S., *op. cit.*

86. Crawford, C. C., Demidovich, J. W., and Krone, R. M. *Productivity Improvement by the Crawford Slip Method: How to Write, Publish, Instruct, Supervise, and Manage for Better Job Performance.* Los Angeles, Calif.: School of Public Administration, University of Southern California, 1984.

87. Clark, C. H. *The Crawford Slip Writing Method.* Kent, Ohio: Charles H. Clark, 1978.

88. Warfield, J. N., et al., *op. cit.*

89. Geschka, H., *op. cit.*

90. Parnes, S. J., Noller, R. B., and Biondi, A. M., *Guide to Creative Action,* rev. ed. New York: Scribner, 1977.

91. VanGundy, A. B. University of Oklahoma, Norman, Oklahoma, 1986.

92. Taylor, J. W., *op. cit.*

93. Whiting, C. S. *op. cit.*

94. Pickens, J. F. Personal communication, 1985.

95. VanGundy, A. B. *Creative Problem Solving: A Guide for Trainers and Management.* Westport, Conn.: Quorum Books, 1987.

96. Warfield, J. N., et al., *op. cit.*

97. Geschka, H., *op. cit.* According to Geschka et al. (Geschka, H., von Reibnitz, U., and Storvik, K., *op. cit.*) Method 6-3-5 was the first brainwriting technique developed. However, some creativity consultants dispute this claim. It also is interesting to note that Geschka, von Reibnitz, and Storvik describe the same version used by Warfield et al.

98. Rickards, T., *op. cit.*

99. Geschka, H., *op. cit.*

100. Phillips, D. J. "Report on Discussion 66." *Adult Education Journal* 7:181–182 (1948).

101. Maier, N. R. F. *Problem Solving Discussions and Conferences.* New York: McGraw-Hill, 1963.

102. *Ibid.*

103. Geschka, H., *op. cit.*

104. *Ibid;* Geschka, H., von Reibnitz, U., and Storvik, K., *op. cit.*

105. Osborn, A. F., *op. cit.*

106. Tauber, E. M. "Discovering New Product Opportunities with Problem Inventory Analysis." *Journal of Marketing* 39:67–70 (1975).
107. Griggs, R. E. "A Storm of Ideas." Reported in *Training* 22:66 (November 1985).
108. Faafeng, O. Personal Communication. Norwegian Management Institute, Oslo, Norway, 1986.
109. Parnes, S. J., Noller, R. B., and Biondi, A. M., *op. cit.*
110. Schaude, G. R. "Methods of Idea Generation." In S. S. Gryskiewicz, ed. *Proceedings of Creativity Week I, 1978.* Greensboro, N.C.: Center for Creative Leadership, 1979.
111. Brooks, J. D. *Review of Operational Mechanisms for Innovative Management Course.* Industrial Studies Program, U. S. Steel Corporation, Pittsburgh, Pennsylvania (no date), p. 3.
112. Souder, W. E., and Ziegler, R. W. "A Review of Creativity and Problem Solving Techniques." *Research Management,* 34–42 (July 1977).
113. Souder, W. E., and O'Keefe, W. M. *Fourteen Useful Techniques for Technical Problem Solving and Creative Thinking.* Technical report funded by the National Science Foundation and the U. S. Agency for International Development, University of Pittsburgh, Pittsburgh, Pennsylvania, 1979.
114. Although SIL uses brainwriting to generate the initial ideas, the Battelle group in Frankfurt has classified it as a brainstorming variation since the major activity of the method is conducted verbally.
115. Warfield, J. N., et al., *op. cit.*
116. Adapted from Schaude, G. R., *op. cit.*
117. Smithers, L. E. *The Story Board.* Hudson, Ohio: The Creative Thinking Center, Inc., 1984.
118. Roth, W. F., Jr. *Problem Solving for Managers.* New York: Praeger, 1985.
119. Smithers, L. E., *op. cit.* The arrangement of the cards for the Creative Thinking approach is identical to that used by Vance. The major difference is in the names given the various types of cards (e.g., headers and subbers) and the use of a required "purpose" card with the Creative Thinking version. Thus, Fig. 4–10 also illustrates the general format of the Creative Thinking Story Board approach.
120. Bauer & Associates. *The Participant's Guide to FASTTRACK.* Ann Arbor, Michigan: Bauer & Associates, 1985. Other related publications by Bauer & Associates include: *The FASTTRACK Facilitator, FASTTRACK, Beyond the Basics, and ACTION-TRACK, Getting It Done Now.*
121. Conway/Miliken & Associates. *Conway/Miliken Communications* 4(2):1–3 (1986).
122. Creative ability is measured using creativity tests developed by E. Paul Torrance (e.g., *Thinking Creatively with Pictures* and *Thinking Creatively with Words.* Scholastic Testing Service, Inc., 1966).
123. Grossman, S., and Catlin, K. *Super Heroes.* Presentation at the 31st Annual Creative Problem Solving Institute. Buffalo, N.Y.: The Creative Education Foundation, 1985.
124. Gordon, W. J. J., *op. cit.*
125. Prince, G. M. "The Operational Mechanism of Synectics." *Journal of Creative Behavior* 2:1–13 (1968).
126. Gordon, W. J. J., *op. cit.*
127. Stein, M. I., *op. cit.*
128. Gordon, W. J. J., *op. cit.*
129. Prince, G. M., *op. cit.*
130. Prince, G. M. "The Mindspring Theory: A New Development from Synectics Research." *Journal of Creative Behavior* 9:159–181 (1975).
131. Khatena, J. "The Use of Analogy in the Production of Original Verbal Images." *Journal of Creative Behavior* 6:209–213 (1972).

132. Khatena, J., "Onomatopoeia and Images: Preliminary Validity Study of a Test of Originality," *Perceptual and Motor Skills* 28:235–238 (1969); "Note on Reliability and Validity of Onomatopoeia and Images," *Perceptual and Motor Skills* 31:86 (1970).

133. Bouchard, T. J., Jr. "A Comparison of Two Group Brainstorming Procedures." *Journal of Applied Psychology* 56:418–421 (1972).

134. Klimoski, R. J., and Karol, B. L. "The Impact of Trust on Creative Problem Solving Groups." *Journal of Applied Psychology* 61:630–633 (1976).

135. Thamia, S., and Woods, M. F. "A Systematic Small Group Approach to Creativity and Innovation: A Case Study." *R & D Management* 14:25–35 (1984).

136. Bosticco, M. *Creative Techniques for Management.* London: Basic Books, 1971.

137. Bujake, J. E. "Programmed Innovation in New Product Development." *Research Management* 12:279–287 (1969).

138. Adapted from Schaude, G. R., *op. cit.*

139. More recently, Geshcka (Geschka, H., personal communication, 1986) has suggested that a series of pictures be shown before the primary stimulus pictures. These initial pictures also should be unrelated to the problem. However, they are intended to help relax the participants and put them in a frame of mind conducive to creative thinking using pictures. Therefore, they should be abstract without as much detail as the primary stimulus pictures. The primary pictures should contain scenes with easily identified objects, such as street scenes, a boat on a river, and so forth. The initial pictures, in contrast, should be general nature scenes, such as leaves on a tree or a beautiful sunset. Typically, the initial pictures will be more appealing aesthetically.

140. *Ibid.*

141. Geshcka, G., von Reibnitz, U., and Storvik, K., *op. cit.*

142. Rickards, T., *op. cit.*

5
Evaluating and Selecting
Ideas

Of the different problem-solving stages, decision making has received the most attention in the academic literature. Moreover, a substantial portion of this literature has been devoted to describing how or why people make decisions, rather than what they should do. Although both descriptive and prescriptive approaches are important, the techniques in this chapter emphasize alternative ways for individuals and groups to evaluate a pool of ideas and select the ones most likely to produce the best solution. As a result, these techniques are not necessarily representative of all the techniques available. Furthermore, methods that are highly quantitative in nature have been avoided. Such methods are more useful for well-structured problems that permit a rational ordering of solution alternatives. The techniques in this chapter, in contrast, have been selected for their applicability to ill-structured problems that require creative solutions. This is not to say that no quantitative procedures have been used; 11 of the techniques use some form of quantitative rating or voting. What have been excluded are techniques that emphasize sophisticated probability estimates.

The 16 techniques that follow can be classified according to their appropriateness for either individuals or groups and their emphasis on either idea evaluation or selection. Seven of the techniques can be classified as being suitable only for groups: Castle Technique, Electronic Voting, Goalstorming, Idea Advocate, Panel Consensus, SPAN Voting, and Sticking Dots. It should be noted that the Panel Consensus technique was developed specifically for use by groups in hierarchical organizations and is not appropriate for use by individuals or a single group of individuals. The remaining techniques will be appropriate for either individuals or groups. Classification of the techniques with regard to evaluation and selection is a difficult task, since most of them combine both activities, first evaluating the alternatives and then providing a way for selecting the best solution. The Castle Technique, Electronic Voting, SPAN Voting, and Sticking Dots, however, would be exceptions since they were designed solely for group voting, with no emphasis upon evaluation.

5.01 Advantage-Disadvantage

This technique is perhaps the most simple and basic of all the evaluation methods. It is also the approach that probably is used most frequently, although not necessarily most effectively. The process typically used is one of listing all the available alternatives, examining the strengths and weaknesses of each, and then selecting the one that best fulfills the problem objectives. Sometimes, this process is further simplified to an examination of each alternative in sequence. That is, during the search for alternatives, the first alternative identified is analyzed with regard to its advantages and disadvantages, and then either rejected or accepted as the problem solution. If the alternative is rejected, then another alternative is selected, analyzed, and accepted or, if rejected, the process is repeated until an acceptable alternative is located. Of the two approaches, the one that attempts to identify all the available alternatives before evaluating them is the one most likely to result in a high-quality solution. The second approach, in which alternatives are evaluated in sequence, is likely to produce a satisfactory solution but not necessarily a high-quality one.

One version of the Advantage-Disadvantage approach involves the following steps:

1. For each alternative, construct a separate table containing three columns.
2. Over the first column, write down the word *Criteria;* over the second column, the word *Advantages;* and over the third column, the word *Disadvantages.*
3. Under the first column, list all of the relevant criteria associated with all of the alternatives.
4. For each criterion, place a check mark in either the second or third column to signify that the criterion is either an advantage or disadvantage.
5. Repeat the entire process for all of the available alternatives.
6. Count the total number of advantages and disadvantages checked for each alternative.
7. Select the alternative receiving the greatest number of checks under the Advantages column.

An example of this procedure is shown in Table 5-1. The problem facing the decision maker is to choose between two job offers that would require a move to a different city. Four advantages are checked for Alternative A and five for Alternative B. If the procedure is strictly followed, the job in Cleveland will be chosen over the job in Dallas. Note that, in this example, only two alternatives are available and it probably was not necessary to construct two separate tables. When there are a large number of alternatives, however, separate tables should be used.

Table 5–1. Example of the Advantage-Disadvantage Technique.

Alternative A

- Dallas -

CRITERIA	ADVANTAGES	DISADVANTAGES
Climate	✔	
Salary		✔
Housing		✔
Schools	✔	
Promotion Opportunities		✔
Public Transportation		✔
Taxes	✔	
Job Responsibilities		✔
Entertainment	✔	
TOTAL:	4	5

Alternative B

- Cleveland -

CRITERIA	ADVANTAGES	DISADVANTAGES
Climate		✔
Salary	✔	
Housing		✔
Schools		✔
Promotion Opportunities	✔	
Public Transportation	✔	
Taxes		✔
Job Responsibilities	✔	
Entertainment	✔	
TOTAL:	5	4

Evaluation   Except for possible use as a preliminary assessment device, the Advantage-Disadvantage technique has little merit as an idea selection approach. A primary weakness is its assumption that all the criteria are equal in weight. In the example described, for instance, it is unlikely that most persons would consider entertainment possibilities in a city to be equal in value with job salary. A second, although lesser, difficulty lies in the quality of the criteria. If any relevant criteria are omitted from consideration, the quality of the final decision is likely to suffer. This is, of course, a drawback associated with all decision-making techniques.

5.02 Battelle Method

The Battelle Method for selecting ideas was developed by H. Ronald Hamilton[1] and his colleagues at the Battelle Institute in Columbus, Ohio. Although originally designed for screening business development opportunities, the method also is useful for screening ideas from other areas.

The Battelle Method represents the second stage in a three-stage corporate development process described by Hamilton. The first stage consists of the identification and generation of ideas and uses Classical Brainstorming as the primary method. This stage is followed by an idea-screening process in which a large number of ideas are filtered and then a few are selected for more in-depth analysis. What has been termed the Battelle Method is drawn from this second stage. In the final stage, ideas surviving the screening process are then subjected to intensive evaluation. The Battelle Method is implemented using the following steps:

1. Generate ideas using Classical Brainstorming.
2. Develop *culling* criteria (low-cost screens) that can be answered with a yes or no response.
   a. If practical, group the culling criteria into successive screening stages.
   b. Compare every idea with each of the criteria.
   c. Eliminate those ideas receiving a no response to any one of the criteria within a screening stage (or to any one criterion if stages are not used).
3. Develop *rating* criteria (medium-cost screens) that can be answered with a yes or no response.
   a. Group the rating criteria into cost-homogeneous units.
   b. Establish a minimally acceptable passing score for each unit.
   c. Eliminate ideas that survived the culling criteria but fall below the minimum score for rating criteria.
4. Develop *scoring* criteria (high-cost screens) using quantitative or qualitative value ranges.
   a. Group the scoring criteria into cost-homogeneous units.
   b. Establish a minimally acceptable passing score for each unit.
   c. Assign a weight to each of the criterion responses and to the criteria themselves.
   d. Using ideas that survived the rating stage, select a value for each criterion and multiply it by the weight of the criterion.
   e. Sum the totals of the criterion scores and compare them with the minimum score.
   f. Eliminate ideas falling below the minimum score.
5. Conduct an in-depth analysis of the surviving ideas and select the most promising one(s).

The basic principle underlying the Battelle Method is that low-cost screens should be applied first, followed by progressively higher-cost screens. The cost of a given screen is determined by the investment in resources required to obtain

Table 5-2. Using Screens to Evaluate a Proposed Apartment Development.

CULLING SCREENS				Yes	No
1. Is the area presently saturated with other similar units?					X
2. Is the present turnover rate of units more than 10 percent?					X
3. Is the population of the market area over 100,000?				X	
			Minimum score is 1.		
			Pass to next stage? Yes	X No	

RATING SCREENS				Yes	No
1. Can the required land be obtained?				X	
2. Can the land be developed within estimated costs?				X	
3. Is the proposed site within commuting distance of at least 30 percent of the market area?					X
			Minimum score is 2.	2 Yes	1 No
			Pass to next stage? Yes	X No	

SCORING SCREENS					
1. Likely return on	Poor	Fair	Good	Weight	Total
investment	1	②	3	3	6
2. Possibility of *no*	Poor	Fair	Good		
cost overruns?	1	2	③	2	6
3. Projected growth	0–4%	5–9%	10% +		
rate of market?	1	2	③	2	6
					18
		Minimum score is 18.	Pass	X Reject	

the information necessary to evaluate an idea. For example, determining if an idea requires an extensive capital investment might represent a low-cost screen if this information can be easily obtained. Determining the potential profit structure, in contrast, might require a higher-cost screen if extensive studies are needed. When a large number of ideas are to be evaluated, it is more logical to eliminate first those ideas that can be more simply evaluated. The pool of ideas then can be reduced considerably, requiring fewer comparisons for subsequent screens. Hamilton cautions, however, that low-cost screens might not always be appropriate. Different evaluation criteria might possess different weights, and the costs of applying a highly weighted criterion and initially eliminating a large number of ideas also must be considered.

Some examples of screens that might be used in developing an apartment complex are presented in Table 5-2. A single-stage culling screen is used in this example in which any ideas not receiving at least one yes response are to be eliminated. The surviving ideas are then subjected to the questions described in the rating form. (This particular list is intended to represent a single cost-homogeneous unit.) Although not shown, numerically rated responses also could be used when considered appropriate for certain criteria—especially those for which it is difficult to establish a yes or no response.

It should be apparent that there will not always be much difference between culling and rating questions. In practice, the difference between the two types of screens is likely to vary as a function of a particular organization's objectives and philosophy. Nevertheless, in developing such questions, it should be remembered that rating criteria generally will be more expensive than culling criteria. From experience in using the Battelle Method, Hamilton reports that rating criteria generally will be ten times more costly than culling criteria; scoring criteria will be two and one-half to ten times more costly than rating criteria and 25 to 100 times more costly than culling criteria.

Those ideas surviving the rating screens are then subjected to a scoring stage. These criteria should be highest in cost relative to the other screens and are typically provided with weights to assist in their evaluation. As shown in Table 5–2, one of the range of values for each criterion has been selected and that value then multiplied by the overall weight for that criterion to obtain a total score. The total scores are then summed and compared with the minimum passing score.

Hamilton offers three tips for using this method: (1) Avoid second-guessing ideas that have been eliminated, (2) do not use the screening process to prove why an eliminated idea should have been rejected, and (3) senior executives should be counseled to avoid giving the impression that their pet ideas require special consideration. All of these tips seem to emphasize that, in order for the method to work, there is little room for personal and/or emotional entanglements.

Evaluation The Battelle Method has certain strengths and weaknesses that should be considered before using it to select ideas. The major advantage of the technique probably lies in its ability to systematically process a large number of ideas in a cost-efficient manner. Because most organizations or departments can only afford to intensively evaluate a few ideas, the use of progressively expensive screens—and the subsequent reduction in the total pool of ideas—allows for a more efficient use of resources. Thus, the evaluation process can be speeded up considerably. The most important benefit, however, is that the method provides structure for a process that is typically handled in a less-than-systematic manner.

There are also several weaknesses that could detract from the method's effectiveness. First, a certain amount of specialized knowledge is required to develop criteria appropriate for a particular stage and to determine whether or not the criteria are interchangeable between stages. Second, some types of ideas might not be suitable for the method or might not justify using the procedure. If only a few ideas have been generated or if the ideas are relatively inexpensive to evaluate, a less complex technique should be used. Third, the definition of what constitutes a cost-homogeneous unit might be difficult to develop for some types of criteria. This difficulty would make it hard to determine how many units to use within a screening stage and, thus, might affect the outcome of the process. Fourth, if upper management is not totally committed to the process or tries to force pet ideas, the method will lose much of its objectivity. Fifth, the process can be considerably hindered by any personality clashes between team members, or if some persons in the group have their own pet ideas. Finally, like any evaluation and screening method, the eventual success of the process will depend upon the quality of the initial problem definition and the ideas generated.

In summary, the Battelle Method is likely to be most effective when (1) a large number of relatively costly ideas need to be evaluated, and (2) the method has the support of top management and the persons involved in implementing it.

5.03 Castle Technique

Many groups have difficulty achieving consensus during decision making. One reason for this may be an overemphasis on finding the one "right" problem solution. To counter this tendency, O'Rourke[2] suggests using the Castle Technique.

This technique was named after its originator, Derek Castle. There are five steps involved for the group leader:

1. Establish a time limit (one hour usually is sufficient).
2. Inform the group that three criteria will be used to evaluate each idea: acceptability (the extent to which an idea satisfies existing goals), practicality (the extent to which an idea satisfies previously established financial and time constraints), and originality (the extent to which an idea makes a significant improvement and provides an elegant solution).
3. Number each idea listed. Give each group member the same number of votes as there are ideas (e.g., if there are 50 ideas, each person receives 50 votes). Instruct group members to vote for each idea with either a yes or a no vote. Votes may not be saved up to use on a favorite idea.
4. Conduct the vote by pointing to each idea in turn and asking the group members to vote either yes or no. No discussion about the ideas is permitted.
5. Point to the two ideas that received the largest number of votes and ask the group to combine these ideas into one idea.

Evaluation   According to O'Rourke, the Castle Technique has the following advantages: (1) group members have equal input into the process of selecting the final idea, (2) the combined idea usually will be better than any of the original ideas, and (3) the high degree of solution ownership created helps insure implementation success. She also notes that setting a time limit allows the group to focus its energies more easily and defers the need to make an immediate decision. The Castle Technique also has the advantages of being simple to use and implement, requires few leader facilitation skills, and uses explicit evaluation criteria. And, like other "pure" voting techniques, the Castle Technique can be useful when there is little time available. The primary weakness of this method is the lack of opportunity for group members to discuss the ideas. Not having this chance to verbally interact and ponder the merits of each idea may result in a low-quality solution. Of course, the Castle Technique was intended to overcome the difficulties in achieving consensus that often occur during such discussions. Thus, the lack of discussion will be a weakness only in groups that have little trouble achieving consensus.

5.04 Creative Evaluation

This is a relatively simple technique that was designed to assist in the organization and evaluation of a large number of ideas. It was developed by Leo Moore[3] to meet a need for a structured approach to the evaluation of ideas generated by brainstorming groups. According to Moore, most brainstorming groups are highly successful in developing ideas but experience considerable difficulty when it comes to selecting from among the ideas generated. In addition, the technique was designed to serve as an idea-screening device for managers who require usable ideas but have little time to spend in sorting through a large number of solution possibilities. Thus, instead of a group generating a large number of ideas and then dumping them on a manager to evaluate, Creative Evaluation attempts to present ideas in a format that will reduce the amount of time required for evaluation. To do this, all ideas are evaluated (by a brainstorming group) in terms of their time and money requirements using the following procedure:

1. A list is made of the ideas generated during the brainstorming session.
2. Using Roman numerals, the group categorizes each idea in one of three ways: I (simple), II (hard), and III (difficult). Simple ideas are those that can be implemented with a minimum expenditure of time and money, hard ideas require a slightly greater expenditure, and difficult ideas require the greatest expenditure.
3. The idea categories are presented to management for additional evaluation.

Evaluation   According to Moore, Creative Evaluation possesses four major advantages: (1) A large number of ideas can be quickly evaluated, (2) the categorization of ideas often will reveal previously unconsidered associations and provide suggestions for new ideas, (3) the idea groupings provide a natural action plan by indicating the order in which the ideas might be implemented (category I ideas would be implemented first, followed by category II and then category III ideas), and (4) the brainstorming group is more likely to become involved in implementation and follow-up of the ideas.

While it is true that ideas can be quickly evaluated using this technique, there is little evidence available (other than anecdotal reports) to attest to the quality and usefulness of the procedure. Obviously, the criteria of time and money will be useful when they are important to the problem situation. Other criteria, however, might be more important for different problem situations. Such criteria as return on investment, technical adequacy, resource availability, reliability, and marketability all could take precedence over or be of equal importance with time and money considerations. Furthermore, using the categorization scheme to guide the implementation of ideas could lead to undesirable outcomes. The fact that an idea requires little time or money to implement should not be used as the sole criterion to determine its order of appearance in an action plan. In most cases, the particular characteristics and requirements of a problem should be used to make this determination.

Even if time and money are judged to be sufficient criteria, the technique apparently relies upon purely subjective estimates of idea difficulty. For most ideas, the evaluation costs will vary considerably. Thus, while some ideas can be easily categorized in terms of their difficulty, the information needed to categorize other ideas will be more costly to obtain. For example, the capital required to produce and market Product A might be quickly calculated using existing data; to project the investment required for Product B, however, a rather lengthy and complex series of calculations might be required. In addition, agreement on the idea categories might not be easily obtained in some groups. If, for example, some group members have a vested interest in an idea, they might be more likely to categorize it as simple to implement. As with all problem-solving groups, considerable attention must be given to group composition.

In general, Creative Evaluation would seem to be most appropriate for a cursory examination of a large number of ideas. Even then, it is most suitable for problems for which time and money are of primary importance (although other criteria could be substituted). However, because of its failure to include an evaluation of the costs involved in obtaining information, an approach using low- and high-cost screens (such as the Battelle Method) might be considered as an alternative.

5.05 Decision Balance Sheet

The Decision Balance Sheet was originally developed by Janis[4] and later expanded upon by Janis and Mann.[5] It was designed to assist individuals in making important decisions by providing a structured format for exploring all relevant alternatives and evaluating the benefits and costs associated with each. Although it has been used primarily in the areas of career choice and health-related decisions, the procedure should be useful for a variety of other decision situations. The balance-sheet procedure involves an analysis of each alternative in terms of four categories of expected consequences:

1. Tangible Gains and Losses for Self. Included in this category are all of the possible effects expected by an individual when choosing a particular alternative. For example, an individual might be in conflict over two alternatives: (1) to continue smoking, or (2) to stop smoking. The expected gains and losses from the first alternative might be receiving daily pleasure but facing the possibility of developing lung cancer. For the second alternative, to stop smoking, the possibility of not getting lung cancer could be listed as a gain while unpleasant feelings and irritability could be listed as losses.

2. Tangible Gains and Losses for Others. The factors in this category pertain to the goals of significant others. A gain that might be expected from a decision to continue smoking would be continued good relations with family and friends, while a loss would be the effects upon the smoker's family should he or she die.

3. Self-Approval or Self-Disapproval. The considerations in this category involve the feelings that people will have about themselves if they make a particular choice. The smoker might expect to feel self-satisfied by quitting smoking but feel guilty if he or she becomes irritable with others.

4. Social Approval or Disapproval. This category pertains to the feelings of significant others who are likely to evaluate either the final decision or the decision maker's competence as a decision maker. If the smoker stops smoking, then friends and family will be expected to approve. A statistician friend of the smoker, in contrast, might disapprove of a decision made on the basis of causation inferred from statistical correlations between smoking and lung cancer.

The procedure for using the Decision Balance Sheet method involves the following steps (adapted and modified from those described by Janis and Mann[6]):

1. On a sheet of paper, list all the alternatives that have been seriously considered.
2. Rank the alternatives in terms of personal preferences, listing the most preferred alternative first, the next most preferred alternative second, and so forth until all the alternatives have been ranked.
3. Select the top two alternatives and think of the positive and negative points of each. List these points and try to think of any other considerations. If necessary, assume that an immediate decision is required and try to list all the relevant pros and cons for the two alternatives.
4. Construct a balance sheet grid for all the alternatives. As shown in Table 5-3, each grid should contain twelve cells arranged into three columns and four rows. The names of the four categories of expected consequences are placed in the first cell of each row. The heading *Positive Anticipations +* is written above the second column, and the heading *Negative Anticipations −* is written above the third column.

Table 5–3. The Balance Sheet Grid.

ALTERNATIVE # _____

	POSITIVE ANTICIPATIONS +	NEGATIVE ANTICIPATIONS −
1. Tangible gains + and losses − for SELF		
2. Tangible gains + and losses − for OTHERS		
3. Self-approval + or Disapproval −		
4. Social approval + or disapproval −		

5. Using the positive and negative features identified for the two alternatives in step 3, fill in a separate grid sheet for both alternatives. Then, fill in the sheets for the remaining alternatives.
6. Review all the grid sheets and try to think of any other considerations that should be included.
7. If possible, develop or obtain a list of pertinent considerations to assist in exploring any neglected pros and cons of the various alternatives. This list can be developed by consulting an expert in the field or reviewing pertinent literature.

8. Group the pertinent considerations into the four category areas and examine the list to determine if any new gains or losses might be suggested. Do this by examining each category in sequence for each alternative.
9. Write down any new considerations in the appropriate cell of each balance sheet. If a consideration does not seem to fit easily into one of the four categories, try to list it in the appropriate positive or negative column, without regard to category type.
10. Using a seven-point scale ranging from hardly important at all (1) to extremely important (7), rate each of the considerations within each cell of every balance sheet.
11. Review the alternatives identified and try to think of any new alternatives that should be included in the analysis. If any new alternatives are are identified, repeat steps 4 through 10. In addition, determine if any of the alternatives should be combined or modified and, if so, repeat steps 4 through 10.
12. Review all the balance sheets and again rank all the alternatives in order of preference. This ranking should be considered tentative since new information about the alternative consequences might be obtained before a decision is required, or second thoughts might develop about some of the alternatives.
13. When a decision must be made, select the best alternative for implementation.

Evaluation   The major strength of this technique lies in the systematic manner in which it forces the decision maker to examine fully an expanded range of alternatives and their expected consequences. The format seems to help stimulate the search for relevant considerations in order to prevent the omission of any alternatives that might result in a high-quality decision. As a result, decision makers should experience less anxiety about their choices and decision outcomes once they have implemented a decision. Such a conclusion has been supported by some research evidence. Based upon ten different studies involving the Decision Balance Sheet (with the assistance of a trained counselor), most subjects who used the procedure reported less postdecisional stress than subjects who did not use the procedure.[7] The effects of the procedure when a counselor is not used are less well known, although it would be expected that greater anxiety would be experienced. The use of a disinterested person—whether trained or untrained—to help guide consideration of the alternatives and their consequences might help to overcome this drawback to some degree.

There is also some evidence that individuals using the procedure will be more committed to a chosen course of action. In one study, for example, Hoyt and Janis[8] compared the attendance records of 40 women who had enrolled for an early-morning exercise class. Half of the women were randomly assigned to a group that used the balance-sheet method to evaluate the pros and cons of regular participation in the class. The remaining 20 women (the control group) used the identical procedure to identify the advantages and disadvantages of smoking cigarettes. After seven weeks of the class, the attendance rate for the women who had filled out a balance sheet relevant to the class was almost twice that of the group who had participated in the irrelevant procedure involving smoking.

In addition to these strengths, there are at least two other advantages associated with the balance-sheet procedure. Because a written record is made of the consequences related to all the alternatives, it is relatively easy to evaluate an implemented decision. Such follow-up can be valuable for making any needed adjustments as well as facilitating the decision-making process should a similar problem arise in the future. The other advantage stems from the two categories for evaluating approval and disapproval of self and significant others. Such nonutilitarian considerations are often neglected in other problem-solving models. Although they will not be a factor in all problems to the same degree, they are a useful addition to the decision-making process.

For effective results in using the technique, however, several considerations must be taken into account. First, all the cells for a given alternative must be filled in completely and accurately. There must be a corresponding negative consequence for each positive consideration listed. Second, the procedure is probably most useful for important decisions, that is, situations in which the choice of alternatives is likely to have a significant impact upon one's self or others. Finally, some persons might find it helpful to use a trained counselor or disinterested second party when analyzing the alternatives. In addition to possibly providing a fresh perspective on the decision, this person also could help insure that the procedure is followed correctly.

It also would be interesting to adapt the procedure to group decision-making situations. Although originally designed and tested with individuals, group decision making also might benefit from some of the procedure's strengths. One approach, for example, would be to have individuals fill out the balance sheets, compare results with other group members, reevaluate their own sheets, and continue this process until some form of consensus is achieved. A final decision then could be made using consensual weightings of the consequences and voting on the alternatives.

One way to summarize the advantages and disadvantages of the Decision Balance Sheet procedure would be to fill in a balance-sheet grid. This has been done in Table 5–4 and is self-explanatory. If other selection techniques were under consideration as alternative procedures, then similar sheets could be completed for each technique.

5.06 Disjointed Incrementalism

This technique was originally developed by Braybrooke and Lindblom[9] as a strategy for assisting decision makers in evaluating social-policy decision

Table 5–4. A Completed Balance-Sheet Grid.

ALTERNATIVE # _____

	POSITIVE ANTICIPATIONS +	NEGATIVE ANTICIPATIONS −
1. Tangible gains + and losses − for SELF	Brings out consequences of alternatives; helps structure the problem; assists in follow-up.	Is time consuming; possibility of some loss in spontaneity.
2. Tangible gains + and losses − for OTHERS	Same as above.	Same as above.
3. Self-approval + or disapproval −	I will feel better knowing that I have attempted to investigate systematically the consequences of the alternatives; I will have more confidence in my final decision.	I might feel that I am being too analytical.
4. Social approval + or disapproval −	Others will be impressed that I took the time to carefully and thoroughly consider the consequences of all the alternatives.	Some persons might wonder why I need a balance sheet to help me make decisions; reliance on such a device might be viewed as a sign of weakness.

alternatives. Although it was designed specifically for social-policy analysis, it also should be useful for other situations involving complex policy decisions and vaguely defined, changing objectives. When the problem objectives are more clearly defined and relatively unchanging, and the number of alternative solutions is limited, however, another method for evaluating alternatives should be selected.

The technique gets its name from the factors characterizing most public-policy environments and from the procedure used to evaluate policy alternatives. The disjointed aspect of the technique refers to the way in which most public-policy problems are analyzed at different times in different locations, without any apparent coordinating efforts, and without the benefit of relevant past experiences. Incrementalism refers to the prescriptions used to compare differences or increments in the consequences of various policy alternatives with one another and with a present policy situation (state). Thus, decisions are made by evaluating the trade-offs possible between an increment of one value and an increment of another value. The logic behind the technique perhaps can be better understood by comparing Disjointed Incrementalism with what might be termed the rational approach to policy decision making.

The rational model is typical of the approach used with most general problem-solving models. A current and a desired state of affairs are determined and then a means is sought to achieve the objectives (so-called means-end analysis). A distinguishing feature of this model is an attempt to consider every possible relevant alternative and then rationally select the alternative with the best potential for solving the problem. A description of this model is shown in Fig. 5–1. As indicated, the present and desired states are determined, information that is relevant to the problem is collected, the possible alternatives are listed, each alternative is compared with the present state of the problem, and then, by ranking, an alternative is selected that is likely to achieve the desired problem state. Note that the rational model also considers increments between alternatives but compares the values of all possible alternatives against the present state of the problem.

The strategy used for Disjointed Incrementalism proceeds somewhat differently, as shown in Fig. 5–2. Because objectives in policy analysis often are vaguely defined and constantly changing, traditional means-end analysis is no longer appropriate. Any evaluation of a gap between current and desired states of a problem will be futile since the gap is unstable and it is unlikely that other persons involved in the policy-making process will agree on the values assigned to different alternatives. As a result, alternatives are not evaluated by asking whether one alternative is of more value than another. Instead, the only question to be considered is whether an increment in one value is desirable and, if it is, whether any of the increment can be traded for an increment of another alternative. Thus, one would not consider if liberty is more precious than security but how much security can be sacrificed for greater liberty. When policy problems are viewed in this way, it is not necessary to list all possible alternatives and then carefully rank them according to their absolute differences—an often impossible task for most social-policy problems.

According to Braybrooke and Lindblom, there are four features that distinguish incremental choice from the rational-choice model:

1. Only those policy alternatives are considered whose known or expected consequent states differ from each other incrementally. Policy states with similar values are not considered.
2. Only those policy alternatives are considered whose known or expected consequences differ incrementally from the current policy state. In addition to being different from each other, the policy alternatives also must be different from the present state of affairs.

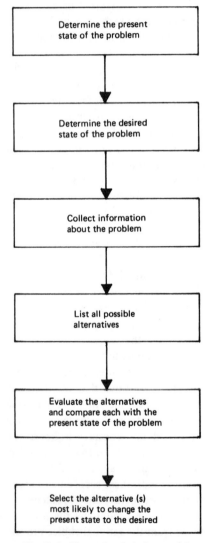

Fig. 5–1. The rational-choice model.

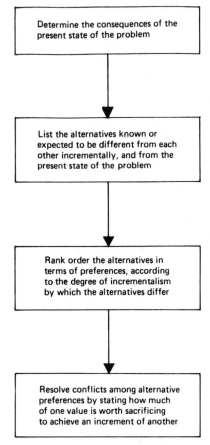

Fig. 5–2. Disjointed incrementalism.

3. A comprehensive analysis of all possible desired states associated with different alternatives is avoided by restricting the analysis to comparisons of the incremental differences between desired states.
4. The selection of policy alternatives involves a preference ranking based upon the increments by which alternatives differ. Those alternatives that are not different from the present state or from each other do not need to be ranked.

Also depicted in Fig. 5–2 is the manner in which problem solvers resolve value conflicts when choosing from among preferred alternatives. Such conflicts often are unresolvable when the rational-choice model is used. If two persons disagree over the values associated with different alternatives, the application of a principle of rational choice or a priorities list is not likely to lead to any form of agreement since such discussions often lead to circular arguments about which alternative is better than the other. If, however, incremental differences are used, resolution is much more likely. For example, if two policy alternatives have as their consequent social states inflation and unemployment, the incremental value between these two states can be compared. This is done by examining the trade-offs possible between the value of one state and another. Thus, the person who favors inflation over unemployment is forced to consider inflation *relative* to unemployment, while the reverse would be true for the person who favors unemployment over inflation. Because these values cannot be ordered in priority, the question to be considered is *how much* of the value in one state can be sacrificed to achieve an increment in another. The conflict is dealt with by determining the relative levels existing in the two alternatives. If unemployment is high, for example, a decrease in this value is evaluated against the possibility of a corresponding increase in inflation. It should be noted that this activity is not static. In most policy situations, information and objectives will change over time, necessitating continual adaptations of the incremental strategy. As a result, many policy problems are alleviated but not completely solved.

Evaluation   A positive feature of Disjointed Incrementalism is its presumed ability to reduce the information-processing demands made upon a problem solver. By restricting the number of alternatives and consequences requiring consideration, the technique can decrease the complexity and uncertainty of a decision environment. In this regard, the technique attempts to use a disordered, fragmented situation for constructive problem-solving purposes. Another positive aspect of the method is its avoidance of the rational model of alternative evaluation when problem objectives and states are likely to change. The current and desired states of a problem are viewed as being dynamic rather than static— a characteristic of most social-policy problems. Thus, the use of adaptive, incremental strategies permits the decision maker to modify policies as the decision environment changes.

On the negative side, the technique's value can be limited by a lack of specific guidelines on how to compare incremental differences and make choices. The skills and policy experiences required to do this can make the technique difficult to apply for persons unfamiliar with policy analysis. In addition to its limited area of application, the technique also is restricted by the ability of problem solvers to generate likely consequences for different policy alternatives as well as the need to rank alternatives. Although the number of alternatives will be reduced greatly when the incremental strategy is used, problems involving large numbers of alternatives still will make information-processing demands upon the problem solver. Finally, the suitability of the method for other than social-policy problems is unknown. It would seem, however, that the method might have limited applicability in many areas due to its descriptive rather than prescriptive orientation.

5.07 Electronic Voting

Groups often use highly efficient procedures for generating ideas but resort to less efficient methods for selecting one or two ideas for implementation or further analysis. Following an efficient procedure by an inefficient one is not likely to result in the selection of the best alternative. At the very least, an inefficient selection procedure is likely to consume time that can render the final selection unusable.

Typically, discussion inefficiency can be characterized in two ways: (1) The group spends too much time discussing an idea for which there is already some degree of consensus, or (2) the group spends too little time discussing an idea perceived to have consensual support when in fact it does not. Neither approach is likely to result in a satisfactory solution, but both can lead to increased frustration among group members—especially when faced with selecting from among a large number of ideas. Obviously, some type of middle-ground procedure would be desirable.

According to Geschka,[10] the Battelle Institute at Frankfurt, Germany, has tried to resolve this problem by the use of an electronic-voting device. The procedure for using the device is as follows:

1. The group discusses a pool of previously generated ideas.
2. Each group member is given a nine-button console that is connected to a visual display screen.
3. When the group is ready to vote, the members individually rate each idea by pushing one of the nine buttons. The buttons correspond to a nine-point rating scale, with a 1 indicating little or no value and a 9 indicating very high value.
4. The results of the voting are displayed on the screen in the form of a tally for each response option. Thus, an idea might receive four 9 votes, two 8 votes, one 7 vote, and so forth.
5. The distribution from the vote tally is examined for any possible inconsistencies. For example, if an idea received eight 9 votes and seven 1 votes but relatively few votes in categories 2 through 8, then the group should discuss the possible reasons behind this pattern. After the discussion, the group votes again and notes the resulting distribution. If this distribution has no inconsistencies, the group moves on to the next idea; if inconsistencies are noted, the process of discussion and voting is repeated. However, if the initial vote results in a pattern requiring no discussion, the group will move immediately to the next idea.

6. Steps 3 through 5 are repeated for each idea. When all ideas have been voted upon, those receiving the highest ratings are selected for implementation or additional analysis.

Evaluation   The Electronic Voting procedure is almost identical to that used by the Nominal Group Technique (NGT) for selecting ideas. The only difference between the two procedures is in the medium used to record vote tallies: NGT uses a chalkboard or flip chart instead of an electronic device. The advantage of either procedure is rather obvious: Each provides group members with an efficient means for determining idea preferences at any point during the group discussion. By receiving such feedback, the group can devote most of its efforts to discussing ideas for which voting preferences are not clearly known or fully crystallized. Of the two methods, however, Electronic Voting would seem to have a slight edge in the speed with which votes can be tabulated and the potential for storing vote tallies in a memory bank for future examination. Furthermore, this edge will be of particular importance when a large number of ideas need to be processed.

On the other hand, both procedures have the potential to be misused if vote tallies are overemphasized to the detriment of group discussion. Voting should be used only to clarify the outcome of group discussions and not as an end in itself. In addition, Electronic Voting has the disadvantage of requiring specialized equipment not needed with less costly, although slower, manual methods. For work groups that rely heavily upon voting-distribution procedures, however, Electronic Voting could be well worth the financial investment.

5.08 Goalstorming

According to Adams,[11] two key managerial responsibilities are goal setting and involving subordinates in decision making. Managers can practice both of these responsibilities by using participative management when establishing corporate goals. To accomplish this, Adams has developed Goalstorming—a combination of brainstorming and goal setting.

Goalstorming is designed to be especially useful when some group members have a vested interest in a particular area, thereby making it difficult to achieve consensus. The process helps overcome this problem by structuring the selection of goals and assigning priorities to them. The primary steps are as follows:

1. Describe the primary corporate objective.
2. List the secondary goals related to the primary objective. For instance, if the objective is profit, secondary goals might be revenue and expense.
3. Subdivide the secondary goals. For example, expenses might be subdivided into categories of labor, raw material, research, inventory, and so forth.

4. Rank all the subdivided goals using the "more-or-less" technique: (a) Randomly select two goals and decide which one is more important, (b) repeat this process of randomly selecting and comparing goals until all goals have been evaluated, and (c) based upon the comparisons, rank the goals in order of importance.

To illustrate how goals might be ranked using the more-or-less approach, suppose that eight goals (A through H) have been generated. If one of these is randomly selected, goal C might be compared with E, then H with B, F with A, and so on until all possible comparisons have been made. If it turns out that goal C was rated as less important than goals B, F, and H, but more important than goals A, D, E, and G, then goal C will be ranked fourth. Other rankings will be obtained in a similar manner.

According to Adams, the group should follow several guidelines when ranking the goals. First, the decision on the relative importance of any one goal must be unanimous. Second, decisions on the importance of one goal over another should not be changed later. Third, difficult decisions sometimes can be resolved by subdividing the goal in question and comparing the subdivisions to the other goal. Fourth, some goals can be combined with others to increase their importance. This often will help resolve disputes. Finally, if any ranking changes are desired, the entire process must be repeated. In addition to these guidelines, Adams also cautions that voting, averaging, or trading votes should be avoided if at all possible. Instead, consensus should be sought.

Evaluation Most of the strengths of Goalstorming derive from its participative approach. Adams notes that involving managers in the goal-setting process provides a formal hearing for a variety of goals and allows managers to have their opinions heard. A related advantage is that managers learn how persons from other areas feel about different goals. In addition, managers should increase their understanding of the corporate objective as well as each other's values. Taken together, all of these benefits suggest that Goalstorming is a task-oriented, team-building process with outcomes beyond mere generation of goals. A primary disadvantage of Goalstorming is that ranking the goals can be an especially tedious and complex process. This is especially true if a large number of goals is involved. To avoid this difficulty, the group should limit the number of goals or conduct an initial screening of the goals using a simpler procedure (e.g., voting). Another weakness might be the need for a moderately skilled facilitator to monitor the consensus-seeking activity involved when goals are compared. Also, some personalities may dominate the discussions or interpersonal conflicts may erupt. Thus, Goalstorming shares most of the positive and negative features of brainstorming.

5.09 Highlighting

Highlighting is a relatively efficient idea evaluation and selection technique developed by Firestien.[12] Idea "hits" are combined into "hotspots" which are modified into workable solutions. It can be used by either individuals or groups using the following steps:

1. Review a list of consecutively numbered ideas and mark any that look interesting or intriguing (idea "hits"). Select these ideas without regard to their workability.
2. Look over all of the hits and identify those that seem to be related to one another. Clusters of such hits are known as "hotspots." List the hits identified for each hotspot.
3. Examine each hotspot and identify what it represents to you. These descriptions can deal with general meanings, implications, and possible consequences of each.
4. Select the one hotspot that best satisfies your needs for the problem. This is your solution. If necessary, combine two or more hotspots to produce a final solution.

Hits and hotspots do not always need to be identified. Sometimes, an idea will stand out right away and it can be used as a solution. It also is possible that none of the hits may be related enough to justify creating hotspots. In this case, one of the hits could be chosen as a solution.

Evaluation The simplicity and ease of use of Highlighting is one of its greatest strengths. Very little training is required and most individuals and groups can master it in a short period of time. Because of its open-ended nature, it also allows for plenty of discussion during group applications. Another strength of Highlighting is identification of hotspots. Combining clusters of related hits usually will lead to an increase in solution quality. Although Highlighting is not designed to structure group decision making, it does provide an efficient way to process and synthesize ideas. About its only weakness is the lack of explicit evaluation criteria. However, if Highlighting is used to screen an initial pool of ideas, another technique (e.g., Weighting Systems) can be used to make specific selections.

5.10 Idea Advocate

One of the methods used at the Battelle Institute of Frankfurt to evaluate ideas is the Idea Advocate.[13] An idea advocate is someone who, during the course of an evaluation session, assumes an assigned role of promoting one particular idea as being most useful. Because an advocate is assigned to every idea, the positive aspects of all of the ideas will be brought out for group examination. The following steps are used for the Idea Advocate method:[14]

1. A list of ideas is presented to a group. Typically, the ideas have been previously generated by the group.
2. The advocate roles are assigned. Assignments are made using any or all of the following criteria: (a) persons who will be responsible for implementing a particular idea, (b) persons who originally proposed an idea, or (c) persons who have a strong preference for an idea. Individuals may advocate more than one idea.
3. As each idea is discussed, the advocate assigned to the idea describes why it would be the best choice.
4. After all the advocate presentations have ended, the group discusses the ideas and presentations and selects the idea that has the most potential for solving the problem.

A minor variation of this technique is known as the Raft Debate.[15] Group members pretend they are on a raft in the ocean. Only one of them can be saved to go on to an island inhabited by an uncivilized people. Each advocate argues why his or her idea must be saved to help the people on the island. The best idea is chosen either by an independent judge or after a discussion among the group members.

Evaluation   This technique will be most useful for situations in which one or more ideas are not likely to get an adequate airing during the evaluation session. When group members have prejudged the available pool of ideas, the discussion during this session might be weighted in favor of these ideas to the neglect of others that have not been favorably prejudged. Thus, the Idea Advocate method can help insure that the strengths of all ideas are thoroughly discussed (assuming, of course, that each idea has an advocate).

There are, however, two possible difficulties associated with this method. First, if there are any major status differences within the group or differences in expertise or access to pertinent information about an idea, some advocates may have an unfair advantage over the others. This advantage might be especially pronounced if any status differences are based upon perceived inequalities of power. For instance, some persons might be reluctant to advocate an idea in opposition to one advocated by their boss. Thus, the method probably will work best when status differentials can be eliminated or at least controlled. A second difficulty with the method is its emphasis upon only the positive aspects of an idea. A more balanced evaluation can be achieved by adding an advocate for negative aspects. Using a devil's advocate and an idea advocate (angel's advocate?)

will create a more natural situation. That is, in a free-discussion evaluation session, many idea strengths and weaknesses are brought out during the course of the discussion. However, when the discussion is structured by assigning specific roles, a more systematic evaluation of the pros and cons of an idea will be possible.

5.11 Panel Consensus

The Panel Consensus technique provides an organization or large group with a systematic and efficient procedure for processing a large number of ideas. Developed in 1970 by Charles Taylor[16, 17] for the Strategic Studies Institute—a U.S. Army activity— it is based upon the concept of an idea funnel. A series of committees or panels, each with their own prescribed role, is used to progressively screen ideas throughout a five-stage process: ideate, screen, select, refine, and decide. A diagram of the technique is shown in Fig. 5-3.

The basic steps involved in implementing the Panel Consensus method are as follows:

1. Ideate. Individuals with some knowledge of the problem area separately ponder the problem for at least 24 hours.
   a. All ideas generated during this stage are carefully compared and the best ones selected.
   b. The resulting ideas are then presented to the first group of panels for processing.
2. Screen. The ideas generated are randomly distributed to a group of 15 screening panels.
   a. Through repeated analysis and assignment of weighted values (on a 1–5 scale), the ideas are gradually narrowed down to a predetermined number.
   b. The best ideas from each panel are then passed on to persons in the next stage.
3. Select. Three select panels are used to further narrow down the number of ideas.
   a. Each panel combines duplicate ideas and compares, analyzes, and evaluates the remaining ideas by assigning weighted values.
   b. A predetermined number of "best" ideas are selected and statements written justifying their selection.
   c. The ideas are then collected and sent on to the next stage.
4. Refine. Ideas at this stage are reviewed by a single panel of upper-level managers.
   a. The panel combines duplicate ideas and compares, analyzes, and evaluates the remaining ideas by assigning weighted values.
   b. This panel may then clarify, expand, or synthesize any ideas as long as their basic substance remains intact.

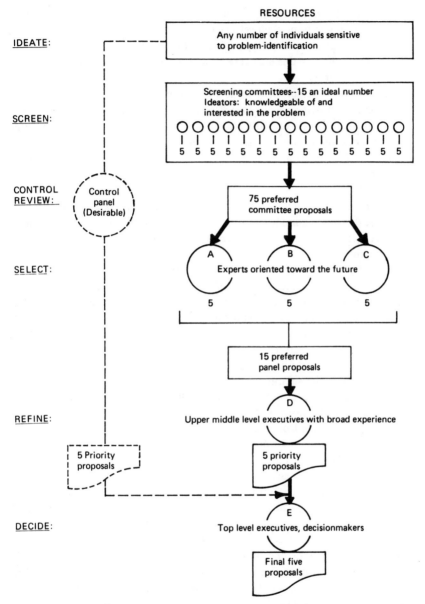

Fig. 5-3. Action levels of the Panel Consensus Technique. Reprinted with permission from the *Journal of Creative Behavior,* Volume 6, No. 3, 1972, published by the Creative Education Foundation, Buffalo, New York.

    c. A predetermined number of "best" ideas are selected and statements written justifying their selection.

    d. The ideas are then collected and sent on to the final stage.

5. Decide. Ideas at this stage are reviewed by a single panel of top organizational managers.

    a. One or more surviving ideas are selected by combining duplicate ideas and comparing, analyzing, evaluating, and assigning weighted values.

    b. For this panel, unlimited discussion of ideas, consideration of implementation problems, and any trade-offs involved are permissible.

    c. The best ideas are selected and submitted to the chief administrator responsible for initiating the process.

There are also five prescribed roles that must be coordinated if the technique is to be successful: administrator, controller, monitor, control review panels, and panel members. Each of these roles fulfills a particular function within the screening process.

Administrator. The administrator is primarily responsible for appointing individuals to panels and the overall coordination of the technique. This person is typically a representative from top management and often delegates most administrative responsibilities to a controller. After assigning individuals to panels, the administrator's other major responsibilities are at the beginning and end of the process. At the outset, the administrator kicks off the technique by describing the problem and its background, explaining the use of the technique, requesting that ideas be submitted, and thanking the participants for their efforts. At the conclusion of the technique, the administrator is responsible for preparing feedback letters concerning the outcome of the idea-screening process.

Controller. The controller provides general assistance to the administrator but is primarily responsible for the direct coordination of all activities. This individual makes sure that the process runs smoothly by (1) assuring that all idea sources remain anonymous, (2) assuring that submitted ideas are uniform in format, (3) assigning code numbers to each idea, (4) maintaining a master idea list, and (5) preparing clean copies of idea lists for use by each successive panel. In fulfilling this role, the controller must remain totally neutral at all times.

Monitor. The monitor is responsible for performing all of the administrative chores of each panel but does not participate in any of the screening activities. Like the controller, it is essential that the monitor remain neutral. Typical duties of the monitor include (1) tabulating weighted values for each individual score sheet, (2) pulling out the highest-scored ideas for further review by other panels or additional review by the same panel, (3) maintaining the prescribed time limit for discussing ideas, (4) assuring that ideas are selected only by balloting and not by taking sides, (5) passing on all idea lists and scoring sheets to the controller, and (6) preparing a follow-up report on the panel's activities.

Because of the monitor's neutrality, the same person may serve on more than one panel. At the highest level, however, the decide panel may use the controller or administrator as its monitor.

Control Review Panels. These panels are optional and may be established at the screen level if at least one of two conditions exist: (1) The number of ideas to be screened is exceptionally large, or (2) there are not enough experts available to perform on the screen panels. The primary task of these panels (one or more may be used) is to make sure that a good idea is not overlooked. Because ideas are randomly assigned to the screen panels, it is possible that one panel might receive a disproportionate number of good ideas. Only a set number of ideas may be selected at this level, and any one screen panel might be forced to choose from among several equally attractive alternatives. The responsibilities of the control review panels include (1) rating every idea on its own merits, (2) categorizing ideas with respect to subject area, (3) combining duplications, (4) selecting the best ideas from each category, (5) developing written justifications of their selections, and (6) passing on the selections to the decide panel. Control review panels may also reword ideas if this will help to assure the quality of an idea. Each of these panels is made up of a monitor and five other persons who should be selected for their particular knowledge of the problem area.

Panel Members. Each stage in the technique, except the ideate state, consists of one or more formally designated panels. These panels constitute the heart of the process and it is within them that the major processing activity occurs. As ideas progress through the successively higher panels, they are subjected to repeated analysis, with panels at the higher organizational levels being the most discriminating in their evaluation.

Although each panel performs the same basic functions, there are certain differences in composition and procedure that warrant further discussion.

Ideate Level. Persons at this level are not really organized into formal panels as such, but they do play a key role in the overall process. Volunteers should be used for this level, and the administrator or controller should emphasize that participants can be uninhibited in their thinking due to the provisions made to protect their identities. A time limit of 24 hours is usually established for the individual generation of ideas. Ideas generated at this level are presented in a prescribed format that includes (1) a brief title of the idea, (2) a brief statement of how the problem is perceived, (3) a concise description of the major highlights of the idea, and (4) a narrative description of how the idea might be implemented. This information should not exceed two pages in length for each idea. If a large number of ideators are used, participants should select their one best idea to submit to the controllers. Once ideas have been received by the controller, the ideation stage must terminate.

Screen Level. Typically, this level consists of 15 panels of 15 individuals each, some of whom may be ideators. Depending upon the number of ideas to be screened and the number of available persons with some knowledge of the problem, fewer than 15 panels can also be used. The major task of panels at this level is to begin reducing the number of ideas by repeatedly reviewing the ideas that have been randomly assigned to each panel. Panels can accomplish this task by rating each idea on a five-point scale and then obtaining a consensus of a predetermined number of "best" ideas (usually five ideas) for every panel. At the end of a three- to four-hour time period, the monitor for each panel then passes the surviving ideas on to the controller for review at the next level.

Select Level. Three panels are used at this level, with each containing five members and a monitor. The members of these panels should be selected by the administrator for their broad experiences and knowledge of the organization and its environment. These persons are typically experts in their fields and are drawn from middle management. Each panel is presented with an identical list of ideas submitted from the screen level and directed to select the five "best" ones (for example) by rating each idea on a five-point scale. After three to four hours, consensus must be achieved within each panel so that the surviving ideas can be passed on to the controller for review at the refine level.

Refine Level. Only one panel is used at the refine level. It should consist of five upper-middle-level executives and one monitor. Because persons at this level should be more knowledgeable about the problem, they may be given more freedom in clarifying, expanding, or synthesizing the ideas presented to them. Any ideas that are substantially altered in meaning must be assigned new code numbers. The refine panel uses the same procedures as the other panels to rate the ideas and reduce their total number to about five remaining ideas. This panel serves an especially important function due to its presumed knowledge about any practical constraints that might automatically eliminate an idea from further consideration.

Decide Level. One panel containing five top managers and a monitor are used to staff this level. It is here that the final decision will be made as to which idea will be used to solve the problem. The same procedure used at other levels is also used at this level to attain consensus on the one best solution. However, any ideas submitted by the control review panels also will be evaluated by the decide panel. Members of the decide panel may also decide to reject all ideas submitted to them.

Evaluation   The Panel Consensus technique possesses the following advantages and disadvantages:

Advantages

1. Encourages participation in problem solving on the part of a large number of organizational members—especially lower-level members who do not always have the opportunity to have their ideas heard by upper-level managers.

2. Through the use of a structured, systematic approach, provides a mechanism for efficiently evaluating a large number of ideas.
3. Avoids direct confrontation and resulting personality conflicts and/or co-ercion by dominant members (by controlling member interaction and using private balloting and an equal rating system for all members).
4. Insures that the basic thought of an idea cannot be easily altered by exter-nal influences.
5. Increases the likelihood of achieving a potential solution through the use of a prescribed time limit and a standardized procedure involving a common task. Thus, the technique reduces the possibility of lobbying for favorite ideas or under-the-table negotiations.
6. Introduces the possibility of greater acceptance of others and tolerance for their ideas by forcing a face-to-face encounter of persons who do not nor-mally work together.
7. Helps overcome language barriers that might develop between experts of different disciplines, since they are forced to communicate with one another to evaluate ideas.
8. Possesses some flexibility in that the technique can be adpated for use in relatively small organizations or with different numbers of ideas (as long as the number of ideas justifies the use of the technique).

Disadvantages

1. Might be more appropriate for large, bureaucratic organizations.
2. Is extremely time consuming—will usually take about a week to process ideas for a typical problem. The advantages of using the technique must be carefully weighed against possible losses due to the time investment of the participants.
3. If a large number of duplicates are generated for a particular idea, some persons might be biased in favor of this idea.
4. If ideas are not properly presented at the outset, subsequent panels might find it difficult to recognize their value. The suggested idea format should be carefully followed.
5. A good working knowledge of organizational constraints on the part of upper-level managers is critical to the potential success of any solution. If some persons at these levels have insufficient or inadequate information, an inappropriate solution might be applied. In this respect, the quality of the final solution will be highly dependent upon the characteristics of the per-sons chosen to fill the various panels.
6. Because of the greater amount of discretion permitted at upper levels in eliminating duplication or in synthesizing or expanding upon ideas, some potentially good ideas can be lost if this process is not skillfully accomplished.

7. Some panels or individuals might be better than others in writing justification statements, and their arguments might appear more persuasive. Such differences in writing skills could possibly influence or bias subsequent reviewers.
8. To avoid possible bias, persons at the decide level must be totally objective and committed to the technique.
9. Factors that are critical in determining when the technique would be appropriate are not well established. As conceived, the technique now seems to be most suitable when the organization is large, there are a large number of ideas to be narrowed down, and the problem justifies the participation of many persons. Unanswered, however, are questions concerning organization size, number of ideas, and the importance a problem should have to justify using the technique.

In general, the Panel Consensus method seems to be most suitable when an organization has an important, ill-structured problem to solve and needs an efficient procedure for evaluating ideas. Equally important will be the organizational members' commitment to using the technique and devoting the time and effort required.

5.12 Reverse Brainstorming

According to Whiting,[18] Reverse Brainstorming (sometimes referred to as negative creativity or the tear-down method) was developed by the Hotpoint Company as a group method for uncovering all possible weaknesses of an idea and/or anticipating what might go wrong when an idea is implemented. It is almost identical to Classical Brainstorming, except that criticisms instead of ideas are generated. However, its use is not restricted to group brainstorming sessions; it can be applied equally well to evaluate ideas generated by other problem-solving methods. Here is the procedure for using Reverse Brainstorming:

1. A group of six to twelve persons is selected (usually the same persons who generated the ideas).
2. The objective of the exercise and the four brainstorming rules are reviewed.
3. The objective and the list of ideas to be evaluated are written on a chalkboard or flip chart.
4. By raising their hands and being recognized by the group leader, the participants suggest a criticism of the first idea on the list.
5. After all criticisms of the first idea have been exhausted, the group begins criticizing the second idea and the process continues until all ideas have been criticized.
6. Using Classical Brainstorming procedures, the group reexamines the ideas to generate possible solutions for each weakness identified.

7. The idea that possesses the fewest number of weaknesses and that will be most likely to solve the problem is selected for implementation.

Evaluation   Often, a large number of ideas is generated during brainstorming sessions (and other approaches). Reverse Brainstorming will not be suitable when there are more than eight or ten ideas to evaluate. If more than this number of ideas is involved, then separate evaluation sessions should be scheduled. As the size of the idea pool increases, so does the complexity involved in reducing the number to a manageable size. For this reason, Reverse Brainstorming is probably most useful for a small number of ideas that have survived an initial screening and when problem outcomes are likely to be serious if a high-quality solution is not selected. Otherwise, the time spent in evaluation might not justify the procedure used.

Another difficulty involved in using this technique stems from its emphasis upon the negative. As pointed out by Whiting, this emphasis can result in a feeling that a potentially good idea should be rejected simply because its weaknesses have been identified. Although such a feeling might not always be a disadvantage, it may present a problem in certain situations. In the area of new-product development, for example, awareness of a potential product's weakness might lead a company to decide against production while a competitor being less aware of the weaknesses might proceed to market the product successfully. Thus, some caution must be exercised to insure that the critical atmosphere of the group does not override the group's enthusiasm for particular ideas or products.

Other considerations involved in using the technique are identical to those associated with Classical Brainstorming. For example, Reverse Brainstorming should be used with an experienced group leader and a group sufficiently motivated and committed to working on the evaluation of ideas. Although there are some differences of opinion with regard to the composition of the group, it is generally recommended that a few disinterested persons be included in the process. Inclusion of such persons often can provide a fresh perspective on the criticisms and on ways of overcoming them.

Finally, there is no reason why techniques other than Classical Brainstorming could not be used to generate solutions for correcting idea weaknesses. In fact, given the negative atmosphere of Reverse Brainstorming groups, one of the many brainwriting variations (e.g., Nominal Group Technique, Brainwriting Pool, Method 6-3-5) might be seriously considered as alternative approaches to use during this phase of the evaluation activity.

5.13 Simulation

When a problem solver is faced with a pool of idea alternatives, an obvious way to select a solution is to apply each alternative to the problem and evaluate its effects. If the first alternative does not provide an adequate solution, then each successive alternative can be applied until one is found that solves the problem. Such an approach, however, would be impractical in most situations since the costs—both in time and money—would prohibit an exhaustive analysis. What is needed is a low-cost approach that will provide a means for estimating which alternative is most likely to solve the problem.

Next to actual implementation, the best estimate of how well an idea will work can be obtained through simulation. That is, the utility of an idea can be estimated by evaluating its effects when tested against a model of the problem situation. A simulation is developed through the following basic steps:

1. Define the problem objectives. Ask: What should a preferred solution be capable of doing?
2. Construct a model of the problem situation. Try to make the model as similar as possible to the actual problem situation.
3. Establish criteria for determining if the problem objective has been achieved. That is, how will you know that a particular idea has solved the problem?
4. Apply each idea to the model and evaluate its effect upon the problem objective.
5. Select the idea that seems to be most capable of solving the actual problem.

A commonly used example of simulation is the wind tunnel. If the problem objective is to design an airfoil capable of producing a certain amount of lift, different airfoil shapes can be tested and measured in an environment that approximates the actual situation in which the airfoil will be used. Another example might be the spinning of an automobile tire at different rates of speed on a roller to evaluate the wear on various tread designs.

Evaluation   Simulation has several advantages that make it an attractive choice for evaluating a number of different problem solutions: (1) It is usually less costly (or potentially so) than actually implementing an idea. The 747 cockpit simulators used for pilot training are expensive but well worth the price when compared to possible loss of human life and a multimillion-dollar aircraft. (2) It permits economical testing of a relatively large number of ideas. (3) Different levels or variations of a desired objective can be tested in relation to several different alternatives or combinations. (4) It avoids reliance upon subjective estimates of the potential utility of an idea. Observing how an idea or solution affects a model of an actual situation can be more reliable than basing selection upon hypotheses derived from a purely subjective information base.

There are, however, several disadvantages to simulation that can outweigh the advantages: (1) Depending upon the problem objective, construction of the model can be a time-consuming and costly task. (2) Because the model only represents an approximation of reality, simulation will be valid only to the extent that reality has been accurately modeled. (3) It is probably most useful for problems that can be physically tested. Physical reality generally can be more easily approximated than social, political, psychological, or economic reality.

If adequate time is available, simulation should be followed by a small-scale field test of the selected solution. Such "pilot" tests, as they are often called, also can help determine the validity of the model used for the simulation.

5.14 SPAN Voting

SPAN[19] Voting is a computer-assisted, numerical rating technique developed by William MacKinnon[20, 21] for pooling individual judgments and synthesizing group decisions. In contrast to group methods that allocate votes directly to options, SPAN Voting indirectly distributes votes among both group members and options. In this way, individual differences in judgmental abilities are taken into account. Thus, persons who consider themselves to be better judges of other group members than the options can allocate most of their votes to other individuals; persons who believe that they are better judges of the options than the other members can distribute most of their votes to the options.

The original SPAN method involves giving a group of individuals a "parcel" of points to distribute to other individuals and/or options in any manner desired. Using the original distribution ratios selected by each individual, the method then continues the process through a series of successive allocation cycles until all of the original points have been distributed among the options. During this process, the parcels for each option cumulate to the terminal cycle where the parcel point totals will be almost equal to the original parcel totals allocated to the individuals. For example, if three individuals are given 100 points each, then there will be almost 300 points distributed among the options at the terminal cycle.

Because of the complexity involved in performing the calculations after the first cycle, a FORTRAN II program (SPAN I)[22] was developed that could accommodate 52 combinations of individuals and options with a limit of 999 cycles. Since this initial program, two programs have been added, both of which have extended the method's capability. SPAN II[23] eliminated the requirement that the numbers given to participants sum to 100. By eliminating this restriction, the program has greater flexibility in the number of allocation methods that can be used and in the type of problems suitable for study. SPAN III[24] built upon the previous programs and introduced a feature that allows participants to assign weights to each of their judgments. SPAN III also increases the number of participant choices by permitting, in addition to an original quota of points, two subquotas, four multiple number assignments, and three dual assignments. Copies of the SPAN III program and its accompanying *SPAN User's Guide*[25] can be obtained by writing to William J. MacKinnon, Department of Psychology, University of Arizona, Tucson, Arizona 85721.

Although it is not absolutely essential, the SPAN Voting procedure almost always will require the use of a computer program, especially for the more complex versions of the method. However, when the number of individuals and options is small (e.g., three individuals and two options), the computations can be made using a desk calculator. While this is a laborious procedure. It is feasible when access to a computer is not possible.

Because of the complexity of the more advanced versions of the method, the following description of the steps for using SPAN will be limited to the initial version (SPAN I). Since the computations for this version can be more easily made using either manual or computer-assisted methods, it should have more general applicability. When more flexibility is desired and a larger number of individuals and options need to be included, then the more sophisticated SPAN III program should be obtained from MacKinnon.

The steps for using the basic version of SPAN Voting are as follows:

1. Each individual is allocated an original quota of points. In most cases, a parcel of 100 points is equally distributed among the participants. When points are allocated in units of 100, the subsequent calculations are greatly simplified. In some situations, however, it might be desirable to weight the parcel allocations among individuals. For exmaple, if individuals A and B are to be given twice as much influence as individual C, then A and B can be given 100 points and C, 50 points. The options, however, always begin with a quota of zero points.

2. The individuals establish the proportions they wish to use in allocating points to other individuals and the options. For example, individual A might designate a proportion of 0.50 for individual B, 0.40 for option 1, and 0.10 for option 2. Individual B, in contrast, might designate 0.60 for individual A, 0.20 for individual C, and 0.20 for option 2. Although the participants can be given complete freedom in determining the proportions, it is generally recommended that a small percentage (such as 5% or 10%) be allocated to at least one of the options. This guideline helps to insure closure on the process; otherwise, the points might continually cycle among the individuals or options.

3. Based upon the proportions he or she has designated, each individual allocates subparcels of points to either the other individuals and/or the options. Once this is done, no further action is required on the part of the individuals. From this stage on, the points are allocated in accordance with the individually designated proportions. The rationale for this procedure is that if participants were to allocate votes in subsequent cycles (and the voting preferences received from others were anonymous), then the new allocations should be similar to those used in the first cycle.

4. Using manual or computer-based calculations, the process continues through as many successive cycles as are needed to distribute all of the points among the options. (The option point parcels are not redistributed; instead, the points allocated to the options cumulate through the different cycles.)

5. The cumulative option totals at the terminal cycle are examined and the option receiving the greatest number of votes is selected as the best alternative.

To demonstrate how SPAN Voting is used, a two-cycle illustration from MacKinnon and MacKinnon[26] is reproduced in Fig. 5–4. Individuals A, B, and C are given 100 points to allocate among each other and the two options. A guideline is established that at least 10% of their allocations must be distributed to either option 1 or option 2. The individuals determine their allocation proportions, the targets of their allocations, and then distribute their votes accordingly. For example, individual A has designated individual B to receive 50% of his or her votes, option 1 to receive 40%, and option 2 to receive 10%. In contrast, individual C has decided to give 90 points to individual B and 10 points to option 2. This allocation format is followed for all successive computations until the terminal cycle is reached. In Fig. 5–4, option 2 has received 76 votes to option 1's 64 votes after two complete cycles. This result does not mean, of course, that option 2 will necessarily receive the highest vote total. The final totals will not be known until all the cycles are completed.

Evaluation   According to MacKinnon[27, 28] and MacKinnon and MacKinnon,[29] SPAN Voting has several advantages to recommend it over other evaluation techniques. One advantage is the provision for equality of voting power. If all the participants are given an equal allocation of points at the beginning of the process, then theoretically any personal influence differences will be equalized. A second advantage involves the effects produced from the successive calculations. Because the calculations are repeated through different cycles, the voting pattern should converge on the member with the greatest perceived judgmental ability. This convergence, in turn, should lead to an increase in final-solution quality. By comparison, more direct voting approaches often wash out the effects produced by having a highly knowledgeable member. Furthermore, the fact that the technique considers preferences about both members and options constitutes a third advantage. By not restricting participants to a single choice among members or options, SPAN Voting should stimulate wider participation in all phases of decision making and result in greater member satisfaction with the process. Finally, the technique possesses flexibility for the types of groups that could use it. For example, in highly cohesive groups, the point allocations will need only to be based upon knowledge of the judgmental abilities of other members. In divided groups, on the other hand, the differences in motives among individuals with regard to group goals will need to be considered in addition to the judgmental abilities of others. If this information is known by the group members, then the cohesiveness of the group should not affect the eventual decision outcomes. In contrast, groups that are divided and use more conventional selection methods often experience difficulty in achieving decision consensus among themselves.

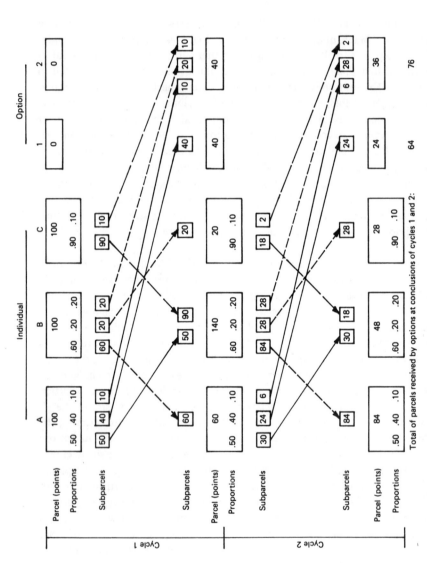

Fig. 5-4. Span computation beginning with hypothetical allocative data for three members and two options and continuing through two cycles. Reprinted from *Behavioral Science*, Volume 14, No. 3, 1969, by permission of James Grier Miller, M.D., Ph.D., Editor.

SPAN Voting, however, is not without its disadvantages. One disadvantage involves group member knowledge of the judgmental abilities of other members. If only a few individuals are knowledgeable about the abilities of others, then the assumption that the voting pattern will converge upon the member with the greatest ability can be erroneous. When only a few members are knowledgeable about the abilities of others, the voting pattern will be more likely to diverge or remain unfocused. Thus, the validity of this information will be critical to the technique's effectiveness. In general, small groups that have worked together for a long time will be more likely to possess accurate information about the relevant expertise areas of others. Even if the members are familiar with each other's abilities, a second disadvantage might involve the attributions that individuals make about others. For example, some individuals might equate such attributes as charisma and decisiveness with judgmental knowledge. When using SPAN Voting, the participants also should be cautioned against the tendency to generalize ability in one area to all others. To some extent, the success of the procedure rests with the accuracy of perceptions about abilities *relevant* to the available options. Expertise in one area is no guarantee that the same individual will be knowledgeable about another, related area. Another difficulty with SPAN Voting could arise at the time it is decided to initiate the process. The go/no-go characteristics of the method rules out the possibility of reevaluating alternatives once the voting has begun. It is therefore important that the alternatives be thoroughly discussed and that all members have an opportunity to ask questions before the points are allocated. Finally, the SPAN approach conceivably might encourage the participants to take less responsibility for the ultimate decision. If the final decision turns out to be ineffective or unsatisfactory, the participants may blame the result on the computer or the persons to whom they allocated their votes. Even if a highly effective or satisfactory solution is produced, feelings of ownership might be diminished due to a lack of control over the process after the initial allocation activity.

Aside from these speculations on the advantages and disadvantages of the SPAN method, at least one published research study has been conducted. In a two-experiment laboratory investigation using college students as subjects, Willis, Hitchcock, and MacKinnon[30] found that the SPAN approach produced higher-quality solutions to hypothetical problems than did more direct voting approaches. In addition, the groups that used the SPAN method reported they were more satisfied with the procedure than did groups using other methods. Although these findings are noteworthy, final conclusions on the method await additional research using "real" groups making "real" judgments.

It should be obvious that the conditions under which SPAN Voting is used will be critical to its eventual effectiveness. Based upon the previous evaluation, the technique is likely to be most effective when (1) the group members are able to accurately perceive differences among themselves in relevant knowledge about the problem, (2) the group is relatively small and has a long history of working together, (3) the group members are able to separate personal expertise from charisma or other personal characteristics unrelated to the options, (4) the group clearly understands how the method works and its rationale, (5) opportunity is provided to discuss the alternatives before the initial votes are allocated (or at least information is made available on the alternatives), and (6) the group is motivated and committed to working as a team.

5.15 Sticking Dots

This technique uses a simple procedure to allow members of a small group to vote directly for their idea preferences. As described by Geschka,[31] the procedure involves giving each group member a fixed number of votes (in the form of self-adhesive, colored dots) and allowing them to allocate the votes in any manner they desire. The steps for this technique are as follows:

1. A list of previously generated ideas is displayed on flip-chart sheets or cards that are pinned to a large wallboard.
2. Each group member is given a sheet of small, self-adhesive colored dots (a different color for each person) corresponding in number to 10% of the total number of ideas listed on the board. Thus, if 100 ideas are listed, each person will be given ten dots.
3. The group members individually evaluate the ideas by sticking the dots next to the ideas they prefer. The dots may be allocated in any manner desired. For example, if each individual is given ten dots, all of the dots may be placed next to one idea, one dot placed next to each of ten different ideas, three dots placed next to one idea and seven next to another, and so forth.
4. The vote tallies are counted and the ideas receiving the greatest number of votes are selected for further analysis or implementation.

Evaluation   A major advantage of this technique is the direct participation it affords group members in the selection process. In addition, the use of color coding to identify individuals can make it easier to conduct a discussion on why people voted the way they did. On the other hand, the openness of the selection procedure might lead to voting conformity should some group members be influenced to vote in accordance with a key opinion leader in the group. Another possible disadvantage may be the use of block voting by a subgroup of individuals who may wish to force their preferences on others.

5.16 Weighting Systems

Whenever a decision must be made to select from among two or more alternatives, a common procedure is to assign weights to the different evaluation criteria. Since not all criteria are likely to be valued equally, such a procedure provides a systematic method for assessing the strengths and weaknesses of each alternative. For example, in the problem used to illustrate the Advantage-Disadvantage procedure, it was noted that not all of the criteria are likely to be given equal weight by the decision maker. If job offers in different cities are considered—as was the case in this example—the criteria of climate and entertainment (Table 5–1) could be valued less highly, for example, then promotion opportunities and job responsibilities. Clearly, a decision made on the basis of a frequency count of advantages would not consider such value preferences. Given the number of criteria involved and the likelihood that different values could be placed upon each, a numerical weighting approach would, instead, be more appropriate.

The general procedure for most weighting methods is to generate a list of evaluation criteria, assign weights to the criteria, rate each alternative against the criteria, and then select the alternative that best satisfies the criteria. One typical procedure involves the following steps:

1. Construct a table containing two more columns than there are alternatives. Thus, if there are five alternatives for a problem, the table will contain seven columns.
2. Write *Criteria* over the first column, *What Should Be* over the second column, and the alternative names over the remaining columns, using one name for each column.
3. Divide each of the alternative columns into two subcolumns. For each alternative, write *What Is* over the first subcolumn and *Subtotal* over the second subcolumn.
4. In column one, write in the criteria desired for the alternatives.
5. In column two (What Should Be), numerically rate the relative importance of each criterion, disregarding the alternatives. Rate each criterion using a number between one and seven. If the criterion is considered to be not at all important, write in a one, if slightly important, a two, and so forth up to the maximum value of seven, very important.
6. Move to the third column and rate the What Is subcolumn for the first alternative using a seven-point scale. A one would indicate that there is only minimal satisfaction of the desired criterion while a seven would indicate near conformance to the criterion. Do this for all the criteria.
7. Fill in the second subcolumn by multiplying each What Should Be value (column two) by each What Is value and write down the product in the Subtotal subcolumn.
8. Repeat steps 6 and 7 for the remaining alternatives.
9. Under the Subtotal subcolumn, add up the products obtained for each alternative.
10. Examine all of the total scores, and decide which alternative should be selected.

Table 5-5. A Weighting System for Choosing a New Job.

CRITERIA	WHAT SHOULD BE	CLEVELAND		DALLAS	
		WHAT IS	SUBTOTAL	WHAT IS	SUBTOTAL
Warm Climate	5	4	20	6	30
High Salary	5	7	35	4	20
Low-Cost Housing	6	4	24	5	30
Good Schools	6	5	30	5	30
Good Promotion Opportunities	7	6	42	4	28
Available Public Transportation	3	4	12	5	15
Low Taxes	3	4	12	5	15
Motivating Job Responsibilities	7	7	49	4	28
Entertainment	2	3	6	4	8

TOTAL: 230   204

Although this procedure might seem complicated, it is actually very simple, as an examination of Table 5-5 will show. Using the same problem described for the Advantage-Disadvantage procedure (Table 5-1), the problem solver lists the criteria desired for a new job in a different city. In this case, the same two cities are involved and the desired criteria are the same for both cities. Under the What Should Be column, each criterion is rated with regard to its importance. (Obviously, different persons will rate the criteria according to their personal preferences and the preferences of those affected by the decision—for example, the problem solver's family.) Promotion opportunities are rated highest, while entertainment possibilities are given the lowest rating. During this activity, the ratings should be done without considering the available alternatives. Otherwise, subsequent ratings of the alternatives might be biased. Next, each alternative is rated with respect to what actually exists. This procedure, of course, will be mostly subjective. For example, although an objective comparison could be made for salary, a comparison of "good schools" would be more subjective. In Table 5-5, salary and motivating job responsibilities have been rated highest for Cleveland, while Dallas is rated highest for climate. The ratings in the What Should Be column are then multiplied by each of the What Is ratings for each alternative to obtain the alternative subtotals. These products are added up and, based upon the totals, the job in Cleveland might be selected as the preferred alternative.

Evaluation When the relative values of different criteria are considered, a much more realistic assessment can be obtained with weighting procedures than is possible when all criteria are considered to be of equal value. There is, of course, some danger involved whenever an attempt is made to quantify value preferences. Any measurement system is only as good as the criteria used to develop it and the validity of the information upon which the ratings are based. In addition, there is probably something to be said for intuitive or gut feelings about an alternative, especially when numerical totals are very close. In the example depicted in Table 5–5, for instance, the problem solver might not want to make a decision based upon a difference of 29 points. Instead, he or she might want to reexamine the weightings given to certain criteria and then make a decision based upon what "feels" right. In many cases, such intuitive reactions are likely to be accompanied by higher-motivation levels for following through on the implementation of an alternative. Obviously, this approach will not be acceptable in all situations, but it certainly would be preferable to overreliance upon quantifiable weights.

The use of intuition then raises the issue of determining the appropriate point in the process for using quantitative versus qualitative approaches. When there are a large number of alternatives to evaluate, Tarr[32] recommends using a quantitative approach to initially screen and reduce the number of alternatives. The remaining alternatives, which should have the greatest likelihood for solving the problem, then can be evaluated using a more subjective procedure. When the number of surviving alternatives is small, the final evaluation process will be greatly simplified. Even this approach, however, has its disadvantages when the costs associated with not solving the problem are perceived to be high. In such situations (and particularly when there does not appear to be one "correct" solution), a quantitative approach can give a problem solver a substantive procedure to use. This, of course, does not mean that the final solution will be of a high quality. Rather, it might serve only to provide the problem solver with a false sense of security.

If there is a large number of alternatives to evaluate, one procedure useful for reducing evaluation complexity is to cluster the alternatives into homogeneous units. For example, alternative technical innovations of a product might be classified according to functional characteristics or areas of application. Grouping information in this manner can reduce considerably the cognitive demands upon the problem solver.

As with all evaluation methods, however, the key to effective use would seem to lie in the quality of the criteria used to judge different alternatives. Typically, these criteria are generated using free association and their quality is limited by the ability of the problem solver to generate valid criteria. To increase the validity and quality of criteria, other methods for generating criteria might be explored. For instance, data generated from some of the redefinitional and analytical methods (especially the Five W's and H technique) could suggest some criteria. During group efforts, various brainwriting approaches also might prove useful for generating criteria.

COMMENTS

The techniques in this chapter range from the very simple to the very complex. The Advantage-Disadvantage and Sticking Dots methods, for example, are extremely easy to apply and require little in the way of special training; the Decision Balance Sheet and Weighting Systems are moderate in complexity; and Goalstorming and the Panel Consensus technique are relatively complex. The degree of simplicity or complexity, however, should not be used as a guide for selecting one of the techniques. Rather, the advantages and disadvantages of each technique, weighted relative to the problem in question, should be the primary selection criterion. Thus, Reverse Brainstorming is simple to use but might not produce an evaluation adequate for selecting alternatives for some types of problems. If, for example, several alternatives appear to be equal in attractiveness, then some rating procedure such as that used in Weighting Systems might be considered. Thus, for extremely complex problems, the use of more than one technique might be indicated. In addition, the amount of time available for evaluation and selection, as well as the importance and risk of the problem will be major factors in choosing a technique. Although not included in this chapter, various computer programs now available for personal computers also might be considered for use as decision aids.

NOTES

1. Hamilton, H. R. "Screening Business Development Opportunities." *Business Horizons,* 13–24 (August, 1974).
2. O'Rourke, P. J. *The Castle Technique: How to Achieve Group Consensus in a Very Short Time with No Argument.* Lyons, Col.: Steamboat Valley Press, 1984.
3. Moore, L. B. "Creative Action–The Evaluation, Development, and Use of Ideas," In S. J. Parnes and H. F. Harding, eds. *A Sourcebook for Creative Thinking.* New York: Scribner, 1962.
4. Janis, I. L. "Motivational Factors in the Resolution of Decisional Conflicts." In M. R. Jones, ed. *Nebraska Symposium on Motivation Vol. 7.* Lincoln: University of Nebraska Press, 1959.
5. Janis, I. L., and Mann, L. *Decision Making.* New York: The Free Press, 1977.
6. *Ibid.*
7. *Ibid.* (cited).
8. Hoyt, M. F., and Janis, I. L. "Increasing Adherence to a Stressful Decision Via a Motivational Balance-Sheet Procedure: A Field Experiment." *Journal of Personality and Social Psychology* 31:833–839 (1975).
9. Braybrooke, D., and Lindblom, C. E. *A Strategy of Decision.* New York: The Free Press, 1963.
10. Geschka, H., personal communication.
11. Adams, R. H. "Goalstorming." *Advanced Management Journal* 44(3):55–61 (1979).
12. Firestien, R. L., and Treffinger, D. J. "Ownership and Converging: Essential Ingredients of Creative Problem Solving." *Journal of Creative Behavior* 17(1):32–38 (1983).

13. Geschka, H., personal communication.
14. Due to the limited amount of information available on this technique, the steps are based upon inferences and interpretations that might not accurately represent how the procedure is used by Battelle.
15. Based upon a description of a Parents Weekend activity at Ohio Wesleyan University (*News & Notes for Parents,* Delaware, Ohio: Ohio Wesleyan University, Fall 1980).
16. Taylor, C. W. "Organizing for Consensus in Problem Solving." *Management Review* 61:16–25 (1972).
17. Taylor, C. W. "Panel Consensus Technique: A New Approach to Decision Making," *Journal of Creative Behavior* 6:187–198 (1972).
18. Whiting, C. S. *Creative Thinking.* New York: Van Nostrand Reinhold, 1958.
19. The letters SPAN originally referred to Successive Proportionate Additive Numeration but were subsequently changed to Social Participatory Allocative Network, presumably to reflect modifications in the technique's methodology.
20. MacKinnon, W. J. "Development of the SPAN Technique for Making Decisions in Human Groups." *American Behavioral Scientist* 9:9–13 (1966a).
21. MacKinnon, W. J. "Elements of the SPAN Technique for Making Group Decisions." *Journal of Social Psychology* 70:149–164 (1966b).
22. MacKinnon, W. J., and MacKinnon, M. M. "The Decisional Design and Cyclic Computation of SPAN." *Behavioral Science* 14:244–247 (1969).
23. MacKinnon, W. J., and Cockrum, D. L. "SPAN II: A Modification of the SPAN Program for Synthesizing Group Decisions." *Behavioral Science* 18:78–79 (1973).
24. MacKinnon, W. J., and Anderson, L. M. "The SPAN III Computer Program for Synthesizing Group Decisions: Weighting Participants' Judgments in Proportion to Confidence." *Behavior Research Methods & Instrumentation* 8:409–410 (1976).
25. Anderson, L. M. *SPAN User's Guide.* Unpublished manuscript. Tucson, Arizona: University of Arizona, 1975.
26. MacKinnon, W. J., and MacKinnon, M. M. *op. cit.*
27. MacKinnon, W. J., *op. cit.,* 1966a.
28. MacKinnon, W. J., *op. cit.,* 1966b.
29. MacKinnon, W. J., and MacKinnon, M. M., *op. cit.*
30. Willis, J. E., Hitchcock, J. D., and MacKinnon, W. J. "SPAN Decision Making in Established Groups." *Journal of Social Psychology* 78:185–203 (1969).
31. Geschka, H. "Methods and Organization of Idea Generation." Paper presented at Creativity Development Week II, Center for Creative Leadership, Greensboro, North Carolina, September 1979.
32. Tarr, G. *The Management of Problem Solving.* New York: Wiley, 1973.

6
Implementing Ideas

Once an idea (or set of ideas) has been selected, the next step is to put the idea(s) into action. This is often easier said than done, however. Numerous obstacles exist in both groups and organizations that can prevent even the best ideas from being implemented. Overcoming such obstacles can be as important as any of the other problem-solving stages.

Because of their complexity at the human and technological levels, most organizations have built-in implementation blocks that must be overcome before an idea can be put into action. Some of these blocks are intentional, having been devised to serve as checks to insure the smooth operation of organizational processes; other blocks are more unintentional and arise from the peculiarities that emerge from an organization's mythology. In addition, there is a third type of block that operates independently of an organization's internal processes. These blocks are usually external to an organization and originate in the immediate task environment. A change in market demand, for example, is an external factor that can block idea implementation.

The act of identifying implementation blocks is a logical consequence of the evaluation and selection phase. In fact, a criterion that should be used to evaluate or select an idea is its likelihood for successful implementation. Recognition that implementation blocks exist often will result in trade-offs being made from among the available alternatives. Such trade-offs are a very real aspect of decision-making activity, and they often lead to selection of the most satisfactory alternative rather than the one seen as being "best" for a problem.

Perhaps the most important element of the implementation stage, however, is careful planning. Effective planning should include consideration of implementation blocks, action steps for implementing an idea, and consequences of each action step. The techniques presented in this chapter emphasize designing action steps and anticipating the consequences of different courses of action. Little mention is made, however, of the implementation blocks that should be considered. Although it is not exhaustive, the following checklist suggests some general concerns that can prevent an idea from being implemented successfully:

1. Are resources (time, personnel, equipment, money, information) adequate for implementing this idea?

2. Do others possess the motivation and commitment needed for succesful implementation?
3. Is the idea likely to encounter "closed thinking" and/or resistance to change in general?
4. Are there procedural obstacles that need to be overcome?
5. Are there structural obstacles in the organization that need to be overcome (e.g., communication channels that might block implementation)?
6. What organizational or managerial policies will need to be overcome?
7. How much risk taking is likely to be tolerated by those responsible for implementation?
8. Are there any ongoing power struggles within the organization—even if unrelated to the idea—that might block implementation?
9. Are there any interpersonal conflicts that might prevent or hinder the idea from being put into action?
10. Is the general climate of the organization one of cooperation or distrust?

Most of these concerns, it should be noted, pertain to human implementation blocks. Next to resource adequacy, such blocks are perhaps the major obstacle that will be encountered when an attempt is made to introduce a new idea.

Three of the techniques in this chapter are designed to assist in the coordination and control of an idea implementation plan. The Program Evaluation Review Technique (PERT) is concerned with insuring that all necessary activities and events are completed according to a prescribed schedule. Because of the complexity involved in constructing a PERT network of events and activities, it is probably most useful for very complex, important implementation projects in which the timing of a large number of events and activities is critical to implementation. A less complex planning and control technique is Research Planning Diagrams (RPDs). RPDs are based upon computer logic to show a sequential flow of events. In contrast to PERT, RPDs have the advantage of using recycling phases for certain activities. Consensus Mapping is intermediate in complexity between PERT and RPDs. A group using Consensus Mapping develops categories of activities and displays them visually. The interrelationships among the categories and the overall implementation sequence also are depicted visually. Although similar to RPDs, Consensus Mapping is not bound by computer flowchart logic. The fourth technique described in this chapter, Potential-Problem Analysis (PPA), is designed to assist problem solvers in systematically anticipating and evaluating any negative consequences of implementation events. A major feature of PPA is the use of probability ratings and estimates of the costs involved in using different preventive actions and contingency plans. To be most effective, PPA should be used before an action plan is implemented and then periodically revised after the action steps are introduced.

6.01 Consensus Mapping

During the transition between idea evaluation and selection and idea implementation, groups often are faced with varying degrees of complexity. This is especially true when they are dealing with ill-structured problems. However, the unstructured nature of most group processes often results in unsatisfactory outcomes. To overcome this limitation, Hart, Boroush, Enk, and Hornick[1] developed the Consensus Mapping technique.

Consensus Mapping was designed to help participants visualize, analyze, and organize ideas that are interrelated and sequence-dependent. To do this, participants create a graphic map that shows clusters of ideas and indicates how they are presumed to be interrelated. The participants modify this map during the course of a discussion. The final map then is used as an implementation guide.

According to its developers, Consensus Mapping is used after ideas have been generated and a preliminary evaluation has been conducted (e.g., ranking the ideas in approximate priority). Typically, two to four groups will be used at one time, along with a facilitator. (Each group should contain from five to nine people.) There are five major steps involved in this idea-structuring process:

1. Search for Structure. Task groups try to identify clusters and categories for grouping the ideas. Individuals first should form their own clusters and then discuss them with the other group members. The goal is to form one classification scheme for each group (members may want to divide themselves into pairs or triads to perform this task). Finally, the ideas should be reclarified, using the classification scheme as a guide. If necessary, new priorities can be assigned to some of the ideas.
2. Development of a "Strawman Map." Staff members collect the schemes developed by each group and consolidate them into one map. All the ideas, categories, and relationships generated by the groups should be incorporated. This map then is presented to the groups as a springboard for further discussion.
3. Map Reconfiguration. The groups study the strawman map and use it as a stimulus for developing custom-made solution maps. These maps can be created by writing ideas on index cards with a wax backing and placing them on sheets of newsprint (*author's note:* Post-It[TM] notes would be easier to use, since the adhesive would not have to be added). A code symbol can be written on each card to indicate where additional information can be obtained. The cards then are shifted from one category to another or modified as desired by the group members. The sheets of newsprint are pinned or taped to a wall in the desired configuration and sequence of activities. Ribbon (or yarn) can be used to depict relationships or flows of information and activities between categories.

4. Presentation in Plenary. The groups reconvene and a representative from each group presents the group's revised map. All participants discuss each map, offering comments and asking questions.
5. Map Consolidation. Representatives from each group meet to produce a single map that incorporates features from all the maps. The final map can be photographed for further analysis later on.

To illustrate how the different maps might be developed, graphical representations are shown in Fig. 6-1, 6-2, and 6-3. The objects in each figure represent activities, while the lines show how they are connected and the sequence involved. Figure 6-1 depicts a simplified strawman map that might be constructed by staff members. Figure 6-2 illustrates hypothetical maps for two task groups, A and B. In this instance, each group has reconfigured the strawman map. Finally, Fig. 6-3 demonstrates how the two maps might be consolidated. Of course, even this map is subject to review and additional revision.

In discussing Consensus Mapping, Hart et al. describe how it has been used to deal with the toxicity of particles emitted from burning coal. After the different stages have gone through, the final map shows a series of activities and connecting arrows. The time frame extends from program initiation on one end of a continuum to a seven- to 10-year final period. Activities include such things as (1) preliminary studies, (2) site selection, (3) preliminary sampling, (4) characterization of samples, (5) development and validation of procedures, (6) choosing of a standard sampling procedure, (7) final site selection, and so forth until the final activity of preliminary risk assessment of the outcome.

Evaluation[2]   Consensus Mapping shares many of the advantages of project management approaches, such as CPM and PERT, while overcoming some of their potential disadvantages. For example, the maps allow group members to analyze the implementation process visually. Consensus Mapping also structures

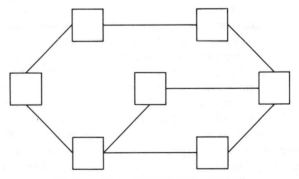

Fig. 6-1. Example of a "strawman map."

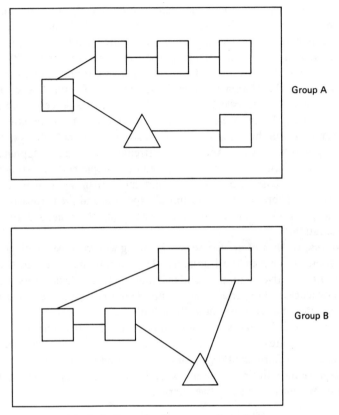

Group A

Group B

Fig. 6-2. Example of map reconfigurations.

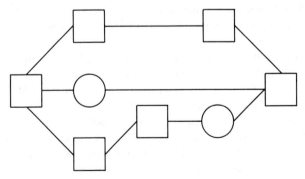

Fig. 6-3. Example of a consolidated map.

the process of categorizing data and demonstrates clearly interrelationships and sequences of activities. However, unlike CPM and PERT, no quantitative estimates are required. Such estimates can be cumbersome if not confusing for many individuals (Consensus Mapping also can be used prior to CPM or PERT and enhance both). This method also combines and improves upon some of the best features of the Nominal Group Technique (NGT), the Castle Technique, and Storyboards. Both brainstorming and brainwriting processes are included, so that the strengths and weaknesses of each are offset to some extent. It is a flexible approach in that its structure can evolve in a number of ways, depending upon the group discussion. Among other strengths, Consensus Mapping requires minimal leader facilitation after the procedure is explained; the strawman map helps keep the discussion productive, maintains momentum, and encourages discussion across different levels of technical expertise; and the emphasis upon consensus helps produce the commitment and motivation needed for effective implementation.

According to Hart et al., Consensus Mapping will work best with groups who receive some training in the technique. However, perhaps the most important variables are effective facilitation and collaboration. The facilitators should have some knowledge and experience in the problem area. And the group members should be capable of cooperating with each other.

The major disadvantages of this technique are that it is relatively time consuming and requires a certain degree of leader facilitation skill and problem knowledge and a fairly high degree of motivation on part of the group members. When compared with more complex and quantitative approaches, however, Consensus Mapping is an attractive alternative.

6.02 Potential-Problem Analysis (PPA)

Most problem solvers recognize that a high-quality solution is no guarantee that a problem will be resolved successfully. If the problem environment is relatively uncertain and only a few elements are under the problem solver's control, any number of difficulties can arise. As stated by Murphy's law: If anything can go wrong, it will.

To prevent problems from occurring during implementation and to reduce their effects should they occur, Kepner and Tregoe[3] have developed a method known as Potential-Probelm Analysis (PPA). Consistent with the basic Kepner-Tregoe approach, PPA is designed in accordance with systematic principles of problem analysis. First, a potential problem is defined in terms of a deviation between what could be and what should be. The precise nature of the potential problem is determined, followed by an assessment of problem risk, causes, likelihood of occurrence, prevention or reduction of effects, and contingency planning. The following are the actual steps used:

1. Define the Objectives. Objectives are "shoulds" that need to occur for a solution to be successfully implemented. Each "should" is an action or event that must be carefully planned to complete the problem-solving cycle. If a "should" does not occur when anticipated, then a potential problem is likely to develop.

2. Generate a List of Potential Problems. This step is commonly referred to as reverse brainstorming (see Technique 5.12) since the problem solver tries to identify everything that possibly could go wrong once a solution has been implemented. According to Kepner and Tregoe, this list is especially important in situations where (a) something new or complex is involved; (b) there is little time available for implementation; (c) a series of activities is critical to implementation or will substantially affect others; (d) a possible solution is missing; (e) many people, activities, or departments are involved; and (f) lines of responsibility are unclear or beyond a manager's area of control.

3. Identify the Specific Nature of Each Problem. In order to adequately analyze each potential problem, the manager should ask: What? Where? When? To What Extent? Because a problem does not exist at this point, the cause of each potential problem is not relevant.

4. Determine the Amonut of Risk Associated with Each Problem. The potential problems should be categorized according to varying degrees of risk. Some problems might be fatal to an implementation plan; some might decrease the chances of success but not be fatal; and others might be only annoying with a minimum amount of risk. To determine in which category a problem belongs, the manager should evaluate each problem according to its potential seriousness and the probability that it will occur. The combination of these two judgments will provide an estimate of overall risk. Problems that involve high risk must be dealt with; problems that involve only moderate risk probably will need to be dealt with; problems that involve little or no risk, however, can be ignored.

5. Search for Possible Causes of Each Problem. The manager should develop a list of the causes that could be associated with each problem. Because most of the causes are only plausible explanations and not based upon fact, the manager must rely upon judgment and experience in developing this list.

6. Estimate the Probability of Occurrence of Each Cause. Again using judgment and experience, the manager should give each cause a probability of occurrence estimate based upon how likely it is the cause will occur if no action is taken. These estimates should be expressed in percentages.

7. Develop Means for Preventing Causes or Minimizing Their Effects. The best way to prevent a potential problem is to take action that entirely removes the possible causes, or at least reduces their likelihood of occurrence. For every problem cause that is eliminated or controlled, the manager will decrease the probability that the problem actually will occur. To determine the likelihood of a cause occurring after preventive action, the manager should estimate this

probability on a scale from zero to 100%. This probability estimate is known as residual probability. Thus, if the probability of cause A occurring is 60% but preventive action A is taken, then the residual probability of the cause might be estimated, for example, at 15% (depending upon the constraints of the particular situation).

8. Develop Contingency Plans for the Most Serious Problems. It often happens that some preventive actions are unsuccessful in significantly reducing or eliminating a cause. In such high-risk situations, the manager should develop contingency plans that specify exactly what actions will be taken if the problem occurs. According to Kepner and Tregoe, contingency plans are essential when there is high risk associated with an operation and a breakdown at one point in the plan is likely to doom the entire operation. However, contingency plans should not be used as substitutes for preventive actions. Preventive actions usually are less costly to implement than contingency plans and always should be used unless it is absolutely certain that contingency plans will produce more efficient results (i.e., involve little expense and effort relative to preventive actions).

PPA can be illustrated with a problem of conducting a market survey to test consumer reaction to several new products. Because of tight production schedules, it is important that the survey be conducted and the results analyzed within prescribed time limits. A project team is established and a PERT network is constructed to guide implementation of the survey. To make sure that the project is completed on schedule, the project manager constructs a table (Fig. 6–4) to analyze potential problems. The team describes the What? Where? When? and Extent? of the project as follows:

What? The survey might not be completed on schedule.

Where? Between the time the questionnaires are printed and the time the survey is conducted.

When? Beginning on the seventh day of the project and continuing to the twenty-third day.

Extent? Three stages of a seven-stage survey process are involved (print questionnaires, select households, and conduct the survey).

Next, the team lists possible problem causes and the probability of occurrence of each, preventive actions, residual probability, and contingency plans. Based upon this analysis, the success of the project is likely to be increased by making arrangements for such things as a backup printer, checking questionnaire proofs, verifying the computer program used to select the households, giving physical exams to the interviewers, and telephoning households immediately prior to the interviews.

Since Kepner and Tregoe described PPA in their book, *The Rational Manager,*[4] several refinements have been added by different users of the procedure. Woods

POSSIBLE PROBLEMS/CAUSES	P[a]	PREVENTIVE ACTIONS	RP	CONTINGENCY PLANS
A. Questionnaires will not be received on time:				
1. Printers go on strike	40	Talk with printers	30	Have a backup printer
2. A major error in printing occurs	20	Check proofs	0	Develop paste-on correction sheets
B. The sample of households will not be representative:				
1. Information is lacking on population characteristics	10	Check other sources	5	Have a standby population of households
2. An error is made in programming the computer	20	Check and verify the program	0	Manually select the sample
C. All of the sample households will not be surveyed:				
1. One or more interviewers become ill	25	Check physical condition	5	Have backup interviewers
2. Some household members fail to keep their appointments	35	Telephone before interview	10	Have backup sample households

[a] P = Probability, RP = Residual Probability.

Fig. 6–4. Potential-problem analysis for a market survey.

and Davies,[5] for example, describe how they modified the basic PPA method for use in an R&D environment. In particular, they added a quantitative estimate of the seriousness of a possible cause as well as an estimate of the costs associated with the preventive actions and contingency plans.[6] They also opted to use a one- to ten-point scale instead of percentages, for all estimates except those involving costs. The cost estimates are made using a three-point scale with choices of low, medium, and high cost.

To illustrate the modifications made by Woods and Davies, Fig. 6–4 has been altered by adding columns for the seriousness and cost estimates. These modifications are shown in Fig. 6–5. By the addition of these estimates, essential contigency plans are clearly shown. However, if low-cost contingency plans can be developed for less critical areas, then they also should be included since the estimates are based upon human judgment and should not be considered infallible.

Another modification of PPA was developed by Van Gundy.[7] It is similar to the Woods and Davies modification in that a seriousness rating has been added to the original approach. It differs, however, in that the cost estimates have been deleted. They have been replaced by quantitative ratings to guide development or preventive actions and contingency plans.

As shown in Fig. 6–6, preventive actions are guided by the result of multiplying each probability rating by each seriousness rating to produce a PS score. The higher this score, the more important it is to develop a high-quality preventive

POSSIBLE CAUSES	Pa	S	PREVENTIVE ACTIONS	RP	C	CONTINGENCY PLANS	C
A. Questionnaires will not be received on time:							
1. Printers go on strike	4	10	Talk with printers	3	L	Have backup printers	H
2. A major error in printing occurs	2	6	Check proofs	0	L		
B. The sample of households will not be representative:							
1. Information is lacking on population characteristics	1	9	Check other sources	1	M	Have a standby population of households	H
2. An error is made in programming computer	2	9	Check and verify the program	0	L		
C. All of the sample households will not be surveyed:							
1. One or more interviewers become ill	3	7	Check physical condition	1	H		
2. Some household members fail to keep their appointments	4	6	Telephone before interview	1	L	Have backup sample households	

a P = Probability, S = Seriousness, RP = Residual Probability, C = Cost, L = Low, M = Medium, H = High

Fig. 6–5. Modified PPA (Woods and Davies version).

action. Development of contingency plans is determined in a similar manner. However, in this case, development of such plans is guided by the product of the PS and RP scores. Thus, all previous decisions are taken into account when contingency plans are developed. Problem causes that have a high probability of occurrence, high seriousness, and high residual probability clearly need to have contingency plans developed. Conversely, such plans will not be needed if the ratings result in a relatively low score.

For example, in Fig. 6–6, the PS X RP score of 120 for a printers' strike obviously is a greater priority than the scores of 0 or 9 for the other potential problems. As a result, a contingency plan needs to be developed only for the possible printers' strike. However, other plans also might be developed for the remaining problems. Deciding how low a score must be to justify additional plans can be determined easily. Develop priority plans first and then any others as time and costs allow.

PROBLEMS/CAUSES	P	S	PS	PREVENTIVE ACTIONS	RP	PS × RP	CONTINGENCY PLANS
A. Questionnaires will not be received on time:							
1. Printers go on strike	4	10	40	Talk with printers	3	120	Have backup
2. A major error in printing occurs	2	6	12	Check proofs	0	0	printers
B. The sample of house-holds will not be representative:							
1. Information is lacking on population charac-teristics	1	9	9	Check other sources	1	9	
2. An error is made in programming the computer	2	9	18	Check and verify the program	0	0	
C. Not all of the sample households will be surveyed:							
1. One or more inter-viewers become ill	3	7	21	Check physical condition	1		
2. Some household mem-bers fail to keep their appointments	4	6	24	Telephone before interview	1		

Fig. 6–6. Modified PPA (VanGundy version).

Evaluation   The major advantage of PPA is its emphasis on a systematic approach for anticipating problems that are likely to prevent a project from being completed successfully.   When potential problems are identified in the early stages of implementation, a project is more likely to proceed as expected.   A second advantage concerns the costs involved in using PPA.   Although the method can be relatively costly to use in the short run, the time and resources consumed in the long run should be much lower.   In other words, an ounce of prevention is worth a pound of cure.   The modifications made by Woods and Davies and VanGundy further strengthen PPA.   The addition of a quantitative seriousness estimate, coupled with the estimates for residual probability and implementation costs, makes it easier to determine areas in which a contingency plan is critical to protect success.   Without such estimates, the costs of a project could increase considerably.   VanGundy's additions strengthen the approach by providing subjective ratings for determining when preventive actions and contingency plans are essential.   Finally, PPA has the advantage of being broadly applicable.   It can be used by either individuals or groups, for simple or complex problems, and in a variety of different problem areas.   In the area of R&D, for example, Woods and Davies suggest that PPA can increase the number of ideas that eventually reach the market as new products.

If not properly used, there also can be certain difficulties in using PPA. First, it is often difficult to identify all possible problems—especially when a project is highly complex. Variations of either brainwriting or brainstorming might help when a project team is attempting to generate potential problem areas. Using a more structured approach in this phase should enhance the quality of the final analysis. Second, if a team is used to conduct PPA, then a climate needs to be established that will be conducive to group interaction. Diagnostic disagreements as well as interpersonal conflicts must be moderated to insure smooth functioning. The use of a skilled project leader is essential for such situations. Finally, a balance must be achieved in the costs of analysis and implementation. For example, although it might be acceptable to have high short-run costs when analyzing potential problems, controls must be used to insure that these costs will not be too high. Spending too much time in potential-problem analysis can doom a project to failure as easily as spending too little time. At some point, a decision will have to be made on when to stop analyzing and start implementing. PPA is just one step in the problem-solving process and it must be used wisely if it is to produce the expected results.

6.03 Program Evaluation Review Technique (PERT)

PERT was designed as a managerial aid for program (or project) planning and control. Once a decision has been made to implement a particular course of action, PERT can be used to insure that all planning and evaluation activities are completed on a timely basis to meet a program's primary objectives. Whether used in engineering, marketing, manufacturing, product development, or human-services programs, PERT has been found useful in coordinating the scheduling of a large number of complex activities. Although large-scale projects will require computerized programs, PERT also can be a valuable aid for the planning and control of less complex projects. It is particularly applicable to one-of-a-kind projects.

PERT originated in 1958 when the U.S. Navy was under pressure to produce the Polaris missile system in record time. Previous to this time, there had been substantial time and cost overruns of major military development contracts. Although some of these overruns could be attributed to overly optimistic contract estimates, there was growing opinion that much of the blame could be laid upon inadequate planning and control techniques. Because the Polaris project involved 250 prime contractors and over 9000 subcontractors, Navy Admiral W. F. Raborn initiated the organization of a special research team to provide the integrated planning and control needed for a project as complex as the Polaris Weapons System program. The team consisted of representatives from the Lockheed Aircraft Corporation, the Navy Special Projects Office, and the management consulting firm of Booz, Allen and Hamilton. The original project name used by the team was Program Evaluation Research Task and the method they used later became known as Project Evaluation and Review Technique. Today, the words Project and Program are used interchangeably.

Because time was of primary concern in the Polaris project, it was the area in which the team concentrated their planning and control efforts. After reviewing other time-based techniques—such as Line-of-Balance, Gantt charts, and milestone reporting systems—the team developed PERT in the form of a graphical-network analysis of the events and activities needed to accomplish a project within certain time limits. Several years later, however, PERT was expanded by other researchers to include the planning and control of project costs. The original approach is now known as basic PERT or PERT/TIME while the more recent method is referred to as PERT/COST. In the discussion that follows, the emphasis will be upon PERT/TIME.

At almost the same time (1957) the original PERT team was beginning its work on the Polaris project, a research team composed of representatives from the duPont company and Remington Rand developed an almost identical approach known as the Critical Path Method (CPM). It was not until 1959, however, that both teams learned of each other's efforts.

CPM was designed to balance the time and cost trade-offs involved in performing routine plant overhauls, maintenance, and construction costs. Like PERT, CPM involves a network analysis for planning and control purposes. Furthermore, both basic PERT and CPM are based upon the same concepts, with PERT using a "critical path" to guide completion of required activities. The major differences between the two approaches are in the notation used, the inclusion in CPM of both time and cost functions, and the fact that CPM uses a single time estimate while PERT uses one or three estimates. In much of the literature that followed the development of these two approaches, CPM, PERT, network analysis, and critical path analysis (to name a few) are generally considered to be names for the same method, even though there are varying degrees of difference among them.

The use of basic PERT requires an understanding of fundamental concepts and terms. Among the important terms are *activities, events, network,* and *dummy.* These terms and the concepts associated with them will be discussed next, followed by a description of how to construct a PERT chart.

Activities Activities are the work efforts of a project that consume time or resources. For example, planning, designing, constructing, and evaluating are all activities that use up units of time or resources. In a PERT network, activities are represented by arrows that have a definable beginning and ending point. Task descriptions and time estimates usually accompany each arrow in a network. The length of an arrow, however, bears no relationship to the expected amount of time required for an activity.

Events   The points where activities begin and end are called events.   Events represent specific accomplishments that occur at particular points in time.   They consume neither time nor resources and function as transition points between activities.   There is no limit to the number of activities that can lead into or out of an event, but each activity must begin and end with an event.   Typically, events are represented in a network by circles, circles with crosses inside, or "beetle" shapes, although other symbols also may be used.

Examples of events and activities are shown in Fig. 6–7.   The events in this network are represented by the numbers in circles while arrows A, B, and C represent activities that immediately precede or follow the events.   Event number 2 is referred to as a "burst" event since more than one activity originates from it.   When an event represents the completion of one or more activities, it is known as a "merge" event.   An example of a merge event is shown in Fig. 6–8, where activities A and B merge on event 3.

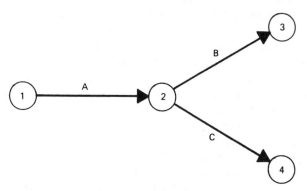

Fig. 6–7. Example of a "burst" point.

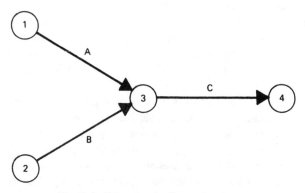

Fig. 6–8. Example of a "merge" point.

Network   A PERT network is a graphical representation of the sequence of activities and events needed to reach an objective. It shows the flow of relationships between activities and events and the order in which they must be accomplished to achieve a project or program objective. When time estimates are added to each activity, a network can aid in controlling project schedules.

Dummy   Although some persons might consider themselves to be one when they first try to develop a PERT network, a dummy is actually an activity of zero duration and zero expenditure of resources. It is usually represented by a dashed-line arrow and is introduced to maintain the logic of a network. As an example, consider the network shown in Fig. 6–9. The project described is one of designing and conducting a market survey. Event 2 is a burst event in which hiring personnel and designing the questionnaire are begun once planning for the survey has been completed. The dashed arrow between 4 and 3 insures that personnel cannot be trained until after the questionnaire has been designed. Obviously, it would be difficult to train the interviewers before the content of the questionnaire was established. The other dashed arrow in Fig. 6–9 (6–5) signifies that the survey is not to be conducted until the questionnaires have been printed. This dummy (6–5) is necessary to insure logic only if a computer is used, while dummy 4–3 is necessary to insure the logic of the network regardless of computer use.

Construction of a PERT Network   The following steps are typical of those used to construct a PERT network:[8]

1. Establish and Define the Project Objective. A team of persons involved in the project meets to determine what the end product should be and insure that it is clearly understood by all team members.

2. Plan the Network. The team develops a list of all the activities needed to achieve the project objective. Whenever possible, activities are broken down into subactivities. The final list is reviewed by the team and changes made if necessary.

3. Construct a Basic Network. The first step involved in developing a network is to construct a skeleton flowchart depicting the relationships between the events and activities. Using the list developed in step 2, the activities are numbered according to the sequence in which they need to occur for the objective to be achieved. For example, the activities used to conduct the market survey (Fig. 6–9) would be numbered as follows:

(1) Plan survey
(2) Hire personnel
(2) Design questionnaire
(3) Train personnel

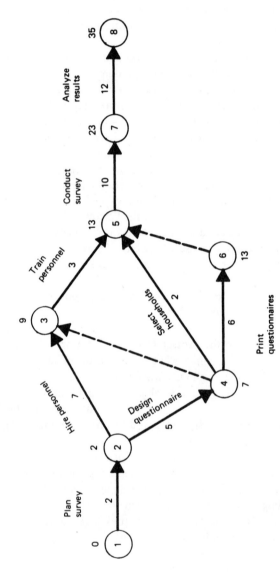

Fig. 6–9. A basic PERT network for a market survey. From PROJECT MANAGEMENT WITH CPM AND PERT, Second edition, by Joseph J. Moder and Cecil R. Phillips © 1970 by Litton Educational Publishing, Inc. Reprinted by permission of Van Nostrand Reinhold Company. The time estimates were developed by the author.

(4) Select households
(4) Print questionnaires
(5) Conduct survey
(6) Analyze results

The corresponding event numbers then are placed in circles (or other symbols), and the network is completed by sequentially joining activities and events. This task can be accomplished by beginning with the start event and working forward to the end event, beginning with the end event and working backward, or beginning with a middle event and working both forward and backward. The typical procedure is to begin with the end event and work backward, although choice of the procedure will depend upon personal preferences.

The flow of events and activities, however, must be developed according to certain rules, some of which will vary in importance depending upon whether or not computers will be used. Among the rules that should be followed are these:

a. An event may not begin until all activities preceding it have been completed.
b. An activity that follows an event may not begin until the event has taken place.
c. The network of arrows does not represent alternate paths; every line in a network must be used to achieve the objective.
d. Each event may occur only once; after an event has taken place, the loop of network activities may not return to it.
e. Only one activity may connect any two events. If more than one activity must connect two events, a dummy activity should be used.
f. A network must begin and end with one event. The initial and terminal events may not have predecessor or successor events.
g. The numbers that represent events in a network may not be duplicated.

Of these rules, the last three (e, f, and g) are necessary to insure compatibility with computer logic for some but not all computer programs. If a network will be constructed manually, then rules e, f, and g are optional. Before the team proceeds to the next step, a poll should be taken among the project team members (and others involved in the project) to determine if there is agreement about the format of the network and the events and activities included in it.

4. Add Detail to the Basic Network. If an analysis of a network reveals that achievement of the objective is likely to be more complex than depicted by the basic network, then more detail should be added. This review of the network is important to insure that no relevant events and activities have been omitted. Otherwise, subsequent calculations of time estimates are likely to be in error. Perhaps the best guide to use in making this analysis is to review all the rules of network construction, especially rules a and b. These rules generally will determine

the amount of detail needed in a network by requiring a sequential examination of the relationships among all events and activities.

5. Collect Time Estimates. A feature that distinguishes PERT from other charting techniques is the use of time estimates to predict the duration of each activity. Although such estimates are usually subjective, they can provide a better estimate of total project time than guessing about an entire project. That is, the sum of individual time estimates is likely to be more accurate than a single estimate when all activities are considered at once.

The estimates should be collected by reviewing them with persons likely to have the most accurate information. The more realistic these estimates are, the more likely it is the project will be completed efficiently. In addition, all estimates should consider the availability of human and material resources. If critical resources will not be available for a specific activity, the estimates must be adjusted accordingly. The persons responsible for these resources are the ones most likely to be aware of their availability and should be consulted whenever possible.

6. Calculate the Expected Time. There are two methods for calculating expected-time estimates. First, there is the single-estimate method, which is simply a prediction of the expected duration of each activity, independent of all other activities. The second method uses three estimates to calculate expected time: optimistic time, pessimistic time, and most likely time. When the three-estimate method is used, the expected time is based upon a weighted average of the estimates, while expected time using the single-estimate method is obtained directly from the initial estimates.

There has been some controversy as to which method is best. For example, the three-estimate procedure has been criticized on the basis of its statistical assumptions and the relatively complex calculations required. On the other hand, the single-estimate procedure has been subject to the criticism that it is too simplistic and will result in grossly inaccurate estimates of total project expected time. It is generally recognized, however, that the choice of estimation method will depend upon the type of project. For operating-level projects of long duration and great uncertainty in regard to estimate accuracy, the three-estimate method is preferable; for master network schedules of relatively short duration and low uncertainty about estimate accuracy, the single-estimate method is preferable. For reasons of simplicity, the discussion that follows will be concerned with the single-estimate method. The reader interested in calculations for the three-estimate method should consult the books listed in the reference section or any of the hundreds of books and articles available on the PERT technique.

Although there may be differences in how individual activity estimates are calculated, the computations involved in calculating the total network estimates are the same. Two sets of calculations are needed for the total network estimates: "forward pass" and "backward pass." The forward-pass computations determine the expected (earliest) start and finish times for each activity and the expected (earliest) time for each event; the backward-pass computations provide the latest-allowable start and finish times for each activity and the latest-allowable time for each event. The forward-pass computations will be described next and the backward-pass computations will be described in step 7. The times for both sets of computations typically are expressed in units such as minutes, hours, days, and weeks.

Forward-pass computations are based upon two assumptions: (1) the start event of a project occurs at zero time, and (2) each activity will start immediately after its predecessor activity has been completed. Based upon these assumptions, the market survey network (with single time estimates) shown in Fig. 6–9 can serve as an example. Each number next to an arrow expresses the expected duration of that activity, while the numbers next to the events are the cumulative time totals for events (in this case, days are used as the time units). Beginning with the start event at time zero, time estimates are made for each subsequent activity until the cumulative total for the network is determined at the end event.

As shown in Fig. 6–9, activity 1–2 is expected to take two days; activities 2–3 and 2–4 are expected to take seven and five days, and the cumulative totals for events 3 and 4 will be nine and seven days, respectively. Event 5, however, is a merge event and the cumulative total for this event must accommodate the event times that preceded it. Thus, once the personnel are trained by the end of three days, a total of 12 days is expected to have elapsed. Once event 4 is completed, however, the activities that follow it (4–5 and 4–6) require two and six days, giving cumulative totals at event 5 of 9 and 13 days, respectively. Thus, there will be three cumulative totals possible for event 5: 12, 9, and 13 days. However, since the survey cannot be conducted until after the questionnaires are printed (the event longest in duration), event 5 is assigned the largest of the three possible cumulative totals. This situation describes the general rule for estimating cumulative merge-event totals: When there is a choice among time estimates terminating at an event, select the largest of the possibilities as the expected date of the event. Continuing with the estimates, event 5 is given an expected duration of 10 days and event 7 a duration of 12 days. Adding the expected duration of activity 7 to the cumulative total at event 7 gives the total cumulative time for the network as 35 days (12 + 23 = 35). The 35-day total represents the longest path through the network and is considered to be the earliest (expected) finish time for the network.

7. Calculate the Latest-Allowable Time. Latest-allowable-time calculations provide estimates of the latest time an event can occur without exceeding the scheduled completion date. These computations are the reverse of forward-pass computations and are referred to as the backward pass. Backward-pass calculations are guided by two rules: (1) The latest-allowable finish time for a network's terminal event should be equal to an arbitrary completion date or to the earliest

expected time determined by forward-pass computations, and (2) when there is a choice among time estimates originating from an event, the smallest of the possibilities should be selected as the latest-allowable time.

Because these computations are the reverse of those used for the forward pass, the individual activity estimates are obtained by subtracting rather than adding the estimated time durations for each activity. This process can be illustrated by again using the example of the market survey network. In Fig. 6–10, the latest time estimates have been added to the earliest time estimates calculated previously in Fig. 6–9. In this case, the latest time has been set as equal to the earliest time of 35 days (event 8). The activity duration of 7–8 is subtracted to provide the latest time for event 7 which is 23, the same as the earliest time. The latest time of 13 for event 5 is found in an identical manner (23 –10 = 13). The latest time for event 6 is 13 since a dummy has zero duration. Event 4, however, has three activities originating from it so the second backward-pass rule must be used. The three possible estimates in this situation are 9 (9 – 0 = 9), 11 (13 – 2 = 11), and 7 (13 – 6 = 7) for activities 4-3, 4-5, and 4-6, respectively. Of these, 7 is the smallest so it is selected as the latest time estimate for event 4. The estimate for event 3 is 10 (13 – 3 = 10) but 2 for event 2 since the differences between activities 2-3 and 2-4 are both 2 (9 – 7 = 2 and 7 – 5 = 2) and no choice has to be made. Finally, the logic of the process is completed by calculating the latest time for event 1 which, of course, will be zero for this network (2 – 2 = 0).

8. Determine the Critical Path. The critical path in a network is the longest path from the start event to the finish event. In Fig. 6–11, the critical path was determined when the cumulative expected time (forward pass) was calculated. All other paths in the network will be shorter, so that if any one activity is delayed, the entire project will be delayed. The critical path is based upon the concept of "slack," which is simply the difference between the earliest and latest times of an event. In Fig. 6–11, for example, slack for each event is shown in boxes. This slack can be used to trace the critical path through those events that have zero slack. In Fig. 6–12, event 3 has positive slack (and is subcritical) so the path shown in double lines follows only the zero-slack events. It must be noted, however, that slack along the critical path can be either positive or negative if an arbitrary completion time is used instead of setting the terminal event's latest-allowable time equal to its earliest (expected) time. In addition, several critical paths might need to be identified for some projects.

9. Update the Network. Because even the best-planned projects have been known to fall apart after they are implemented, it is usually necessary to make certain adjustments to network activities and events. Such adjustments are referred to as updating the network and involve either observable changes in the progress of a project or changes in future plans. Human or material resources will not always be available when anticipated, or more resources might become available and alter the original project's objectives or its scope. In the market

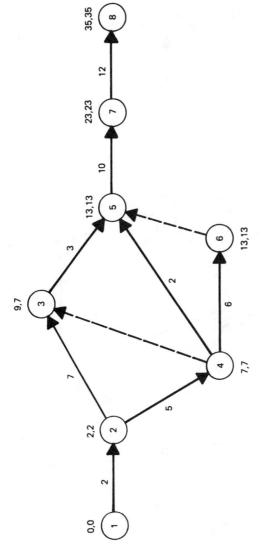

Fig. 6-10. PERT chart showing earliest and latest time estimates.

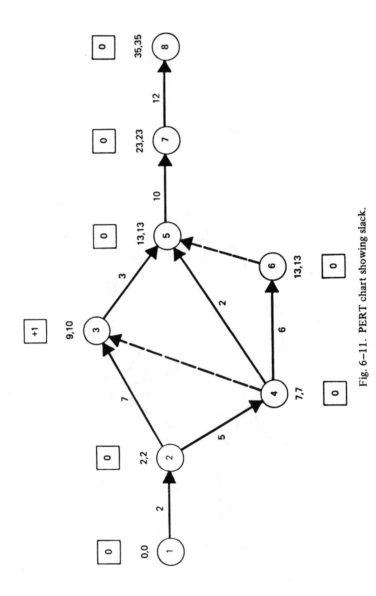

Fig. 6-11. PERT chart showing slack.

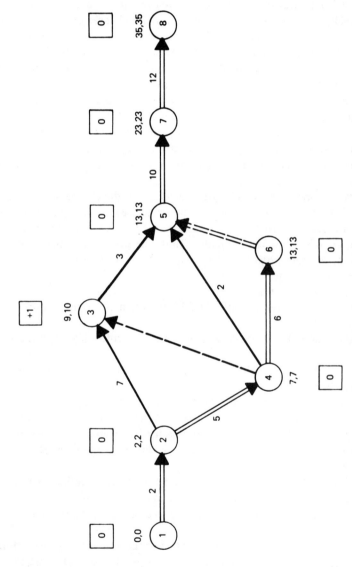

Fig. 6–12. PERT network showing slack and the critical path (double lines).

survey example, for instance, delays could be caused by a shortage of personnel to conduct the survey, or a printer's strike could increase the amount of time needed to print the questionnaires. On the other hand, a new source of personnel might become available enabling the surveyers to conduct more interviews than originally anticipated. Thus, whenever major changes occur, the network of events and activities is likely to be affected. The major advantage of critical-path identification is in knowing where time can be made up should any of the activities along the critical path slip (i.e., require more time than originally estimated). Because the total network slack shown in Fig. 6–12 is only + 1, a slippage of one day is all that will be allowable for the project to be completed by the expected time. Thus, if it is discovered that it will take four days instead of three to train personnel for a market survey, the lost time might be made up by only using six days to hire the personnel instead of the expected seven days. Depending upon the nature of the changes, other updating activities could be made accordingly.

Whenever a change occurs, however, the effect of the change upon the entire network must be considered. New activities might need to be developed or original ones modified or deleted. In addition, such changes usually will involve determination of a new critical path. Thus, the updating activity should be viewed as an ongoing process to be conducted at regular intervals throughout the duration of the project.

To summarize, construction of a PERT network involves the following steps:

1. Establish and Define the Project Objective. A project team agrees upon an end product.

2. Plan the Network. Make a list of all activities needed to achieve the project objective.

3. Construct a Basic Network. Sequentially link together project activities and events and assign numbers to each event. A network typically is constructed by starting with the terminal event and working backwards, using specific rules as guidelines. After agreeing upon the basic format of the network, the team moves on to the next step.

4. Add Detail to the Network. Review all of the relationships between activities and events to insure there have been no omissions. As a guide to this activity, review the network construction rules to determine if there have been any violations.

5. Collect Time Estimates. Consult with relevant others and gather information about the expected duration of each activity. Try to make sure that the estimates will be as accurate as possible.

6. Calculate the Expected Time. Using either the single- or three-estimate method, determine the expected (earliest) time of occurrence for each event.

Beginning with the start event and working forward, write the time estimates along the activity arrows and record the cumulative time totals above each event number. This operation is known as the forward pass.

7. Calculate the Latest-Allowable Time. Beginning with the terminal event and working backwards, subtract the expected time duration of each activity from its expected cumulative finish time. Write the cumulative latest-allowable time total above the start event of each activity. This operation is known as the backward pass.

8. Determine the Critical Path. For each event, subtract the expected (earliest) time cumulative totals from the latest-allowable-time cumulative totals. This calculation identifies the amount of slack for each network path (assuming that the expected and latest times for the terminal event are equal). Trace the critical path through the network events that have zero slack. This line will be the longest possible one that can be drawn through the network.

9. Update the Network. Periodically review progress of the project and make any adjustments necessary to correct time estimates and the critical path. The extent of the adjustments possible, however, will depend upon the amount of available network slack.

Evaluation   The preceding description of basic PERT has been rather superficial in its scope and depth of analysis. Since its development, PERT methodology has become increasingly sophisticated, and a more comprehensive description would exceed the space limitations of this book. In this regard, two major omissions bear mentioning. One omission is the recent emphasis on including resource allocation procedures and cost elements in the PERT planning process—especially time-cost trade-off procedures. The second omission concerns the various mathematical topics involved in implementing complex PERT networks. Although both of these omissions and others might be considered serious to some, the description presented should be adequate for most simple projects. Nevertheless, the reader considering the use of PERT (or other critical-path methods) would be wise to consult the numerous resources available on this topic, regardless of project complexity. As presented, the description is intended to serve only as a general introduction.

It also should be noted that numerous computer programs now exist for personal computers. These programs greatly simplify most of the tedious and complicated aspects of project management. Thus, PERT now should be accessible to more people.

There are at least seven advantages associated with PERT. First, and perhaps most important, it forces managers and others responsible for a project to carefully plan the events and activities needed to reach the objective. Second, forced planning makes it possible to easily identify the pattern of relationships that exist among events and activities. Third, it increases the ability of managers to predict and anticipate delays and provides guidelines on how to make up time lost by such delays. Thus, overall coordination of a project is enhanced greatly. Fourth, the network schedule helps minimize the risks of overlooking essential activities and events. Fifth, the updating procedure provides the flexibility needed to make necessary adjustments when a breakdown in the initial plan occurs. The network also enables a manager to quickly determine the current status of a project at any time during the project. Sixth, if properly used, it can help develop more cohesive teams and insure greater commitment to the project. Seventh, the graphical presentation of the network makes it easier to train new project managers or quickly brief persons who might be periodically involved with the project.

PERT also has certain disadvantages associated with it. Because of the growing complexity of the technique and the fact that it frequently requires computer programming, many operating managers find it difficult to understand and use. Koontz and O'Donnell,[9] for example, report on a survey that showed many companies using PERT networks, but only for informational purposes and not for actual control of a project. Many companies now find it helpful to condense large, complex networks into subnetworks containing major-event clusters. Another difficulty encountered in using PERT is that it is not appropriate for all types of projects. When it is impossible to make realistic time estimates and when a project involves routine planning of recurring tasks, another approach will be more suitable. PERT is also a very time-consuming technique, especially for projects involving large numbers of events and activities and requiring coordination among many different persons. This disadvantage need not present a problem, however, if the cost-efficiency of a project outweighs the time and effort required to develop and monitor it.

PERT will not guarantee better management planning, but it can help increase the quality of planning when it is used appropriately. By forcing managers to plan, it helps create an environment conducive to planning and control. Like other techniques, PERT only will be as good as the quality of information and human judgment that goes into it.

6.04 Research Planning Diagrams (RPDs)

Most managers use a variety of methods to assist in planning and controlling their work activities. Some of these methods involve relatively simple flowcharts, while others involve complex networks of probability estimates and require computer programming. Somewhere in between these types of methods are Research Planning Diagrams (RPDs) that incorporate features of both. RPDs are like simple flowcharts in their depiction of activity sequences without using great detail; they are like more complex methods in their compatibility with probability estimation and computer programming. However, unlike most network methods,

RPDs have the advantage of permitting activities to be recycled throughout the planning procedure. As with most methods, RPDs have features that make them more appropriate in some situations than in others. For projects that require recycling of activities and are too complex for simple flowcharts but not complex enough for network methods, RPDs provide a useful compromise.

RPDs are constructed using logic borrowed from computer flow diagrams. The major guidelines used in constructing RPDs are (1) list specific actions within rectangular boxes, (2) list decision points within diamonds, (3) depict completion needs (terminal points at which one activity must be finished before another may begin), and (4) use "escape routes" to provide opportunities to rethink or reexamine an activity—especially if major obstacles arise. When these guidelines are used, the actual construction of a RPD is a relatively simple process:

1. State the project objectives, being sure to specify the desired end result.
2. List the actions needed to complete the project, starting with the first required activity and then listing the remaining activities in their required order of occurrence.
3. For each activity, list the important questions that must be answered before succeeding activities can begin. These questions will function as the decision points in the diagram and must be answered with a yes or no response.
4. Using the information in steps 2 and 3, begin constructing the diagram. Start with the first required activity and then sequentially list each subsequent activity and decision point. Use arrows to connect the activities and decision points and to show the flow of action through the diagram. When necessary, assign time estimates to the activities and probability estimates to the decision points. These estimates, however, should be considered optional.
5. If a response to a decision point is difficult to determine or presents a major obstacle to project completion, use a "rethink" response. Such responses indicate that the flow of events at this point requires reappraisal. Typically, these situations develop when information is unavailable or inadequate to indicate the specific nature of the next activity or decision point.

To illustrate the use of RPDs, a portion of the diagram used to develop this book is presented in Fig. 6–13. (To comply with flowchart logic, a start should have been located at the top of the diagram but was omitted due to space limitations.) The first activity was to review the relevant literature to determine the need for the book and its possible scope and format. As shown in the right-side portion of this box, it was estimated that this activity would take 21 days to complete. If the first decision point had been answered with a no, then the concept would have been reconsidered and additional literature searched. In this case, however, the need for the book was answered with a yes, and the next three activities were carried out at approximately the same time. Work was begun on a book prospectus, discussions were conducted with others on the feasibility of the book, and a search was begun to determine which publishers might be interested in the book. It was estimated that all three of these activities would take about 14 days, since that was the estimated length of the activity with the longest duration. The completion-need symbol that follows these activities indicates that all of the preceding activities must be completed before the questions at the next decision point can be asked. If the idea for the book had not been considered feasible at this point, then a major rethink would have been required. Since the idea was considered feasible, the prospectus was sent out for review. An unfavorable response (no) following this activity would have led to another rethink and possible selection of other publishers (a recycling event). A yes response to the last decision point depicted would lead to the next activity (not shown), conducting an intensive literature search. The diagram would then continue until the terminal activity had been reached.

The diagram described in Fig. 6–13 is a rather simple example of how RPDs might be used. More complex examples are also possible but typically will require computer programming. Quickenden, Davies, and Woods,[10] for example, discuss how they used the IBM GPSS computer simulation package to plan production of an encapsulated powder using a new process. Because of the need to include precise probability estimates, hand calculation of the various transactions involved would have been prohibitive. To overcome this obstacle, a basic RPD was constructed and then translated into a format compatible with the computer program. The computer then used information provided from the basic diagram to calculate cumulative probability estimates for each day of the project. During the 23 days of the project, a graphical presentation of the project showed that the probability of success increased up to day 16 and then declined sharply. Obviously, such information would be indispensible for planning complex projects.

Evaluation   The major advantages of RPDs are that they (1) help predict critical points at which a project is likely to fail, (2) help make decision criteria explicit, (3) indicate clearly any necessary recycling activities (although in more complex diagrams the recycling can become obscured), (4) are highly compatible with computer simulations and time and cost estimates, (5) are easier to construct than critical-path-network methods (e.g., PERT) and avoid the requirement for dummy activities, and (6) provide a visible description of the sequence of required activities while clearly showing the interaction among the activities.

RPDs also share some of the possible weaknesses characteristic of other planning methods. For example, too much reliance upon diagrams and especially computer simulation of them would be dysfunctional for relatively simple projects. Thus, the availability of computer packages might make it tempting to indiscriminately apply them to all projects. On the other hand, there is also the possibility that computer programs will be avoided when they should be used. The complexity of a project and the requirements and importance of probability estimates can be used to help determine when computers might be cost-efficient

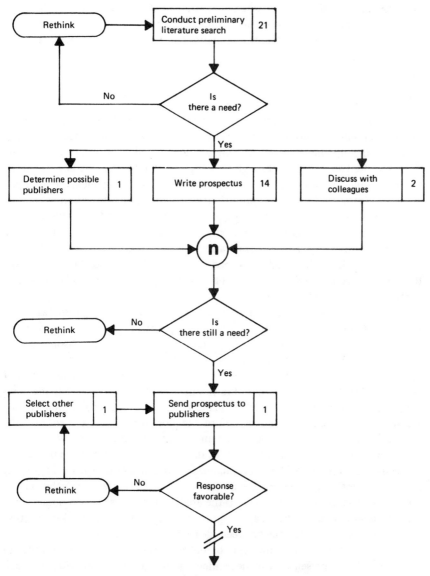

Fig. 6–13. A partial research planning diagram.

to use. Finally, the effects of using a team approach to RPDs need to be considered. In relatively heterogeneous groups it can be difficult to achieve consensus on which activities should be included, their order of appearance, and estimates of time and probability. In contrast, a homogeneous group—in which most members possess identical information and have similar values regarding the information—is much more likely to achieve consensus. These weaknesses, however, are probably minor when compared to the possible benefits that can be gained from using RPDs or other similar methods. As with any technique, care must be taken to use RPDs in situations in which they are likely to be of the most help at the least cost to the user.

COMMENTS

The core of any implementation plan involves assigning specific responsibilities in terms of who will do what, where, when, and how. Beyond these considerations, a timetable needs to be developed and steps taken to insure that the actions specified are followed through to completion. However, the key to success for any implementation strategy is commitment. The individuals who implement an idea must be just as committed to seeing it put into action as the person or persons who developed it. Once an idea is "sold" to the people who can authorize its implementation, commitment is much easier to obtain. The selling of an idea, however, can be a frustrating and often unrewarding task for idea originators. Although not all ideas need to be sold, there are at least two factors that can determine selling success: (1) the selling context, and (2) the selling content.

The context factor refers to such elements as the timing of the sale, the relevance of the intended audience, and the support provided by other persons in influential positions. Timing is important for rather obvious reasons. At the time an attempt is made to sell an idea, consideration must be given to events or attitudes that might negatively affect the outcome of a sale. If a new product concept is proposed, for example, the timing will obviously be bad if the company has just experienced a severe financial loss with a similar product. The second factor pertains to the selection of the most appropriate audience for the presentation. Presenting an idea to an unreceptive audience or one which is not in the position to do anything about it can be the surest way to have it killed or endlessly tied up in the "proper channels." Organizations with a history of being unreceptive to innovations are most likely to present such buffers to creativity. The third context factor is the ability of the presenter to obtain some type of sponsorship for the idea. Support of a person or group in a key position often can make the difference between idea acceptance or rejection.

Content factors refer to the style of the presentation itself. The manner in which an idea is presented can determine its likelihood of adoption as much as the context factors. The following is a partial list of factors to be aware of when proposing an idea to management:

1. Use simple language; avoid technical terms unless the audience is familiar with them.
2. Use a clear statement of need for the idea; provide facts that originally stimulated the need for the idea. That is, describe the problem your idea will solve and explain why it needs to be solved.
3. Present both the pros and cons of the idea; avoid one-sided presentations that might distort the idea's worth.
4. Provide evidence to suggest why the idea will work and why it should be better than another idea; avoid making exaggerated claims about its worth.
5. Stress key points when selling the idea; avoid unnecessary details.
6. Anticipate questions and develop responses to them.
7. Be persistent. If you really believe in the idea, you should be willing to fight for it. However, be careful not to become overly antagonistic.

NOTES

1. Hart, S., Boroush, M., Enk, G., and Hornick, W. "Managing Complexity Through Consensus Mapping: Technology for the Structuring of Group Decisions." *Academy of Management Review* 10:(3):587–600 (1985).
2. Although presented as a decision-making technique, Consensus Mapping is designed to assist in solution consolidation and implementation. Consensual decision making is involved, but only indirectly in making implementation choices. The authors describe a solution in terms of an action plan. As used in this book, however, a solution is a product of idea evaluation and selection. An action plan then needs to be developed to implement it. This difference in perspective and terminology, however, should not detract from the technique's usefulness.
3. Kepner, C. H., and Tregoe, B. B. *The Rational Manager.* Princeton, N.J.: Kepner-Tregoe, Inc., 1976.
4. *Ibid.*
5. Woods, M. F., and Davies, G. B. "Potential Problem Analysis: A Systematic Approach to Problem Predictions and Contingency Planning—An Aid to the Smooth Exploitation of Research." *R & D Management* 4:25–32 (1973).
6. Kepner and Tregoe use a quantitative estimate of problem seriousness in the decision-making cycle of their basic technique but do not include it when describing PPA.
7. VanGundy, A. B. Managing Group Creativity: A Modular Approach to Problem Solving. New York: AMACOM, 1985.
8. The following sources were used to develop the step-by-step description: Barnetson, P., *Critical Path Planning: Present and Future Techniques,* Princeton, N.Y.: Brandon/Systems Press, 1970; Iannone, A. L., *Management Program Planning and Control with PERT, MOST and LOB,* Englewood Cliffs, N.J.: Prentice-Hall, 1967; Miller, R. W., *Schedule, Cost, and Profit Control with PERT,* New York: McGraw-Hill, 1963; Moder, J. J., and Phillips, C. R., *Project Management with CPM and PERT,* New York:

Van Nostrand Reinhold, 1970; Stines, D. M., and Murphy, M. M., *Modern Management Methods: PERT and CPM,* Boston: Materials Management Institute, 1963.

9. Koontz, H., and O'Donnell, C. *Essentials of Management.* New York: McGraw-Hill, 1974.

10. Quickenden, M. A. J., Davies, G. B., and Woods, M. F. "The Use of Research Planning Diagrams." *R & D Management* 2:63–68 (1972).

7
Eclectic and Miscellaneous Techniques

The 14 techniques in this chapter have been roughly classified as being either eclectic or miscellaneous, although the distinction between some of these techniques and those presented in other chapters might seem somewhat arbitrary. The eclectic approaches combine two or more techniques to achieve a particular objective, while the miscellaneous techniques include two or more problem-solving stages and, in most cases, emphasize the process aspects of problem solving. Three of the eclectic techniques also stress problem-solving stages but have been classified as eclectic because of their primary emphasis upon combining different methods.

Of the eclectic techniques, the Bobele-Buchanan method, Creative Problem-Solving, and Value Engineering use major problem-solving stages. These techniques also will be valuable for training in creative thinking. The Coca-Cola method was designed specifically for new-product development and should be most useful for this purpose. Lateral Thinking is appropriate for redefining problems, generating ideas, and training in creative thinking. All of these approaches would be suitable for use by either individuals or groups.

The miscellaneous techniques are more diffuse in their commonality. The Delphi method and the Nominal Group Technique include two problem-solving stages (generation and selection of ideas), while the other miscellaneous techniques emphasize all of the stages. Two of these techniques are unique in their emphasis upon both the task and group process aspects of problem solving. Phases of Integrated Problem Solving and Problem-Centered Leadership both provide guidance for task and social-facilitation processes. In contrast, the other techniques described in this book are oriented more towards structuring the task and provide little or no guidance on handling group discussions. The Decision Seminar, Nominal Group Technique, Phases of Integrated Problem Solving, and Problem-Centered Leadership are designed for use only by groups, while the other methods can be used by either individuals or groups. It also should be noted that the Delphi method, and Nominal Group Technique could be used for generating ideas, and the Kepner-Tregoe method would be especially helpful for analyzing problems and evaluating and selecting ideas.

ECLECTIC TECHNIQUES

7.01 Bobele-Buchanan

Most creative solutions are obtained through convergent and divergent types of thinking. Convergent thinking involves assessing the information associated with a problem and then systematically converging upon a problem solution; divergent thinking is just the opposite—different solutions are sought by spreading out from an idea in different directions.

The Bobele-Buchanan technique is a five-step problem-solving method that uses different types of thinking at each stage in the process. To encourage such thinking, different formal problem-solving techniques are used, as well as case studies and exercises in creative thinking. The Bobele-Buchanan method was developed by H. Kenneth Bobele and Peter Buchanan—Canadian management consultants—as an alternative to the case-study method of teaching managerial problem solving.[1] It was originally designed to be presented in three 80-minute class sessions, not including outside reading assignments. With some minor modifications, it can be tailored easily to fit different problem-solving situations. The five basic steps used to implement the process are

1. Identify the problem
2. Generate alternatives
3. Define the criteria
4. Design an action implementation plan
5. Build feedback systems

Before presenting the five-step process, Bobele and Buchanan begin their class sessions by having the participants spend 15 minutes reading a case study involving a packaging problem. The participants are asked to individually analyze the situation, generate alternatives, and select the best alternative along with their reasons for doing so. The case study is discussed next, followed by a presentation on human information processing and its relation to managerial problem solving and decision making. The five-step problem solving process is then presented.

1. Identify the Problem. Five different activities are used for this step. First, a convergent definition of the problem is sought using the Kepner-Tregoe approach of defining a problem in terms of an aberration from some expected standard or norm. Second, problem symptoms are listed and possible causes deduced (the "detective" approach). Third, six questions are asked about the problem to further analyze it: Who? What? Why? Where? When? How? Fourth, if information is still perceived to be insufficient, two questions are asked: What information do I need to solve the problem? and Who has that

information? Finally, the fifth activity involves presenting the group with a case study and having them practice the problem identification procedure.

2. Generate Alternatives. When an instructional class session is held, the participants use practice exercises before generating ideas. To emphasize the need for divergent thinking during this step, the participants are first asked to generate a list of all possible uses for a toothpick, followed by an exercise involving the problem of how to draw one continuous line through nine dots arranged in columns and rows to form a square. The rules of Classical Brainstorming are presented, and the group once again generates a list of possible uses for a toothpick. The group is then given practice in developing lateral thinking skills through the use of a random-word generator known as the "Think Tank"[2] (a box containing words printed on pieces of plastic which are dropped out a few at a time). Practice in using the Think Tank is achieved by brainstorming on all possible uses for a brick. The practice exercises conclude with the presentation of a case study involving conflict between management and sales personnel. Group members are asked to role-play the managers using the problem identification step, and then the entire group attempts to generate solutions using Classical Brainstorming.

3. Define the Criteria. The process of defining criteria that a solution must meet is basically a convergent-thinking activity. Emphasis in this step is upon comparing each generated idea against a specific list of criteria. Bobele and Buchanan suggest using criteria such as (a) time, both long- and short-term; (b) cost; (c) social considerations to the organization; (d) risk to the manager; (e) ease of implementation; and (f) the potential for the idea to create additional or bigger problems. Lateral Thinking (a divergent-thinking activity) also could be used in this stage. Priorities for the criteria also should be established, and a solution selected using these priorities.

4. Design an Action Implementation Plan. Little information is provided by the authors for using this step. The central activity seems to involve devising a strategy that can be used for implementing the solution previously selected. This activity would be classified as being convergent.

5. Build Feedback Systems. The final step in the process is essentially a convergent-thinking activity. It involves designing an information collection procedure for monitoring the performance of the chosen solution. Because most organizational environments are dynamic, any solutions implemented will be only temporary. Thus, feedback systems provide a way for sensing any changes related to the problem solution.

When presented as a classroom activity, the Bobele-Buchanan method concludes with the class applying the five-step process to a case study and discussing the procedure and its outcome. The procedure for using the five-step problem-solving process can be summarized as follows:

1. Identify the Problem
   a. Use the Kepner-Tregoe approach to analyze the problem.
   b. List the problem symptoms and possible causes.
   c. Ask: Who? What? Why? Where? When? How? to analyze the problem.
   d. Ask: What information do I need to define the problem? and Who has that information?
2. Generate Alternatives
   a. Use Classical Brainstorming.
   b. Use the Think Tank idea generator or Lateral Thinking.
3. Define the Criteria
   a. Compare each alternative against such criteria as time, costs, social considerations to the organization, risk to the manager, ease of implementation, and the possibility that the alternative could create additional or larger problems.
   b. Use Lateral Thinking.
   c. Establish criteria priorities.
   d. Select the solution that best satisfies the priorities.
4. Design an Action Implementation Plan
   a. Devise a strategy for implementing the optimal solution.
   b. Implement the solution.
5. Build Feedback Systems
   a. Develop a procedure for monitoring the effects of the chosen solution upon the problem.
   b. Change or adapt the solution to fit changing environmental conditions.

Evaluation As an eclectic technique, the Bobele-Buchanan method is probably more useful as a procedure for practicing creative thinking than it is for actually solving problems. The approach seems to suffer most from a lack of specificity in describing the operations used. From the description of the process provided by the authors, it is difficult to know exactly how to apply many of the procedures —especially steps 4 and 5. The steps also seem to be inadequately conceived. Identifying the problem is mixed with defining and analyzing the problem, and no provision is made for determining how criteria priorities should be established. In addition, a step for selecting alternative solutions probably should follow the step for defining criteria.

The positive feature of this technique is its emphasis upon an eclectic approach. Kepner-Tregoe, Classical Brainstorming, and Lateral Thinking are combined to produce a procedure that is broader in scope and presumedly more useful than more narrowly developed techniques (i.e., those emphasizing a single problem-solving stage). The most important aspect of an eclectic approach, however, is the rationale used to combine the different methods. Bobele and Buchanan base their rationale upon the concepts of divergent and convergent thinking—commonly discussed elements of the creative process. To some extent they have been successful in tying in both types of thinking, primarily because of the techniques they used—Kepner-Tregoe uses convergent thinking while Classical Brainstorming and Lateral Thinking use divergent thinking. The placement of these techniques within specific stages, however, could be a limiting factor. A better procedure might be to use techniques that would provide for both types of thinking within each of the steps. Kepner-Tregoe and Wishful Thinking, for example, could be jointly used to analyze a problem. The best way to insure both convergent and divergent thinking, however, would be to use Creative Problem Solving. Each stage of this approach begins with divergent thinking and ends with convergent thinking.

Finally, the authors report results of some preliminary research on their approach. The number of solutions produced by students before they used the five-step process was compared with the number of solutions produced by the same students after they participated in the process. Results indicated that an average of 5.98 solutions were produced before training and 9.51 were produced after training. No mention was made, however, of the statistical significance of these results (i.e., could the results have been produced by chance alone?). Furthermore, without a comparison group that does not receive the training, no meaningful conclusions can be drawn from these findings.

Even if it is assumed that an increase in ideas does result from using the technique, two additional factors must be considered. Firts, the *quality* of ideas produced by the method is an unknown element, especially in relation to "real" problem-solving groups. Second, the results were based upon use of the entire training activity, which included assigned readings, discussion of case studies, practice exercises, and lectures on the problem steps. There is no way of knowing how successful the approach would be if applied as a technique—using only the problem steps—rather than as a complete training activity. Until more research is available, it would probably be best to consider the Bobele-Buchanan method as more suitable for problem-solving training than as a specific problem-solving technique. However, it must be noted that—with a few exceptions—the same criticism can be made about most creative problem-solving models.

7.02 Coca-Cola

In 1969, J. E. Bujake,[3] a development associate in the Coca-Cola Company's Foods Division, reported on his experiences in using a four-step process designed to stimulate creative thinking in the area of new-product development. According to Bujake, technological advances in computers and laboratory equipment have accelerated the amount of progress made in the research and development (R&D) field over the last 50 years. Such advances, however, cannot substitute for the creative insights needed to initiate and implement R&D programs.

New-product development is especially problematic since much of the creative effort used in this area is relatively hit-or-miss. In an attempt to introduce some structure into this process, Bujake suggests using "programmed innovation." The four steps used to produce programmed innovation are

1. Opportunity search
2. Form evolution
3. Concept expansion
4. Concept development

1. Opportunity Search. The purpose of this step is to search for and identify areas that could be used for new-product development. During the course of this activity, background material is gathered that will be used to generate new concepts in the other steps of the process. To help in exploring potential-product areas, Bujake suggests using either Attribute Analysis (Attribute Listing) or Systems Analysis.

Attribute Analysis is used by listing all of the uses and desirable and undesirable attributes of a product in as general a manner as possible. The listing is then discussed and analyzed in a group session, with any new concepts added as they occur. The major focus of this activity, however, is upon combining desirable characteristics in such a way that any undesirable characteristics are either minimized or eliminated. As an example, Bujake describes how a new breakfast food might best combine such attributes as texture, flavor, aroma, compactness, and convenience.

Bujake's description of how Systems Analysis can be used to explore new-product areas is similar to the procedure used for the Input-Output technique. When all possible inputs and outputs associated with a product area are analyzed, new concepts can be created in the process of trying to improve the system's efficiency. To illustrate, Bujake describes new concepts developed from an analysis of a "system" involving packaged breakfast foods. The activities involved in a breakfast, for example, could be broken down into the stages of preparation, serving, and clean-up. In looking at ways to make these activities more efficient the problem solvers could conceive of a new product that might be ready to eat, prepared by individuals for their own consumption, and have disposable or edible containers. Thus, the need for all three activities would be eliminated.

2. Form Evolution. Using the material generated in the first step, an attempt is made to create unusual product-concept forms. The method used to accomplish this is Morphological Analysis. Different product states and product forms are first listed in a matrix and then the different combinations are examined for new concepts. A foam state and a flake form, for example, could be combined to suggest a foam flake that would combine the unique features of

each (e.g., the porousness of foam and the crispness of flakes). A few of the new forms that have evolved from the matrix analysis would then be selected for the next step.

3. Concept Expansion. This step involves the generation of a large number of alternative ways for looking at the attributes and concepts developed in the previous stages. The purpose of this activity is to provide maximum flexibility in selecting the concepts to be used for further development. To do this, Bujake suggests using Classical Brainstorming or the Trigger Method. Using the Trigger Method to illustrate this step, Bujake describes how the concept of a foam flake could be expanded to be applicable as a breakfast food. A food might be developed, for example, that (a) contains aromatic flavors permeating a porous flake, or (b) a foamed shell encasing a filling that would be used in a toaster, or (c) a foam structure constructed like a sandwich and containing textured bacon and egg flavors. After a number of different product concepts are analyzed, one is selected for further development. If it proves to be unworkable, then a new concept is selected and the process continues.

4. Concept Development. The fourth and last step of the process has as its goal the development of a problem solution. The method employed to do this is Synectics. To describe how Synectics could be used to develop a concept into a practical solution, Bujake uses the example of the sandwich-like structure generated in the previous step. The Problem as Given (PAG) is the original concept of the foamed sandwich structure. This is then followed by the Purge stage and then the Problem as Understood (PAU). Using fantasy, the PAU might be defined in terms of how a material can be made to blow itself up. During the Excursion, the next Synectics stage, an analogy—such as nuclear fission—might be applied to the problem, followed by a Force Fit stage to combine elements like pressure, compression, heating, and so forth. Finally, a viewpoint is created, such as using a mixture under pressure to create a foamed structure containing different textures, flavors, and aromas. The viewpoint then must be subjected to critical evaluation by experts to determine its feasibility. If the viewpoint is not seen as feasible, then a new concept can be selected for development or the viewpoint can be used as the basis for additional concept development.

Evaluation   In discussing this process, Bujake notes that its most valuable feature is its systematic emphasis. Specifically, the sequence of steps should result in solutions of higher quality than could be obtained with a less organized approach. The actual techniques used for each step, however, can be varied to suit the problem. Synectics and/or the Trigger Method, for example, could be used for all of the steps depending upon the problem, although Bujake recommends using a variety of techniques whenever possible.

In addition to the strengths and weaknesses associated with the particular techniques used by Bujake in his program, there are a number of concerns specifically related to the Coca-Cola approach. The advantages and disadvantages of the Coca-Cola method are listed below.

Advantages

1. The process described by Bujake actually involves two steps: idea finding and idea refining. Idea finding is the objective of the opportunity search step, while the next three steps progressively refine the ideas (concepts) until a practical solution is achieved. As a result, a typically unstructured, hit-or-miss process is provided with some degree of structure to guide idea development.

2. In addition to providing structure, the method also can have a positive effect upon an organization's creative atmosphere. According to Bujake, the involvement of persons from different backgrounds can foster cooperation and provide greater interaction among members of different work groups. A likely by-product of such interaction is greater acceptance of new ideas throughout an organization.

3. Although originally developed for innovation in new-product development, the method could be applied to a variety of other areas, such as engineering, marketing, and research.

4. Perhaps the major advantage of the process, however, is its eclectic nature. By drawing upon a variety of techniques, the method is especially suitable for broad-scope problems that require a multimethod approach. For such problems, methods used in isolation are seldom adequate to provide the necessary degree of idea refinement.

Disadvantages

1. Although the process provides different methods for analyzing a problem and generating ideas, it fails to provide much structure for evaluating and selecting ideas. After the first step, the selection of ideas for further refinement apparently is left to the discretion of the group members or the group leaders. If a low-quality idea is selected early in the process, much time and effort can be wasted in recycling back to an earlier step. The process could be improved considerably by inserting selection criteria (possibly based upon screens of varying cost) at the end of the second, third, and fourth steps.

2. The method requires a group of at least four or five highly trained individuals. While the training requirements for Attribute Analysis, Systems Analysis, and Morphological Analysis are not exceptionally high, Classical Brainstorming, the Trigger Method, and especially Synectics do require a high level of training on the part of the group members and particularly the group leader. Practice in the different techniques would seem to be essential to insure effectiveness of the method.

3. The process probably will be of greatest value when used with members who have diverse backgrounds and when the problem is medium or broad in scope. Although diversity of membership is important for most group creativity methods, the appropriateness of the process for broad-scope problems makes this requirement all the more important. When a problem is open-ended and not well defined, different perspectives can help to expand the number of potential alternatives. If the method is used with narrow-scope problems, however, the talents as well as the time of the group members will be wasted. The more clearly defined the problem, the less will be the need to refine it using multiple methods. Related to this concern is the possibility that group members will become so attached to the process that they will try to apply it to all the problems they encounter. Like most problem-solving methods, the Coca-Cola approach used must be applied selectively and not viewed as a cure-all for any problem that might come along.

In summary, the process described by Bujake has the major advantages of being structured, eclectic, and suitable for broad-scope problems that require successive refinements of generated ideas. The major disadvantages of the process involve the absence of idea evaluation and selection procedures, the need for member and leader training in the different techniques, and the inappropirateness of the method for well-defined, narrow-scope problems.

7.03 Creative Problem-Solving (CPS)[4]

Since first presented by Osborn, Classical Brainstorming has spawned many different variations and related techniques. One of the most notable of these is the Creative Problem-Solving (CPS) program developed by Sidney J. Parnes, chairman of the board of the Creative Education Foundation and professor of creative studies at the State University College at Buffalo, New York. Since the 1950s, Parnes has been actively involved in developing creativity training programs, evaluating and researching the concept of creativity, and—through the Creative Education Foundation—conducting annual institutes on creative problem solving.[5]

The training program Parnes and his associates[6] have developed will be used to present CPS as a creative problem-solving technique. This description will be supplemented by the work of Isaksen and Treffinger[7] as well as VanGundy.[8] Parnes's original model was preceded by recognition of a "mess" that must be refined and clarified before beginning the process. Isaksen and Treffinger have added a sixth stage (Objective Finding) which formalizes the activities involved in assessing the "mess."

Although it might be an oversimplification, CPS is basically an expanded version of Classical Brainstorming structured within a framework of major problem-solving stages and incorporating a variety of techniques to fulfill the objectives of the stages. In addition to Classical Brainstorming, CPS draws upon Checklists, forced-relationship methods, Morphological Analysis, and Synectics. Each of these can be used at different times during the process.

The six stages of the CPS process are

1. Objective finding
2. Fact finding
3. Problem finding
4. Idea finding
5. Solution finding
6. Acceptance finding

Each of these stages begins with a divergent activity and ends with a convergent activity. Throughout the process, the guiding principle is deferred judgment. Except for the task of selecting a solution, all evaluation must be suspended during the divergent part of each stage so that a freewheeling, open climate can be maintained.

1. Objective Finding. The first stage is designed to narrow the focus for problem-solving efforts. The divergent portion of Objective Finding begins with a search for concerns, challenges, and opportunities that need to be confronted. Convergence then is used to select the most important objective area. Isaksen and Treffinger suggest identifying outcomes and obstacles to facilitate divergence during this stage. Outcomes can be aided by generating a list of "Wouldn't it be nice if (WIBNI) . . .?" statements. For instance, "WIBNI:

a. I had trouble deciding how to spend my money?"
b. supervisors offered more praise than punishment?"
c. I could learn everything in a book by just looking at it?"

In a similar manner, obstacles can be generated using "Wouldn't it be awful if (WIBAI) . . .?" statements. For example, "WIBAI:

a. No one ever paid any attention to what I said?"
b. My boss never shared what he expected of me?"
c. I had to do the same thing over and over again in my job?"

Any other concerns, challenges, and opportunities thought of also would be written down.

Convergence during Objective Finding involves identifying important areas to work on. These are known as "hits." Next, the hits are examined to identify areas of commonality. Any hits that seem to share something in common should be combined. These combinations are known as "hotspots." Using the hits and hotspots as stimuli, the problem solver then develops problem statements. From the outcomes and obstacles generated in the example, some potential statements would be the following:

a. In what ways might I reward my boss to praise me more often?
b. In what ways might I gain access to an optical text scanner?
c. In what ways might I learn more about what my boss expects of me?
d. In what ways might I introduce more variety into my job?

The most important statement would be selected for the next stage. Selecting this statement can be guided by the criteria of ownership and outlook. Ownership criteria are concerned with how much influence the problem solver has over a problem as well as his or her motivation level. Outlook criteria involve such things as familiarity with a problem, its urgency to be resolved, and its stability.

2. Fact Finding. The objective of this stage is to gather all information related to the problem. This can be accomplished by dividing a sheet of paper into three columns: wants, sources, and obtained information. The wants column should contain a list of questions about the information needed to clarify and understand the problem. In writing these questions, it is important that only fact-oriented questions be developed. Questions that require judgment should be avoided. For example, What are the specifications for this equipment? is fact oriented; but Should I buy this equipment? is evaluative. Separation of fact from opinion, however, must be done with great care. What is fact to one person might be opinion to another. To avoid destructive conflicts, it is probably better to record such opinions as facts whenever a conflict is likely. All of the wants should be listed without regard to the availability of information. The second column of the sheet should then contain all the potential sources of information, followed by the actual information, when obtained, in the third column. Another highly recommended way to stimulate divergence during Fact Finding is to use the Five W's and H method (Chapter 3). The responses to each of the W and H questions can be used as stimuli to prompt new problem viewpoints.

Convergence during Fact Finding again can be aided by using hits and hotspots. All the important data are identified first (hits), followed by combinations of hits (hotspots). After completing this stage, the problem solver should have a better idea of the problem needing resolution. If possible, a refined version of the problem statement developed during Objective Finding should be the final product.

3. Problem Finding. The Problem Finding stage involves the gradual development of the broadest possible statement of the problem. By beginning with the original fuzzy statement of the problem and progressing toward a broad statement,

a problem solver can examine a large number of alternatives that will make the problem more conducive for Idea Finding. One method typically used to expand the problem statement is the Why Method (Chapter 3). This technique poses questions in such forms as: In what ways might (IWWM) . . .? In this case, the original statement is posed and then why? is asked of the statement. For example, consider the problem, IWWM we obtain an auxiliary heating system for our factory? A why question would be, Why do we want to obtain an auxiliary heating system? A possible answer might be, To keep warmer during the winter. This response then is restated as a new problem: IWWM we keep warmer this winter? A new response is generated for this question and the process continues until a high level of abstraction is achieved. In addition to the Why Method, other problem redefinitions should be generated by examining the responses to the Five W's and H method. These responses frequently can suggest new problem statements or unique viewpoints.

Convergence during Problem Finding involves using hits and hotspots to develop the best possible problem statement. Important redefinitions generated during divergence should be noted and combined, whenever possible, into one statement. Development of this statement should be guided by at least two criteria. First, a problem statement should contain no more than one problem. Second, major criteria should not be included in a statement. For instance, the following statement would be inappropriate: IWWM we keep warm this winter at a cost of less than $100 per month? The cost factor is a criterion that places a constraint upon potential ideas.

Problem Finding concludes with selection of the most promising statement. According to Parnes,[9] even though one problem statement might be better than another, Idea Finding usually is influenced by the different problem viewpoints generated during Problem Finding. As a result, Idea Finding invariably benefits from the "stretch" for a variety of viewpoints. Such stretches can help stimulate many unique ideas during Idea Finding.

4. Idea Finding. The eclectic nature of the CPS process is particularly evident during this stage. To generate possible ideas during divergence, a number of different techniques can be used. Perhaps the most common approach is to use Classical Brainstorming. The four brainstorming principles are presented to the group, the need to separate idea generation from idea evaluation is stressed, and special emphasis is given to the principle of deferred judgment. A second approach is to use forced relationships in which two apparently unrelated objects or ideas are forced together to produce a novel product. Another variation of this approach involves the manipulation of nouns and verbs. For example, one of two nouns, such as "paper" and "soap," is converted to a verb and a relationship forced between the two. Thus, "soap" might be converted to "soaps" and forced together with paper to suggest a paper impregnated with soap that could be used as an easily removable label for a jar. Osborn's checklist method[10]

represents a third approach to Idea Finding. Idea-spurring questions such as: Put to other uses? Adapt? Modify? Magnify? Minify? Substitute? Rearrange? and Combine? can be applied to objects or ideas to suggest new ideas. A fourth approach is to use analogies from the Synectics technique, and a fifth approach is to use Morphological Analysis. Whatever technique is selected to generate ideas, the most important consideration is that all judgment must be deferred during divergence. In addition to these specific methods, Parnes also suggests that Idea Finding might benefit further by introducing movement into the group. Thus, when group members have an idea to offer, the leader might instruct them to walk to a board or chart and write the idea down themselves. Divergence during Idea Finding is accomplished by reviewing all the ideas generated and noting hits and hotspots. It is especially important that ideas be combined when feasible (the hotspots). Often, a couple of fairly weak ideas can be integrated to produce one strong idea. The Idea Finding stage should finish with selection of two or three of the most promising ideas. This final selection process sometimes can be guided by selecting one or two of the most important evaluation criteria and judging each idea against them. However, be cautious when using such an approach. Many potentially useful ideas can be omitted from further consideration when only one or two criteria are used.

5. Solution Finding. The previous stages dealt with divergent and convergent searches for objectives, facts, problems, and ideas. This stage also uses divergent and convergent activities, but in two different ways. The first activity is to diverge and generate a list of criteria for evaluating solutions. Then, the most important criteria are selected (convergence). The second activity involves diverging and developing the best possible solution. Using the ideas selected from Idea Finding, the problem solver makes the necessary modifications and combinations to improve the ideas as much as possible. (Of course, one of the ideas from the previous stage may be in workable form already and require no additional effort.) Selection of the best solution (convergence) can be aided using a systematic procedure such as Weighting Systems (Chapter 5).

6. Acceptance Finding. The last stage of the CPS process is concerned with developing and evaluating ways to implement a final solution. Because the solution selected from the previous stage is still regarded as tentative, the objective of Acceptance Finding is to insure that it will be accepted by other persons involved. There are at least four ways to do this. This first way is to use an implementation checklist that contains questions such as the following: What are the possible objections likely to be raised about this idea and how might they be countered? In what ways could other persons help to implement this idea? Where is the best location to implement this idea? What would be the best time to implement this idea? Are there any ways in which this idea can be tested before implementation? A second method is to use a who, what, where, when, why, and how checklist. One way to use this method is to construct three

columns on a sheet of paper using the headings what; who, where, and when; and why and how. Ideas are generated for each column and the best ones from each column selected. These ideas can then be forced together to suggest new implementation ideas. A third method of insuring acceptance is to use protective thinking. This simply involves considering ways to protect the integrity of one's ideas. Of these methods, protective thinking is probably the least useful and should be used in conjunction with one of the other methods. A fourth way to assist solution implementation is to use structured techniques such as Consensus Mapping or Potential Problem Analysis (Chapter 6). These techniques accomplish much of what the other methods do, but do it in a more systematic manner.

When this stage is used, three guidelines should be followed: (1) the principle of deferred judgment should be emphasized, (2) individuals or two-person teams should be responsible for developing action plans rather than involving the entire group (unless the plan is important to the group), and (3) several different implementation plans often are advisable for people problems, but only one plan typically will be required for problems involving mechanical objects.

To illustrate how the CPS process might be used, an example of a problem-solving situation described by Parnes will be disucssed. (Because it was not included in the original version of CPS, Objective Finding is not described in this example.) It should be remembered that there is some flexibility in how the different stages can be used. Thus, the methods employed in this example are only representative.

The situation described by Parnes[11] involves a school-bus driver who has had several near-miss accidents caused by a boy who is constantly starting fights with other children on the bus. This behavior persisted even though the other children complained, the boy was reprimanded by the principal, and appeals were made to the boy's parents. The bus driver considered spanking the boy but was told by the principal that to do so could result in a law suit.

To begin the Fact Finding stage, a three-column sheet is developed to list wants, sources, and obtained information. As an example of the wants column, a question might be asked such as, Does the boy have personal or family problems? The sources of information may be the boy's parents or teachers, and the information obtained from these persons might reveal that the boy has no personal or family problems. Similar information will then be used to fill in the rest of the columns while keeping in mind the principle of deferred judgment.

In the Problem Finding stage, a question might be asked such as, In what ways might we get the boy to settle down? Then, from the question of why the boy needs to be settled down, a broader statement may emerge, such as, In what ways might peace be achieved on the bus? Although many other questions can be posed, this broadened statement will be used as an example of a question that might be selected for further work in the next stage.

With the problem now more clearly defined, potential solutions are generated during the Idea Finding stage. When Classical Brainstorming is used as the idea generation method, three ideas are produced: (1) Separate the boy from the other children, (2) allow the other children to decide what to do with the boy, and (3) assign the boy to the role of bus monitor. The first two ideas are selected as having the most potential for solving the problem.

To help in selecting one of these ideas, a criteria checklist is developed in the fourth stage of the process—Solution Finding. Three criteria are agreed upon: (1) the effect on the objective, (2) the effect on the boy, and (3) the effect on the other children. The ideas are then rated 1 (poor), 2 (fair), or 3 (good) on each of these criteria. The results of the rating indicate that the first idea (separating the boy) receives ratings of fair, poor, and good, respectively, on the criteria. A decision then is made to retain this idea for possible future consideration. The second idea is rated good on all three criteria and is selected for immediate implementation after modifying it using another idea (in this case, punishing misbehavior). A solution is then selected: Motivate the other children to keep the boy under control.

Once this solution is selected from among the others that could have been developed, it is time to begin Acceptance Finding. A three-column sheet is constructed with the headings: what (implementation ideas); who, where, and when; and why and how. Ideas are generated under each heading. In the what column, an idea is selected such as: Have the children think of an activity to do during the bus ride. The who, where, and when column provides the following choice: The other children in the school will have a contest, beginning the following week, to select an activity for the bus rides. The third column (why and how) yields the selection: A tape recorder or suggestion box will be used to record the ideas. This solution is then implemented and, it is hoped, the problem will be solved.

Evaluation   Before the evaluation of the CPS method is begun, it should be mentioned that the description of the process probably does not do justice to the work that Parnes has put into his creative-training programs. There are many variations of CPS that have been used to enrich the creative-thinking process. The sheer volume of this material, however, precludes a more comprehensive description. Nevertheless, it is felt that the basic elements of the CPS model have been adequately conveyed. In addition to the books by Parnes and his associates, the reader interested in more detailed information about CPS can write to: The Center for Studies in Creativity, State University College at Buffalo, Chase Hall, 1300 Elmwood Avenue, Buffalo, New York 14222.

It probably would be accurate to say that the Creative Problem-Solving method continues where Osborn's Classical Brainstorming approach leaves off. This is not surprising since Osborn founded the Creative Education Foundation and exerted much influence on Parnes' ideas about creative thinking.

While both approaches place heavy emphasis upon brainstorming principles and assumptions, CPS has expanded upon Osborn's original method by stressing the alternation between divergent and convergent thinking in each of the problem-solving stages. In addition, CPS is eclectic, making use of a variety of problem-solving methods within each of the stages. The fundamental element of all the stages, however, is the brainstorming principle of deferred judgment. Thus, to criticize the CPS approach is also to criticize Classical Brainstorming, although the reverse would not necessarily be true. Because the advantages and disadvantages of Classical Brainstorming are discussed elsewhere (Chapter 4), they will not be repeated here. There are, nevertheless, certain features of CPS that are unique to it and these will be described next.

Besides any advantages that might be associated with Classical Brainstorming, there are at least four major strengths of CPS. The first strength concerns its extension of the brainstorming method to include specific problem-solving stages. In addition to the idea-getting and idea evaluation stages of Osborn's method, CPS uses these stages (Idea Finding and Solution Finding) and adds four additional stages to round out the process. Furthermore, all of the CPS stages are more comprehensive in both their description and use. The Solution Finding stage, for example, prescribes the use of a specific activity to generate selection criteria as well as how to select ideas for further consideration. A second major strength of CPS is its emphasis upon training to use the method. In fact, CPS probably is more of a training program than it is a specialized problem-solving technique. Unfortunately, most of the research on the training program has been limited to investigations of the brainstorming elements of the process to the exclusion of other techniques in the program. The eclectic nature of CPS is a third strength of the approach. With the combination of brainstorming with Checklists, forced relationships, Morphological Analysis, and Synectics, a greater arsenal of approaches is available to use in solving different types of problems. The fourth strength of the CPS method is an outgrowth of its eclectic nature. Not only does CPS use a variety of techniques, but it is flexible in their application. That is, CPS does not rigidly specify which techniques must be used within the different stages. (The only major exception would be the use of brainstorming principles throughout the process. Brainstorming, however, is the core element upon which the other techniques are built.) This added flexibility gives CPS an advantage over other eclectic approaches that are more fixed in their use and application of different techniques.

As mentioned, CPS also is subject to most of the weaknesses associated with Classical Brainstorming as well as those specific to the technique. CPS can be used by individuals working alone or by a group; often, it alternates between the individual and the group. When used by a group, it has several weaknesses that it might share with other group methods. The first major weakness concerns its emphasis upon training. Although this can be considered a strength, it is also a weakness since the effectiveness of the CPS method might be directly related to the degree of training received by the group members in using the approach. As with some other group methods (e.g., Synectics), the training requirement also might be dependent upon the type of problem. The strength of the technique in its flexibility of application also carries with it a major weakness. Because some discretion can be used in selecting different techniques for different stages, group leader diagnostic ability is necessary. Furthermore, the effectiveness of a leader's diagnostic skills is likely to be diminished due to the lack of research available on what techniques will work best with what problems, and in what problem-solving stages.

In spite of these weaknesses, some empirical research supports the usefulness of CPS overall and in comparison with other approaches. Research on the model itself generally has resulted in favorable outcomes.[12] Although not conclusive, empirical research which has compared CPS to other models also has been fairly positive.[13] One study attributes much of the confusion over the model's effectiveness to difficulties involved in interpreting statistical results. Using an analytical tool known as "meta-analysis," Rose and Lin[14] evaluated 46 research studies. Their results indicated that CPS appeared to be a more effective creative problem-solving training method than many other well-known procedures.

In summary, it can be said that the major strengths of CPS are its emphasis upon different problem-solving stages, its eclectic nature, and its flexibility in applying different techniques. The major weaknesses would appear to be the training requirements needed for the group members and the level of leader diagnostic skills necessary to use the method. There also is considerable evidence which supports the effectiveness of CPS in training creative problem-solving performance.

7.04 Lateral Thinking

Lateral Thinking was developed by Edward de Bono,[15] a British physician and psychologist, to provide a method for escaping from conventional ways of looking at a problem. It is not so much a formal technique as it is a method for developing new attitudes to apply to the thinking process. The method is based upon the premise that the human mind naturally processes and stores information in accordance with a specific patterning system. Because of the logic built into this system, however, new idea development is hindered. The mind can create, recognize, or use patterns, but not change them.

The purpose of Lateral Thinking is to disrupt these patterns by introducing discontinuity. To do this requires (1) being aware of the patterning system of the mind, (2) knowing the difference between vertical and lateral thinking, (3) applying special techniques, and (4) using a new operational word (PO). The patterning system already has been briefly discussed, so the following description will focus upon the remaining elements in the process.

2. Vertical and Lateral Thinking. Vertical thinking relies upon the traditional principles of logical analysis. Ideas are developed by proceeding on a continuous path from one bit of information to another. If the steps along the path are followed correctly in sequence, it is easy to determine when the end of the path (or the goal) has been reached. Lateral thinking, in contrast, is not so logical. The steps used to reach the end of the path might be taken in a haphazard manner and without any logically apparent sequence. Once the end of the path is reached, its validity never can be determined by the method used to reach it. The fact that the end of the path has been reached is the only conclusion necessary—the steps used to get there require rationalization, not logical justification. Specific differences between the two types of thinking are described in Table 7-1. In general, Lateral Thinking is an approach for breaking away from the mind's logical patterning to create the attitude necessary to generate new ideas. Vertical thinking, on the other hand, relies upon this logical patterning to produce specific ideas based upon the obvious.

3. Special Techniques. There are three major activities used to promote Lateral Thinking: awareness, alternatives, and provocative methods. Some of these activities involve techniques that are similar or identical to those described elsewhere in this book; other activities were developed by de Bono to assist specifically in the lateral-thinking process.

Awareness. The activities in this category are used to redefine and clarify current ideas. Before new ideas can be generated or old ideas rejected, current ideas must be clearly understood. de Bono suggests that five different areas be examined: (a) dominant ideas, (b) tethering factors, (c) polarizing tendencies, (d) boundaries, and (e) assumptions.

a. Dominant ideas. These must be identified to determine how the problem is currently being viewed. It is important that they be defined clearly so that the subsequent generation of ideas will not be limited in scope. In the search for dominant ideas, it should be remembered that there is usually more than one dominant idea and that different people might identify different dominant ideas.

b. Tethering factors. These are usually overlooked factors that are always assumed to be included in a problem situation. The importance of this area is suggested by de Bono's example of car parking rates: It is usually assumed that the average hourly rate will be lower the longer the car is parked. It is conceivable, however, that a situation might exist when this assumption would not be valid. The objective of reducing the number of commuter cars parked to make room for shoppers, for example, could be achieved by charging more per hour the longer a car is parked. The existence of tethering factors needs to be identified to determine how restricted a possible solution might be.

c. Polarizing tendencies. This situation occurs whenever a problem contains an either-or type of situation. A common example is the confrontation between environmentalists and energy-resource developers. Because only one of the groups can be satisfied, the number of ways to review the problem is reduced.

Table 7-1. Major Differences Between Lateral and Vertical Thinking.

LATERAL THINKING	VERTICAL THINKING
1. Tries to find new ways for looking at things; is concerned with change and movement.	1. Tries to find absolutes for judging relationships; is concerned with stability.
2. Avoids looking for what is "right" or "wrong." Tries to find what is different.	2. Seeks YES/NO justification for each step. Tries to find what is "right."
3. Analyzes ideas to determine how they might be used to generate new ideas.	3. Analyzes ideas to determine why they do not work and need to be rejected.
4. Attempts to introduce discontinuity by making illogical jumps from one step to another.	4. Seeks continuity by logically proceeding from one step to another.
5. Welcomes chance intrusions of information to use in generating new ideas; considers the irrelevant.	5. Selectively chooses what to consider for generating ideas; rejects any information not considered to be relevant.
6. Progresses by avoiding the obvious.	6. Progresses using established patterns; considers the obvious.
7. Increases the odds that a solution will be found; avoids any guarantees.	7. Guarantees at least minimal success in finding a solution.

d. Boundaries. The boundaries of a problem will limit the amount of "space" available in which to solve it. Many boundaries involving organizational problems exist only in the minds of the perceivers, having developed from long-existent mythology of how the organization operates and is affected by its environment. Persons who develop unique solutions by ignoring commonly accepted boundaries are often accused of cheating. The classical problem of how to draw four lines through nine dots, without lifting up the pencil or retracing, is a typical example. As shown in Fig. 7-1, one solution to this problem is to ignore the apparent boundary formed by the arrangement of the dots and use the area outside to help draw the lines. Unless problem boundaries are considered, many solutions will only be variations on old ideas.

e. Assumptions. Assumptions are present in every problem and are used as the material for building ideas. Because it is often difficult to determine if an assumption is valid, attention should be directed from evaluating assumptions to simply recognizing that they exist. The number of assumptions present in most problems makes it impractical to devote time to ascertaining their validity. If the problem solver tries to become aware of their existence, new ideas might result.

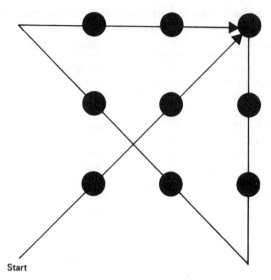

Start

Fig. 7–1. A solution to the nine-dot problem.

While there will be some overlap between these areas, the most important factor to consider when using them is that they are intended only to identify and not to evaluate current ideas.

Alternatives. The activity of alternatives involves a conscious effort to produce as many different ways as possible for looking at a problem. The objective is to find a variety of different approaches, not the best one. Because Lateral Thinking does not require justification of assumptions, problem analysis is not a major concern. Instead, effort should be directed toward escaping from old ideas and assumptions. There are seven different techniques available for this activity: (a) avoidance devices, (b) rotation of attention, (c) change of entry point, (d) quota of alternatives, (e) concept changing, (f) fractionation, and (g) bridging divisions.

a. Avoidance devices. Avoidance is essentially an attitude that is developed by attempting to ignore old ideas and being open to new ways for viewing a problem. de Bono uses an example of ways to make a hole. An old idea might suggest using a conventional drill bit. For some situations, however, a square hole might be more suitable.

b. Rotation of attention. Many people have a learned response that has conditioned them to focus their attention on the core of a problem. To escape from old ideas, however, attention should be shifted to other parts of the problem. The development of no-fault auto insurance represents an example of rotating attention. When there is an accident, the core of the situation for an insurance company is how to best settle the claim. Focusing attention on the time and personal costs to the customer involved, however, presents a different aspect of the problem, with no-fault insurance as a possible by-product.

c. Change of entry point. The starting point used to analyze a problem can direct the search for possible solutions. A fresh perspective on a problem often can be obtained by recognizing a usual entry point and then deliberately looking for some other entry point not usually considered. One way to do this is to work backwards from a problem's terminal or endpoint. In one instance, a problem on how to relieve traffic congestion in a downtown area used cars parked on the street as an entry point. Each office building was then required to maintain separate parking facilities. This solution, however, only increased the congestion by encouraging more car travel. The problem was eventually solved by concentrating upon the movement of cars in and out of the area (a different entry point), suggesting the need for some type of mass transit.

d. Quota of alternatives. Another way of forcing the deliberate search for alternative ways of looking at a problem is to establish artificial quotas. de Bono suggests using no more than five different alternatives as a goal. If too many alternatives are set as a quota, the search can become discouraging and often end with alternatives only slightly different from one another. The important point is that it is not the number or "correctness" of alternatives that should be sought. Rather, it is the qualitative difference between alternatives that is desired.

e. Concept changing. The purpose of concept changing is to avoid a fixed way of looking at how a problem is expressed. The successful market for mobile homes, for example, might be attributed to a concept change. When a mobile home is viewed as a vehicle rather than a home, it becomes exempt from building codes and real estate taxes. As another example, a car company was faced with the problem of paying high import taxes on small foreign pick-up trucks. With the addition of two rear-facing seats in the bed of the truck, the concept of a truck was changed to a car, thereby subjecting it to lower taxes.

f. Fractionation. When used with Lateral Thinking, fractionation involves dividing a problem up into any arrangement of parts without regard to logical subdivisions. Vertical thinking, in contrast, involves breaking a problem down into its functional subcomponents in such a way that the "correctness" of the subdivisions can be justified. When Lateral Thinking is used, there is no correct way to subdivide a problem, since the objective of the procedure is to produce a new way of looking at a problem. For example, a problem of how to increase passenger traffic on an airline might be divided into two parts: attractiveness to passengers and profitability.

g. Bridging divisions. Another way to produce new ways of looking at a problem is to put together two apparently unrelated concepts (the opposite of fractionation). Doing this directs attention away from how two aspects of a problem might be different and toward how they might be similar. The concepts of advertising and marketing, for example, could be considered together to suggest a new sales strategy.

Provocative Methods. While awareness methods are used to recognize current ideas about a problem (identification) and alternatives serve to break away from old ideas (avoidance), provocative methods are intended to assist in developing new ideas. The purpose of these latter methods is to introduce discontinuity into the thinking process by changing the way of looking at a problem. The techniques within this category can be divided into those that produce change from within a problem and those that produce change from without or outside a problem. Change from within can be introduced by using two methods: (a) reversal, and (b) distortion and exaggeration; change from the outside involves five methods: (c) exposure, (d) cross-fertilization, (e) problem switching, (f) analogies, and (g) random-word stimulation.

a. Reversal. With the reversal technique, new ideas can be suggested by examining the current direction of a problem and turning it completely around, inside out, or upside down. As an example, de Bono describes a situation in which meters are used to discourage car parking. If the situation is reversed to encourage parking, an idea can develop to give out-of-town shoppers a ticket to park free one day each week at a meter, thus spreading out the parking load and possibly discouraging parking by daily commuters. As with all Lateral Thinking methods, it is not the correctness of the reversal that counts, but the fact that the perspective on the problem is changed.

b. Distortion and exaggeration. A method similar to the reversal procedure is to change a part of a situation or to take it to an extreme. In contrast to reversals, the direction of the change is not specified. Many of the art works produced by Picasso provide a vivid example of this technique, with his distorted and exaggerated depictions of the human body. Another example might involve a quality-control problem in a manufacturing plant. The situation could be exaggerated to the extent that every product was viewed as being faulty. This alteration might then suggest the idea of completely redesigning the product line.

c. Exposure. The first of the methods that can be used to introduce change from the outside is exposure. This method is similar in purpose to Nonlogical Stimuli in that ideas are generated by considering things that are apparently unrelated to the problem. As an example, de Bono suggests wandering around in stores. If a plastic duck were to be noticed and examined, it might suggest the nature of some organizational problems: those that are above the surface and those that are hidden or below the surface. For the exposure method to work, there must be a willingness to consider the possible significance of an irrelevant object or event. Furthermore, the method is likely to be more successful if a specific problem is being considered at the time of exposure.

d. Cross-fertilization. This method is similar to the exposure method except that the stimulation is provided by people instead of things. For cross-fertilization to be effective, the people listened to should be from fields entirely unrelated to the problem. The procedure involves asking experts from other fields how they would solve the problem using methods from their areas. An attempt can then be made to apply these methods to the problem.

e. Problem switching. This method, for developing a new problem perspective, combines the mechanisms of both exposure and cross-fertilization. The basic procedure is to stop concentrating on one problem and switch to another. The situation for using problem switching must be constructed so that it is easy to return to an old problem once new ideas have been suggested by the second problem. One difficulty with this approach is that not everyone will be in a position where they have the freedom to alternate between different problems.

f. Analogies. The use of analogies to analyze a problem has been previously discussed in Chapter 4. There are, however, some specific points made by de Bono that are worth considering. First, analogies are used by translating the problem into an analogy, refining and developing the analogy, and then translating back to the problem to judge the suitability of the analogy. If an analogy is selected that is too similar to the problem, little will have been gained. Second, analogies that are concrete and specific should be selected over more abstract ones. Finally, analogies should describe a specific, well-known process.

g. Random-word stimulation. This method is similar to the Catalog technique. A word is selected from a dictionary or specially prepared word list and a link sought between the word and the problem. In its purest form, the word should be selected using a table of random numbers to choose a page in a dictionary and then a position on a page. For most problems, however, a less-than-random procedure is probably adequate. One important point in using this method is to stay with a word once it is selected. Premature judgment about a word's relevance could result in many useful ideas being overlooked.

4. A New Operational Word. The last method used to disrupt the mind's logical patterning system is to use a new operational word developed by de Bono: PO. PO is a symbol to indicate that the principles of Lateral Thinking should be applied. Just as the word NO is used in vertical thinking to logically reject an idea, PO is intended to convey the attitude that a new patterning system is to be used by introducing discontinuity. In essence, YES and NO are not to be considered as part of one's problem-solving language when Lateral Thinking is used.

One major concept used with PO is the intermediate impossible. While vertical thinking seeks to determine if an idea can be accepted or rejected, PO—as used in Lateral Thinking—provides a third alternative. Instead of placing a value on an idea, the word PO indicates that judgment should be deferred, even if the idea initially appears to be unacceptable. PO signals that the worth of an idea lies in its ability to spark new ideas and jot just a final solution for a problem.

The word PO can be operationalized in many different ways. For example, when the intermediate impossible is used, an idea pertaining to ways for reducing supermarket thefts might be stated as: PO all food should be given away free. With Lateral Thinking, an idea for a food club might then be developed.

PO also can be used to escape from names, labels, or classifications. If, for example, PO drinking glass is said, new ways can be sought for applying the characteristics of a drinking glass to an apparently unrelated problem—such as ideas for designing car seats.

In summary, the Lateral Thinking method is an attitude for restructuring problems. Logical, step-by-step analysis of a problem is rejected in favor of developing new thinking patterns that will provide new ways of looking at a problem. The major premise is that any method that will provide a different perspective is valid. Three primary activities are used to stimulate lateral thinking: awareness, alternatives, and provocative methods. Awareness activities involve examining current ideas by looking at

    a. Dominant ideas
    b. Tethering factors
    c. Polarizing tendencies
    d. Boundaries
    e. Assumptions

The purpose of alternatives is to produce as many ways as possible for looking at a problem with the goal of avoiding old ideas. The following devices are used to produce alternatives:

    a. Avoidance devices
    b. Rotation of attention
    c. Change of entry point
    d. Quota of alternatives
    e. Concept changing
    f. Fractionation
    g. Bridging divisions

Provocative methods attempt to introduce discontinuity by suggesting new ideas using methods such as:

    a. Reversal
    b. Distortion and exaggeration
    c. Exposure
    d. Cross-fertilization
    e. Problem switching
    f. Analogies
    g. Random-word stimulation

Finally, PO is suggested as a new operation to signal that the principles of Lateral Thinking should be used.

The previous sections have described methods that individuals can use to develop a lateral-thinking attitude. Some people, however, might find it difficult to fully develop this attitude when working in isolation and without the benefit of a structured format. Another way that lateral thinking can be encouraged is to use a structured, formal group setting. Formal settings have the advantage of providing a special situation that people can exploit to avoid the logical thinking emphasized in their everyday lives. On the other hand, formal settings have the potential of being incorrectly perceived as a process in themselves, rather than as situations in which the principles of Lateral Thinking can be applied.

One formal setting, which de Bono suggests using, is Classical Brainstorming. The main advantages provided by brainstorming sessions as a setting for Lateral Thinking are (1) the formality inherent in the process, (2) the provision for separate idea generation and evaluation stages, and (3) the stimulation provided by face-to-face discussion. While brainstorming sessions can be useful for promoting the use of Lateral Thinking, de Bono suggests that other formal settings can be equally useful. Because the elements of Classical Brainstroming are discussed in Chapter 4, they will not be repeated here.

Evaluation   It is difficult to conveniently "fit" Lateral Thinking into one of the traditional problem-solving stages. It appears to be both a problem analysis and idea generation method. de Bono, however, has emphasized using Lateral Thinking as a way to escape from old ways of looking at a problem and to develop new ways. Because of this and its many different methods, Lateral Thinking has been classified as an eclectic technique.

The complexity, depth, and breadth of Lateral Thinking makes it difficult to capsulize for presentation to others, let alone describe a step-by-step fashion. Consistent with the philosophy of avoiding vertical thinking, most of the material describing Lateral Thinking is anything but logical or sequentially patterned. This is both a strength and a weakness of the approach. It is a strength because it acknowledges that creativity cannot always be attained through the use of an all-encompassing, step-by-step problem-solving technique; it is a weakness because of the lack of structure it provides in guiding the application of its various methods. As Bosticco[16] notes, the concept of lateral thinking is "difficulty both to talk about and write about. . . ."

In general, the most positive feature of Lateral Thinking is its emphasis upon developing new ways for looking at problems; its most negative feature is that it is extremely difficult to recondition the human mind—even if the method is applied in a formal setting. This point, however, also could be made about most other creative methods.

Nevertheless, the use of formal settings does seem to be a step in the right direction for encouraging the use of Lateral Thinking. de Bono's suggestion to use Classical Brainstorming (or other similar situations) as a formal setting, however, might limit the method's potential. As de Bono describes the use of brainstorming sessions, the only prevalent Lateral Thinking methods involved are cross-fertilization and random stimulation—methods that naturally occur during formal brainstorming activities. A more fruitful approach would be to design a formal setting that deliberately accommodates the other methods used to promote Lateral Thinking. Methods from each of the three primary activity areas (awareness, alternatives, provocative methods) could be loosely structured into a systematic framework that incorporates the major problem-solving stages. If this were done, the user of Lateral Thinking would be provided with a relatively logical format. Ideally, the strengths of both vertical and lateral thinking could be exploited in this manner. Because it is difficult for the human mind to completely break away from sequential patterning, such a framework would conceivably satisfy this constraint and, at the same time, provide a comprehensive, formal setting for encouraging lateral thinking. At the very least, the methods described by de Bono to promote lateral thinking should be valuable by themselves as individual approaches for redefining problems and generating ideas.

7.05   Value Engineering (VE)[17]

Value Engineering (VE) was developed by Lawrence D. Miles,[18] a purchasing agent at the General Electric Company in the 1940s. Also known as Value Management, Value Analysis, Value Improvement, and Value Assurance, it has been enriched by various practitioners over its 40-year history.[19] Its success at improving product design, especially in terms of reducing cost, led to its use in other manufacturing companies, and eventually to all types of organizations, including construction, services, and even government.[20] Value Engineering clauses occur in all major U.S. government procurement contracts and many grant programs.

Value Engineering is a problem-solving technique that is well adapted to industry. Although not limited to engineers, it is especially useful for dealing with technical problems in organizations. It has its own technical society, the Society of American Value Engineers (S.A.V.E.) (600 South Federal Street, Suite 400, Chicago, Illinois 60605), with chapters around the country and affiliated societies around the world. The *Proceedings* of their annual conferences are available in many large libraries and contain advice from people who have applied the process.

Value Engineering takes a broader approach to problem solving than many other techniques. Not only does it lay out steps for an individual or group to follow in approaching a problem, it also addresses issues such as team composition, project selection, structure of a VE support system in organizations, and even contract language to encourage or require suppliers to apply the VE process.

Value Study   The basic mechanism of VE is the value study: the formation of a team of individuals from various departments and/or disciplines who use the

VE methodology to develop action plans or solution alternatives. Value studies can be formed around almost any goal or problem for which an organization desires improved alternatives. One of the most common uses is reducing the cost of a product or service without harming the quality, worth, or reliability. These studies can last from a few hours to over 100 hours.

In most cases, the VE team also takes responsibility for initiating and supporting the implementation of the ideas developed by the study. The team may present the ideas to key decision makers and follow up on implementation. Or, the team may act on its own and work within the policies and procedures of the organization.

The Job Plan   The steps or process used in a value study are known as a job plan. As often happens when creative people are involved, the processes used to conduct value studies are as varied as their developers. For example, Miles[21] uses the stages (1) Mind Tuning, (2) Information, (3) Analysis, (4) Creativity, (5) Judgment, (6) Development, and (7) Planning; Fallon[22] uses these stages: (1) Preparation, (2) Information, (3) Analytic, (4) Creative, (5) Evaluation, (6) Presentation, and (7) Implementation; Mudge's[23] process involves the stages (1) Information, (2) Functional Analysis, (3) Creativity, (4) Analytical, and (5) Implementation.

Although each version highlights different aspects of the VE process, they seem to mirror the Osborn-Parnes[24] five-stage Creative Problem Solving approach. The information stages correspond to Fact Finding, the analytical stages to Problem Finding, the creativity stages to Idea Finding, the Judgment/Evaluation/Analytical stages to Solution Finding, and the remaining stages are similar to Acceptance Finding.

Each of the major stages recognizes that problem solving benefits from a shift in thinking mode (Mind Tuning), a search for more information is often helpful (Information), an attempt should be made to reframe the problem statement (Function Analysis), a divergent search for ideas is necessary (Creative), judgment should be deferred until after the creative phase (Evaluation), and further refinement and selling frequently are required for selected ideas (Development, Planning, Presentation, and Implementation).

As with Creative Problem-Solving, a variety of techniques may be used within each of the stages. Experienced value specialists often will supplement their efforts with a variety of problem-solving and team-building approaches. For instance, checklists frequently are used to guide the Information and Implementation stages, Classical Brainstorming is relied upon for the Creative phase, and decision matrices are used during the Evaluation stage. Nevertheless, a core process is common to all VE studies.

An important aspect of VE is its ability to analyze problems and develop new perspectives (Problem Finding in the CPS model). In this stage, VE uses the concept of value and the technique of Function Analysis to gain insight into a problem. A major assumption is that a given problem must be reunderstood to achieve a high-quality solution. The ultimate aim of VE is improvement of the value of whatever is being studied. To achieve this goal, a VE team must thoroughly understand relevant aspects of value before trying to improve a problem.

Value and Function   Value is a multidimensional concept. A rough definition of value is the ratio between worth and cost. To improve value, it is not enough simply to seek an increase in the benefits or to reduce the costs. Rather, it is necessary to pay attention to both simultaneously.

To illustrate, consider the question, "Which is the better value, a Chevy Nova or a Cadillac?" Several responses are possible, such as, "It depends upon whom you ask," "I'd rather have the Cadillac," and "The Nova is the best buy." VE can clarify this discussion with the concept of function. A function is what something does for you. If you consider the function to be "transport the driver to work," both cars will perform the task equally well. However, since the Nova is less expensive, it is the better value *in this situation.*

Because things generally have more than one desired function, the value may be different in another situation. For example, a sales executive might value the function, "I want to impress customers." Since most people will be more impressed by the luxury car, the Nova will be a terrible value—even though it costs less. Of course, if your customers are impressed by thriftiness, the Nova is unquestionably the better value. Thus, for any product, service, or decision, the value is the net result of many different function/cost comparisons.

To help explore and integrate these many functions and function/cost relationships, a technique called Function Analysis Systems Technique (FAST) or Function Modeling has been developed.[25] It involves mapping various types of functions and their relationships.

Functions can be divided into three types: basic, secondary, and supporting. Although differences between these types sometimes are not clear, some examples may provide clarification.

Basic functions are those required of a design to perform its primary purpose. Thus, the basic function of a car would be transportation. Although a car can perform a variety of functions, it cannot be sold as a new car unless it can transport people.

Secondary functions are those required by a current design but not required or needed by a user or consumer. For example, one function of most automobile engines is "move piston." Although it is true that a car will stop moving if the piston stops, the function of the piston is secondary to the user. For the user, a car without pistons (such as the rotary engine) would be satisfactory as long as it performed the desired function of transportation.

In contrast to basic and secondary functions, supporting functions are any enhancements to a design. The decor of a car's interior, for instance, may serve the function "impress passengers." Although impressing passengers may be important to a car's owner, it certainly is not required for the car to perform its basic function.

The differences among function types often is difficult to determine or agree upon. In the examples, transporting drivers may be the basic function as seen by some people; others, however, might argue that transporting passengers is the basic function. In practice, each problem-solving group makes a different distinction. Such inconsistencies usually present no major problems, since the processes of agreeing upon and discussing the functions often will open the door to many creative solutions.

Different functions also can be mapped to show the relationships among the different types. For example, a map can be used to show how certain secondary functions operate to provide specific basic and supporting functions.

Many different mapping formats can be used. In Fig. 7-2, one example of a function map is shown using the example of a coffee cup. The column on the left illustrates a conceivable relationship among coffee cup functions. The column on the right describes components referred to by each function. Thus, the supporting function of "protect user" is dealt with by using a handle and a certain thickness of the cup. (Note that the functions serve as problems resolved by the components.)

In more complex projects, each secondary and supporting function could have its own secondary functions. For example, a supporting function in the coffee cup example was "project image." A secondary function for this function could be "apply ink." On other projects, "apply ink" could be defined further as "clean surface," "prepare ink," "spray ink," "dry ink," "inspect image," and so forth.

After a team discusses how different aspects of an existing design fit a function, a cost can be computed for each function. When this computation is done, each cost should add up to no more than the actual cost of the cup. For example, a two-dollar mug may be valued at only ten cents in the basic function of holding coffee. The rest of the cost, however, might go toward thickening the cup to keep the coffee warm, toward protecting the user from heat, and for various decorative or marketing uses.

The Function Modeling approach can be used for a variety of problems or products. In the example, Function Modeling also could have been used for any type of cup, be it plastic foam or fine china. The only restriction is that the team must understand the function process and be familiar with the relevant technology.

Once a team has completed the Function Modeling process, it should be familiar with the problem and all of its various features and requirements. If so, the team is ready to search for potential solutions.

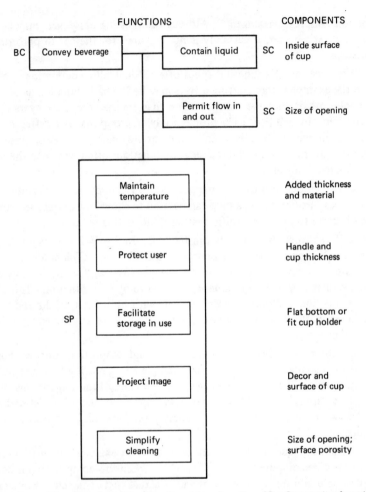

Note: BC = Basic function, SC = Secondary function, SP = Supporting function

Fig. 7-2. Example of function modeling.

Idea Generation Conventional wisdom about creativity might question the value of providing a team with so much detailed problem information. Some people might expect information overload to reduce creativity. However, instead of using brainstorming or other techniques at the same time, the team now can focus its efforts on one function at a time. For instance, if improving a typewriter is the problem, a team might focus upon the function "apply ink." Then, it might shift its focus to functions such as "reduce energy consumption," "hold paper," and "simplify cleaning."

During these sessions, a synergistic vision often develops among the team so that they begin to function as one. As a result, ideas often emerge which solve several subproblems at once. New synergy also may occur during the final stages of the process, when action plans for implementation are developed.

The Value Engineering process does not stop when a solution is found. Other aspects of VE involve working upon acceptance and implementation of the solution until improvements are in effect.

Evaluation   Value Engineering is more than a singular problem-solving technique. Its strategies for managing innovation, writing contracts, choosing projects, and selecting the people to be involved in creative efforts all contribute toward a unique process. Used alone or with other techniques, VE provides a powerful tool for improving existing designs or decisions. Furthermore, VE is especially useful in organizations for problems involving products, services, policies, or administrative procedures, to name a few areas. For new-product invention, the process is useful but requires an exceptionally experienced leader. It can be especially useful in converting the rough ideas of inventors into detailed designs appropriate for successful production and marketing. In addition, VE also can be beneficial for personal and interpersonal types of problems.

As a problem-solving technique, VE has the advantages of CPS: emphasis upon different problem-solving stages, eclectic nature, and flexibility in applying other techniques. In addition, value and function analysis are powerful ways to analyze many different values and requirements of a complex problem and to bring a diverse group to a shared understanding and common language.

Nevertheless, VE is perhaps best used as a technique for handling complex, interdisciplinary projects within organizations. While anyone can benefit from asking, "What am I trying to accomplish with this?" and "How else could I accomplish that?"; VE will be used most productively, however, when an interdisciplinary team can focus all of its knowledge and resources upon a problem.

When used with a team, VE provides each person with a similar understanding of the problem—especially about the various trade-offs and values. As a result, idea generation is facilitated and combinations of ideas increase the overall value by simultaneously addressing many issues. However, such teams do require a leader with strong facilitation skills.

This need for a leader who can deal with interpersonal and interdepartmental conflicts, facilitate creativity, lead the integration of ideas, and motivate team members to follow up on ideas is a major disadvantage of VE. It usually takes several years of training and experience to do this job adequately. However, an expert in facilitating creativity who understands organizations can pick up the technique in a relatively short time.[26]

MISCELLANEOUS TECHNIQUES

7.06   Decision Seminar

The Decision Seminar is a complex, broad-based, social policy analytical tool developed by Harold Laswell.[27] It requires participants to evaluate problems in terms of their past, present and future. Data from these analyses are recorded and evaluated using a variety of resources, problem-solving requirements, and an overall problem-solving strategy.

The Problem-Solving Strategy   According to Burgess and Slonaker,[28] there are four major activities involved in the problem-solving component of a typical Decision Seminar. Each of these activities also contains many subactivities and problem-solving stages for analyzing a particular social context. The problem-solving strategy also is supplemented by various resources and problem-solving requirements.

The problem-solving strategy used during the Decision Seminar consists of (1) analyzing a problem using the Social Process Model, (2) refining examination of the model using eight values, (3) developing a "contextual map" using a decision process to refine the problem further, and (4) using specific analytical procedures (the five "intellectual tasks") to guide the group in a continuing examination of the problem.

The Social Process Model   Information used to guide problem solving is acquired and refined using seven broad categories:

1. Participants—the relevant actors and institutions who interact in the social context.
2. Perspectives—the expectations, preferences, and beliefs of the participants.
3. Situations—the specific locations where the participants interact. Situations should be analyzed in detail by describing and clarifying specific points of interaction and the reason for their occurrence.
4. Base-values—the participants' assets and liabilities relevant to the goals and objectives being evaluated. In other words, "Who can do what for (or to) whom?"
5. Strategies—the manner in which base-values are used to affect outcomes. A number of different strategies might be examined in any given setting. For instance, the group might examine formal and informal programs that acquire additional units of some value, values that are exchanged for other values, or asset values used to offset the effects of liabilities.
6. Outcomes—the way in which values are distributed. Participants generally will perceive outcomes to be either desirable or undesirable.
7. Effects—any change in perceived values for the participants that result from value outcomes.

As an example of the Social Process Model, Burgess and Slonaker describe a situation involving educational policy-making. The participants are a board of education in a particular city. The board is elected rather than appointed because of problems perceived to exist with the math curriculum. The perspectives are that the board expects its directives to be carried out, feels threatened by potential negative publicity the issue may generate, and believes the problem to be urgent. The situation is the inadequate math curriculum brought to the board's attention by the superintendent. It is assumed that the board members communicated privately with one another prior to the meeting and that they will discuss the issue at their next meeting. In analyzing base-values, it is revealed that the board's assets involve the power to fire and hire, the authority to make financial decisions, limited access to publicity media, and contact with significant community groups. Liabilities are an inability to control the media as a result of an unfavorable editorial. Strategies include communication with other board members, allocating funds to appoint a committee to study the matter, and publicly disclosing the problem to gain credibility. Outcomes for this problem are the steps prescribed for gaining more information (e.g., establishing the committee). Finally, effects are determined to be the interest and financial support that resulted in establishing the committee. This action helped direct attention to the first step of "The Decision Process."

Value Analysis. Once the Social Process Model has been examined, the next major activity is to refine this information by analyzing eight key values: (1) power (victory or defeat in war or elections), (2) enlightenment (news and scientific discoveries), (3) wealth (transfer and ownership of income), (4) well-being (health care and recreation), (5) skill (instruction and being proficient), (6) affection (expressing intimacy, friendship, and loyalty), (7) respect (honor and recognition), and (8) rectitude (acceptance into religious or ethical associations).

Each of the seven Social Process Model categories can be evaluated against these values. For example, participants might be analyzed in terms of the power institutions involved (e.g., legislatures and executive branches of government) or enlightenment institutions (e.g., news media and universities). Some institutions also might be described as possessing a number of different values. Parochial schools, for instance, support enlightenment, skills, and rectitude. After participants are analyzed, the other categories then can be analyzed using the values in a similar manner.

The Decision Process. Analysis of a problem often can be aided by developing a contextual map that describes major problem aspects and their interrelationship. The Decision Seminar uses a seven-step process. Such a process helps to identify and further refine roles of the participants and the arenas in which they operate. The seven steps are

1. Intelligence—gathering and processing information
2. Promotion—making and promoting policy/decision recommendations

3. Prescription—developing and prescribing general policy rules
4. Invocation—deciding how to monitor adherence to the policy rules
5. Application—applying the general rules
6. Appraisal—evaluating effectiveness of the rules
7. Termination—terminating the policy

Each of these decision functions has referent institutions which specialize in that particular function. As a result, the participants and institutions being analyzed can be located. Thus, mass media and social research organizations perform intelligence functions, legislative hearings perform promotion functions, city councils are involved with prescribing policies, special administrative units deal with invocation, and the courts and legislative commissions perform application and appraisal functions, respectively. Termination functions would be handled by the same decision units, depending upon the particular policy under consideration.

Analytical Procedures. The last component of the Decision Seminar's problem-solving strategy involves use of an analytical sequence. This sequence provides a sense of continuity for the seminar participants. In addition, it offers a common procedural language. The analytical procedures are operationalized as "five intellectual tasks" for evaluating policy-related problems:

1. Goal clarification—identifying possible future states of the problem
2. Trend description—examining similarities and discrepancies between previous and current events in regard to desired future states
3. Analysis of conditions—determining what factors have affected the direction and size of the trends.
4. Projection of developments—predicting the likely future of goals (and possible discrepancies), given current policies.
5. Invention, evaluation, and selection of alternatives—determining what goals and actions will encourage achievement of the desired goal states.

Problem-Solving Requirements A second major aspect of the Decision Seminar is concerned with three broad problem-solving requirements. These requirements are (1) contextuality, (2) multimethodology, and (3) specification of objectives and purposes.

Contextuality. Contextuality refers to the understanding gained by examining a problem in terms of its past, present, and future. The past provides a perspective for interpreting the present and anticipating future contingencies. Using an accumulation of data about the problem, seminar participants seek to represent the problem—as realistically as possible—in its social context. The better the problem is represented, the more realistic will be the social-policy alternatives generated.

Multimethodology.   The complexity of social processes and the demands of systematically managing data about these processes require use of a multimethod approach.   To develop a sense of control and understanding about a problem, typical seminars rely upon such exotic-sounding aids as "contextual mapping," "developmental constructs," and "prototyping." Other less exotic methods include program budgeting, operations research, systems analysis, forecasting, linear and dynamic programming, brainstorming, and computer simulation and gaming.

Objectives and Purposes.   The objectives and purposes of the seminar must be explicated clearly at the outset. The seminar participants need to understand the relevance of a particular social context. Without this understanding, their motivation, as well as their ability to analyze a problem, will be diminished. The objectives should be stated flexibly to allow for continuing revision. Moreover, they should be developed through consensual decision making.

Resources for Problem Solving   The third major component of a Decision Seminar is resources.   Resources support the other components and enable them to be carried out.   Problem solving resources consist of (1) a permanent core group, (2) a permanent location, (3) audio-visual aids, (4) outside experts, (5) record keeping, and (6) research.

Permanent Core Group.   The participants in a seminar must be committed to its purposes and be active in its meetings and discussions. Although some members may come and go, the seminar should be viewed as an ongoing enterprise.   Otherwise, there will be no sense of continuity or culture which are needed to facilitate the problem-solving process. The seminar members—usually numbering no more than 15—are expected to participate in discussions, give special reports, make agenda suggestions, and help evaluate the seminar process.

Permanent Location.   The Decision Seminar should be located in a permanent chart and map room that is devoted exclusively to continuing problem-solving activity.   Displays of data and visual aids are located in this room to enhance the seminar's analytical procedures.   Maintaining all of the problem-solving aids in one room makes it easier to examine social context in detail during every session. Also, with the data always on display, new members will not need to receive extensive briefings.

Audio-Visual Aids.   The typical Decision Seminar uses a variety of graphs, trend lines, three-dimensional models, films, and audio and video recordings. Along with a permanent location, such aids encourage a focus upon the entire social context of a problem and make it easier to examine relationships among problem elements.   In addition, audio-visual aids help stimulate information recall and imagination while the participants consider alternative future states. Because of the emphasis upon new-information acquisition, the audio-visual aids must be revised continuously.

Outside Experts. The core group develops a disciplined, cumulative data base that serves to increase problem familiarity over time. New perspectives sometimes are needed, however, to keep the information system open and allow information to be refined and expanded. Such needs can be met by periodically bringing in outside experts to add to the data base. Combining contributions of outside experts with the core group's own knowledge will increase understanding of a problem's social context. To remain fresh, the core group must be challenged constantly with new issues.

Record Keeping. Record keeping involves two functions: (1) formulating an agenda to guide consideration of a problem's past, present, and future, and (2) developing a set of minutes for each meeting. The agenda for each seminar session specifies how the content will be dealt with. For example, an agenda might describe how institutional goals will be examined for the previous five years and then used as the context to evaluate current goals and develop future goals. Minutes of the sessions (usually transcribed from audio tapes) provide continuity between meetings, serve as a way to verify statements and recover information, and stimulate the design of research studies.

Research. The open-ended nature of the Decision Seminar makes it an ideal forum for collecting and analyzing data. With its high information requirements and the inquiry process used by the core group, the seminar often assumes a conceptual orientation. However, whether the focus is abstract or concrete, data must be continually revised, analyzed, and accepted or rejected.

Evaluation The overall strength of the Decision Seminar is its potential to focus the efforts of a number of people using a variety of resources upon a single policy issue. Because attention is concentrated rather than diffused, high-quality solutions are more likely to result. The seminar has other advantages:

1. It uses a common procedural language to guide implementation of the problem-solving strategy and other aspects of the seminar.

2. Using the "five intellectual tasks" to refine understanding about a policy issue helps reduce interpersonal conflict and keeps the discussion focused upon the task.

3. An ideal opportunity is provided to research a problem using laboratory and field research methodologies. Both basic and applied research issues can be confronted.

4. The use of cumulative information provides a valuable data base for guiding policy analysis and decision making. It also improves problem perspectives by allowing participants to increase their familiarity and understanding.

5. The use of a permanent core group provides the continuity needed to deal with complex and unpredictable social-policy issues. The addition of problem experts as temporary members further enhances the seminar by multiplying the information base and improving its quality.

6. The emphasis upon contextuality is a significant contribution to problem analysis. Examining the past and present to provide a perspective on the future increases problem familiarity quickly. It allows the participants to shift back and forth between detail and the whole. Thus, new insights are obtained which can prompt new approaches.

7. Flexibility of the seminar allows formation of subgroups to investigate less important issues or deal with subproblems of a larger issue.

The Decision Seminar also has certain disadvantages, such as the following:

1. The relative complexity of the seminar makes it difficult for group members to learn the steps involved. More importantly, the complexity hinders actually using all the processes of the seminar. A skilled facilitator and training for the participants would seem to be essential.

2. Depending upon the type of problem dealt with, the seminar may be too removed from the problem to develop a proper perspective. For instance, one application of the seminar dealt with a problem in a public school located several hundred miles from the seminar room.

3. It is relatively easy to lose sight of the ultimate objective and get tied up in details of the seminar as well as details of the problem.

4. Unless objectives are established and agreed upon at the outset, conflicting purposes often can develop. The result is a loss of focus upon the problem.

5. Managing the amount of data required can cause difficulties. Acquiring, storing, retrieving, and presenting data must be monitored carefully. Otherwise, quality of the data base will be lessened and resulting decisions will be less than satisfactory.

Although not available at the time the original seminars were established, there now are a variety of computer resources that can be brought to bear upon this problem. For instance, there now are easy-to-use relational data base and chart display programs for personal computers. Computers also can be used to analyze some problems interactively—even when the members are geographically dispersed. Another technological advance for data management is a board used to record and store data. It is designed much like a standalone chalkboard, and data written on it can be stored in memory and then printed out from a built-in printer. Transcribing from charts would be eliminated. ·

6. Because of the time commitment required, participant motivation can be a problem. The members must be committed to working on a problem for a set period of time. If the composition of the core group varies too much over time, needed continuity will be lost.

7.07 Delphi

The Delphi technique was developed at the RAND corporation in the early 1950s to obtain expert opinion on how many Soviet atomic bombs would be required to do a specified amount of damage in the United States.[29] Since then, the technique has been employed in technological forecasting, public-policy analysis, educational innovations, program planning, and a variety of other areas. The essential feature of the Delphi method is its emphasis upon developing expert consensus about a topic through an anonymous seris of mailed questionnaires. The initial questionnaire poses a broad question to which responses are sought, summarized, and then sent back to participants in a second questionnaire for possible modification. Anywhere from three to five questionnaires then might be used to repeat the process until consensus is achieved or the problem is sufficiently answered. Although not specifically designed to generate creative responses to problems, the Delphi technique can be adapted easily for this purpose.

Ten major steps involved in implementing a three-questionnaire version of the technique have been described by Delbecq, Van de Ven, and Gustafson:[30]

1. Develop the Delphi question (problem).
2. Select and contact the respondents.
3. Select the sample size.
4. Develop and test questionnaire #1.
5. Analyze results of questionnaire #1.
6. Develop and test questionnaire #2.
7. Analyze results of questionnaire #2.
8. Develop and test questionnaire #3.
9. Analyze results of questionnaire #3.
10. Prepare final report and send to respondents.

The Delphi approach typically involves three different groups: decision makers, staff, and respondents. Decision makers are individuals responsible for implementing the final decision. A work group of five to nine persons (including staff) is usually created by the decision makers to guide the process of developing and analyzing questionnaires, evaluating collected data, and revising questionnaires if necessary. The staff group is directed by a coordinator who should have experience in using the Delphi method and be familiar with the major problem. The staff coordinator's primary duties involve supervising a support staff in typing, mailing questionnaires, processing some results, and scheduling meetings. Respondents typically are experts on the problem who agree to respond to the questionnaires.

1. Develop the Delphi Question (Problem). This step begins with formulation of the broad question by the decision makers. The key element of this step is to develop a question that will be clearly understood by the respondents. If the question is misunderstood or subject to multiple interpretations, the entire

process can be wasted. The staff members also play a critical role during this step. Staff personnel should question the decision makers to insure that they understand what the decision makers want to do and how the results will be used. Close coordination between staff and the decision makers is essential throughout the entire process.

2. Select and Contact the Respondents. The characteristics of the individuals selected to receive questionnaires will determine the quality of the final product. Delbecq et al. recommend that participants be selected on the basis of their (a) sense of personal involvement in the problem (b) possession of relevant information, (c) motivation to spend time on the Delphi process, and (d) perception of the value of information they will obtain from the other participants. When the purpose of the process is to develop creative solutions, special attention should be given to identifying qualifications of specialists in the problem area. This way, the solutions are more likely to be practical.

Respondents are selected using a nomination process. The work group of decision makers and staff should select a target population and then seek nominations from well-known, knowledgeable individuals. (In some cases, a more random selection process may be used if expert opinion is not a major criterion.) Whenever possible, the participants then should be contacted by phone or in person to explain the purpose of the process, describe their responsibilities, and answer any questions.

3. Select the Sample Size. The Delphi technique has been used with anywhere from four or five respondents to more than 100, although a typical sample will contain about 20–30 participants. The actual sample size selected will depend upon the purpose and objectives desired. If development of creative solutions is the objective, a group of about 15–20 specialists in the area should be sufficient. If a broad-based response is sought for opinions on a particular topic or issue, 100 or more people might be included. Whatever sample size is selected, it must be remembered that increasing sample size will increase the amount of coordination required. Size therefore must be tailored to the resources available for implementation.

4. Develop and Test Questionnaire #1. The initial questionnaire poses the broad problem to the respondents. Although no specific format is necessary, the questionnaire generally contains a couple of open-ended questions or asks for examples of possible problem solutions. A cover letter including a statement of purpose, use of the results, instructions, and a response deadline also should be included. If responses are not received from a participant within one week of the response deadline, a follow-up letter should be mailed to encourage a response.

5. Analyze Results of Questionnaire #1. The critical objective of this step is to summarize all responses in such a way that they can be understood clearly by the respondents in the second questionnaire. The work group records each

response on an index card, sorts the cards into common categories, develops consensus on labels for each category, and prepares summaries reflecting the content of the categories.

6. Develop and Test Questionnaire #2. The second questionnaire is developed using the responses summarized from questionnaire #1. The focus of this questionnaire should be upon (a) identifying areas of agreement and disagreement, (b) providing an opportunity to clarify meanings, and (c) establishing tentative priorities placed on topics or solutions. Respondents are typically asked to vote on items summarized from the first questionnaire. This can be done with an agree/disagree type of response or ranking procedures. In addition, respondents should be encouraged to add comments or to clarify their perceptions of any items. After completion, questionnaire #2 should be tested with a small group of nonparticipants, revised if necessary, and then mailed to the participants.

7. Analyze Results of Questionnaire #2. The task of the work group at this step is to count the number of votes for each item and summarize any comments made. Votes can be counted using a vote tally sheet that shows the item number, the number of persons voting for it, how they rated it, and the total vote for the item. Comments can be analyzed using a procedure similar to that used for analyzing questionnaire #1: comments can be placed on cards, the cards sorted into categories, labels assigned to the categories, and summary statements written for each category. A key function of the work group at this stage is to determine if the information provided will help solve the problem or be useful in some other way. If the information is not considered useful at this point, the work group can alter the type of questions asked or terminate the process altogether.

8. Develop and Test Questionnaire #3. The third and final (in this illustration) questionnaire is designed to pull together the entire Delphi process. Results from the second questionnaire are summarized for the participants, who then are asked to record a final vote for each item. If the number of items is not large, respondents may rank order the items in terms of their importance or usefulness. Care also should be taken to insure that the original meaning of an item is not lost in summarization. After it has been developed, the questionnaire should be tested and then mailed to the respondents.

9. Analyze Results of Questionnaire #3. The results from Questionnaire #3 are analyzed using the same procedure followed to analyze questionnaire #2.

10. Prepare Final Report and Send to Respondents. One purpose of this step is to provide the respondents with a summary as a gesture of courtesy for their participation. The report should contain a review of the original problem, the goals of the process, the procedure used, the final results, and, if possible, a description of any decisions made as a result of the Delphi procedure.

Evaluation The Delphi technique has been widely used for a variety of forecasting purposes with more or less favorable results. Before the Delphi technique is used to generate ideas, its strengths and weaknesses should be evaluated to determine its suitability for a particular problem. The following major advantages and disadvantages should be considered:

Advantages

1. Provides a convenient way to involve persons who might be geographically distant from one another.
2. Permits anonymous responding and minimizes group conformity pressures.
3. Eliminates the sometimes harmful psychological barriers often found in groups; prevents individual domination and avoids any form of disruptive interpersonal conflicts.
4. Uses an idea evaluation stage in addition to idea generation.
5. Makes possible the generation of a large number of ideas.
6. Written responses force respondents to seriously consider their ideas, allowing for greater crystallization of thought. Thus, higher-quality ideas often emerge.
7. Keeps attention focused directly on the problem (i.e., is task centered).
8. Each participant has an equal opportunity to contribute; all ideas are given equal consideration.
9. Produces more accurate estimates of predictions than face-to-face confrontations.

Disadvantages

1. Is extremely time consuming. A typical Delphi process will take at least a month and a half to implement and requires a large amount of coordinating effort by the work group.
2. Requires a relatively high level of participant skill in written communication.
3. Requires a relatively high level of participant motivation to stay with the entire process.
4. Does not provide any social-interaction benefits for participants.
5. Fails to provide an opportunity for verbal clarifications.
6. Any participant conflicts over ideas are dealt with only by pooling votes; no opportunity is provided for verbal compromises in thinking.
7. When it is used for forecasting purposes, it will be of unknown value since it is difficult to predict the future accurately. Also, it can be difficult to separate forecasting desires from forecasting predictions.
8. The unstructured nature of the initial question can be frustrating to persons who require more structure in the form of some minimal idea stimulation.
9. Requires a certain skill level on the part of the work group to summarize the questionnaires accurately and clearly.

Although a few negative results have been obtained,[31] research on the Delphi technique generally has been positive. For instance, Campbell[32] found that two-thirds of the scientific predicitons made in 1964 using Delphi has come true by 1970, and Erffmeyer and Lane[33] found that Delphi produced the highest-quality solutions when compared with consensus, interacting, and Nominal Group Technique (NGT) groups. A major issue about the technique's validity concerns the number of questionnaire rounds required. Martino[34] suggests that a minimum of four rounds may be needed to achieve sufficient convergence. Support for this proposition has been found by Erffmeyer, Erffmeyer, and Lane.[35]

In general, the Delphi technique is suitable for idea generation only if it is not practical to bring participants together and if time is not a major constraint. Otherwise, its advantages could be obtained more easily with another method, such as the Nominal Group Technique.

7.08 The Idea Generator[TM]

The Idea Generator[TM] was developed by Experience in Software, Inc. (2039 Shattuck Avenue, Suite 401, Berkeley, California 94704)[36] as a computer software program for generating ideas. It is based upon Gerard Nierenberg's *The Art of Creative Thinking*[37] and is appropriate for either individuals or groups. Three stages prompt users in describing a problem, generating ideas, and evaluating ideas. The major stages follow:

1. Describe the problem. This stage is concerned with collecting basic background information and developing a good understanding of the problem. The primary activities are
   a. Describe the situation. State it in the most useful way possible. The statement should be clear and specific, and should not include any particular solution or approach.
   b. List the desired goals. The goals should be specific and nonoverlapping, and should include time limits as appropriate. Enter each goal on a single line and rate its importance using a one- to nine-point scale.
   c. Describe the people involved. Include people who can help change the situation, those who might be affected by it, and those whose approval will be important for solution implementation.
   If any problem solutions occur during this stage, record them on the Idea Screen. At the conclusion of this stage, the program generates a Summary Report.
2. Generate ideas. While all judgment is deferred, a variety of techniques can be used to stimulate ideas. The program prompts users in working with the following techniques:
   a. Consider similar situations. Adapt previous solutions that worked for the current problem.

b. Examine metaphors that might help prompt ideas. Use the metaphorical situation as a source of unrelated stimuli. Unlike the first technique, metaphors do not have to fit the situation exactly.

c. Use a new perspective. Think of how someone else might solve the problem.

d. Focus upon each goal individually. Pretend that each goal is the only one. This technique will help prevent premature closure on possible solutions.

e. Reverse the problem goals. State the opposite of each goal and think of ways to achieve it. Use these ways as stimuli for suggesting practical ideas for achieving the original goal.

f. Focus upon the people involved. Identify the positive and negative qualities of people who might be helping or hindering resolution of the problem. Use these qualities as stimuli for generating ideas.

After all possible ideas are generated, the final step in this stage is to conduct a preliminary idea evaluation. Rephrase any poorly worded ideas, group related ideas, combine related ideas, or record any new ideas stimulated by the previous ideas. The program then generates a Summary Report for this stage.

3. Evaluate the ideas. The last stage of the program involves a careful selection and assessment of the most promising ideas. This process is guided using the following activities:

a. Choose ideas to evaluate. Begin by stating evaluation objectives. For instance, an objective might be to select one "best" idea, a few, or many ideas. Using the objective as a guide, select desired ideas. Rate each idea intuitively using a one- to nine-point scale. Depending upon the outcome of this activity, the program may suggest other evaluation activities or terminate the process.

b. Rate ideas using the goals. If required, further refine the ideas by rating each one in terms of how well it satisfies the original goals (at this point, the goals may need to be revised). The program will display a weighted average of the ratings for each of the ideas. Note any large discrepancies between these ratings and your intuitive ratings.

c. Evaluate costs, benefits, and effects upon people. A final evaluation activity involves examining the potential costs and benefits of an idea upon people. An idea that affects a large number of people in a positive way obviously will be more desirable than an idea that affects people negatively.

As with the other stages, the program will generate a Summary Report of what was accomplished during this stage. Results of the entire process also can be printed out for later evaluation. This report can be used to assist implementation of ideas or loaded into another program for additional processing.

Evaluation   The Idea Generator^{TM} program is an exceptionally well conceived and presented software package for facilitating resolution of a variety of problem situations. Most problem-solving techniques must be mastered by the user before their potential can be exploited fully. Using a computer program, in contrast, relieves the problem solver of much of the learning effort that must be expended before problem solving even can begin. The Idea Generator^{TM} does an excellent job of structuring the process and guiding the user. Although it has a few minor weaknesses, it more than compensates for these by adhering to basic creative-thinking principles throughout and by its flexibility of application.

In addition to those already mentioned, its major advantages include the following:

1. It is relatively easy to use and requires no in-depth knowledge of computers. It is "user friendly."
2. Ideas are recorded on an Idea Screen for future reference. The screen is always accessible so that previous ideas can be used to stimulate new ones.
3. A "Help" function makes it easy to get assistance in using the program.
4. As with many other problem-solving processes, it can be adapted easily for use with groups.
5. The Summary Reports provided at the end of each stage increase problem understanding and can serve as stimuli for new ideas and suggest improvements for previous ones.
6. Due to the "magic" of computers, all problem-solving data can be placed into other software programs designed as outliners or word processors. Once there, the data can be manipulated in a number of different ways to encourage creative thinking.
7. The instruction manual is well documented and exceptionally easy to follow. All operations are explained in easy-to-understand, plain English. Troubleshooting questions and answers also are included, as is an excellent index.
8. Because data are stored as computer files, it is easy to return to previous stages of the process or make revisions and general editorial changes.
9. The idea generation portion of the process uses both related and unrelated problem stimuli. The use of metaphors and reversals is especially commendable. With proper use, these techniques are capable of producing diverse problem perspectives and the unique ideas that often accompany them.
10. The evaluation component stresses both intuition and use of weighted criteria.

Although limited in number and not of major consequence, some potential disadvantages of the program are the following:

1. Like any problem-solving technique, The Idea Generator^{TM} is not a panacea. People are needed to solve ill-structured problems. Thus, the program is an excellent tool, but it obviously cannot replace human thinking.
2. The number of idea generation techniques is rather limited. However, the same criticism can be made of other similar approaches, such as the Osborn-Parnes Creative Problem Solving model.
3. A more detailed description (with specific examples) in the manual of how to use some of the techniques might be helpful. Of course, this disadvantage does not detract from the program or the problem-solving process.
4. Listing specific problem goals (which also function as evaluation criteria) at the outset of the process may introduce unnecessary constraints during the later stages. The manual cautions that the goals should be as accurate as possible since they will be used as criteria during evaluation. However, this caution may not be sufficient. On the other hand, the manner in which the goals are used during idea generation to prompt new ideas can offset this potential weakness somewhat. In any event, initial goals should be used cautiously and flexibly.
5. Maximum benefit is not likely to be obtained from using the program alone. As with any similar approach, supplemental reading, training, and experience in applying the process all will help provide optimal use.

Computer-aided problem solving is not for everyone. However, with the proliferation of personal computers, The Idea Generator^{TM} can be a useful tool for assisting those who do like interacting with computers.

7.09 Idea Tracking

The Idea Tracking technique was developed by Frank Armstrong[38] as a systematic creative-thinking method. His basic premise is that most people do not stay on a "tracking line" of creative thought when solving problems. In particular, people often fail to approach similar problems in similar ways, primarily because they are unaware of how they dealt with the problem the first time. To remedy this situation, he suggests Idea Tracking as a practical alternative. Idea Tracking consists of the five major steps:

1. Assessing the situation
2. Defining the problem
3. Use of the subconscious in creativity
4. The idea-producing session
5. Use of judgment in selecting the best idea

Check rules also have been developed for each of the steps as implementation guides. A synopsis of these check rules, as described by Armstrong, is presented next.

1. Assessing the Situation
   a. Defer opinions about the problem.
   b. Locate the most common assumption about the problem and evaluate its validity.
   c. Ask endless questions and look for the one factor that will be more important than others.
   d. Determine the validity of all sources of information.
   e. Ask: What date? What time? How many? How few? How long ago? How recently? How big? How small?
2. Defining the Problem
   a. Develop a tentative definition of the problem.
   b. Collect, organize, and analyze all relevant information about the problem.
   c. Examine each word of the problem definition for accuracy, completeness, appropriateness, and clarity.
   d. Seek the opinion of others about the meaning of the problem.
3. Use of the Subconscious in Creativity
   a. Look at the problem statement before going to bed at night and while on vacation.
   b. Frequently refer to the written statement to provide a possible new stimulus.
4. The Idea-Producing Session
   a. Put everything else out of your mind and concentrate on producing ideas.
   b. Write down all ideas; after pursuing one line of thought for a while, begin a new one.
   c. When you have finished producing ideas, compare each one with the original problem objectives.
5. Use of Judgment in Selecting the Best Idea
   a. Use a period of time to allow the ideas to "simmer."
   b. Seek criticism of the ideas from others.
   c. Develop a balance sheet to show the strengths and weaknesses of each idea.
   d. After narrowing down the pool of ideas, compare a few of the best ones with the original problem statement.

Evaluation Idea Tracking is really a rational problem-sovling model that incorporates use of the unconscious to produce creative solutions. Although it is systematic, it probably will be most useful for well-structured or semi-structured problems rather than as a procedure for ill-structured problems. Since described by Armstrong in 1960, many other methods have emerged that should be more useful. Nevertheless, Idea Tracking is simple to use and might prove to be helpful as a checklist for certain types of problems. The use of the subconscious for developing creative solutions, however, is similar to the Free Association method and might be too limiting for producing unique solutions unless used with other stimulation sources.

7.10 Kepner-Tregoe

This technique was developed by Kepner and Tregoe[39] as a practical approach for managers to use in analyzing problems and making decisions. According to the authors, most problem-solving activity proceeds in a piecemeal fashion with little apparent order or logic; although the major elements of the problem might be explored, there is no systematic way to determine what information is relevant and how it should be used. The Kepner-Tregoe approach, in contrast, was designed to provide an efficient, orderly method for showing managers: what to do, when to do it, and what information to use and how to use it.

The basic Kepner-Tregoe procedure consists of two cycles or phases: problem analysis and decision making. The problem analysis cycle is designed to guide the process of finding problem causes, while the decision-making cycle assists the decision maker in taking action. Each of these cycles is further subdivided into seven stages.

Problem Analysis The seven stages of the problem analysis cycle are described below.

1. Identify Problem Areas by Comparing Actual Performance with What Should Be Happening. A problem can be defined in terms of a deviation that exists from an expected performance norm. To know when a problem exists, a manager must be knowledgeable of current standards. For a situation to be classified as a problem, there must be (a) recognition that an undesirable deviation exists between what actually is and what should be, and (b) motivation on the part of the manager to find a problem cause and correct the deviation. Once the possible deviations have been recognized, the manager proceeds to the next stage.

2. Examine the Problem Areas, Establish Priorities, and Select a Problem. Quite often, a number of different problem areas will be identified in the first stage. In order to narrow these down to some workable number, it is necessary to use a systematic procedure. To do this, the manager should examine all identified problem areas, eliminate deviations that are acceptable (i.e., those within tolerance limits), and then gather all available information on the remaining

problem areas. Using this information, the manager should examine the problems to determine if any problems have been inappropriately combined or clustered together. A frequent mistake, for example, is to group a number of problems under the heading "communication problems." If such clustering has occurred, the problems should be broken down and specific deviations identified. Next, priorities need to be established so that the most important deviations can be selected for further analysis. This is done by asking three questions about (a) the urgency of the deviation, (b) its seriousness, and (c) its general trend and growth potential. In addition, the focus of the priorities needs to be considered. Managerial judgment is required to evaluate the priorities since problem importance may vary among managers. Any priorities established should be viewed as tentative because priorities often will change. Finally, before moving on to the next stage, the manager should determine if the cause of the priority problem is known or unknown. If the cause is clearly known, then the remaining problem analysis stages can be omitted and the manager can proceed directly to the decision-making cycle. If, however, there is any doubt about the cause of the problem, the manager should go on to the next stage of the problem analysis cycle.

3. Determine the Precise Nature of the Problem by Describing Its Identity, Location, Time, and Extent; Describe What is Not Included in the Problem. The purpose of this stage is to define the problem boundaries as specifically as possible, that is, to determine what is and what is not. Precise specification of a problem is a difficult task since most persons have a tendency to begin immediately searching for problem causes. By precisely specifying what the problem is and is not, the possible causes of the problem can be more clearly identified. The procedure to do this involves asking questions about *what* the deviation is and is not, *where* the deviation is observed and where it is not, *when* the deviation is and is not observed, and the *extent* to which the deviation is or is not observed. Kepner and Tregoe suggest that a worksheet can be used as an aid for sorting information into the different categories.

4. Examine the Problem Specification (What Is and Is Not) and Identify Those Characteristics That Distinguish What the Problem Is from What It Is Not. In order to locate the one change responsible for producing the deviation, it is necessary to look for clues that might indicate the nature of the change. When distinctions between the is and is not characteristics of the problem are analyzed, it is often possible to identify features unique to what the problem is and is not. For instance, the problem might be characterized as occurring only in one specific location at one specific time. These features then can be used to further narrow down the search for a cause.

5. Examine the Problem Distinctions to Determine Relevant Changes That Could Have Caused the Problem. Using the distinctions identified in the previous stage, the problem solver should attempt to isolate the one change primarily

responsible for the problem. In this stage, it is important that only relevant changes be examined. That is, only those changes likely to have produced sharp distinctions should be examined. All forms of speculation should be avoided during this stage. Only the facts used to specify the problem should be considered.

6. Using the Relevant Changes Identified, Deduce Possible Causes of the Problem. The changes identified in the previous stage are only tentative causes of the problem. The purpose of this stage is to reduce the number of probable causes by making deductions or hypotheses involving cause and effect. Thus, it might be hypothesized: The explosion occurred because of a defective value. By using the relevant changes associated with the distinctions between the is and the is not, the problem solver will be guided in the search for possible causes. The final product of this stage should be a list of specific, testable hypotheses about the relationship between problem causes and an observed deviation.

7. Test the Possible Causes of the Problem by Determining the Extent to Which They Explain What Is and Is Not Characteristic of the Problem. To avoid premature or false conclusions about possible problem causes, hypotheses should be tested by looking for any exceptions that might explain the deviation. After examination, some causes might be found that produce the deviation, but only when certain conditions are present. Such causes can be eliminated since there can be only one change capable of producing the deviation. To be valid, the selection of the primary cause must be based upon an explanation that satisfies both the is and is not aspects of the problem. Thus, a defective valve can be the primary cause of an explosion if and only if other possible sources of the explosion and effects associated with these causes can be ruled out. To be considered the primary cause, the valve alone must be verified as being responsible for the explosion.

A brief case study described by Kepner and Tregoe[40] can help illustrate problem analysis. In the "Case of the Plugged Spray Guns," crews working for a street department in a large city reported that their spray guns suddenly began to plug up one day while on a job. Every time the guns plugged up, the crews stopped working and cleaned out the guns with paint thinner. The solution was only temporary, however, as the guns soon began to plug up again. Finally the superintendents of the crews met with the departmental manager to discuss the problem.

In this case, the problem area was easily identified. The deviation was simply that the guns should not be plugging up when they did (stage 1). Only one problem area existed, and the major priority was to determine the cause of the problem (stage 2). Specifying the problem (stage 3) in terms of what, where, and extent was relatively easy: The clogging developed in the spray nozzles, occurred with all of the work crews throughout the city, and completely prevented the guns from operating. The when of the problem was more difficult to identify.

Some of the superintendents disagreed as to when the clogging occurred. After repeated questioning, the manager finally determined that the guns clogged up when they were first used each time and remained clogged until the paint thinner was used. The manager then began to look for distinctions (stage 4). One of the superintendents noted that the most distinctive feature of the problem was that the guns were clean before each painting job. Although this information could be viewed as contradictory, the manager decided to examine it to determine if there were relevant changes that could have caused the problem (stage 5). When the superintendents were asked about any changes observed when cleaning the guns, one man reported that some paint thinner always remained in the guns after they had been cleaned. From this information, they hypothesized that it might be the paint thinner that was causing the clogging (stage 6). This hypothesis was tested by experimenting with the paint thinner (stage 7). It was discovered that residual thinner would coagulate and clog the guns as soon as paint entered the nozzle. However, this explanation required testing for exceptions, since the same brand of thinner had been used for many years and the problem only had recently developed. After searching for additional information, it was found that one manufacturer of the thinner recently had changed some ingredients that tended to clog when used with the thinner made by another manufacturer of the same brand. Changing the type of thinner used quickly solved the problem.

Decision Making   After the cause of the problem has been determined from the problem analysis cycle, actions need to be taken to solve the problem. It is at this point that the decision-making cycle is initiated. Below are the seven stages of this cycle.

1. Establish the Specific Objectives to Be Accomplished in Terms of Expected Results and Available Resources. The purpose of this stage is to develop a set of standards against which the solution alternatives can be evaluated. The objectives should be stated in precise, specific terms. Thus, an objective to increase profit is too broad and should be restated to specify: What type of profit? How much? Where? and When? Another consideration involved in establishing objectives is to determine the expected results. These expectations can be determined by asking questions pertaining to desired accomplishments, specific problems to be corrected, intended directions, required activities, areas to be avoided, and so on. Finally, the available resources need to be considered. The resources should be evaluated in terms of five general categories: (a) personnel, (b) money, (c) material, (d) time, and (e) power (energy, authority). These categories then can be used as guides for determining the operating limits within which the decision must be made.

2. Classify the Objectives in Order of Importance by Listing Must and Want Requirements. In most problem situations, the objectives will not be of equal importance. Some objectives will be absolutely essential while others might be

desirable but not essential to making a decision. To distinguish between important and nonessential objectives, a list should be developed spelling out the musts and wants. A must specifies the minimum and maximum limits for the expected results and available resources. (To be considered as a potential problem solution, the alternatives generated in the third stage must fall within these prescribed limits.) Objectives classified as wants express relative advantages and disadvantages. Thus, a want objective could be stated as: I would like to use more equipment than the resources limit allows. When some wants are considered to be more important than others, numerical weighting procedures can be used. One procedure involves assigning a weight of one to the least important objective and considering how much more important another objective is when compared with it. For example, a 4 could be assigned to this second objective, indicating that it is seen as being four times as important as the least important objective. Another procedure would be to rate, independently, all of the objectives on a one- to ten-point scale, noting the relative importance of each objective.

3. Develop Alternative Courses of Action. The previous stages should have produced the requirements needed to generate alternatives. When it is known how the objectives will be achieved and the relative emphasis to be placed upon different objectives, generation of alternatives should be relatively simple. The process for doing this involves reflecting upon past experiences and separately examining each objective to determine implications or actions that might help to attain the objective. Some alternative courses of action will already exist, while others will have to be developed from scratch. Regardless of the source of the alternatives, however, it is important that a rational and logical strategy be developed to satisfy the standards established by the objectives.

4. Compare Each Alternative Against the Musts and Wants Developed for the Objectives. During this stage, the alternatives are evaluated individually to determine which one (or combination) has the most potential for achieving the stated objectives. Each alternative should be compared with each of the must and want objectives. When the comparison is with a must objective, a decision is made to retain an alternative by indicating either go, or no go. Alternatives that exceed limits of the must objectives are eliminated from further consideration. When alternatives are compared with the want objectives, each alternative should be rated numerically using either a ten-point scale or a rank-ordering procedure. Such scores or ranking, however, do not reflect the importance placed upon the objectives. Instead, the numerical ratings are intended to provide a measure of the ability of each alternative to achieve the want objectives. Thus, to obtain an overall evaluation, the ratings for each alternative should be multiplied by the weightings previously assigned to each want objective. This way, both the performance assessment and the importance of that performance will be considered for each alternative. In addition, numbers should not be used as substitutes for human judgment. All of the decisions made during the cycle are based upon facts and experiences and not arbitrary use of numerical scores.

5. Make a Tentative Decision by Selecting the Best Alternative. It is not until the fifth stage of the decision-making cycle that a decision is actually made on a potential course of action. Using the weightings from the previous stage, the problem solver should select the alternative receiving the highest score as a tentative means for achieving the objectives. In many cases, this choice will be a combination of several alternatives that might satisfy part of an objective. The final alternative selected, however, must be the one that will completely satisfy all the requirements of the objectives.

6. Evaluate Any Possible Adverse Consequences of the Alternative Selected. Events external to a problem solver often will change over time. In addition, some alternatives will create new problems by introducing change into a system. Therefore, it is important to consider and evaluate the adverse consequences that might be associated with the tentative alternative. It is obviously much easier to discover and correct problems in advance than to deal with them once a course of action has been implemented. To insure successful implementation, effects of the alternative upon other things and the effects of other things upon the alternative should be considered. Kepner and Tregoe recommend examining nine different areas as potential sources of problems: (a) people (motivation, skills, health), (b) organization (relationships, communications), (c) external influences (economic trends, competition, legal and government), (d) facilities and equipment (space, flexibility, location), (e) ideas and processes (security, adaptability), (f) material (sources and availability, quality, handling and storage), (g) money (capital, costs and expenses, return), (h) output (quality, quantity, pace and timing), and (i) personal influences (goals and plans, family interests). To obtain a more precise estimate of the adverse consequences, a numerical weighting system (similar to that used to weight the want objectives) can be used to evaluate the seriousness of the consequences. In addition, a numerical rating of the likelihood of the consequences occurring also should be attempted. If the seriousness and likelihood ratings are multiplied, an index of overall threat can be obtained. The combination of this index and human judgment then can be used to determine how (or if) the alternative should be put into action.

7. Carefully Plan Implementation of the Decision by Establishing Procedures to Eliminate or Minimize Adverse Consequences; Follow Up on the Decision to Make Sure That the Specified Actions Are Carried Out. This stage has two primary objectives: to prevent the occurrence of the adverse consequences identified in the previous stage, and to carefully design a plan for implementing and following up the decision. Prevention of adverse consequences can be accomplished by analyzing their possible causes and taking action to eliminate them, or by developing contingency plans to deal with unwanted problems should they occur. A specific procedure, Potential-Problem Analysis, has been developed by Kepner and Tregoe for this purpose. (A detailed discussion of this procedure can be found in Chapter 6.) The implementation and follow-up plan involves the following steps:

a. Establish an implementation schedule and reporting procedures for evaluating progress.
b. After instructions for implementing the decision have been given, check to insure they have been received and are clearly understood.
c. Assign specific areas of responsibility for carrying out the decision, and check for understanding.
d. Establish a timetable of specific dates for measuring progress made on correcting the problem.
e. Establish a feedback system to provide information whenever the plan encounters a major obstacle.

It is critical that careful attention be given both to the analysis of potential problems and to the implementation and follow-up of the final decision; otherwise, much effort in the preceding stages will have been wasted.

To illustrate how the stages of the decision-making cycle are used to take action on a problem, a situation borrowed from Kepner and Tregoe[41] will be described. The situation involves a manager who is notified that his house will be torn down to make way for a new superhighway. He is told he has 60 days to buy a new house and that he will receive a fair price for his current home. Because this situation does not require problem analysis, the manager can begin immediately to make decisions.

He begins the process by establishing specific objectives (stage 1). He wants a house that will meet the needs of his family yet be within the price range he can afford. Among the objectives he considers are monthly payment, number of bedrooms and baths, distance to work, availability for occupancy, and the amount of money he has in the bank. Thus, in this situation, the primary resource concerns are money and time.

Having listed these tentative objectives, the manager then proceeds to make a specific list of must and want requirements (stage 2). For the must requirements, he decides that the new house must not require a down payment in excess of $30,000 nor a monthly payment in excess of $1,500. In addition, the house must have at least four bedrooms and two baths, be located within 45 minutes' driving time from his office, and be ready for occupancy within 60 days. After establishing these limits for the must objectives, the manager then lists the want requirements. Among these objectives he includes such factors as the lowest possible monthly payment, nearby public transportation, convenience to schools, maintenance costs, probable resale value, adequacy of landscaping, and a large kitchen with an attractive view. Using a ten-point scale, he assigns each objective a weight, with a 1 indicating low importance and a 10, high importance. He assigns the monthly payment the highest weight, followed by convenience to schools, maintenance costs, resale value, public transportation, landscaping, and a large kitchen.

Next, the manager takes his list to a real estate agent who provides the manager with three houses (A, B, and C) that satisfy all of the must requirements and seem to fit most of the want requirements (stage 3). Using the information he obtains about these houses, he checks each one against the must objectives (stage 4). One of the houses (B) requires a $370 monthly payment, so it is eliminated from any further consideration. The remaining houses then are compared against the individual want objectives by using a ten-point scale to indicate the worth of that objective. These weights are multiplied by the original weights to derive a total weighted score for each house. House A is given a score of 804 while house C is given a weighted score of 848. Using these weightings, the manager tentatively selects house C as the best alternative (stage 5).

To assess any possible adverse consequences of his tentative decision, the manager considers potential problems associated with houses A and C (stage 6). For example, marks in the basement of house C indicate a possible flooding problem, and the beginning construction on a new shopping center could mean heavier traffic in front of the house. He also reexamines house A and finds that one of his subordinates lives across the street, which could mean awkward socializing, and his wife tells him that there are few children in the neighborhood in the same age group as their children. He writes down all of these adverse consequences and rates each one, again using a ten-point scale. He constructs two columns for each alternative; in the first column, he rates the probability that the consequence will occur, and in the second column he rates the seriousness of the consequence. He then multiplies the ratings together and, on the basis of these ratings, selects house A. Because the manager did not consider the possible awkward social relationship with his subordinate to be serious, and because there was little he could do to increase the number of children in the neighborhood, there was nothing that could be done to minimize or eliminate the consequences or to follow up on the decision (stage 7). As it turned out, however, the people who eventually bought house C were greeted with nine inches of water in their basement the following winter.

To summarize, problem analysis and decision making involve the following stages:

Problem Analysis

1. Compare what should be happening with what is happening.
2. Establish problem priorities and select a problem to work on.
3. Specify the problem deviation in terms of what, where, when, and to what extent.
4. Identify characteristics that distinguish what the problem is from what it is not.
5. Examine the distinctions to determine changes which could have caused the problem.

6. Deduce possible problem causes.
7. Test the possible problem causes.

Decision Making

1. Establish the specific objectives to be accomplished in terms of expected results and available resources.
2. Classify the objectives in order of importance by listing must and want requirements.
3. Develop alternative courses of action.
4. Compare each alternative against the must and want requirements.
5. Make a tentative decision by selecting the best alternative.
6. Evaluate any possible adverse consequences of the alternative selected.
7. Carefully plan implementation of the decision by establishing procedures to eliminate or minimize adverse consequences; follow up on the decision to make sure that the specified actions are carried out.

In addition to their book, *The New Rational Manager,* Kepner and Tregoe also conduct training programs designed to develop skills in using their procedures. Persons interested in obtaining information about these programs can write to Kepner-Tregoe, Inc., Research Road, Box 704, Princeton, New Jersey 08540.

Evaluation A major strength of the Kepner-Tregoe approach is its emphasis upon a systematic procedure for analyzing problems and making decisions. By emphasizing the need to systematically search for problem causes, the technique helps insure that information will be efficiently used; by emphasizing the need to systematically evaluate decision alternatives, the probability of achieving a high-quality decision is increased. Economy of time and effort are obviously the most distinguishing features of this method. The procedure also assists managers in knowing where they (or their subordinates) are at any one point in the problem-solving process and provides a record for checking problem analysis after decision making has begun. Furthermore, it can help prevent premature development of conclusions about problem causes, insure that alternatives are not generated until objectives have been established, and provide a screen for efficiently filtering alternative courses of action.

Another strength of the method is its compatibility with either individual or group problem-solving situations. Although not fully discussed by Kepner and Tregoe in their book, a group approach has the potential to increase the quality of the problem analysis and decision-making cycles. Involving subordinates also should lead to greater subordinate commitment in implementing decisions. If subordinates are included, however, consideration must be given to the level of subordinate motivation and the extent to which their acceptance of a decision will be critical to effective implementation. In addition, a certain level of managerial skill will be required to deal with any interpersonal or substantive conflicts that might arise. According to Stech and Ratliffe,[42] several different versions of group decision making could be tried with the Kepner-Tregoe approach. For example, a group might try to achieve consensus on the must and want requirements and on the weights given to each want. Next, individuals could compare the alternatives with the requirements before reconvening to discuss selection of the best alternative. Based upon individual ratings of the solutions, an averaging procedure then could be used to determine which alternative should be selected.

Although the Kepner-Tregoe approach is suitable for complex problems with a known or limitied number of alternative solutions, it is probably less suited for problems with an unknown or infinite number of solutions. Because it assumes there can be only one cause of a problem, it will not be quite as useful for problems in the areas of new-product development or tehcnological innovation. Such problems are concerned primarily with generating ideas, any number of which might provide an acceptable solution. The Kepner-Tregoe approach, in contrast, is concerned more with identifying problem causes and selecting from among already identified alternatives. For this reason, the approach lacks some of the spontaneity required to develop innovative solutions to unstructured problems. The procedures used to analyze problems and make decisions could be improved by including idea stimulation aids to assist in generating objectives, musts and wants, and alternative courses of action. A second consideration involved in using the procedure is that it might not be suitable for relatively simple problems. In particular, problems that are narrow in scope probably do not justify use of all the different stages and cycles. Kepner and Tregoe recognize this point and recommend that managers use their own judgment in deciding if the entire approach would be appropriate or if it might be better to use a more abbreviated version. Another consideration is the method's failure to *explicitly* differentiate between low- and high-cost screens. Decisions involving the testing of problem causes or evaluating of alternative courses of action are made without regard to the possible costs of these activities. Although this will not be a problem for all situations, it is an issue that needs to be considered. Most evaluation activities consume time and other resources that must be weighed against the need to achieve the problem objectives. Quantitative cost estimates might be introduced to help alleviate this problem.

7.11 Nominal Group Technique (NGT)

The Nominal Group Technique (NGT), developed by Andre Delbecq and Andrew Van de Ven,[43] combines features of both brainstorming and brainwriting to produce a method that has been widely used in a variety of organizations for program-planning purposes. The format of the technique permits written recording but verbal discussion of all ideas generated. In addition, provision is made for systematically evaluating and selecting ideas once they have been generated. The NGT process involves the following basic steps:

1. Silent generation of ideas in writing
2. Round-robin recording of ideas
3. Serial discussion for clarification
4. Preliminary vote on item importance
5. Discussion of the preliminary vote
6. Final vote

1. Silent Generation of Ideas in Writing. The group leader gives a group of five to nine persons a written statement of the problem and reads it aloud to them. The group then silently writes down their ideas without discussion with others. The leader should avoid any detailed clarification of the problem, such as providing specific examples. In addition, the leader should function as a working member of the group and try to model good behavior by writing silently and discouraging those who do not.

2. Round-Robin Recording of Ideas. After a designated period of time (five or ten minutes), the idea generation phase is terminated and all ideas are recorded on a flip chart or chalkboard visible to the group. The leader asks each group member to read aloud an idea which is then recorded in front of the group. This activity continues by recording one idea from each person in turn until all of the ideas have been recorded. Ideas should be recorded as rapidly as possible using brief statements in the original words of the person who developed the idea. Duplicate ideas may be deleted, but variations on an idea are encouraged. During this step, there should not be any discussion of the ideas listed.

3. Serial Discussion for Clarification. The purpose of this step is to clarify the meaning, importance, and logic behind each idea. The leader points to each idea and asks for questions or comments. Agreement or disagreement with an idea may be encouraged, but depth of the discussion should be controlled by the leader to insure that a heated debate does not develop. The activity during this step should be viewed as a group responsibility, permitting individuals to refrain from commenting on their own idea if they desire. After allowing a reasonable and equitable (if possible) amount of time to discuss each idea, the leader should move on to the fourth step.

4. Preliminary Vote on Item Importance. Step four involves a group method for aggregating the perceived importance of each idea to arrive at an independent judgment of the most important or "best" idea. The procedure for accomplishing this objective is as follows:

a. The participants select between five and nine priority ideas from the entire list (the actual number being determined by the total number in the list—the more ideas on the list, the more priority ideas should be selected).

b. The participants write their ideas on 3 X 5 cards (one idea per card) and record the number of the idea (from the master list) at the upper left-hand corner of the card.

c. The participants carefully read over their selected ideas and rank each one by assigning a number 5 to the most important or best idea, a 1 to the least important or worst idea, and so on, until all of the ideas are ranked. The participants then record the number ranks in the lower right-hand corner of each card and underline the number three times to avoid confusion with the idea number.

d. The leader collects the cards and shuffles them to maintain anonymity of the votes.

e. The leader records the votes on a visible chart or chalkboard by listing the idea number in one column and all of the ranked scores for each idea number in a second column.

f. The vote tallies are counted and the idea receiving the greatest number of votes is noted.

For some types of problems, the NGT process can terminate with the fourth step if a clear picture of voting preferences has emerged. For other problems, however, a more refined selection procedure might be desired. In this event, the fifth and sixth steps should be added.

5. Discussion of the Preliminary Vote. If this step is selected, the voting tally sheet can be examined for any peculiar voting patterns and/or items can be discussed that seemed to receive too many or too few votes. An example of a peculiar voting pattern might be a situation where an idea receives three 5 votes and three 1 votes. Such a discrepancy could be examined to determine if there were differing perceptions as to the meaning or logic behind the idea. Clarification through discussion could then affect the final vote (step 6) differently than had no discussion taken place. An item receiving what is perceived to be too many or too few votes could also be discussed for the same purpose of clarification and possible modification of the final vote. If ideas are discussed in any manner, the leader should make it clear that the discussion is being held only to clarify and not to persuade anyone that they should change their original vote.

6. Final Vote. The procedure used to obtain a final vote usually is identical to that used to obtain the preliminary vote (step 4). A rating procedure also can be used, although it is probably not advisable to do so unless fine discriminations can be made between the ideas. Whatever procedure is used, the final vote helps provide a sense of closure for the NGT process.

The setting used to conduct an NGT meeting also can be an important element in the process, especially if more than one group is used. The room used to conduct the meeting should be large enough to accommodate the different groups, each containing between five and nine persons seated in a U-shaped fashion around a table. Obviously, the tables should be placed far enough from each other so that one group's discussion is not likely to interfere with another's. When more than one group is used, one leader can conduct the entire process if recorders are used at every table. It is probably wise, however, not to conduct an NGT meeting with more than three or four groups at one time. The reader interested in a more detailed discussion of the NGT process should refer to the excellent book by Delbecq, Van de Ven, and Gustafson.[44]

Evaluation The advantages of using NGT are the following:

1. Provides equality of participation among group members. In a less structured group, personality or status differences often sway the direction of group discussions.
2. Provides separate stages for idea generation and evaluation.
3. Provides both task and social-emotional satisfactions for participants.
4. Written generation of ideas increases a sense of commitment to the task.
5. Permits open confrontations over disagreements; ideas, not individuals are contested.
6. Produces a large number of ideas.
7. Provides a sense of closure often not found in less-structured group methods.

The disadvantages of using NGT follow:

1. Preparation and facilities required prohibit using it as a spontaneous technique.
2. Requires a highly skilled leader who is knowledgeable about the process.
3. Lacks flexibility in only being able to deal with one problem at a time.
4. Requires a certain amount of conformity on the part of participants; not all persons will be comfortable with the degree of structure involved.

NGT has been written about and researched extensively since it first appeared in the literature.[45] Numerous studies have compared it with the Delphi technique, Classical Brainstorming, and various interacting procedures. In most of these studies, NGT has produced more ideas than the other approaches.[46] Stephenson, Michaelson, and Franklin[47] observed that NGT participants preferred NGT to interacting methods and believed that it produced significantly more and higher-quality ideas, was more efficient, increased member participation, and provided more of a sense of accomplishment. However, not all studies have found NGT to be superior in idea quality. Erffmeyer and Lane,[48] for example, found that Delphi, consensus, and interacting groups all yielded higher-quality ideas than NGT.

In spite of these findings, it must be noted that some results may be affected by methodological problems. For instance, Price[49] observed that groups in his NGT study were led by leaders who lacked training in the method employed.

The group leaders received instructions on how to behave rather than training in actually using the different approaches compared. In addition, no attempt was made to evaluate effectiveness of the group leaders. Although these problems may not detract from all comparative studies, they certainly must be considered.

Bartunek and Murnighan[50] suggest that NGT can overcome many of its weaknesses if it is used flexibly and modified slightly. According to Bartunek and Murnighan, two major disadvantages of NGT are its lack of public participation in decision making and inappropriateness for ill-structured problems. Individual voting eliminates many of the difficulties that plague interacting groups, but the consequent lack of discussion and anonymity reduce commitment and possible implementation success. Ill-structured problems are inappropriate for NGT since they typically require discussion for purposes of clarification. Because NGT neglects this discussion activity, the wrong problem might be solved. To counter both of these weaknesses, Bartunek and Murnighan propose certain modifications to the NGT process.

To increase group-member participation, they suggest one of three possible public voting procedures: (1) Vote for one idea at a time, with a minimum number of votes needed for selection; (2) vote as described in procedure 1, but eliminate the idea with the fewest votes prior to additional voting, and allow discussion (or silent thinking) between votes; (3) Use a "black ball" procedure in which an idea is eliminated when rejected by a minimum number of group members. Discussion is permitted during these votes to determine reasons for rejecting an idea.

To accommodate ill-structured problems, Bartunek and Murnighan propose that the NGT process be modified as follows:

1. Individuals generate ideas silently using the round-robin technique.
2. The leader asks the members to determine if the ideas all address the same problem. If the responses are affirmative, the group moves on to the next NGT step; if the responses are negative, the remainder of the modified process is followed.
3. The ideas are organized into similar categories.
4. The ideas are presented and explained to the entire group.
5. Individuals generate additional ideas, present them using the round-robin procedure, and add them to the appropriate category.
6. Using one category at a time, the leader conducts a discussion to clarify each idea.

When using this modified procedure, the leader should allow periodic pauses in the process. During these pauses, the group should discuss if they are dealing with the right problem. The primary focus of these discussions should be to validate assumptions about the original problem. Another pause activity would be to evaluate the adequacy of ideas generated. Although these modifications will not insure success with NGT, they can increase its usefulness.

7.12 Packcorp Scientific Approach (PakSA)

The PakSA technique was developed by Jack Taylor[51] to meet the need for a comprehensive, broadly applicable technique of creative thinking. PakSA stands for the Pack Corp Scientific Approach, named in honor of the Packaging Corporation of America where Taylor worked as director of management development. According to Taylor, nine steps are involved in implementing the technique:

1. Pick a problem.
2. Get knowledge.
3. Organize knowledge.
4. Refine knowledge.
5. Digest.
6. Produce ideas.
7. Rework ideas.
8. Put ideas to work.
9. Repeat the process.

1. Pick a Problem. Picking a problem involves two activities: (a) defining the problem, and (b) defining your objective. To define a problem correctly, you should state it in writing in specific terms. To ask, How can we increase productivity? is too broad. A better way to define this problem would be to make specific declarative statements about what is wrong. Thus, you should state that there are too many machine setups required, that delivery of incoming materials is too slow, or that it takes too long to train new personnel. To define your objective, you need to state the specific end result you desire. For example, if your problem is a toaster that is difficult to clean, your objective might be to develop a new way of toasting bread that involves a way to catch crumbs.

2. Get Knowledge. The most important part of this step is to collect facts relevant to the problem. Taylor cautions that it is often difficult to know what a fact is—there might be only evidence and assumptions that must be tested for validity. Facts can be gathered by studying written references on the subject, experimenting, exploring, and discussing the problem with informed people. Focus only on gathering information, not ideas. Above all, put the facts in writing and try to check their accuracy. To evaluate the validity of facts, Taylor suggests asking questions pertaining to the reliability, sufficiency, internal consistency, impartiality, comprehensiveness, and predictive validity.

3. Organize Knowledge. The purpose of the third step is to order all of the collected information into a logical format. The more complex the problem, the

greater the need to organize the information. Taylor suggests using scrap books, card indexes, computers, or whatever will help to sort and classify the pertinent data in writing. Once information about the problem is organized into some sensible form, you will be better prepared to attempt solving the problem.

4. Refine Knowledge. This step seeks to explore any patterns that might underlie the data. In particular, a search should be made to find similarities and differences, analogies, cause and effect relationships, and principles and laws. In other words, how are the data related? If possible, the facts about the problem should be disassembled and then put together again so that a new, more creative definition of the problem emerges. This can be accomplished using other creative methods such as Input-Output or Checklists.

5. Digest. The goal of this step is to incubate the problem by allowing the subconscious mind to work. At this point in the process, the problem should be put aside and some other, unrelated activity engaged in. The problem solver could relax, rest, or play while the subconscious is given a chance to develop its "second wind." Only then should the next step be attempted.

6. Produce Ideas. If the previous steps have been followed, a feeling of inspiration or insight now should emerge. Studying the problem should be intensified and all ideas written down as they occur. It is especially important to avoid judging any ideas but, instead, concentrate on generating as many alternatives as possible.

7. Rework Ideas. Once generated, many ideas produce a level of enthusiasm that can cause the problem solver to overlook possible flaws. All generated ideas should be evaluated objectively against the original objectives and criteria. Thus, before applying any idea, it should be scrutinized thoroughly and then reworked, if necessary, into a more applicable form.

8. Put Ideas to Work. Three suboperations are involved in this step. First, a decision must be made on which alternatives to select. Taylor describes five methods that can be used: (a) the saturation approach (apply all the ideas), (b) the intuitive approach (mull over the ideas until a decision comes to mind), (c) the ranking approach (establish criteria and rank each idea against the criteria), (d) the known-odds approach (choose the ideas that have the best probability of being successful), and (e) the statistical-analysis approach (calculate the mathematical expectation of achieving a favorable outcome). Second, the ideas must be sold to others who must accept (buy) the ideas before they can be implemented. To do this, five basic guidelines should be used: (a) plan the sale by deciding who, when, and where, and by examining all the selling points, (b) give others enough time to digest the ideas and their implications, (c) invite others to participate in discussing the ideas' strengths and weaknesses, (d) demonstrate or illustrate how the ideas would work, and (e) show others how the ideas will benefit them. Finally, the third operation involves teaching others any new methods or skills that might be required to put the ideas to work.

9. Repeat the Process. The ninth and final step is to repeat the entire process. The purpose in doing this is to increase the odds that a better idea might be produced the second time and to receive practice in using the PakSA technique so that it becomes a natural way of thinking.

Evaluation Although Taylor contends that PakSA is a "complete" and "universally applicable" creative-thinking technique, not everyone would agree with him. Given the state of the art at the time (1961) he introduced his method, PakSA probably was a useful contribution. Taylor provided a structured, systematic approach at a time when most methods focused upon only how to produce ideas without considering other elements of the problem-solving process. Today, his technique still has validity in being systematic and structured.

PakSA could have been classified as eclectic because of Taylor's suggestion to use other available methods during the refine knowledge step. It is almost inconceivable that he did not make the same suggestion for the produce ideas step. Certainly, there is nothing preventing the use of other techniques during this step, but he does fail to explicitly mention this. His suggestion, instead, is to concentrate on the problem until new ideas emerge—essentially an unstructured, free-association method. Nevertheless, Taylor's emphasis upon evaluating the validity of facts and organizing and refining knowledge does make the technique worthy of consideration. As a method for generating ideas, however, other techniques should be consulted.

7.13 Phases of Integrated Problem Solving (PIPS)

When a group is faced with a problem to solve, it must deal with two major issues: (1) the task, and (2) the group process. The task issue concerns those activities —usually sequential—that, if followed, will lead to a problem solution; the group-process issue pertains to interpersonal activities of the group in working together to solve a problem. Both issues must be dealt with by a group if it expects to solve its problems.

Resolution of these two issues requires different skills. Resolving the task issue requires learning specific procedures to use in guiding a group toward a solution. These procedures generally are intended to provide the structure needed to focus upon achievement of a problem solution. After a little practice, most groups are able to master these skills if the procedure is clearly presented. Group-process issues, in contrast, cannot be so easily learned. The interpersonal and social aspects of group interaction require that behavioral skills—as opposed to task skills—be learned.

While both types of skills are equally important, most group problem-solving techniques have emphasized development of task skills. Learning how to use a sequential procedure is obviously easier than learning a set of human-relations skills. The problem, however, is how to get a group to concentrate upon both task and process issues. Most groups have a tendency to direct their attention to the task at hand, while interpersonal concerns often are ignored or given secondary consideration.

One possible solution to this problem has been advanced by William Morris and Marshall Sashkin,[52] who developed PIPS as a new model for prescribing group problem-solving procedures. In their model, task issues are dealt with using a six-phase sequential format. Each of the phases contains five questions that must be answered by consensus before the group can move on to the next phase. Such a format is not unique when compared with previous models. The PIPS model, however, is distinguished by the use of a similar format for dealing with group-process issues. As each of the task questions is posed, a corresponding process question also must be asked. Morris and Sashkin refer to the behaviors covered by these two question areas as "acts" (task concerns) and "interacts" (process concerns). The six major phases of the model are

1. Problem definition
2. Problem solution generation
3. Ideas to action
4. Solution action planning
5. Solution evaluation planning
6. Evaluation of the product and the process

1, Problem Definition. The purpose of this phase is to avoid making incorrect assumptions about the nature of the problem. In many instances, a group will look only at a problem symptom or a subpart of the actual problem. The task activities involved in testing problem assumptions are (a) searching for information about the problem, (b) developing a detailed understanding of the specifics of the general problem situation, and (c) examining and developing consensus on the goals the group would like to achieve. Corresponding to these activities are the process activities that include (a) making sure all group members are involved in the information search, (b) encouraging individuals to openly share their information about the problem, and (c) working toward consensus on the desired goal. After the problem has been explored, clarified, and defined, the activities for this phase should be terminated when a mutually agreed upon definition is attained and all members of the group have been consulted on their agreement with the final problem statement. The agreed upon statement is then recorded in writing.

2. Problem Solution Generation. Because most people tend to be solution oriented rather than problem oriented, groups often will select one of the first few solutions presented. In doing so, they may overlook potentially better solutions. The activities of this phase are intended to force the group to consider

many different possible solutions and to suspend judgment until all the ideas have been generated. The specific tasks activities are (a) using Classical Brainstorming to generate ideas, (b) elaborating and refining the ideas generated, and (c) developing a tentative list of specific solutions. The accompanying process activities are (a) encouraging all group members to participate in the brainstorming activity, (b) discouraging all criticism of ideas, and (c) encouraging cooperation when listing solutions. The phase is concluded by checking to see that everyone is aware of the final list of alternatives.

3. Ideas to Action. The objective of this phase is to select a solution that will be capable of solving the problem. The major task activities include (a) evaluating the strengths and weaknesses of each idea, (b) considering ways of combining several potentially good solutions into one idea, and (c) selecting a tentative solution to apply to the problem. Corresponding process activities include (a) insuring the group members avoid nonproductive criticism of each other's ideas, (b) resolving differences of opinion on the best combination or best way to modify ideas, and (c) working toward consensus as to the best alternative to implement. When the solution intended for testing is agreed upon, it is recorded in writing and the group moves on to the next phase.

4. Solution Action Planning. Problem-solving groups often assume that they have finished the major portion of their job once a tentative solution has been generated. Failure to develop a detailed action plan, however, can reduce the chances of successfully solving the problem. The purpose of this phase is to direct the group in the development of a step-by-step plan to use in implementing the solution. This is accomplished using the following major task activities: (a) listing the steps needed to implement the solution, (b) identifying the resources essential for accomplishing each step, and (c) assigning responsibilities for carrying out each step. The corresponding process activities are (a) insuring that all group members participate in developing the action steps, (b) insuring that group members adequately evaluate the potential of the available resources to aid in implementing the action steps, and (c) developing commitments to carry out the assigned responsibilities. The phase concludes by recording the action steps in writing along with a description of who is responsible for each step and the time schedule for carrying out the required activities.

5. Solution Evaluation Planning. By using this phase, the group is provided with an ongoing learning experience about the success of their solution. Regardless of whether the solution appears to be successful or unsuccessful in solving the problem, it is necessary to know what is working and what is not. Although solutions seldom can be classified as being totally successful or unsuccessful, an evaluation of what is happening as the solution is applied can be useful for making minor adjustments or improvements. The major task activities are (a) developing measures for describing the degree of success achieved by each action step in the action plan, (b) monitoring the results of each action step by developing

a timetable, and (c) outlining contingency plans for modifying action steps if needed. The process activities are (a) insuring that all group members contribute to the development of success measures, (b) insuring that all group members feel comfortable with the timetable developed, and (c) establishing commitments for implementing contingency plans. The final activity for this phase is to write down the solution evaluation criteria, the evaluation plan, and the date of the next evaluation meeting.

6. Evaluation of the Product and the Process. This phase of the model is used after sufficient time has elapsed to permit final evaluation of the solution outcome and the group process. If the problem or a part of it has not been resolved successfully, the group should recycle to one of the previous phases; if the problem was resolved, the group should determine what is necessary to prevent the problem from occurring again. In addition, group-process activities should be evaluated. The major task activities for this phase include (a) looking at the effects of the solution in comparison to the objectives established earlier, (b) determining if any new problems have been created, and (c) determining what, if any, future actions might be required. The process activities include (a) evaluating the extent of group-member participation, (b) evaluating how free the members felt in expressing themselves and supporting others, and (c) looking at exactly what the group has learned about itself and its ability to use the PIPS model. The process terminates with a discussion on the general adequacy of the group's problem-solving procedures.

Guidelines for Using the PIPS Model PIPS is intended to serve two functions: (1) as a means to learn and practice problem-solving procedures and skills, and (2) as a monitoring device for observing a real group and providing it with feedback on its activities. When used in an organizational setting to work on "real" problems, Morris and Sashkin recommend using a ten-step procedure that involves (1) stating the meeting's purpose, (2) selecting a problem, (3) discussing PIPS, (4) dividing the group into observers and problem solvers, (5) arranging the setting, (6) beginning work on the problem, (7) stopping to examine the definition of the problem, (8) continuing work on the problem, (9) repeating for each problem-solving phase periods of stop action and work, and (1) discussing and evaluating the work session.

Regardless of whether PIPS is used for training or actual problem solving, the same questionnaire instrument is used to structure the problem-solving activity. The questionnaire for each phase begins with a general focusing question and ends with a written statement of the product for that phase. These elements help to direct the group's activity and provide a sense of closure. The questionnaire used for the first phase is reproduced in Fig. 7–3. The complete instrument and instructions for its use can be found in either of the two references cited for Morris and Sashkin.

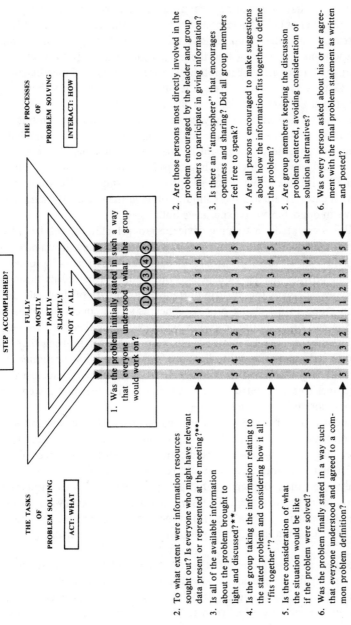

THE TASKS
OF
PROBLEM SOLVING

ACT: WHAT

TO WHAT EXTENT WAS THE
STEP ACCOMPLISHED?

FULLY
MOSTLY
PARTLY
SLIGHTLY
NOT AT ALL

THE PROCESSES
OF
PROBLEM SOLVING

INTERACT: HOW

1. Was the problem initially stated in such a way
   that everyone understood what the group
   would work on?   ① ② ③ ④ ⑤

2. To what extent were information resources sought out? Is everyone who might have relevant data present or represented at the meeting?**   5 4 3 2 1   1 2 3 4 5   2. Are those persons most directly involved in the problem encouraged by the leader and group members to participate in giving information?

3. Is all of the available information about the problem brought to light and discussed?**   5 4 3 2 1   1 2 3 4 5   3. Is there an "atmosphere" that encourages openness and sharing? Did all group members feel free to speak?

4. Is the group taking the information relating to the stated problem and considering how it all "fits together"?   5 4 3 2 1   1 2 3 4 5   4. Are all persons encouraged to make suggestions about how the information fits together to define the problem?

5. Is there consideration of what the situation would be like if the problem were solved?   5 4 3 2 1   1 2 3 4 5   5. Are group members keeping the discussion problem centered, avoiding consideration of solution alternatives?

6. Was the problem finally stated in a way such that everyone understood and agreed to a common problem definition?   5 4 3 2 1   1 2 3 4 5   6. Was every person asked about his or her agreement with the final problem statement as written and posted?

*Reprinted by permission from *Organizational Behavior in Action, Skill Building Experiences*, W. C. Morris and M. Sashkin. Copyright ©1976, West Publishing Company. All rights reserved.
**If additional information is found to be necessary, this information should be obtained before going further with the discussion.

Use the next page of questionnaire to record, in detail, the final problem statement

Fig. 7–3. Phase I of the PIPS technique: problem definition.*

In using the instrument, Morris and Sashkin suggest that every group member be given a copy and that two members be given the responsibility of group observers. One observer should be responsible for the task items and the other, the process items. When the group begins its discussion of the problem, the observers are responsible for insuring that the group moves smoothly through each phase and that they adequately accomplish each step. So that all members will be able to participate as problem solvers, the observer responsibilities should be rotated among the group members for each phase.

Use of the observer role also can vary as a function of group size. In smaller groups (around five persons) a facilitator could assume one of the roles and have only one other person observe; in groups of from six to nine persons, three or four members could serve as observers; in groups larger than ten, two subgroups could be created with one group doing the problem solving and the other, the observing. In all cases, group members should rotate in their roles to insure that all persons have an opportunity to experience both roles.

Because PIPS is essentially a training device, a group facilitator will be indispensable. This individual should provide follow-through on any group-process issues, make sure that all members rotate through the observer and problem-solver roles, and provide general guidance to the group as it proceeds through each of the phases. Perhaps the most important responsibility of the facilitator is to assist the group in discussing process concerns at the conclusion of each phase and at the end of the entire procedure when evaluating their effectiveness in using the instrument. The facilitator is also responsible for insuring that all group members clearly understand the directions for using the PIPS questionnaire. The directions should describe the format of the questionnaire and instruct participants to feel free to interrupt the discussion if they feel that a step has been deleted or incorrectly followed.

The instrument is used by having the participants read each question and rate the group's performance on a question using a one- to five-point scale. If a group member gives a rating below 5 (indicating the step has not been fully accomplished), then the entire group should review their performance on that step. It is only when the group agrees that a step has been fully accomplished that it can move on to the next step. To insure that the participants will correctly follow the recommended procedure for using the questionnaire, the group should make a verbal commitment before beginning the problem-solving process.

Evaluation   Morris and Sashkin report that the PIPS model has been used with groups from the fields of education, science, youth services, and medicine, among others. There seems, however, to be little or no research evidence available to attest to the model's effectiveness. Whether or not the model works better with some groups than others or in different situations is not known. As with most problem-solving methods, the evaluation that follows will be limited until more research is available.

Advantages

1. Emphasizes both task and process aspects of group problem-solving activity (hence the name "Integrated Problem Solving"); handles the complex issue of group processes by structuring activities designed to promote learning of behavioral skills.
2. Separates idea generation and evaluation stages.
3. Provides feedback to a group on its progress in task and process activities, both during and after the problem-solving phases.
4. Eases the role of the group facilitator by providing structure for both task and process activities.
5. Includes phases for monitoring the ongoing effects of a solution (phase 5) and for evaluating the final product and the overall process. This feature sharply differentiates PIPS from many other problem-solving models that tend to terminate the process once action plans have been developed.
6. Reduces interpersonal threat to group members by not focusing on any one individual.
7. Places equal emphasis upon both skill development and task orientation.

Disadvantages

1. Requires full commitment of the group members. If part or all of the group is unwilling or reluctant to follow the procedure, conflict and other inappropriate behaviors can result.
2. The questionnaires can be time-consuming and frustrating to use for persons accustomed to a more conventional, less structured process. For some persons, PIPS may provide too much structure.
3. Although structure is provided for both task and process elements, the group facilitator still must possess certain skills necessary for directing problem-solving and interpersonal activities.
4. If not skillfully handled by the facilitator, the group can become bogged down with concern over procedural matters.
5. If severe process issues develop (e.g., interpersonal conflicts, dominance, status and power issues), the structured procedure for group-process concerns might be inadequate. In this event, the need for a highly skilled facilitator will be even more critical.
6. The generation of ideas is limited to the procedure used in Classical Brainstorming. Other methods—especially brainwriting techniques—can be equally or more useful.
7. Prescribing desired behaviors for the group members can result in some loss in spontaneity. In particular, solutions might be less innovative and unique than those produced with methods that require less rigid adherence to a set of prescribed guidelines.

In general, the PIPS model is probably most valuable as a training tool for group problem solving. It should prove useful as a format for solving "real" problems *only* if the group members possess the motivation and commitment needed to stick with the questionnaire and carry out each of the steps specified. Although Morris and Sashkin contend that PIPS will be internalized after "a few uses," it should not be used as a group's primary problem-solving approach unless they have demonstrated that they have indeed internalized both the method and the philosophy of PIPS. Once a group has shown they can use the approach successfully, its constraints should become less evident and the approach more "natural" to the persons involved. The trick, of course, is to establish the initial level of motivation needed to attempt using the model.

7.14 Problem-Centered Leadership (PCL)

Most of the group techniques presented in this book emphasize task activities. With the exception of the PIPS method, all the techniques provide a structured approach for solving problems but provide little information on how group leaders should deal with group-process activities. Invariably, the assumption is made that group leaders need to possess certain skills and that, somehow, "good" leaders will automatically come to a group with these skills.

Although it is true that different techniques require different levels of leader skill, there are situations that require a high degree of leader ability to coordinate and guide group discussion. In particular, there is some evidence to suggest that the most difficult problem situation for a group leader to handle is one in which there is a strong need to develop a solution that is both high in quality and acceptable to the group members. Such situations are especially difficult when relevant knowledge and information about a problem are possessed only by the leader or one or two other persons, either internal or external to the group. In such situations, the leader can be placed in the position of sacrificing quality at the expense of acceptance, or vice versa. If the leader pushes for quality, the acceptance needed to implement a solution might be missing; if the leader pushes for acceptance, then quality might not be achieved.

In an attempt to provide a solution to this dilemma and provide more structure for group-process activities, Miner[53] has developed a leader skill-enhancing approach known as Problem-Centered Leadership (PCL). This approach is based almost entirely upon the work of Maier[54] and emphasizes the behaviors that leaders should use during a five-stage problem-solving process. The five stages of the PCL approach are presented next, followed by a discussion of the specific leader behaviors recommended for each stage. The five stages are

1. Presentation of the problem and relevant information
2. Initial discussion of the situation
3. Continued discussion

4. Solution generation and decision making

5. Determination of decision acceptance

Because Miner's description of the stages is rather limited, the majority of the material used to describe the stages has been taken from Maier.[55] In weaving in Maier's material, an attempt has been made to present a more detailed description of leader behaviors, without losing the basic meaning intended by Miner. Nevertheless, the author must assume full responsibility for any interpretations that go beyond those originally intended by Miner.

1. Presentation of the Problem and Relevant Information. Because the manner in which a problem is presented can set the mood for the entire meeting, it is important that the leader carefully plan the way the problem will be introduced. It is especially important that the leader avoid creating a defensive atmosphere. If group-process obstacles are to be avoided, the leader must approach the problem in a way that stresses the constructive aspects of the situation. According to Maier, there are six guiding principles leaders should use during this stage to aid the problem-solving process and prevent "emotional responses and confusion."

a. State the problem in situational rather than behavioral terms. The rationale behind this principle is that it often is easier to change situations than it is to change people. For example, a behavioral statement such as, How can we get the employees to be mofe careful? would be better stated as, How can we make the employees' jobs more safe? The latter avoids a biased statement of the problem situation while, at the same time, it creates a situation in which the number of potential solutions is greatly expanded.

b. Avoid suggesting alternative solutions. Although it is natural for group leaders to come to a meeting with preconceived solutions, such thoughts should be suppressed to encourage freedom of thought among the group members. Leaders who present their own solutions usually receive two reactions. One reaction by the group member is to automatically accept the solutions based upon their face value. When this occurs, the group learns to become dependent upon the leader and to avoid assuming responsibility for developing problem solutions. The second type of reaction occurs when the group criticizes the leader's initial suggestion. When this situation occurs, the leader is immediately put on the defensive and the rest of the discussion is generally downhill from there. The best approach is to encourage the members to freely explore the problem area rather than to restrict the discussion by imposing a specific direction of exploration.

c. State the problem so that it incorporates mutual interests. The purpose of this principle is to increase the motivation level needed to solve a problem. If the group members can be shown how they might benefit from solving the problem, they will be more likely to cooperate with each other in working toward a solution.

d. Include only one specific objective in the problem statement. Many problem solutions are capable of achieving a variety of objectives. Some of these objectives will result in positive and negative outcomes that are really by-products of the intended objective. Including a specific description of the primary objective will thus help prevent confusion about the difference between by-products and the original objective. As an example, Maier cites the widespread use of employee suggestion plans that are reported to have both positive and negative consequences. Unless a specific objective is stated, it will be difficult to know whether the problem is how to get ideas from employees or how to create employee interest in company problems, both of which have positive and negative by-products. To prevent confusion, the leader should give attention to just one specific objective and, for the time being, put aside considerations involving positive and negative outcomes of different solutions.

e. State the problem as briefly as possible. Some group leaders have a tendency to present long-winded descriptions of a problem. Often this is due to failure on the leader's part to have prepared a clear problem statement to present to the group; other times, a leader is initially greeted with silence after describing the problem and then feels compelled to elaborate. Regardless of the reason behind lengthy statements, the end result is usually confusion on the part of the group members. Solutions and objectives can become mixed, and misunderstanding can result if the leader attempts to restate the original description. Thus, the leader should carefully prepare a clear, succinct statement; not become upset with silence; and avoid attempts at restating the problem.

f. Share only essential information. Most problem statements are accompanied by some indication of the amount of relevant information the leader has about the problem. Such information can be valuable to the group, providing a perspective on problem constraints and their authority to act on the problem. In supplying this information, the leader should do three things: (1) Clearly separate facts as given from interpretation of facts; an appearance of trying to influence decisions of the group should be avoided. (2) Present only the information needed to clarify and understand the problem; more detailed information can be introduced later in the discussion. (3) Use no more than five minutes to present the problem information needed by the group to begin working on the problem.

2. Initial Discussion of the Situation. The purpose of this stage is to begin dealing with the emotions and feelings of the group. Some types of problems—especially those in which participants have considerable personal investment—are likely to evoke behaviors that are not conducive to conducting a problem-solving discussion. By being aware of this, the leader can determine the state of mind of the participants and structure the initial discussion to give vent to any pent-up feelings. Maier suggests using two different procedures for dealing with these feelings: giving assurance, and releasing expression of feeling in harmless channels.

Giving Assurance. This procedure is especially important when management is introducing a change likely to be seen as a threat by subordinates. In most cases, more threat will be seen when there is more uncertainty associated with a proposed change. Often, a change will be introduced without explaining what new responsibilities and skills will be required, how worker interpersonal relationships will be affected, and management's general expectations. To help alleviate threat, leaders should be realistic in their assurances and inform workers that it is not absolutely essential that they accept a change. Being realistic helps to convey an attitude of sincerity to the workers by indicating that management could have overlooked something and is willing to consider any objections and suggestions the workers might have. Informing workers that they do not need to accept the change can create a free-choice situation whereby workers can try the change on a trial basis or test different ways of solving the problem.

Releasing Expression of Feeling in Harmless Channels. When superiors criticize subordinates and their ideas, they often—without knowing it—discourage subordinates from openly and freely expressing their feelings. As a result, unexpressed feelings can accumulate over time, lend to additional frustration, and culminate in harmful consequences. A subordinate's outburst in reaction to an apparently harmless comment, for example, could simply reflect feelings that have built up as a result of some previous situation. Obviously, a group discussion is not likely to be productive as long as such feelings persist. The way to alleviate this type of situation is to provide subordinates with acceptable outlets for venting their frustrations. Maier recommends five guiding principles leaders can use to help subordinates express their feelings:

a. Be sensitive to guarded expressions of resentment. At the beginning of a meeting, a leader often will make a statement and fail to acknowledge the verbal reactions of the subordinates. If these reactions are loaded with emotion and go unheeded by the leader, the subordinates might be less likely to participate in the discussion later on.

b. Introduce long pauses to encourage expressions of feeling. When presented with a problem statement, a group usually needs some time to digest what has been said. If the leader is uncomfortable with silence and continues to talk and restate the problem, the group will be encouraged to assume a passive role in the subsequent discussion. In contrast, by waiting for and appropriately responding to an initial response, the leader will encourage other group members to participate more spontaneously.

c. Accept expressions of feeling. The group leader should actively try to accept feelings rather than disagreeing or rejecting them. In doing this, the leader will convey an attitude to the group that will indicate their ideas and themselves as individuals are both worthy of attention. The leader does not need to agree with an idea to convey acceptance—only indicate that the idea is worthy of being heard.

d. Try understanding thoughts and feelings rather than evaluating them. For many group leaders, this is a difficult principle to apply. The roles of supervisor and group leader often conflict since a supervisor is expected to evaluate rather than just to understand. Problems involving communication failures and misunderstandings, however, are less likely to occur if evaluation and judgment are suppressed. When a subordinate suggests an idea, the leader should try to understand what is being said, ask other group members if they understand the content and feeling of the statement, and, if necessary, ask the person to provide elaboration to clarify the statement. In addition, the leader can check for understanding by reflecting the *feelings* of the person suggesting an idea. This means that the leader should restate the comment in his or her own words.

e. Involve all group members in the discussion. One trap that discussion leaders often find themselves in is a lengthy two-way interchange with one of the participants. If this occurs frequently, other participants will be discouraged from making contributions. To avoid this trap and encourage wider participation, the leader should (1) introduce long pauses (2) ask the entire group what they think about an expressed idea, (3) check for agreement with an idea and request additional viewpoints, and (4) provide opportunities to indicate agreement or disagreement, without using up too much discussion time.

3. Continued Discussion. In this stage of the process, the leader begins to move the group in the direction of examining the problem situation. The objective is to explore a problem's positive and negative aspects. To do this, the leader can ask questions to surface issues not previously considered. In particular, the focus of the questions should be upon the possible consequences of different actions that might be taken to deal with the problem. Such questions can be especially important when the group becomes bogged down on a particular topic or when it seems to lose its momentum. Otherwise, if the discussion is progressing smoothly, the leader can adopt a more relaxed approach and, as needed, periodically provide brief summaries of the discussion.

4. Solution Generation and Decision Making. After the problem and relevant information have been presented, feelings dealt with, and the problem examined, it is time to begin the process of generating, evaluating, and selecting ideas. The leader has three primary functions to perform during this stage: (a) stimulating the generation of ideas or solutions, (b) guiding the group in evaluating the ideas and solutions, and (c) helping the group select a final solution.

Idea Stimulation. There are four ways a leader can help stimulate idea production. First, the leader can *delay the process of reaching a solution.* At the beginning of the group discussion it is natural for the participants to begin focusing upon solutions rather than the problem. A greater number of higher-quality solutions, however, can be achieved if the leader requires the group to spend time discussing and analyzing the problem. Second, the leader can *insure that idea getting is separated from idea evaluating.* If each idea is criticized as it is suggested, many imaginative solutions will be lost. To avoid this situation, the leader should structure the discussion to include separate stages for generating and evaluating ideas, much like those used for brainstorming sessions. Third, the leader must take an active part in *dealing with agreement and disagreement* among the group members. Too much of either can limit the number of ideas produced. If the group seems to be too much in agreement, the leader should create disagreement by presenting a controversial viewpoint or by asking for a discussion on the advantages and disadvantages of an idea; if there is too much disagreement, the leader should act as a mediator by turning emotional statements into situational problem descriptions. Finally, the leader can help stimulate idea production by *periodically summarizing the discussion.* Summaries can be helpful in (a) getting a discussion back on course, (b) checking for understanding through restatement, (c) increasing communication within the group, (d) improving the leader's listening skill (thus, the leader can offer more constructive suggestions), (e) making periodic reviews of the ideas suggested, (f) indicating and measuring progress, and (g) separating a problem into its different components. For the actual generation of solutions, Maier suggests using Osborn's brainstorming procedure.

Idea Evaluation. There are also four ways a leader can help evaluate ideas. First, the leader can assist the group in *examining the advantages and disadvantages of each solution.* This is especially important in groups divided in their opinion about a solution. If this is the case, then the leader can ask the whole group to consider the positive and negative aspects of a solution. By placing advantage and disadvantage columns on a chalkboard, the leader can guide the group in working together to discuss the merits of each proposed solution. A second way leaders can help evaluate ideas is by *exploring supporting evidence.* In situations in which there does not appear to be one superior solution, it may be difficult to achieve consensus. To avoid this situation, the leader can require the group to analyze all available facts that might support one solution over another. Third, the leader can facilitate evaluation by *using stalemates constructively.* Stalemates often occur when facts are presented in support of two different solutions. If it does not appear the stalemate can be easily resolved, the leader can suggest that other facts be obtained or that the group move on to consider other solutions. Finally, the leader can assist idea evaluation by *exploring any new problems created by solutions.* When evaluating different solutions, groups often will concentrate upon whether or not a solution is likely to achieve a desired objective. The leader, however, should encourage the group to also consider any possible costs involved in implementing a solution. If one solution seems likely to create more serious new problems than another, then the least costly solution will be preferred.

Selection of a Final Solution. After the group has generated and evaluated solutions, one solution must be selected for implementation. In some situations, this task will be more complicated than in others, depending upon the size of the group, the needs and values of its members, and the number and quality of available alternatives from which to choose. Obviously, when the group is large, the members have conflicting opinions, and there are many available alternatives, the selection process will be more difficult than if the opposite situation exists. During this activity, there are two ways a leader can help the group reach a decision: considering conservative versus liberal alternatives and action versus no action, and reducing a list of many solutions.

Conservative versus liberal alternatives; action versus no action. Many decisions involve elements of risk the decision maker must weigh when selecting potential courses of action. When information is limited about possible future problem states, for example, a risky decision will be made if it is decided not to wait for additional information (a liberal alternative). On the other hand, a decision to wait and see what will happen is a more conservative approach. A decision to expand a company product line into a new market area would exemplify these two choice situations. If the market forecast is seen as being unreliable, a decision to enter the market will be risky, although the possible gains could be high; if a decision is made to postpone action, then the possibility of loss will be lower while the possibility of gain will also be lower (assuming, of course, that timing of the entry is a key factor in this case). According to Maier, it is the leader's responsibility to overcome conservative attitudes. To do this, the leader must impress upon the group that a failure to act relegates problem outcomes to events external to the group. Among the ways Maier recommends to resolve conflicting attitudes of conservativism and risk are (a) integrate the alternatives, (b) test the alternatives to see how well they work, and (c) treat failure to agree as a problem in itself.

Reducing a list of many solutions. Quite often, when a group develops a large number of solutions, conflict will exist among preferred alternatives. This especially will be the case when many members have their own "pet" solutions. To reduce the number of solutions and yet maintain member acceptance of the process, Maier suggests a relatively simple procedure. The steps for this procedure are:

a. The solutions on a master list are given consecutive numbers.
b. Each person selects three to five of their favorite solutions from this list by jotting down the numbers corresponding to the solutions they selected.
c. The preferences are tabulated by asking for a show of hands to indicate how many persons selected each solution.
d. Those solutions receiving the largest number of votes are examined to determine how they might be integrated or combined.

At the conclusion of the solution generation and decision-making stage, it is not always necessary to progress through the activities of generating, evaluating, and selecting solutions. In some cases, it should be possible to proceed directly from generating to selecting, without considering evaluation activities. According to Maier, this can be done when (a) the value of a solution lies more in individual differences of opinion than in the interrelationship of facts, and (b) the facts are well known and require no additional examination.

5. Determination of Decision Acceptance. Once a decision is made to select a particular solution, there is no guarantee it will be accepted by all group members. Some members might agree with the general content of the decision but disagree with or misunderstand specific details. In order to gain the acceptance often (but not always) needed to implement a solution, the leader should provide the group with a carefully prepared summary of the final decision. This summary should contain sufficient detail so that all aspects and implications of the decision can be clearly understood. In addition, the leader should check with the group to determine if they have a need to modify, add to, delete, or clarify any meanings described in the summary.

Summary The Problem-Centered Leadership (PCL) approach, as developed by Miner and based upon the work of Maier, was designed to provide group leaders with specific skills for conducting problem-solving discussions. The prescribed behaviors are not "canned"—in the sense that there is no step-by-step format to follow—but, instead, rely upon a leader's ability to evaluate a situation and apply the appropriate behaviors. The stages of the PCL approach can be summarized as follows:

1. Presentation of the Problem and Relevant Information
   a. State the problem in situational rather than behavioral terms.
   b. Avoid suggesting alternative solutions.
   c. State the problem so that it incorporates mutual interests.
   d. Include only one specific objective in the problem statement.
   e. State the problem as briefly as possible.
   f. Share only essential information.
      i. Separate facts as given from interpretation of facts.
      ii. Present only clarifying information.
      iii. Use no more than five minutes to present information.
2. Initial Discussion of the Situation
   a. Give assurance to group members.
      i. Be realistic.
      ii. Inform group members that they do not have to accept a change.
   b. Allow expressions of feeling to be released in harmless channels.
      i. Be sensitive to guarded expressions of resentment.
      ii. Introduce long pauses to encourage expressions of feeling.
      iii. Accept expressions of feeling.
      iv. Try to understand rather than evaluate thoughts and feelings.
      v. Involve all group members in the discussion.
3. Continued Discussion
   a. By asking questions, make the group consider problems and issues not previously considered.

      b. If the discussion is progressing smoothly, participate only by providing brief summaries of topics discussed.
4. Solution Generation and Decision Making
      a. Stimulate the generation of solutions.
          i. Delay the process of reaching a solution.
          ii. Separate idea getting from idea evaluating.
          iii. Deal with agreement and disagreement.
          iv. Periodically summarize the discussion.
      b. Assist in the evaluation of solutions.
          i. Examine the advantages and disadvantages of each solution.
          ii. Explore supporting evidence.
          iii. Use stalemates constructively.
          iv. Explore any new problems created by solutions.
      c. Assist in the selection of solutions.
          i. Deal with conflicts between conservative and liberal solution alternatives by integrating or testing the opposing alternatives, or by treating failure to agree as a separate problem.
          ii. Reduce a large list of solutions by having participants vote for a specified number of preferences, tabulating the results, and integrating or combining those solutions receiving the greatest number of votes.
5. Determination of Decision Acceptance
      a. Provide the group with a carefully prepared, detailed summary of the final decision.
      b. Ask the group to modify, add to, delete, or clarify any meanings described in the summary.

Evaluation   As previously noted, some liberty was taken in using the work of Maier (from whom the stages and associated concepts were derived) to fill in the problem-solving stages described by Miner. Although there is considerable overlap between the work of these two individuals, the following evaluation will be colored somewhat by this blending of material. The advantages of the PCL approach seem to include the following:

1. PCL provides specific guidelines for leader behavior that traditionally have been ignored by other group problem-solving methods. The effectiveness of other methods is often assumed to be independent of leader behavior, except for the task of facilitating the progression of the group from one step to another. The PCL approach, however, allows group leaders to vary their behaviors in accordance with the specific problem-solving situation.

2. Research by Miner indicates that extensive leader training in using the method might not be necessary. In a laboratory study, Miner[56] compared the PCL approach with the Nominal Group and Delphi methods. Although the

leaders of the PCL groups were given only 30 minutes of instruction, the PCL groups outperformed the groups using the other two methods.

3. The emphasis upon the social-emotional aspects of group discussion permits feelings to be vented and can result in less conflict among group members.

4. The emphasis upon open expression of ideas and full participation of all group members should help increase the number and possibly the quality of ideas generated.

5. A major advantage of PCL is the emphasis it places upon obtaining member acceptance of solutions. Although other techniques might be structured better for generating ideas, PCL might result in more successfully implemented ideas (if, of course, implementation is contingent upon member acceptance).

6. PCL separates idea generation and idea evaluation activities. As a result, higher-quality solutions should be produced.

The disadvantages of the PCL approach seem to include the following:

1. PCL requires an exceptionally high degree of leader skill and experience in working with groups. Especially critical is the leader's ability to appropriately diagnose a discussion situation. Although Miner reports success in using a short training period, the artificiality of the problem used (a role-playing exercise) and the nonrandomness of his subject selection procedure make his results less than conclusive. It is possible, for example, that the subjects used as leaders possessed qualities or experiences that allowed them to incorporate the method easily into their own personal leadership styles. Until more research is available—using both real and artificial problems and laboratory and actual work settings—the ease with which leaders can be trained in the concepts of the method and effectively apply them will remain unknown.

2. Although PCL provides a leader with structure for applying behavioral skills, it provides little structure for analyzing problems or generating ideas. Maier mentions using Osborn's brainstorming procedure, but Miner fails to describe any specific solution generation method. PCL is even more deficient in this area than the PIPS method. Thus, the group-process aspects of problem solving are structured while the content or task activities are relatively unstructured. Without research to verify the problems created by structuring one aspect of the problem-solving process but not the other, it will remain to be seen whether this is really a disadvantage. It would seem, however, that the answer will vary with the problem and the characteristics of the group members. It might be inappropriate, for example, to spend time and money training leaders for groups that seldom have destructive disagreements.

3. The PCL method provides little guidance on how to implement solutions.

4. The fact that ideas are generated through verbal interaction could reduce the quantity of solutions produced but possibly not the quality. In a study comparing PCL with Classical Brainstorming, NGT, and a third interactive group

procedure, Price[57] obtained results suggesting that group interaction contributes to a reduction in idea quantity.

The most important factor to consider when deciding to use PCL is whether or not it can be an effective problem-solving device for typical group leaders. The answer is probably a qualified no. If the majority of group leaders are able to easily grasp the basic concepts of PCL and integrate them with their personal leadership styles, then the method will be useful for problems in which disagreement and conflict (both substantive and interpersonal) among group members is likely to occur. On the other hand, because of the lack of structure it provides for analyzing, generating and, to some extent, evaluating solutions, the method will not be useful for problems typically encountered by most groups. Until more research is conducted, PCL would seem to be most appropriately used as a general training device for group leaders. The skills learned then could be applied along with a more structured, task-oriented approach.

COMMENTS

One danger in classifying techniques according to major problem-solving stages is that many potentially useful techniques might be overlooked that otherwise could prove useful for a particular stage. The techniques in this chapter are especially vulnerable in this regard since they combine two or more techniques or problem-sovling stages but have not been classified as being appropriate for any one problem-solving stage. The Delphi and Nominal Group Technique, for example, generally are considered to be idea generation techniques but were classified under the miscellaneous category because of the explicit provisions they make for selecting the ideas generated. On the other hand, Classical Brainstorming also uses a procedure for selecting ideas, but it is not particularly explicit. For this reason, and the fact that Classical Brainstorming is universally considered to be an idea generation method, it was not classified in the miscellaneous category. The rationale used to classify any of the techniques in this book is probably less important than the specific contributions they can make to problem solving in general.

NOTES

1. Bobele, H. K., and Buchanan, P. J. "Training Mangers to be Better Problem-Solvers." *Journal of Creative Behavior* 10:250–255 (1976).
2. According to Bobele and Buchanan, the Think Tank was developed by Savo Bojicic and its use has been described by Edward de Bono (*Think Tank,* Toronto: Think Tank Corporation, 1973).
3. Bujake, J. E. "Programmed Innovation in New Product Development." *Research Management* 4:279–287 (1969).
4. Creative Problem-Solving, capitalized with Problem-Solving hyphenated, refers only to Parnes's program and should not be confused with the more general area of creative problem solving.

5. Information about the annual Creative Problem Solving Institutes can be obtained by writing to The Creative Education Foundation, 437 Franklin Street, Buffalo, New York 14202.
6. Parnes, S. J., Noller, R. B., and Biondi, A. M. *Guide to Creative Action*. New York: Scribner, 1977.
7. Isaksen, S. G., and Treffinger, D. J. *Creative Problem Solving: The Basic Course*. Buffalo, N.Y.: Bearly Limited, 1985.
8. VanGundy, A. B. *Creative Problem Solving: A Guide for Trainers and Management*. Westport, Conn.: Quorum Books, 1987.
9. Parnes, S. J. Personal communication.
10. Osborn, A. F. *Applied Imagination*, 3rd ed. New York: Scribner, 1963.
11. Parnes, S. J., et al., *op. cit.*
12. Parnes, S. J., and Brunelle, E. E., "The Literature of Creativity (Part 1)," *Journal of Creative Behavior* 1:52–109 (1967); Parnes, S. J., and Noller, R. B., "Applied Creativity: The Creative Studies Project (Part 1)," *Journal of Creative Behavior* 6:11–20 (1972).
13. Torrance, E. P., "Can We Teach Children to Think Creatively?" *Journal of Creative Behavior* 6:114–143 (1967); Mansfield, R.S., Busse, T. V., and Krepelka, E. J., "The Effectiveness of Creativity Training," *Review of Educational Research* 48:517–536 (1978).
14. Rose, L. H., and Lin, H-T. "A Meta-Analysis of Long-Term Creativity Training Programs." *Journal of Creative Behavior* 18:11–22 (1984).
15. de Bono, E. *Lateral Thinking: Creativity Step by Step*. New York: Harper & Row, 1970.
16. Bosticco, M. *Creative Techniques for Management*. London: Basic Books, 1971, p. 121.
17. The original draft of this section was written by Chris Barlow, president of Appleseed Associates and a certified value engineer. He also provided many helpful comments and assisted in revising this section.
18. Miles, L. D. *Techniques of Value Engineering and Analysis*. 2nd rev. ed. New York: McGraw-Hill, 1971.
19. Major books also include Fallon, C., *Value Analysis*, 2nd rev. ed., Irving, Texas: Triangle Press, 1980; Mudge, A. E., *Value Engineering*, New York: McGraw-Hill, 1971.
20. National Academy of Sciences. *Value Engineering in Federal Construction Agencies*. Washington, D.C.: NAS Printing Office, 1969.
21. Miles, L. D., *op. cit.*
22. Fallon, C., *op. cit.*
23. Mudge, A. E., *op. cit.*
24. Osborn, A. F., *op. cit.;* Parnes, S. J., *op. cit.*
25. Barlow, C. *Why and How: An Introduction to the Concepts and Techniques of Function Analysis*. Shaker Heights, Ohio: Appleseed Associates, 1981.
26. Barlow, C. *Conducting a Value Management Study: A Basic Guidebook*. Shaker Heights, Ohio: Appleseed Associates, 1982.
27. Laswell, H. D. "The Technique of Decision Seminars." *Midwest Journal of Political Science* 4:213–236 (1960).
28. Burgess, P. M., and Slonaker, L. L. *The Decision Seminar: A Strategy for Problem-Solving* (a briefing paper). Columbus, Ohio: The Mershon Center of The Ohio State University, 1978.
29. Dalkey, N., and Helmer, O. "An Experimental Application of the Delphi Method to the Use of Experts." *Management Science* 9:458–467 (1963).
30. Delbecq, A. L., Van de Ven, A. H., and Gustafson, D. H. *Group Techniques for Program Planning*. Glenview, Ill.: Scott, Foresman, 1975.

31. Gustafson, D. H., Shukla, R. K., Delbecq, A., and Walster, G. W. "A Comparative Study of Differences in Subjective Likelihood Estimates Made by Individuals, Interacting Groups, Delphi Groups, and Nominal Groups." *Organizational Behavior and Human Performance* 9:280–291 (1973).

32. Campbell, R. M. *A Methodological Study of the Utilization of Experts in Business Forecasting.* Unpublished Doctoral Dissertation. Los Angeles: University of California at Los Angeles, 1966.

33. Erffmeyer, R. C., and Lane, I. M. "Quality and Acceptance of an Evaluative Task: The Effects of Four Group Decision-Making Formats." *Group & Organization Studies* 9:509–529 (1984).

34. Martino, J. P. *Technological Forecasting for Decision Making.* New York: Elsevier Science Publishing, 1983.

35. Erffmeyer, R. C., Erffmeyer, E. S., and Lane, I. M. "The Delphi Technique: An Empirical Evaluation of the Optimal Number of Rounds." *Group & Organization Studies* 11:120–128 (1986).

36. Nierenberg, G. I. *The Idea Generator*™ *User's Manual.* Berkeley, California: Experience in Software, Inc., 1985.

37. Nierenberg, G. I. *The Art of Creative Thinking.* New York: Cornerstone Library (Simon & Schuster), 1982.

38. Armstrong, F. A. *Idea Tracking.* New York: Criterion, 1960.

39. Kepner, C. H., and Tregoe, B. B., *The Rational Manager,* Princeton, New Jersey: Kepner-Tregoe, Inc., 1976; Kepner, C. H., and Tregoe, B. B., *The New Rational Manager,* Princeton, New Jersey: Kepner-Tregoe, Inc., 1981.

40. Kepner, C. H., and Tregoe, B. B., *op. cit.,* 1976, pp. 138–140; Kepner, C. H., and Tregoe, B. B., *op. cit.,* 1981, pp. 67–68.

41. Kepner, C. H., and Tregoe, B. B., *op. cit.,* 1976, pp. 195–206.

42. Stech, E., and Ratliffe, S. A. *Working in Groups.* Skokie, Ill.: National Textbook Company, 1976.

43. Delbecq, A. L., et al., *op. cit.*

44. *Ibid.*

45. For example, Sink, S. D., "Using the Nominal Group Technique Effectively," *National Productivity Review* 2:173–184 (1983); Chung, K. H., and Ferris, M. J., "An Inquiry of the Nominal Group Process," *Academy of Management Journal* 14:520–525 (1971); Souder, W. E., "Effectiveness of Nominal and Interacting Group Decision Processes for Integrating R & D Marketing," *Management Science* 23:595–605 (1977).

46. Stumpf, S., Freedman, R., and Zand, D., "Judgmental Decisions: A Study of Interactions Among Group Membership, Group Functioning and the Decision Situation," *Academy of Management Journal* 22:765–782 (1979); Van de Ven, A. H., and Delbecq, A. L., "Nominal Versus Interacting Group Processes for Committee Decision Making Effectiveness," *Academy of Management Journal* 14:202–212 (1971).

47. Stephenson, B. Y., Michaelson, L. K., and Franklin, S. G. "An Empirical Test of the Nominal Group Technique in State Solar Energy Planning." *Group & Organization Studies* 7:320–334 (1982).

48. Erffmeyer, R. C., and Lane, I. M., *op. cit.*

49. Price, K. H. "Problem-Solving Strategies: A Comparison by Problem-Solving Phases." *Group & Organization Studies* 10:278–299 (1985).

50. Bartunek, J. M., and Murnighan, J. K. "The Nominal Group Technique: Expanding the Basic Procedure and Underlying Assumptions." *Group & Organization Studies* 9:417–432 (1984).

51. Taylor, J. W. *How to Create Ideas.* Englewood Cliffs, N.J.: Prentice-Hall, 1961.

52. Morris, W. C., and Sashkin, M. *Organization Behavior in Action, Skill Building Experiences,* St. Paul, Minnesota: West, 1976; Morris, W. C., and Sashkin, M., "Phases of Integrated Problem Solving (PIPS)," In J. W. Pfeiffer and J. E. Jones, eds., *The 1978 Annual Handbook for Group Facilitators,* La Jolla, Calif.: University Associates, Inc., 1978.
53. Miner, F. C., Jr. "A Comparative Analysis of Three Diverse Group Decision Making Approaches." *Academy of Management Journal* 22:81–92 (1979).
54. Maier, N. R. F., *Principles of Human Relations,* New York: Wiley, 1952; Maier, N. R. F., *Problem Solving Discussions and Conferences: Leadership Methods Skills,* New York: McGraw-Hill, 1963.
55. *Ibid.*
56. Miner, F. C., Jr., *op. cit.*
57. Price, K. H., *op. cit.*

Bibliography

Adams, J. L. *Conceptual Blockbusting: A Guide to Better Ideas,* 2nd ed. New York: Norton, 1979.

Adams, R. H. "Goalstorming." *Advanced Management Journal* 44(3):55–61 (1979).

The Advanced Technology Staff. "Bionics." In G. A. Davis and J. A. Scott, eds. *Training Creative Thinking.* Huntington, N.Y.: Krieger, 1978.

Allen, M. S. *Morphological Creativity.* Englewood Cliffs, N.J.: Prentice-Hall, 1962.

Anderson, L. M. *SPAN User's Guide.* Unpublished manuscript. Tucson, Arizona: University of Arizona, 1975.

Armstrong, F. A. *Idea Tracking.* New York: Criterion, 1960.

Arnold, J. E. "The Creative Engineer." *Yale Scientific Magazine* 12–23 (March 1956).

Barlow, C. *Why and How: An Introduction to the Concepts and Techniques of Function Analysis.* Shaker Heights, Ohio: Appleseed Associates, 1981.

Barlow, C. *Conducting a Value Management Study: A Basic Guidebook.* Shaker Heights, Ohio: Appleseed Associates, 1982.

Barnetson, P. *Critical Path Planing: Present and Future Techniques.* Princeton, N.Y.: Brandon/Systems Press, 1970.

Barrett, F. D. "Creativity Techniques: Yesterday, Today, and Tomorrow." *Advanced Management Journal* 43:25–35 (1978).

Bartunek, J. M., and Murnighan, J. K. "The Nominal Group Technique: Expanding the Basic Procedure and Underlying Assumptions." *Group & Organization Studies* 9:417–432 (1984).

Bauer & Associates. *The Participant's Guide to FASTTRACK.* Ann Arbor, Mich.: Bauer & Associates, 1985.

Bauer & Associates. *The FASTTRACK Facilitator.* Ann Arbor, Mich.: Bauer & Associates, 1985.

Bauer & Associates. *FASTTRACK, Beyond the Basics.* Ann Arbor, Mich.: Bauer & Associates, 1985.

Bauer & Associates. *ACTIONTRACK, Getting It Done Now.* Ann Arbor, Mich.: Bauer & Associates, 1985.

Bobele, H. K., and Buchanan, P. J. "Training Managers to Be Better Problem Solvers." *Journal of Creative Behavior* 10:250–255 (1976).

Bosticco, M. *Creative Techniques for Management.* London: Basic Books, 1971.

Bouchard, T. J., Jr. "A Comparison of Two Group Brainstorming Procedures." *Journal of Applied Psychology* 56:418–421 (1972).

Bouchard, T. J., Jr. "Training, Motivation, and Personality as Determinants of the Effectiveness of Brainstorming Groups and Individuals." *Journal of Applied Psychology* 56: 324–331 (1972).

Bouchard, T. J., Jr. "Whatever Happened to Brainstorming?" *Journal of Creative Behavior* 5:182–189 (1971).

Braybrooke, D., and Lindblom, C. E. *A Strategy of Decision.* New York: The Free Press, 1963.

Brightman, H. J. "Differences in Ill-Structured Problem Solving Along the Organizational Hierarchy." *Decision Sciences* 9:1–18 (1978).

Brooks, J. D. *Review of Operational Mechanisms for Innovative Management Course.* Industrial Studies Program, U. S. Steel Corporation, Pittsburgh, Pennsylvania (no date), p. 3.

Bry, A., with Bair, M. *Visualization: Directing the Movies of Your Mind.* New York: Barnes & Noble, 1978.

Bujake, J. E. "Programmed Innovation in New Product Development." *Research Management* 12:279–287 (1969).

Burgess, P. M., and Slonaker, L. L. *The Decision Seminar: A Strategy for Problem-Solving* (a briefing paper). Columbus, Ohio: The Mershon Center of The Ohio State University, 1978.

Burns, M. G. "A Comparison of Three Creative Problem-Solving Methodologies." *Dissertation Abstracts International* 45:341A (1984).

Campbell, J. P. "Individual Versus Group Problem Solving in an Industrial Sample." *Journal of Applied Psychology* 52:205–210 (1968).

Campbell, R. M. *A Methodological Study of the Utilization of Experts in Business Forecasting.* Unpublished Doctoral Dissertation. Los Angeles: University of California at Los Angeles, 1966.

Center for Creative Leadership, *Potential Problem Analysis.* Greensboro, North Carolina: Center for Creative Leadership, 1979.

Chung, K. H., and Ferris, M. J. "An Inquiry of the Nominal Group Process." *Academy of Management Journal* 14:520–525 (1971).

Clark, C. H. *The Crawford Slip Writing Method.* Kent, Ohio: Charles H. Clark, 1978.

Conway/Miliken & Associates. *Conway/Miliken Communications.* 4:(2):1–3 (1986).

Crawford, C., and Demidovich, J. *Crawford Slip Writing Method: How to Mobilize Brainpower by Think Tank Technology.* Los Angeles, California: School of Public Administration, University of Southern California, 1983.

Crawford, C. C., Demidovich, J. W., and Krone, R. M. *Productivity Improvement by the Crawford Slip Method: How to Write, Publish, Instruct, Supervise, and Manage for Better Job Performance.* Los Angeles, California: School of Public Administration, University of Southern California, 1984.

Crawford, R. P. *The Techniques of Creative Thinking.* Englewood Cliffs, N.J.: Prentice-Hall, 1954.

Crosby, A. *Creativity and Performance in Industrial Organization.* London: Tavistock Publications, 1968.

Crovitz, H. F. *Galton's Walk.* New York: Harper & Row, 1970.

Cummings, L. L., Hinton, B., and Gobdel, B. C. "Creative Behavior as a Function of Task Environment: Impact of Objectives, Procedures, and Controls." *Academy of Management Journal* 18:489–498 (1975).

Dalkey, N., and Helmer, O. "An Experimental Application of the Delphi Method to the Use of Experts." *Management Science* 9:458–467 (1963).

Davis, G. A., Roweton, W. E., Train, A. J., Warren, T. F., and Houtman, S. E. *Laboratory Studies of Creative Thinking Techniques: The Checklist and Morphological Synthesis Methods.* Technical Report No. 94, Wisconsin Research and Development Center for Cognitive Learning, University of Wisconsin, 1969.

Davis, G. A., and Scott, S. A., eds. *Training Creative Thinking.* Huntington, N.Y.: Krieger, 1978.

de Bono, E. "Information Processing and New Ideas—Lateral and Vertical Thinking." *Journal of Creative Behavior* 3:159–171 (1969).

de Bono, E. *Lateral Thinking: Creativity Step by Step.* New York: Harper & Row, 1970.

de Bono, E. *Lateral Thinking for Management.* New York: American Management Association, 1972.

de Bono, E. *PO: A Device for Successful Thinking.* New York: Simon & Schuster, 1972.

de Bono, E. *Think Tank.* Toronto: Think Tank Corporation, 1973.

Delbecq, A. L., and Van de Ven, A. H. "A Group Process Model for Problem Identification and Program Planning." *Journal of Applied Behavioral Science* 7:466–492 (1971).

Delbecq, A. L., Van de Ven, A. H., and Gustafson, D. H. *Group Techniques for Program Planning.* Glenview, Illinois: Scott, Foresman, 1975.

Dreistadt, R. "The Use of Analogies and Incubation in Obtaining Insights in Creative Problem Solving." *The Journal of Psychology* 71:159–175 (1969).

Duncker, K. "On Problem Solving." Translated by L. S. Lees. *Psychological Monographs* 58, No. 5 (1945).

Dunnette, M. D., Campbell, J. P., and Jaastad, O. "The Effects of Group Participation on Brainstorming Effectiveness for Two Industrial Samples." *Journal of Applied Psychology* 47:10–37 (1963).

Eberle, R. *Scamper: Games for Imagination Development.* Buffalo, N.Y.: D.O.K. Press, 1972.

Erffmeyer, R. C., Erffmeyer, E. S., and Lane, I. M. "The Delphi Technique: An Empirical Evaluation of the Optimal Number of Rounds." *Group & Organization Studies* 11: 120–128 (1986).

Erffmeyer, R. C., and Lane, I. M. "Quality and Acceptance of an Evaluative Task: The Effects of Four Group Decision-Making Formats." *Group & Organization Studies* 9:509–529 (1984).

Faafeng, O. Personal communication. Oslo, Norway: Norwegian Management Institute, 1986.

Fallon, C. *Value Analysis,* 2nd rev. ed. Irving, Texas: Triangle Press, 1980.

Field, R. H. G. "A Critique of the Vroom-Yetton Contingency Model of Leadership Behavior." *Academy of Management Review* 4:249–257 (1979).

Firestien, R. L., and Treffinger, D. J. "Ownership and Converging: Essential Ingredients of Creative Problem Solving." *Journal of Creative Behavior* 17(1):32–38 (1983).

Fulmer, R. M. *The New Management.* New York: Macmillan, 1974.

Gawain, S. *Creative Visualization.* Mill Valley, Calif.: Whatever Publishing, 1978.

Geschka, H. "Methods and Organization of Idea Generation." Paper presented at Creativity Development Week II, Greensboro, N.C.: Center for Creative Leadership, September 1979.

Geschka, H. Personal communication, 1986.

Geschka, H., Schaude, G. R., and Schlicksupp, H. "Modern Techniques for Solving Problems." *Chemical Engineering* 91–97 (August 1973).

Geschka, H., von Reibnitz, U., and Storvik, K. *Idea Generation Methods: Creative Solutions to Business and Technical Problems.* Columbus, Ohio: Battelle Memorial Institute, 1981.

Gick, M. L., and Holyoak, K. J. "Analogical Problem Solving." *Cognitive Psychology* 12: 306–355 (1980).

Goldner, B. B. *The Strategy of Creative Thinking.* Englewood Cliffs, N.J.: Prentice-Hall, 1962.

Gordon, W. J. J. "Operational Approaches to Creativity." *Harvard Business Review* 34: 41–51 (1956).

Gordon, W. J. J. *Synectics.* New York: Harper & Row, 1961.

Graham, W. K. "Acceptance of Ideas Generated Through Individual and Group Brainstorming." *Journal of Social Psychology* 101:231–234 (1977).

Gregory, C. E. *The Management of Intelligence.* New York: McGraw-Hill, 1967.

Griggs, R. E. "A Storm of Ideas." Reported in: *Training* 22:66 (November 1985).

Grossman, S. R. "Releasing Problem Solving Energies." *Training and Development Journal* 38:94–98 (1984).

Grossman, S. R., and Catlin, K. "Super Heroes." Presentation at the 31st Annual Creative Problem Solving Institute. Buffalo, New York: The Creative Education Foundation, 1985.

Gustafson, D. H., Shukla, R. K., Delbecq, A., and Walster, G. W. "A Comparative Study of Differences in Subjective Likelihood Estimates Made by Individuals, Interacting Groups, Delphi Groups, and Nominal Groups." *Organizational Behavior and Human Performance* 9:280–291 (1973).

Haefele, J. W. *Creativity and Innovation.* New York: Van Nostrand Reinhold, 1962.

Hallacy, D. S., Jr. *Bionics: The Science of "Living" Machines.* New York: Holiday House, 1965.

Hamilton, R. "Screening Business Development Opportunities." *Business Horizons* 13–24 (August 1974).

Hart, S., Boroush, M., Enk, G., and Hornick, W. "Managing Complexity Through Consensus Mapping: Technology for the Structuring of Group Decisions." *Academy of Management Review* 10(3):587–600 (1985).

Herbert, T. T., and Yost, E. B. "A Comparison of Decision Quality Under Nominal and Interacting Consensus Group Formats: The Case of the Structured Problem." *Decision Sciences* 10:358–370 (1979).

Hicks, H. G. *The Management of Organizations.* New York: McGraw-Hill, 1967.

Higbee, K. L., and Millard, R. J. "Visual Imagery and Familiarity Ratings for 203 Sayings." *American Journal of Psychology* 96:211–222 (1983).

Hoffman, L. R. "Homogeneity of Member Personality and Its Effect on Group Problem Solving." *Journal of Abnormal and Social Psychology* 58:27–32 (1959).

Holyoak, K. J., Junn, E. N., and Billman, D. O. "Development of Analogical Problem-Solving Skill." *Child Development* 55:2042–2055 (1984).

Hoyt, M. F., and Janis, I. L. "Increasing Adherence to a Stressful Decision via a Motivational Balance-Sheet Procedure: A Field Experiment." *Journal of Personality and Social Psychology* 31:833–839 (1975).

Iannone, A. L. *Management Program Planning and Control with PERT, MOST and LOB.* Englewood Cliffs, N.J.: Prentice-Hall, 1967.

Isaksen, S. G., and Treffinger, D. J. *Creative Problem Solving: The Basic Course.* Buffalo, N.Y.: Bearly Limited, 1985.

Jablin, F. M. "Cultivating Imagination: Factors That Enhance and Inhibit Creativity in Brainstorming Groups." *Human Communication Research* 7:245–258 (1981).

Janis, I. L. "Motivational Factors in the Resolution of Decisional Conflicts." In M. R. Jones, ed. *Nebraska Symposium on Motivation Vol. 7.* Lincoln: University of Nebraska Press, 1959.

Janis, I. L., and Mann, L. *Decision Making, A Psychological Analysis of Conflict, Choice, and Commitment.* New York: The Free Press, 1977.

Jensen, J. V. "A Heuristic for the Analysis of the Nature and Extent of a Problem." *Journal of Creative Behavior* 12:168–180 (1978).

Jensen, J. V. "Metaphorical Constructs for the Problem-Solving Process." *Journal of Creative Behavior* 9:113–123 (1975).

Keane, M. "On drawing Analogies When Solving Problems: A Theory and Test of Solution Generation in an Analogical Problem-Solving Task." *British Journal of Psychology* 76:449–458 (1985).

Keen, P. G. W. "Evolving Concept of Optimality." In M. K. Starr and M. Zeleny, eds. *Multiple Criterion Decision Making.* Amsterdam: North-Holland, 1977.

Kepner, C. H., and Tregoe, B. B. *The Rational Manager.* Princeton, N.J.: Kepner-Tregoe, Inc., 1976.

Kepner, C. H., and Tregoe, B. B. *The New Rational Manager.* Princeton, N.J.: Kepner-Tregoe, Inc., 1981.

Khatena, J. "Note on Reliability and Validity of Onomatopoeia and Images." *Perceptual and Motor Skills* 31:86 (1970).

Khatena, J. "Onomatopoeia and Images: Preliminary Validity Study of a Test of Originality." *Perceptual and Motor Skills* 28:235–238 (1969).

Khatena, J. "The Use of Analogy in the Production of Original Verbal Images." *Journal of Creative Behavior* 6:209–213 (1972).

Klimoski, R. J., and Karol, B. L. "The Impact of Trust on Creative Problem Solving Groups." *Journal of Applied Psychology* 61:630–633 (1976).

Koberg, D., and Bagnall, J. *The Universal Traveler.* Los Altos, Calif.: William Kaufmann, Inc., 1976.

Koontz, H., and O'Donnell, C. *Essentials of Management.* New York: McGraw-Hill, 1974.

Laswell, H. D. "The Technique of Decision Seminars." *Midwest Journal of Political Science* 4:213–236 (1960).

Laverty, F. "Creative Ideas Through Circumrelation." *Journal of Creative Behavior* 8: 40–46 (1974).

MacCrimmon, K. R. "Managerial Decision Making." In J. W. McGuire, ed. *Contemporary Management, Issues and Viewpoints.* Englewood Cliffs, N.J.: Prentice-Hall, 1974.

MacCrimmon, K. R., and Taylor, R. N. "Decision Making and Problem Solving." In M. D. Dunnette, ed. *Handbook of Industrial and Organizational Psychology.* Chicago: Rand McNally, 1976.

McKim, R. H. *Experiences in Visual Thinking.* Monterey, Calif.: Brooks/Cole, 1972.

MacKinnon, W. J. "Development of the SPAN Technique for Making Decisions in Human Groups." *American Behavioral Scientist* 9:9–13 (1966).

MacKinnon, W. J. "Elements of the SPAN Technique for Making Group Decisions." *Journal of Social Psychology* 70:149–164 (1966).

MacKinnon, W. J., and Andersen, L. M. "The SPAN III Computer Program for Synthesizing Group Decisions: Weighting Participants' Judgments in Proportion to Confidence." *Behavior Research Methods and Instrumentation* 8:409–410 (1976).

MacKinnon, W. J., and Cockrum, D. L. "SPAN II: A Modification of the SPAN Program for Synthesizing Group Decisions." *Behavioral Science* 18:78–79 (1973).

MacKinnon, W. J., and MacKinnon, M. M. "The Decisional Design and Cyclic Computation of SPAN." *Behavioral Science* 14:244–247 (1969).

McPherson, J. *The People, the Problems and the Problem-Solving Methods.* Midland, Mich.: Pendell, 1967.

Madsen, D. B., and Finger, S. R., Jr. "Comparison of Written Feedback Procedure, Group Brainstorming, and Individual Brainstorming." *Journal of Applied Psychology* 63: 120–123 (1978).

Maginn, B. K., and Harris, R. J. "Effects of Anticipated Evaluation on Individual Brainstorming Performance." *Journal of Applied Psychology* 65:219–225 (1980).

Maier, N. R. F. *Principles of Human Relations.* New York: Wiley, 1952.

Maier, N. R. F. *Problem Solving and Creativity in Individuals and Groups.* Belmont, Calif.: Brooks/Cole, 1970.

Maier, N. R. F. *Problem Solving Discussions and Conferences; Leadership Methods and Skills.* New York: McGraw-Hill, 1963.

Mansfield, R. S., Busse, T. V., and Krepelka, E. J. "The Effectiveness of Creativity Training." *Review of Educational Research* 48:517–536 (1978).

Martino, J. P. *Technological Forecasting for Decision Making.* New York: Elsevier Science Publishing, 1983.

Miles, L. D. *Techniques of Value Engineering and Analysis,* 2nd rev. ed. New York: McGraw-Hill, 1971.

Miller, R. W. *Schedule, Cost, and Profit Control with PERT.* New York: McGraw-Hill, 1963.

Miner, F. C., Jr. "A Comparative Analysis of Three Diverse Group Decision Making Approaches." *Academy of Management Journal* 22:81–92 (1979).

Moder, J. J., and Phillips, C. R. *Project Management with CPM and PERT.* New York: Van Nostrand Reinhold, 1970.

Moore, L. B. "Creative Action—The Evaluation, Development, and Use of Ideas." In S. J. Parnes and H. F. Harding, eds. *A Sourcebook for Creative Thinking.* New York: Scribner, 1962.

Morris, W. C., and Sashkin, M. *Organization Behavior in Action, Skill Building Experiences.* St. Paul, Minn.: West, 1976.

Morris, W. C., and Sashkin, M. "Phases of Integrated Problem Solving (PIPS)." In J. W. Pfeiffer and J. E. Jones, eds. *The 1978 Annual Handbook for Group Facilitators.* La Jolla, Calif.: University Associates, Inc., 1978.

Mudge, A. E. *Value Engineering.* New York: McGraw-Hill, 1971.

National Academy of Sciences. *Value Engineering in Federal Construction Agencies.* Washington, D.C.: NAS Printing Office, 1969.

Nierenberg, G. I. *The Art of Creative Thinking.* New York: Cornerstone Library (Div. of Simon & Schuster), 1982.

Nierenberg, G. I. *The Idea Generator*™ *User's Manual.* Berkeley, Calif.: Experience in Software, Inc., 1985.

Olson, R. W. *The Art of Creative Thinking.* New York: Barnes & Noble, 1980.

O'Rourke, P. J. *The Castle Technique: How to Achieve Group Consensus in a Very Short Time with No Argument.* Lyons, Colo.: Steamboat Valley Press, 1984.

Osborn, A. F. *Applied Imagination,* 3rd ed. New York: Scribner, 1963.

Papanek, V. J. *Design for the Real World.* New York: Pantheon Books, 1972.

Papanek, V. J. "Tree of Life: Bionics." In S. J. Parnes, R. B. Noller, and A. M. Biondi. *Guide to Creative Action,* rev. ed. New York: Scribner, 1977.

Parnes, S. J. "Idea-Stimulation Techniques." *Journal of Creative Behavior* 10:126–129 (1976).

Parnes, S. J., and Brunelle, E. E. "The Literature of Creativity (Part 1)." *Journal of Creative Behavior* 1:52–109 (1967).

Parnes, S. J., and Meadow, A. "Development of Individual Creativity Talent." In C. W. Taylor and F. Barron, eds. *Scientific Creativity: Its Recognition and Development.* New York: Wiley, 1963.

Parnes, S. J., and Noller, R. B. "Applied Creativity: The Creative Studies Project (Part 1)." *Journal of Creative Behavior* 6:11–20 (1972).

Parnes, S. J., Noller, R. B., and Biondi, A. M. *Guide to Creative Action,* rev. ed. New York: Scribner, 1977.

Pearson, A. W. "Communication, Creativity, and Commitment: A Look at the Collective Notebook Approach." In S. S. Gryskiewicz, ed. *Proceedings of Creativity Week I, 1978.* Greensboro, N.C.: Center for Creative Leadership, 1979.

Phillips, D. J. "Report on Discussion 66." *Adult Education Journal* 7:181–182 (1948).

Pickens, J. F. Personal communication, 1985.

Price, K. H. "Problem-Solving Strategies: A Comparison by Problem-Solving Phases." *Group & Organization Studies* 10:278–299 (1985).

Prince, G. M. "The Operational Mechanism of Synectics." *Journal of Creative Behavior* 2:1–13 (1968).

Prince, G. M. *The Practice of Creativity.* New York: Harper & Row, 1970.

Prince, G. M. "The Mindspring Theory: A New Development from Synectics Research." *Journal of Creative Behavior* 9:159–181 (1975).

Quickenden, M. A. J., Davies, G. B., and Woods, M. F. "The Use of Research Planning Diagrams." *R & D Management* 2:63–68 (1972).

Rickards, T. *Problem-Solving Through Creative Analysis.* Essex, U.K.: Gower Press, 1974.

Rickards, T., and Freedman, B. L. "Procedures for Managers in Idea-Deficient Situations: An Examination of Brainstorming Approaches." *Journal of Management Studies* 15: 43–55 (1978).

Rickards, T., and Freedman, B. L. "Procedures for Managers in Idea-Deficient Situations: A Note on Perceptions of Brainstorming Users Obtained from a Cross-Cultural Pilot Study." *Journal of Management Studies* 15:347–349 (1978).

Rose, L. H., and Lin, H-T. "A Meta-Analysis of Long-Term Creativity Training Programs." *Journal of Creative Behavior* 18:11–22 (1984).

Roth, W. F., Jr. *Problem Solving for Managers.* New York: Praeger, 1985.

Schaude, G. R. "Methods of Idea Generation." In S. S. Gryskiewicz, ed. *Proceedings of Creativity Week I, 1978.* Greensboro, N.C.: Center for Creative Leadership, 1979.

Schnelle, W. *Interactional Learning.* Publisher and date of publication unknown.

Shore, S. *Creativity in Action* (monthly newsletter). Sharon, Connecticut.

Simon, H. A. *The New Science of Management Decision,* rev. ed. Englewood Cliffs, N.J.: Prentice-Hall, 1977.

Simon, H. A. *The Science of the Artificial.* Cambridge, Mass.: MIT Press, 1969.

Sink, S. D. "Using the Nominal Group Technique Effectively." *National Productivity Review* 2:173–184 (1983).

Smithers, L. E. *The Story Board.* Hudson, Ohio: The Creative Thinking Center, Inc., 1984.

Souder, W. E. "Effectiveness of Nominal and Interacting Group Decision Processes for Integrating R & D Marketing." *Management Science* 23:595–605 (1977).

Souder, W. E., and O'Keefe, W. M. *Fourteen Useful Techniques for Technical Problem Solving and Creative Thinking.* Technical report funded by the National Science Foundation and the U. S. Agency for International Development, University of Pittsburgh, Pittsburgh, Pennsylvania, 1979.

Souder, W. E., and Ziegler, R. W. "A Review of Creativity and Problem Solving Techniques." *Research Management* 34–42 (July 1977).

Stech, E., and Ratliffe, S. A. *Working in Groups.* Skokie, Ill.: National Textbook Co., 1976.

Stein, M. I. *Stimulating Creativity, Volume 1, Individual Procedures.* New York: Academic Press, 1974.

Stein, M. I. *Stimulating Creativity, Volume 2, Group Procedures.* New York: Academic Press, 1975.

Stephenson, B. Y., Michaelson, L. K., and Franklin, S. G. "An Empirical Test of the Nominal Group Technique in State Solar Energy Planning." *Group & Organization Studies* 7: 320–334 (1982).

Stines, D. M., and Murphy, M. M. *Modern Management Methods: PERT and CPM.* Boston: Materials Management Institute, 1963.

Street, W. R. "Brainstorming by Individuals, Coacting and Interacting Groups." *Journal of Applied Psychology* 59:433–436 (1974).

Stumpf, S., Freedman, R., and Zand, D. "Judgmental Decisions: A Study of Interactions Among Group Membership, Group Functioning and the Decision Situation." *Academy of Management Journal* 22:765–782 (1979).

Summers, I., and White, D. E. "Creativity Techniques: Toward Improvement of the Decision Process." *Academy of Management Review* 1:99–107 (1976).

Tarr, G. *The Management of Problem Solving.* New York: Wiley, 1973.

Tauber, E. M. "HIT: Heuristic Ideation Technique—A Systematic Procedure for New Product Search." *Journal of Marketing* 36:58–61 (1972).

Tauber, E. M. "Discovering New Product Opportunities with Problem Inventory Analysis." *Journal of Marketing* 39:67–70 (1975).

Taylor, C. W. "Organizing for Consensus in Problem Solving." *Management Review* 61: 16–25 (1972).

Taylor, C. W. "Panel Consensus Technique: A New Approach to Decision Making." *Journal of Creative Behavior* 6:187–198 (1972).

Taylor, D. W., Berry, P. C., and Block, C. H. "Does Group Participation When Using Brainstorming Facilitate or Inhibit Creative Thinking?" *Administrative Science Quarterly* 3:23–47 (1958).

Taylor, J. W. *How to Create Ideas.* Englewood Cliffs, N.J.: Prentice-Hall, 1961.

Thamia, S., and Woods, M. F. "A Systematic Small Group Approach to Creativity and Innovation: A Case Study." *R & D Management* 14:25–35 (1984).

Torrance, E. P. *Thinking Creatively with Pictures* and *Thinking Creatively with Words.* Scholastic Testing Service, Inc., 1966.

Torrance, E. P. "Can We Teach Children to Think Creatively?" *Journal of Creative Behavior* 6: 114–143 (1967).

Van de Ven, A. H., and Delbecq, A. L. "The Effectiveness of Nominal, Delphi, and Interacting Group Decision Making Processes." *Academy of Management Journal* 17:605–621 (1974).

Van de Ven, A. H., and Delbecq, A. L. "Nominal Versus Interacting Group Processes for Committee Decision-Making Effectiveness." *Academy of Management Journal* 14:203–211 (1971).

VanGundy, A. B. Course taught on creative problem solving, Norman, Oklahoma: University of Oklahoma, 1980.

VanGundy, A. B. *A Typology of Techniques for New Product Idea Generation.* Paper presented at the Sixth Annual Conference of the Product Development and Management Association. Philadelphia, Pennsylvania, 1981.

VanGundy, A. B. "How to Get the Idea That Leads to the Product." Chicago, Illinois, *The National New-Products Conference* (May 8–9, 1984).

VanGundy, A. B. *108 Ways to Get a Bright Idea.* Englewood Cliffs, N.J.: Prentice-Hall, 1983.

VanGundy, A. B. *Managing Group Creativity: A Modular Approach to Problem Solving.* New York: AMACOM, 1984.

VanGundy, A. B. *Product Improvement CheckList (PICL).* Point Pleasant, N.J.: Point Publishing Co., 1985.

VanGundy, A. B. "The New Product Creative Process." Chicago, Illinois, *The National New-Products Conference* (May 1–2, 1985).

VanGundy, A. B. *Creative Problem Solving: A Guide for Trainers and Management.* Westport, Conn.: Quorum Books, 1987.

VanGundy, A. B. *Stalking the Wild Solution: A Problem Finding Approach to Creative Problem Solving.* Buffalo, N.Y.: Bearly Limited, 1987.

Von Fange, E. K. *Professional Creativity.* Englewood Cliffs, N.J.: Prentice-Hall, 1959.

Vroom, V. H., and Yetton, P. W. *Leadership and Decision Making.* Pittsburgh Press, 1973.

Wakin, E. "Component Detailing." Presentation at the 31st Annual Creative Problem Solving Institute, Buffalo, New York (June 1985).

Wallas, G. *The Art of Thought.* New York: Harcourt, 1926.

Warfield, J. N., Geschka, H., and Hamilton, R. *Methods of Idea Management.* Columbus, Ohio: The Academy for Contemporary Problems, 1975.

Warren, T. F., and Davis, G. A. "Techniques for Creative Thinking: An Empirical Comparison of Three Methods." *Psychological Reports* 25:207–214 (1969).

Whiting, C. S. *Creative Thinking.* New York: Van Nostrand Reinhold, 1958.

Williams, F. E. *Foundations of Creative Problem Solving.* Ann Arbor, Mich.: Edward Brothers, Inc., 1960.

Willis, J. E., Hitchcock, J. D., and MacKinnon, W. J. "SPAN Decision Making in Established Groups." *Journal of Social Psychology* 78:185–203 (1969).

Woods, M. "The Brainwriting Game." *Creativity Network* 5:7–12 (1979).

Woods, M. F., and Davies, G. B. "Potential Problem Analysis: A Systematic Approach to Problem Predictions and Contingency Planning—An Aid to the Smooth Exploitation of Research." *R & D Management* 4:25–32 (1973).

Zwicky, F. *Discovery, Invention, Research Through the Morphological Approach.* New York: Macmillan, 1969.

Index